TANTRUM

TANTRUM

JULES FEIFFER

FANTAGRAPHICS BOOKS

FANTAGRAPHICS BOOKS
7563 Lake City Way NE
Seattle, WA 98115

Fantagraphics Books edition prepared by Gary Groth, Kim Thompson, Ilse Thompson, and Evan Sult. Special thanks to Jules Feiffer.

Originally published by Alfred A. Knopf, Inc. First edition: October, 1979
First Fantagraphics Books edition: November, 1997

To receive a full-color catalogue from Fantagraphics Books, call 1-800-657-1100 or 1-206-524-1967.

ISBN: 1-56097-282-3

Printed in Canada

THERE WAS a Jules Feiffer cartoon in the mid-sixties in which a baby, hardly old enough to walk, catalogues the grievances inflicted upon it by its parents, each indignity accompanied by a soothing "Mommy loves baby. Daddy loves baby."

"Whatever that word 'love' means," says the baby, essaying its first steps, "I can hardly wait till I'm big enough to do it to *them*."

When I first discovered Jules Feiffer I was... what? Four years old? Five, maybe? This was in England, in 1964 or 1965, and the book was a hardback blue-covered edition of *The Explainers*, Feiffer's 1962 collection, and I read it as only a child can read a favourite book: over and over and over. I had little or no context for the assortment of losers and dreamers and lovers and dancers and bosses and mothers and children and company men, but I kept reading and rereading, trying to understand, happy with whatever comprehension I could pull from the pages, from what Feiffer described as "an endless babble of self-interest, self-loathing, self-searching and evasion." I read and reread it, certain that if I understood it, I would have some kind of key to the adult world.

It was the first place I had ever encountered the character of Superman: there was a strip in which he "pulled a chick out of a river" and eventually married her. I'd never encountered that use of the word "chick" before, and assumed that Superman had married a small, fluffy, yellow baby chicken. It made as much sense as anything else in the adult world. And it didn't matter: I understood the fundamental story—of compromise and insecurity—as well as I understood any of them. I read them again and again, a few drawings to a page, a few pages to each strip. And I decided that when I grew up, I wanted to do that. I wanted to tell those stories and do those drawings and have that perfect sense of pacing and the killer undercut last line.

(I never did, and I never will. But any successes I've had as a writer in the field of words-and-pictures have their roots in poring over the drawings in *The Explainers*, and reading the dialogue, and trying to understand the mysteries of economy and timing that were peculiarly Jules Feiffer's.)

That was over thirty years ago. In the intervening years the strips that I read back then—in *The Explainers*, and later, in discovered copies of *Sick*, *Sick*, *Sick* and *Hold Me!*—have waited patiently in the back of my head, commenting on the events around me. ("Why is she doing that?" "To lose weight." / "You're not perfection... but you do have an interesting offbeat color... and besides, it's getting dark." / "What I wouldn't give to be a non-conformist like all those others." / "Nobody knows it but I'm a complete work of fiction.")

So. Time passed. I learned how to do joined-up writing. Feiffer continued cartooning, becoming one of the sharpest political commentators there has ever been in that form, and writing plays and films and prose books.

In 1980, I got a call from my friend Dave Dickson, who was working in a local bookshop. There was a new Jules Feiffer book coming out, called *Tantrum*. He had ordered an extra copy for me.

I had stopped reading most comics a few years earlier, limiting my comics-buying to occasional reprints of Will Eisner's *The Spirit*. (I had no idea that Feiffer had once been Eisner's assistant.) I was no longer sure that comics could be, as I had previously supposed, a real, grown-up, medium. But it was Feiffer, and I was just about able to afford it. So I bought *Tantrum* and I took it home and read it.

I remember, mostly, puzzlement. There was the certainty that I was in the presence of a real story, true, but beyond that there was just perplexity. It was a real "cartoon novel." But it made little sense: the story of a man who willed himself back to two years of age. I didn't really understand any of the whys or whats of the thing, and I certainly didn't understand the ending.

(Nineteen is a difficult age, and nineteen year olds know much less than they think they do. Less than five year olds, anyway.)

I was at least bright enough to know that any gaps were mine, not Feiffer's, for every few years I went back and reread *Tantrum*. I still have that copy, battered but beloved. And each time I read it, it made a little more sense, felt a little more right.

But with whatever perplexity I might have originally brought to *Tantrum*, it was still one of the few works that made me understand that comics were simply a vessel, as good or bad as the material that went into them.

And the material that goes into *Tantrum* is very good indeed.

I reread *Tantrum* a month ago.

Now, as I write this, I'm in spitting distance of Leo's age, with two children rampaging into their teens. I know what that place is. And I have a two year old daughter—a single minded, self-centred creature of utter simplicity and implacable will.

And as I read it I found myself understanding it—even recognising it—on a rather strange and personal level. I was understanding just why Leo stopped being forty-two and began being two, appreciating the strengths that a two year old has that forty-two year old has, more or less, lost.

Leo's drives are utterly straightforward, once he's two again. He wants a piggy-back. He wants to be bathed and diapered and fussed over. As a forty-two year old he lived an enervated life of blandness and routine. Now he wants adventure—but a two year old's adventure. He wants what the old folktale claimed women want: to have his own way.

Along the way we meet his parents, his family, and the other men-who-have-become-two-year-olds. We watch him not burn down his parents' home. We watch him save a life. We watch his quest for a piggy-back and where it leads him. It's sexy, surreal, irresponsible and utterly plausible.

Everyone, everything in *Tantrum* is drawn, lettered, created, at white-hot speed: one gets the impression of impatience with the world at the moment of creation—that it would have been hard for Feiffer to have done it any faster. As if he were trying to keep up with ideas and images tumbling out his head, trying to capture them before they escaped and were gone.

Feiffer had explored the relationship between the child and the man before, most notably in "Munro," his cautionary tale of a four year old drafted in the US army (later filmed as an Academy Award-winning short). Children populated his *Feiffer* strip, too—not too-smart, little adult *Peanuts* children, but real kids appearing as commentators or counterpoints to the adult world. Even the kids in *Clifford*, Feiffer's first strip, a one-page back-up to the *Spirit* newspaper sections, feel like real kids

(except perhaps for Seymour, who, like Leo, is young enough still to be a force of nature).

Tantrum was different. The term 'inner child' had scarcely been coined when it was written, let alone debased into the currency of stand-up, but it stands as an exploration of, and wary paean to the child inside.

When the history of the graphic novel (or whatever they wind up calling long stories created in words and pictures for adults, in the time when histories are appropriate) is written, there will be a whole chapter about *Tantrum*, one of the first and still one of the wisest and sharpest things created in this strange publishing category, and one of the books that, along with Will Eisner's *A Contract with God*, began the movement that brought us such works as *Maus*, as *Love and Rockets*, as *From Hell*—the works that stretch the envelope of what words and pictures were capable of, and could not have been anything but what they were, pictures and words adding up to something that could not have been a film or a novel or a play: that were intrinsically comics, with all comics' strengths.

I am delighted that Fantagraphics has brought it back into print, and after reading it, I have no doubt that you will be too...

Neil Gaiman
March 1997

TO

E.C. SEGAR
ROY CRANE
and
WILL EISNER

1

METAMORPHOSIS

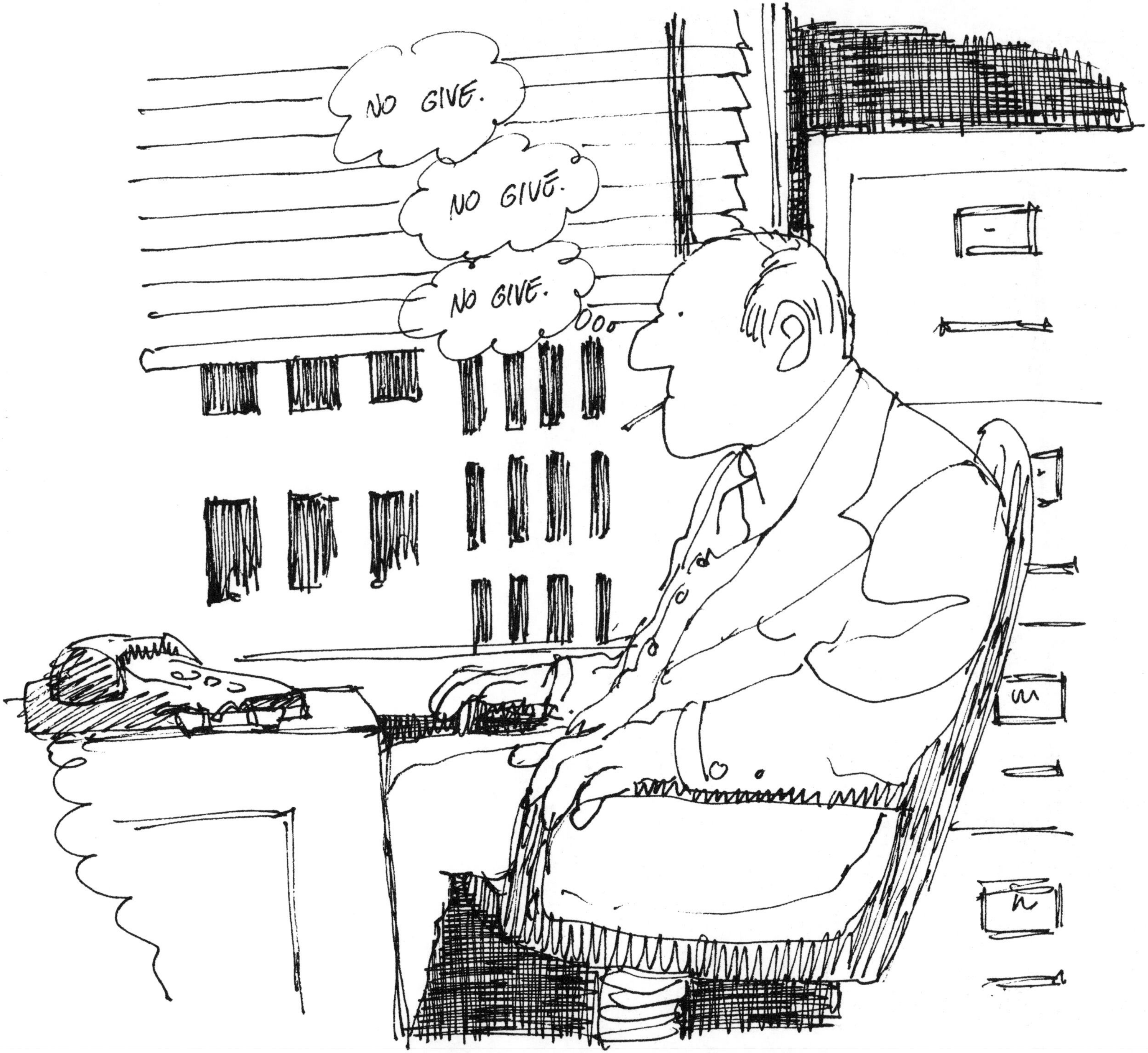
NO GIVE.
NO GIVE.
NO GIVE.

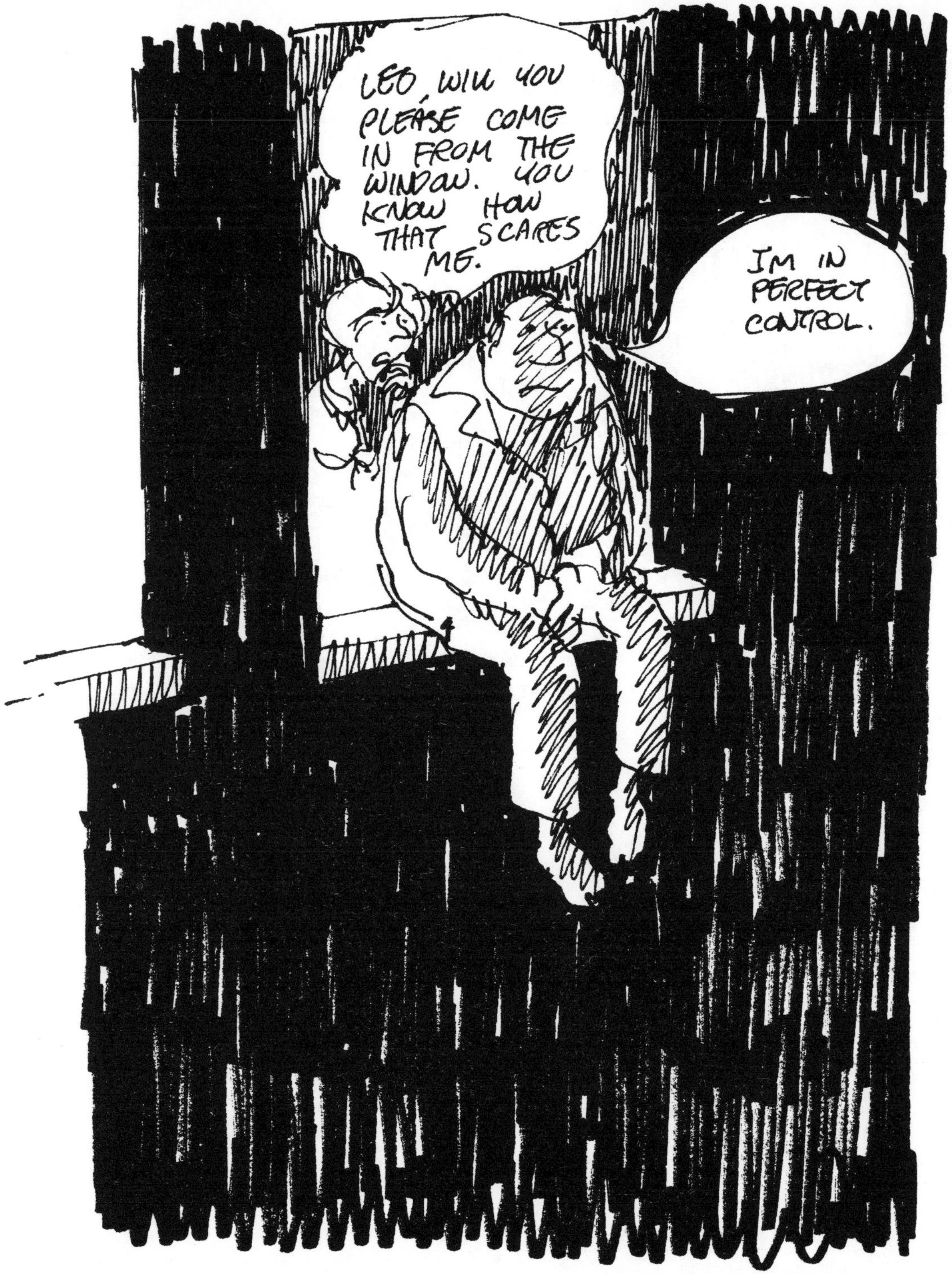
LEO, WILL YOU PLEASE COME IN FROM THE WINDOW. YOU KNOW HOW THAT SCARES ME.
I'M IN PERFECT CONTROL.

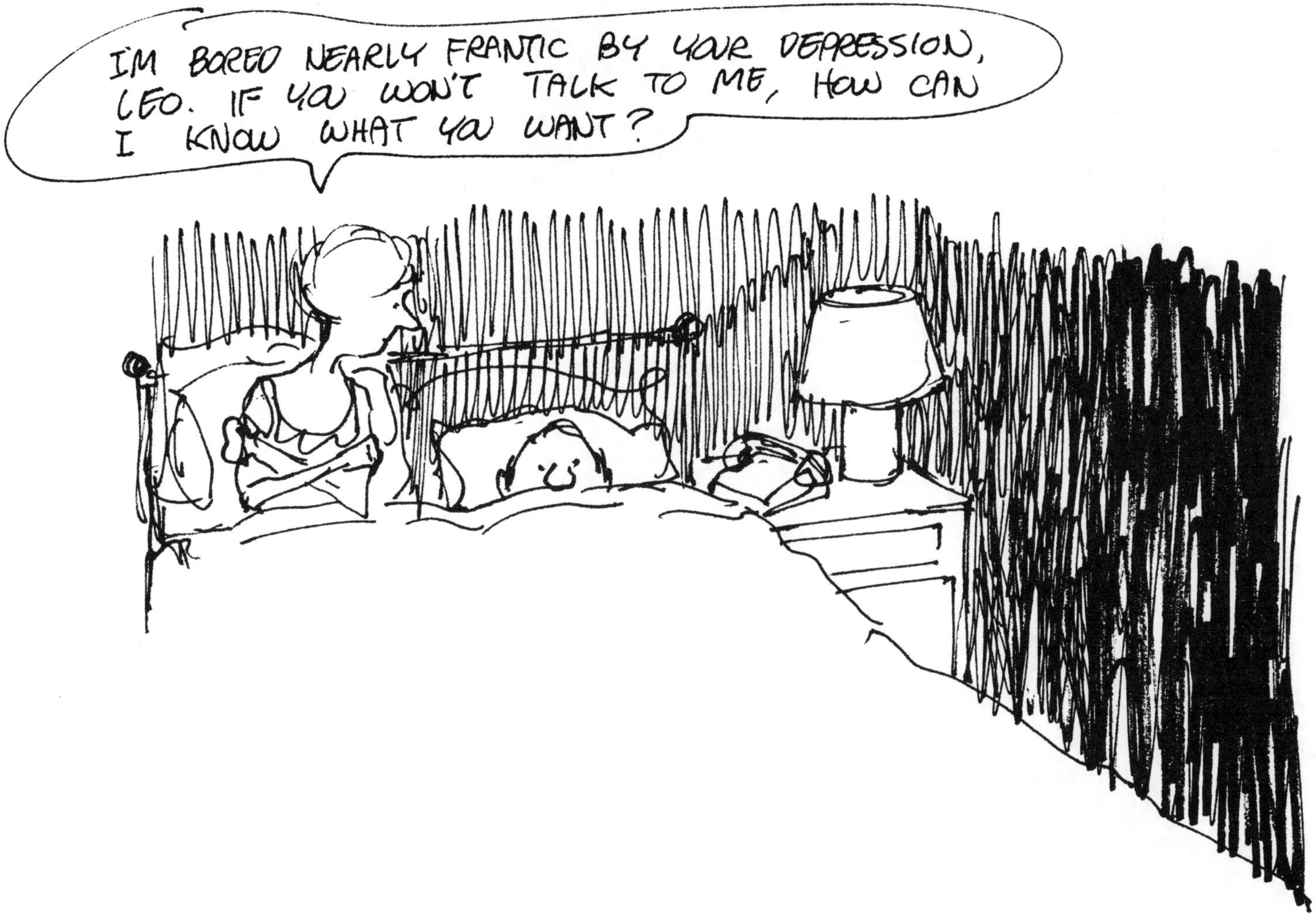
IM BORED NEARLY FRANTIC BY YOUR DEPRESSION, LEO. IF YOU WON'T TALK TO ME, HOW CAN I KNOW WHAT YOU WANT?

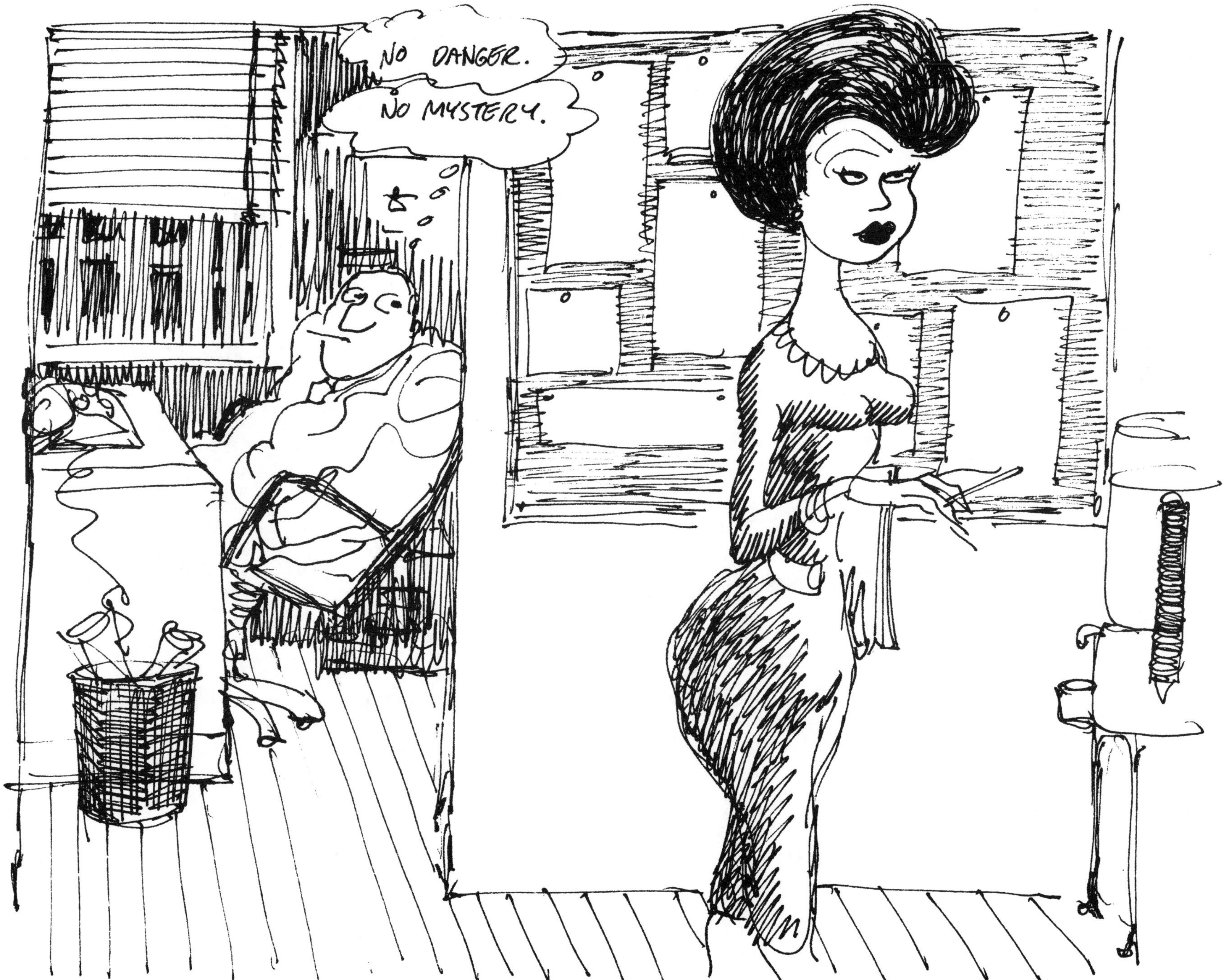
NO DANGER.
NO MYSTERY.

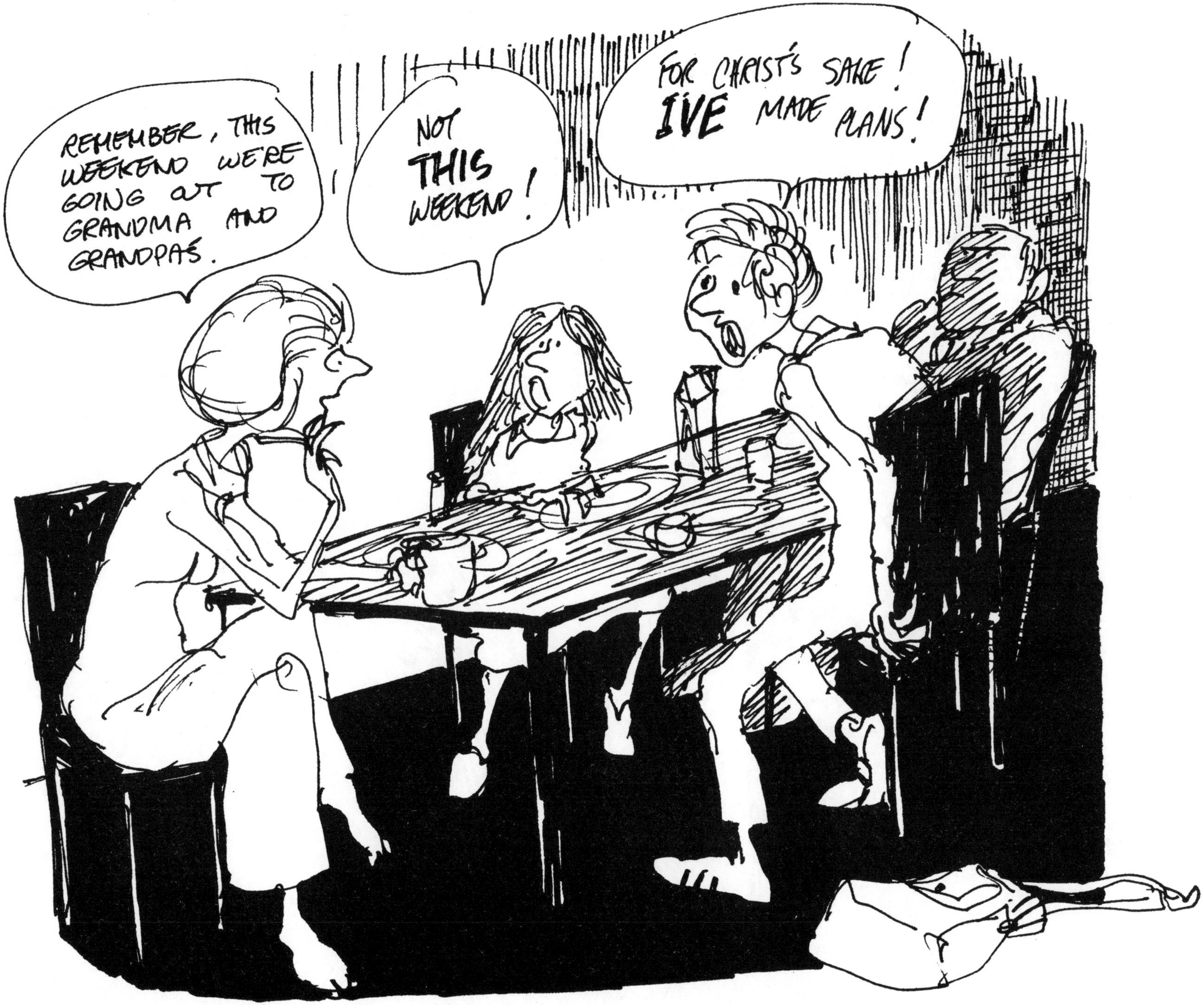
REMEMBER, THIS WEEKEND WE'RE GOING OUT TO GRANDMA AND GRANDPA'S.
NOT THIS WEEKEND!
FOR CHRIST'S SAKE! IVE MADE PLANS!

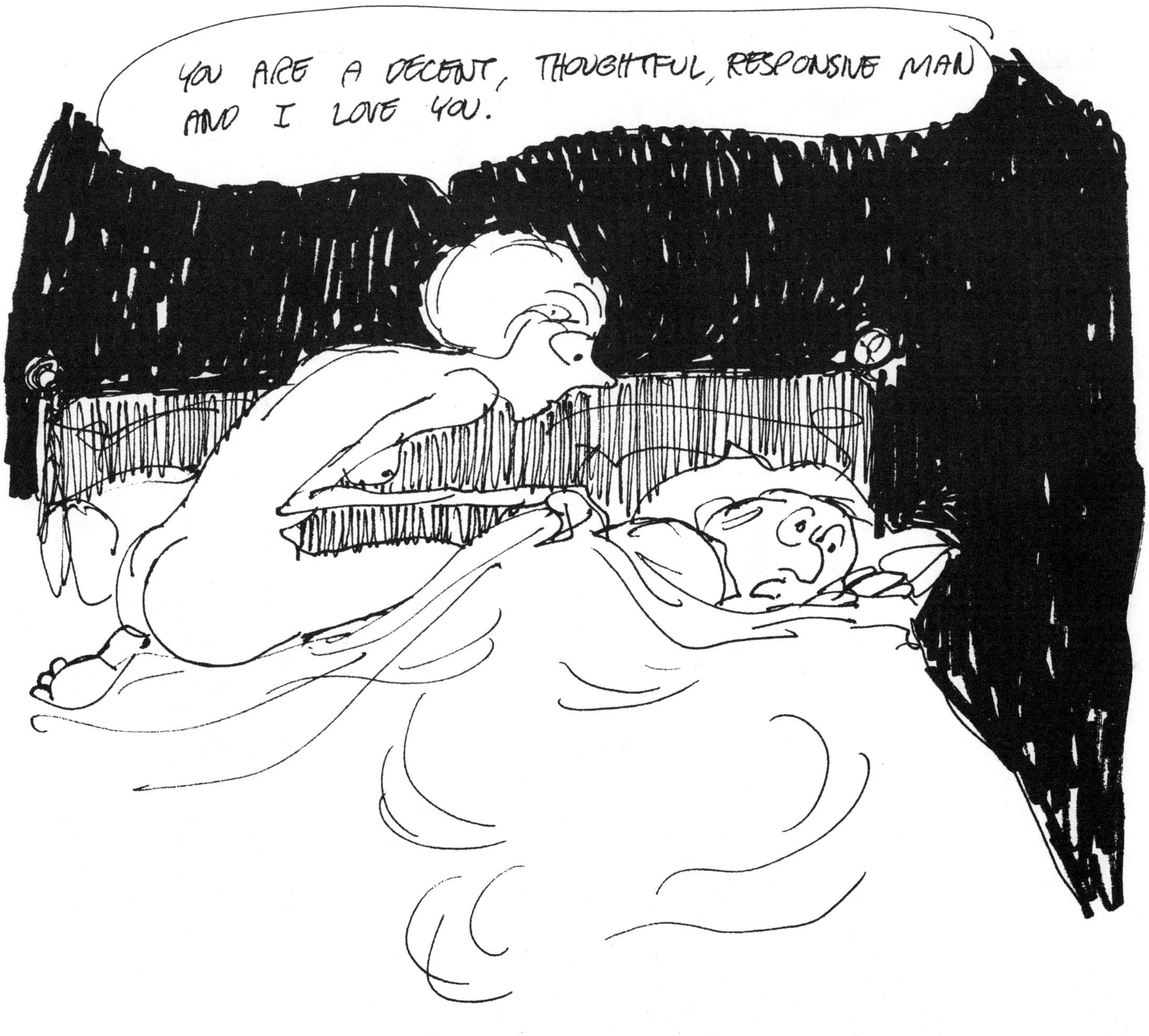
YOU ARE A DECENT, THOUGHTFUL, RESPONSIVE MAN AND I LOVE YOU.

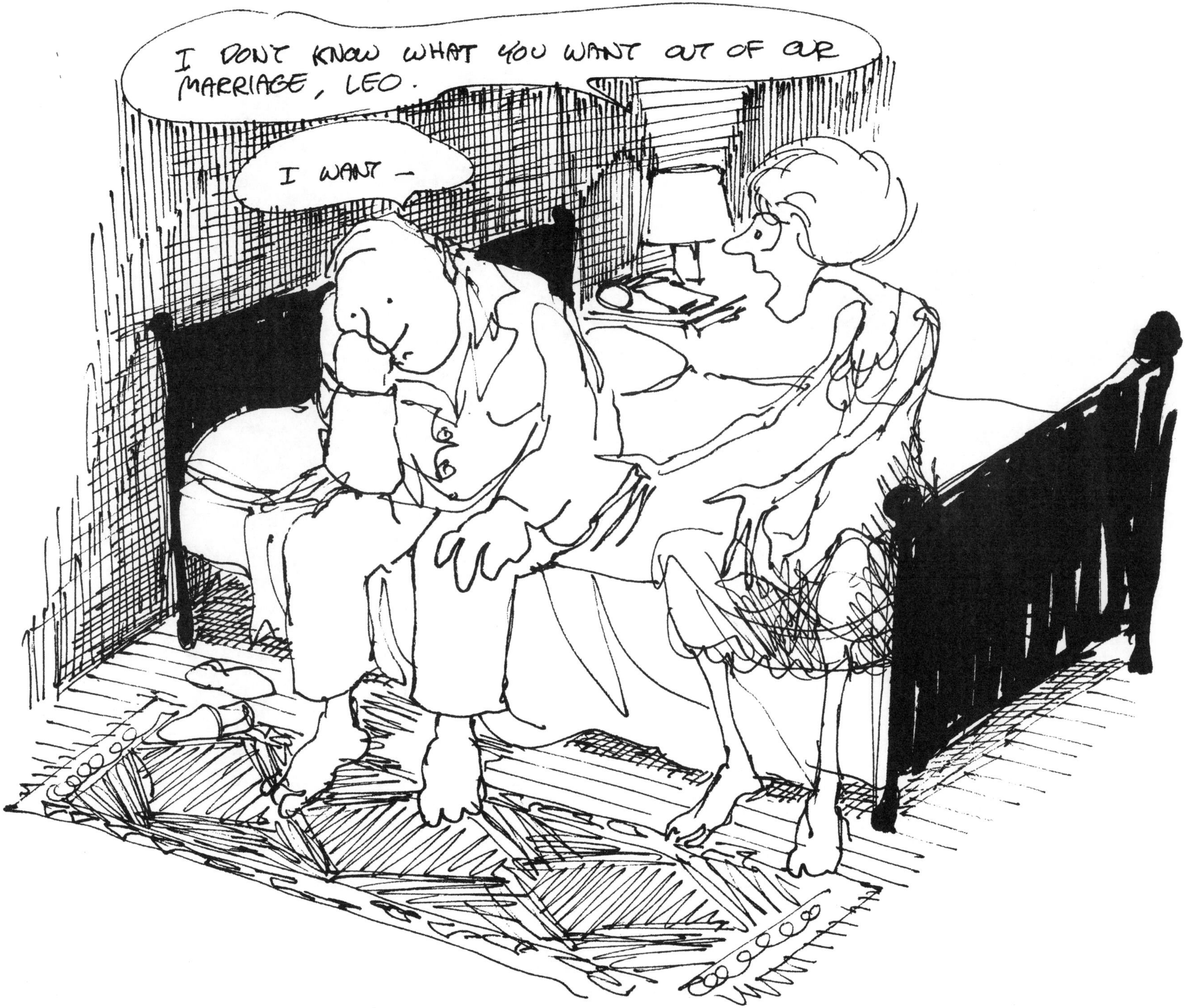
I DON'T KNOW WHAT YOU WANT OUT OF OUR MARRIAGE, LEO.
I WANT –

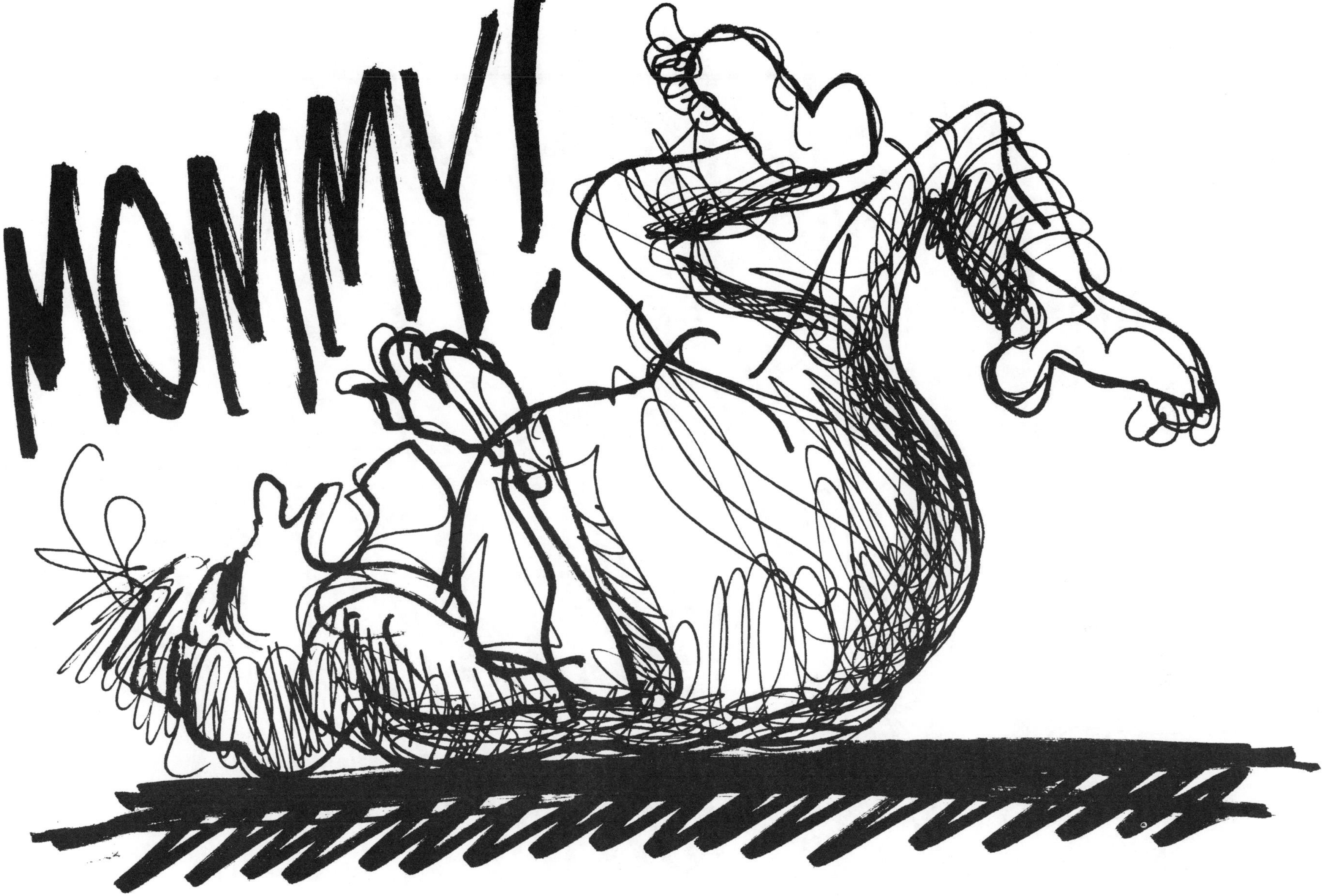
MOMMY!

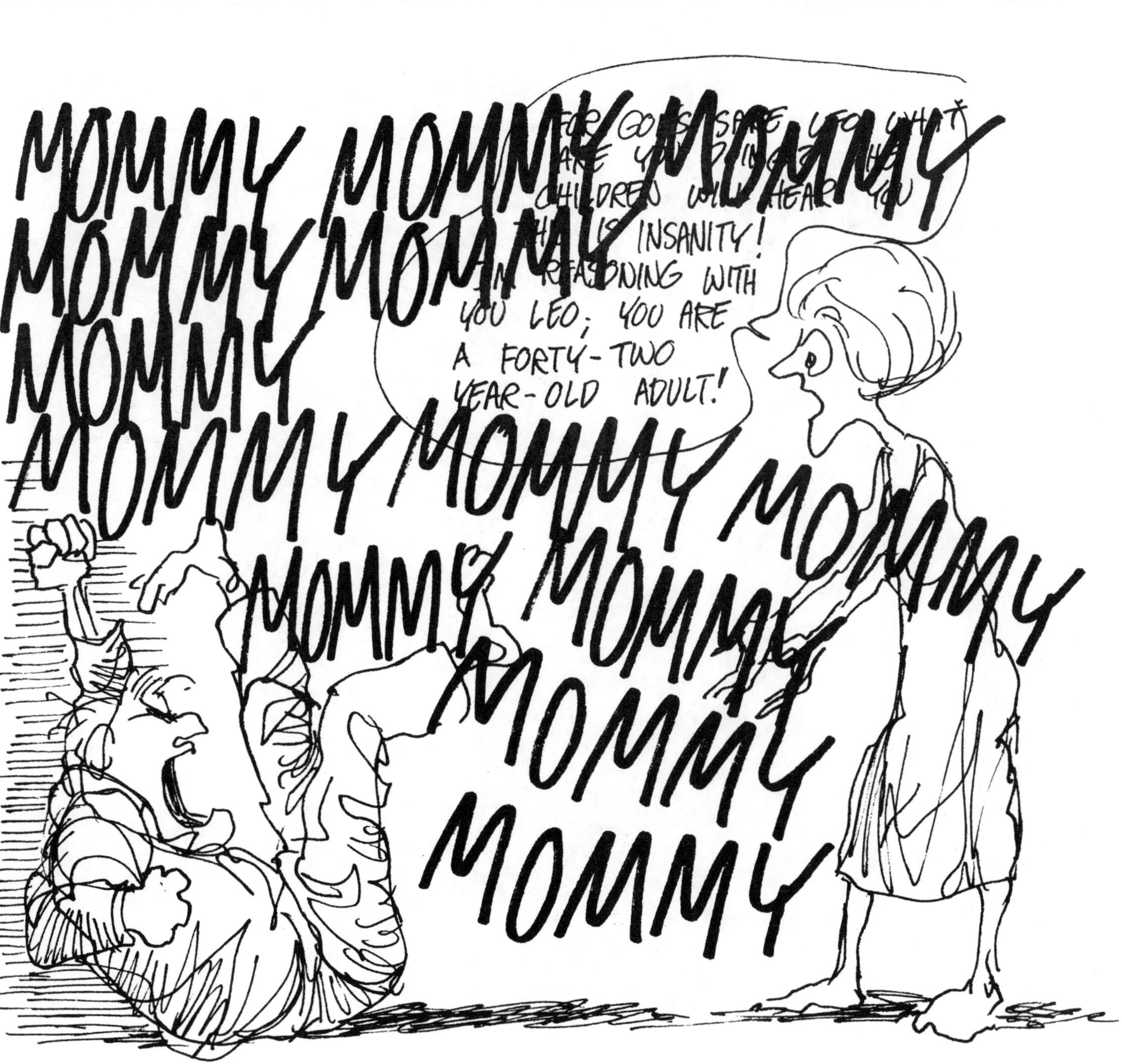

MOMMY MOMMY MOMMY
MOMMY MOMMY
MOMMY
MOMMY MOMMY MOMMY
MOMMY MOMMY
MOMMY
MOMMY
INSANITY!
YOU LEO; YOU ARE
A FORTY-TWO
YEAR-OLD ADULT!

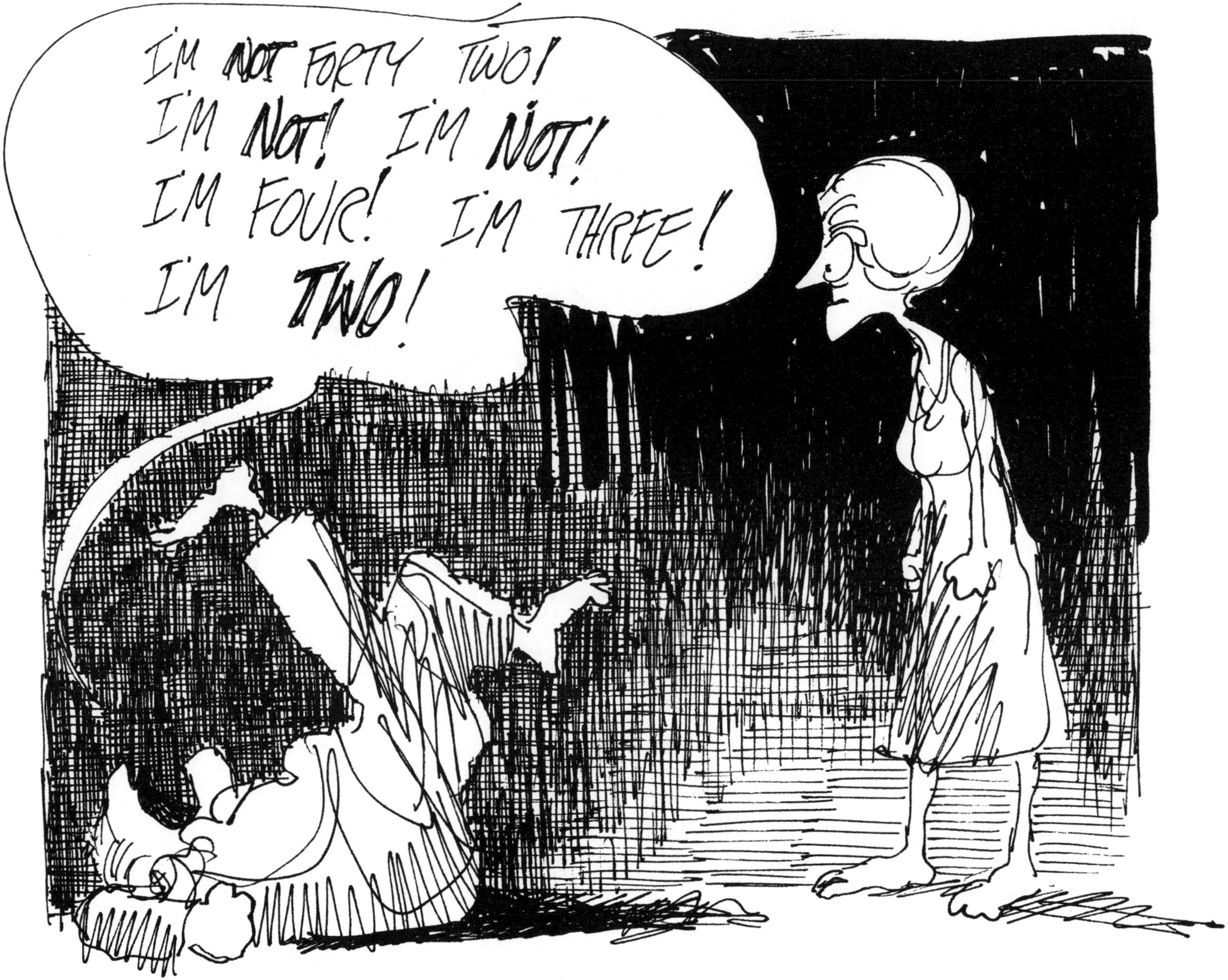
I'M NOT FORTY TWO! I'M NOT! I'M NOT! I'M FOUR! I'M THREE! I'M TWO!

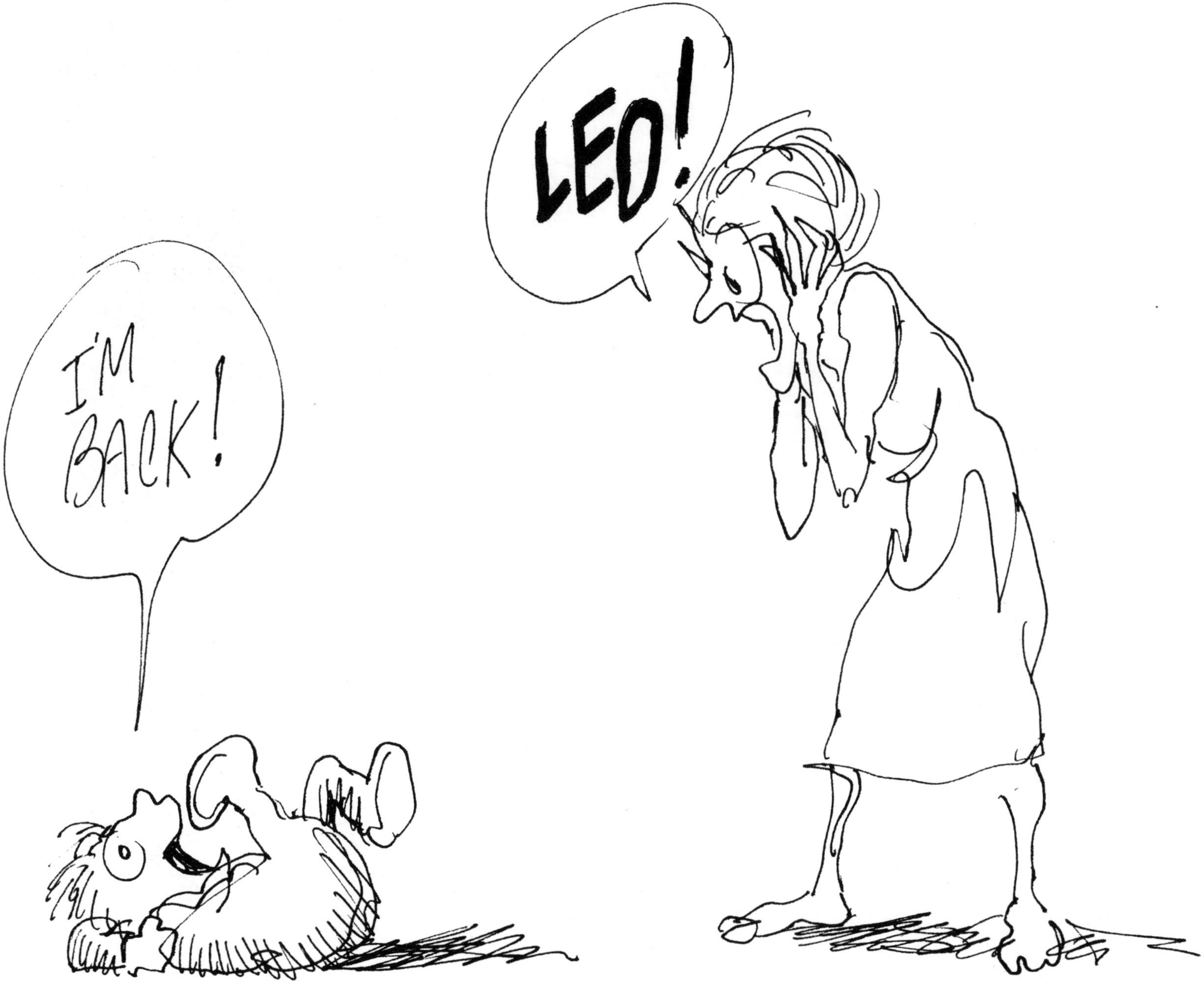
I'M BACK!
LEO!

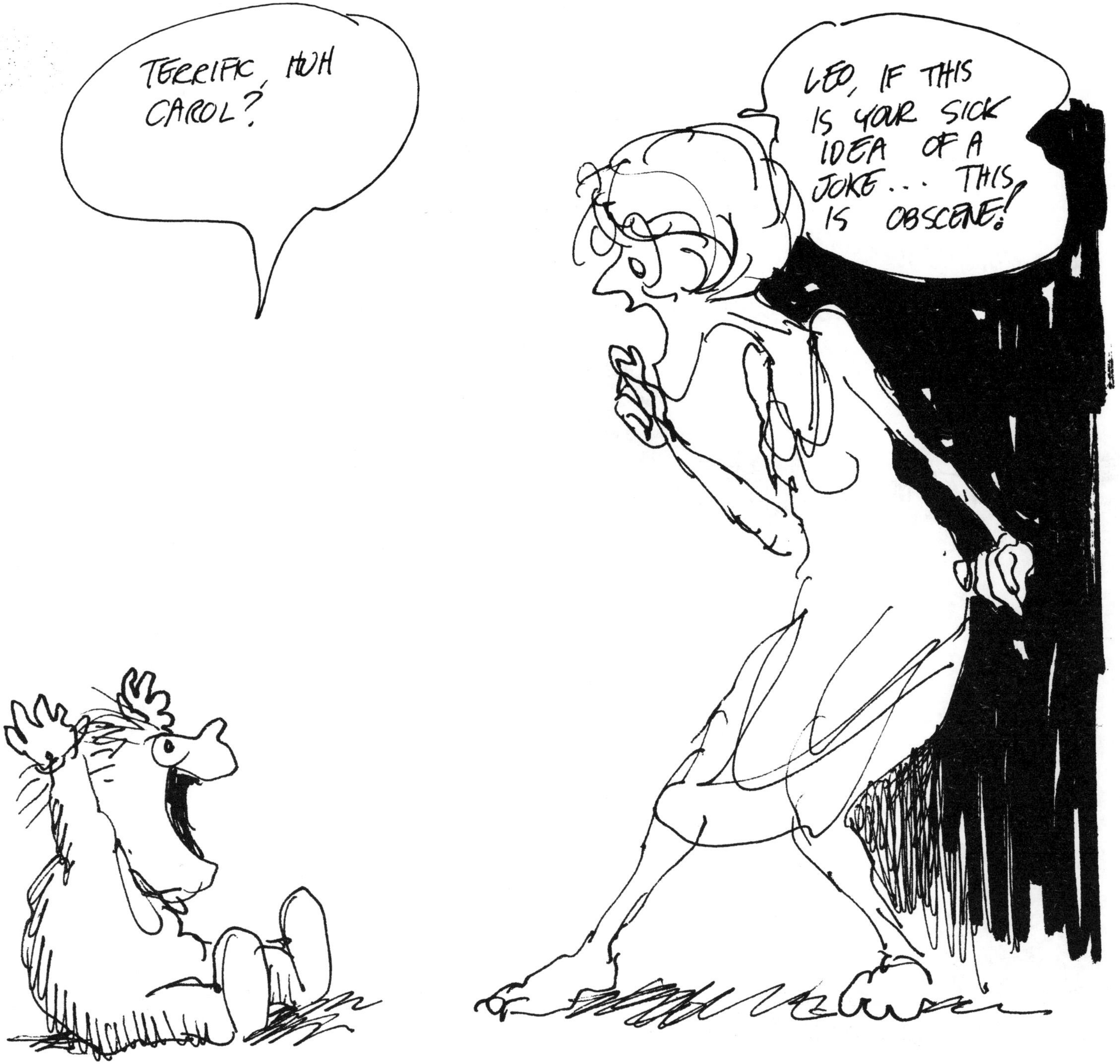
TERRIFIC, HUH CAROL?
LEO, IF THIS IS YOUR SICK IDEA OF A JOKE... THIS IS OBSCENE!

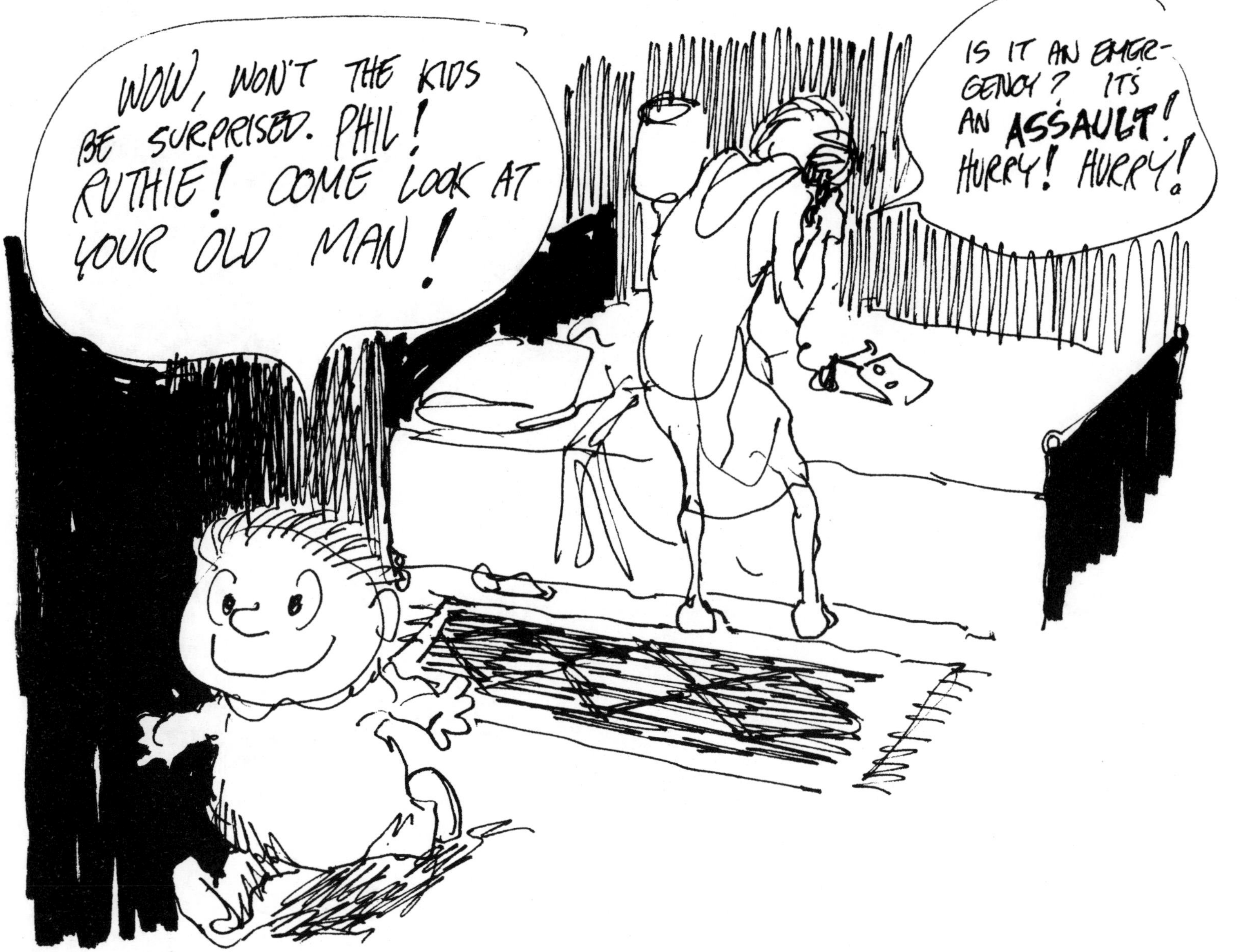
WOW, WON'T THE KIDS BE SURPRISED. PHIL! RUTHIE! COME LOOK AT YOUR OLD MAN!
IS IT AN EMERGENCY? IT'S AN ASSAULT! HURRY! HURRY!

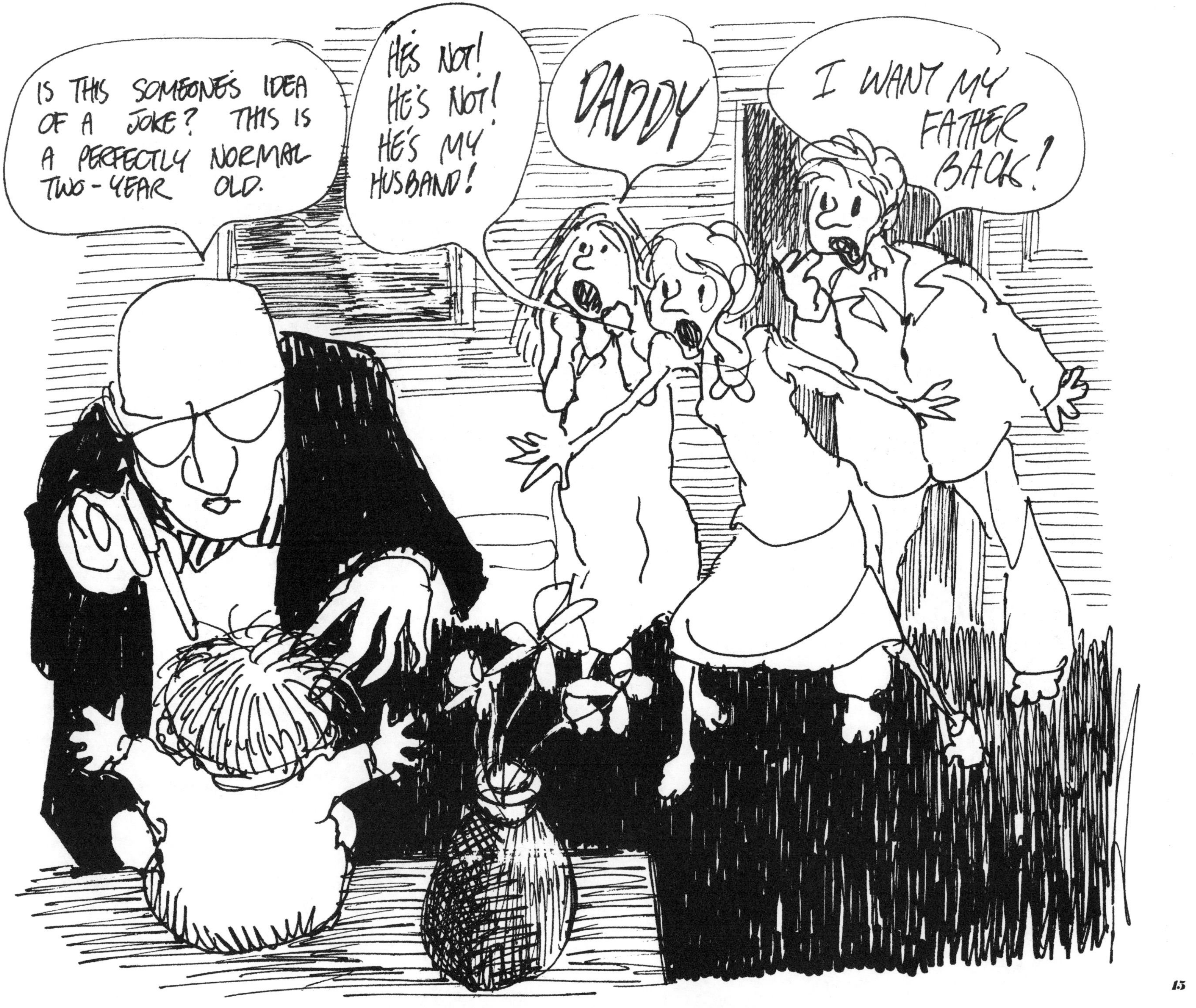
IS THIS SOMEONE'S IDEA OF A JOKE? THIS IS A PERFECTLY NORMAL TWO-YEAR OLD.
HE'S NOT! HE'S NOT! HE'S MY HUSBAND!
DADDY
I WANT MY FATHER BACK!

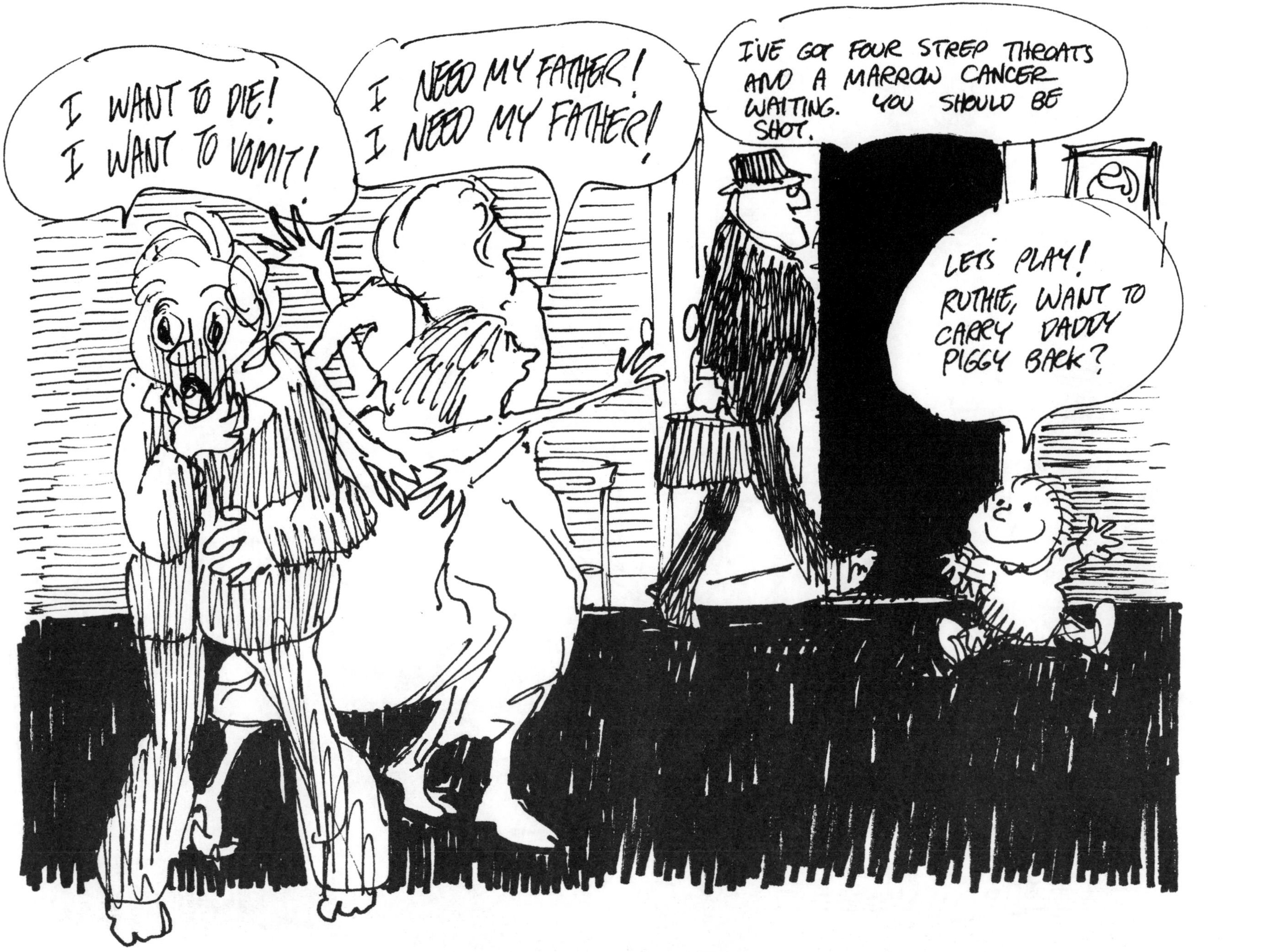
I WANT TO DIE! I WANT TO VOMIT!
I NEED MY FATHER! I NEED MY FATHER!
I'VE GOT FOUR STREP THROATS AND A MARROW CANCER WAITING. YOU SHOULD BE SHOT.
LETS PLAY! RUTHIE, WANT TO CARRY DADDY PIGGY BACK?

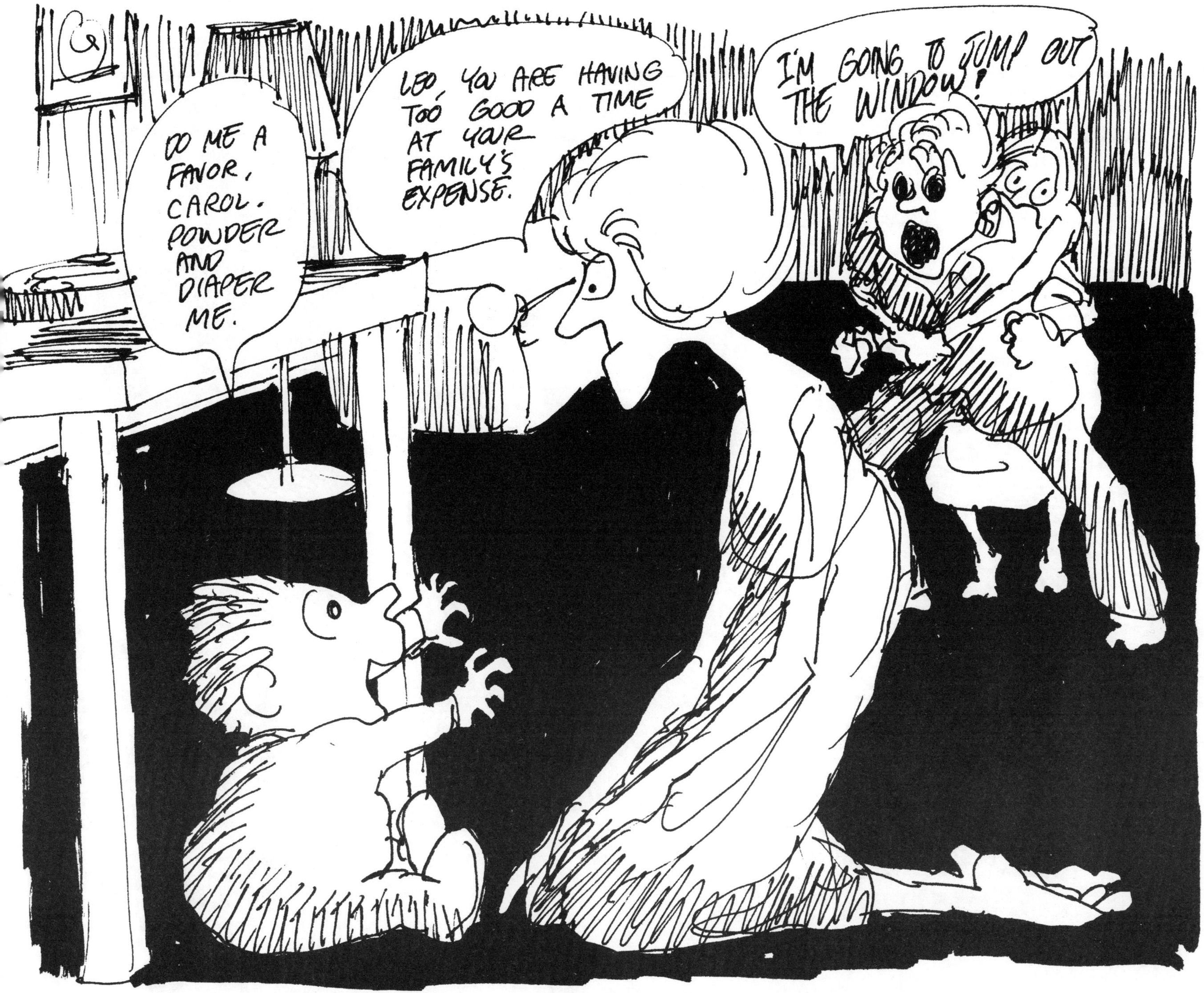
DO ME A FAVOR, CAROL. POWDER AND DIAPER ME.
LEO, YOU ARE HAVING TOO GOOD A TIME AT YOUR FAMILY'S EXPENSE.
I'M GOING TO JUMP OUT THE WINDOW!

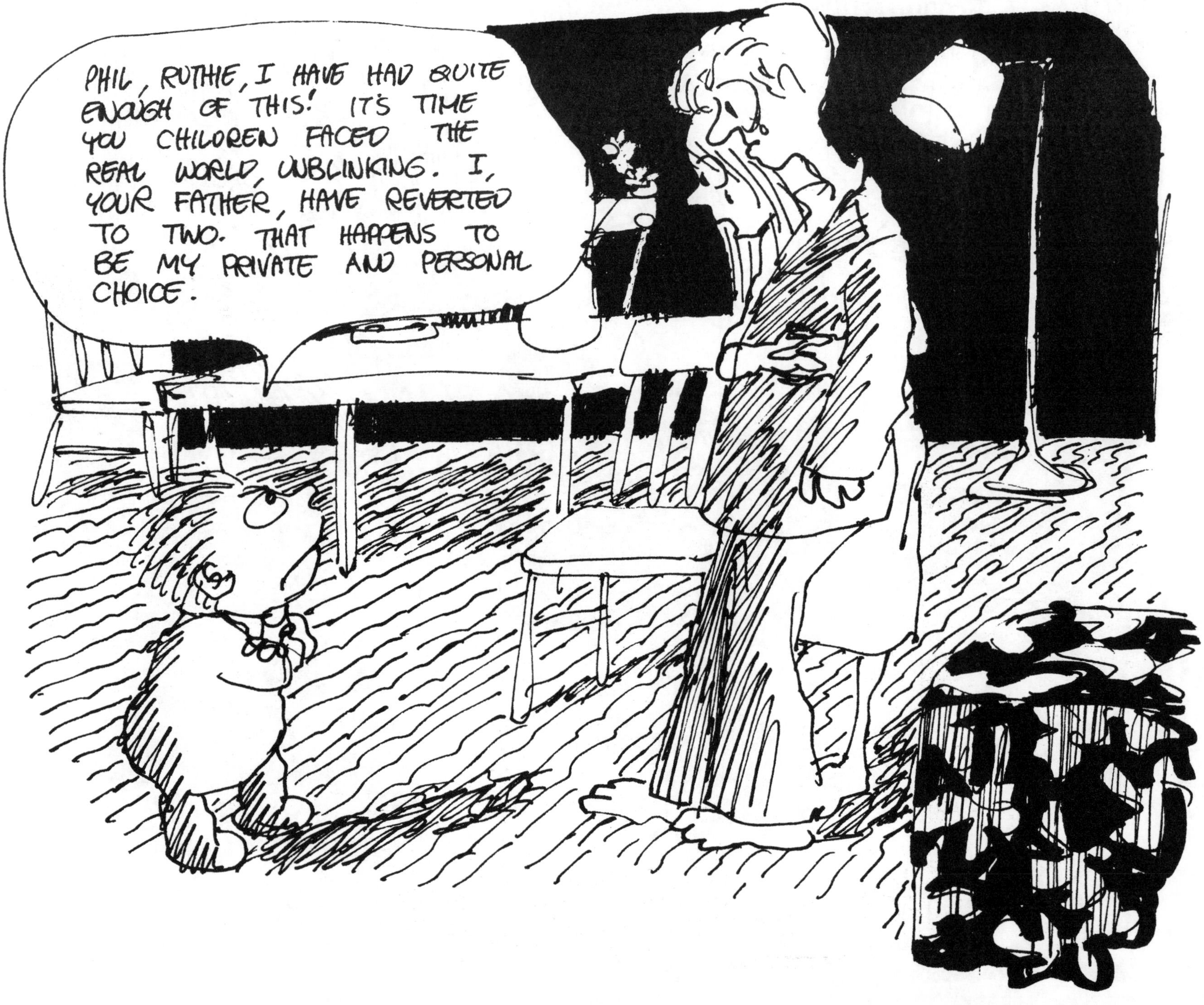
PHIL, RUTHIE, I HAVE HAD QUITE ENOUGH OF THIS! IT'S TIME YOU CHILDREN FACED THE REAL WORLD, UNBLINKING. I, YOUR FATHER, HAVE REVERTED TO TWO. THAT HAPPENS TO BE MY PRIVATE AND PERSONAL CHOICE.

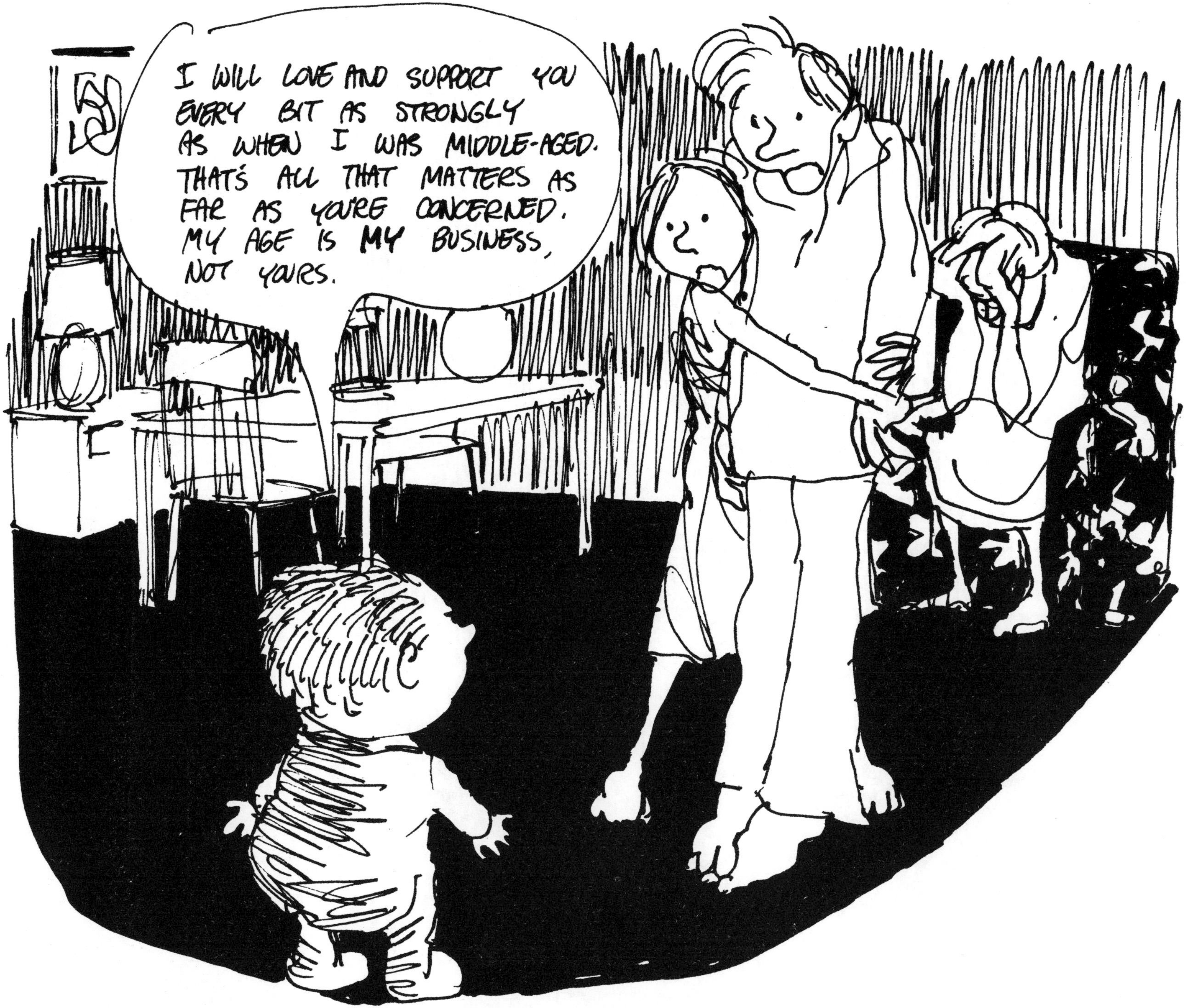
I WILL LOVE AND SUPPORT YOU EVERY BIT AS STRONGLY AS WHEN I WAS MIDDLE-AGED. THAT'S ALL THAT MATTERS AS FAR AS YOU'RE CONCERNED. MY AGE IS MY BUSINESS, NOT YOURS.

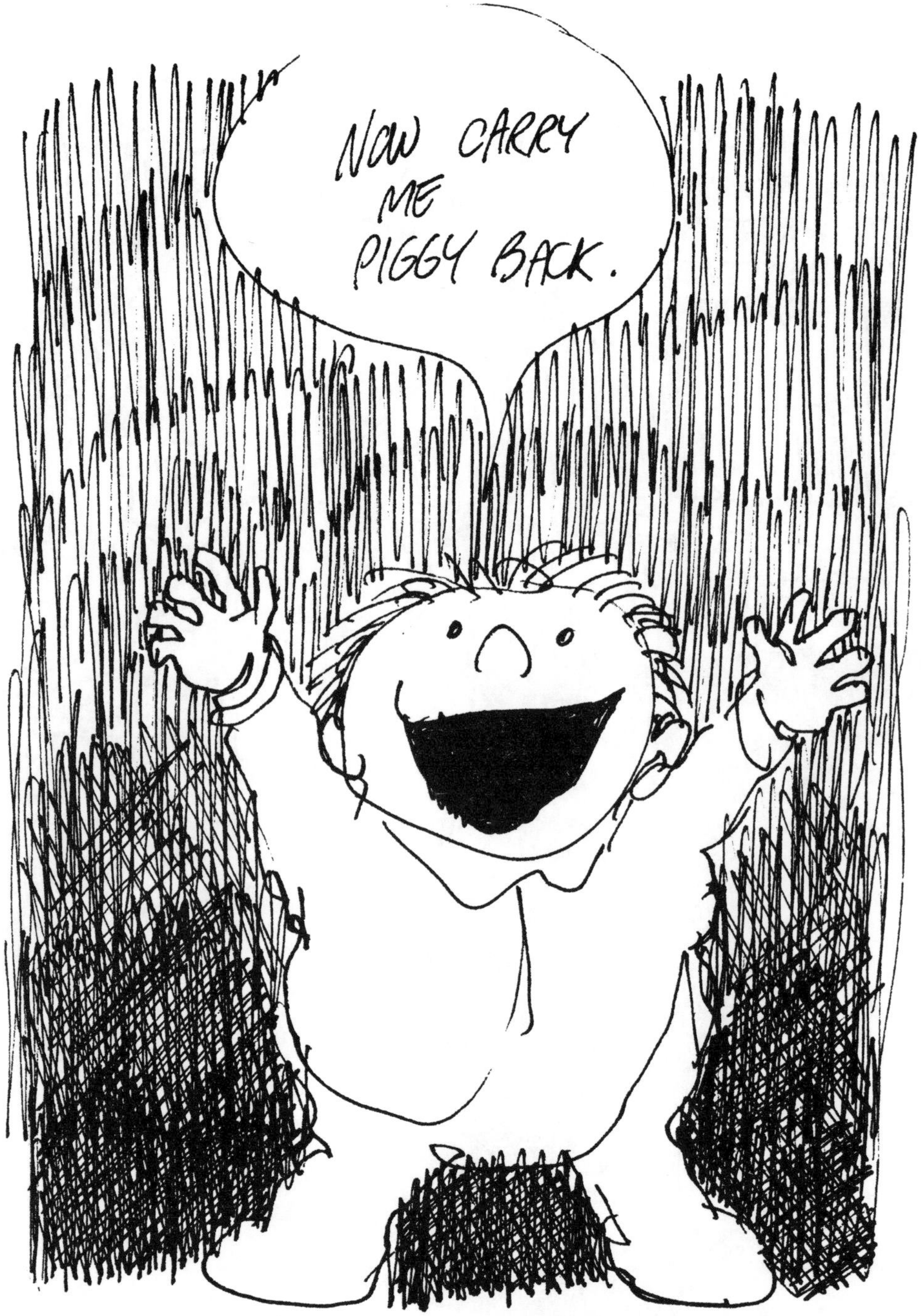
NOW CARRY ME PIGGY BACK.

HOMECOMING

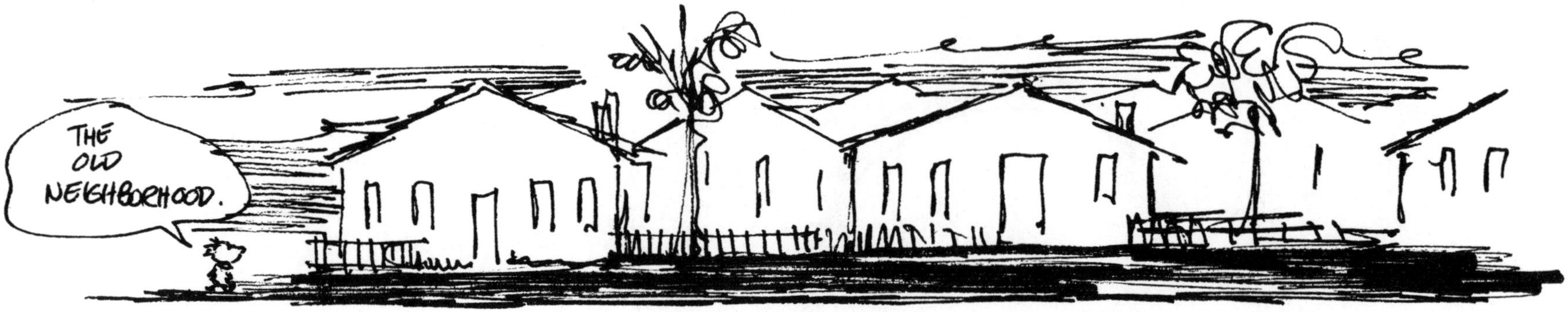
THE OLD NEIGHBORHOOD.

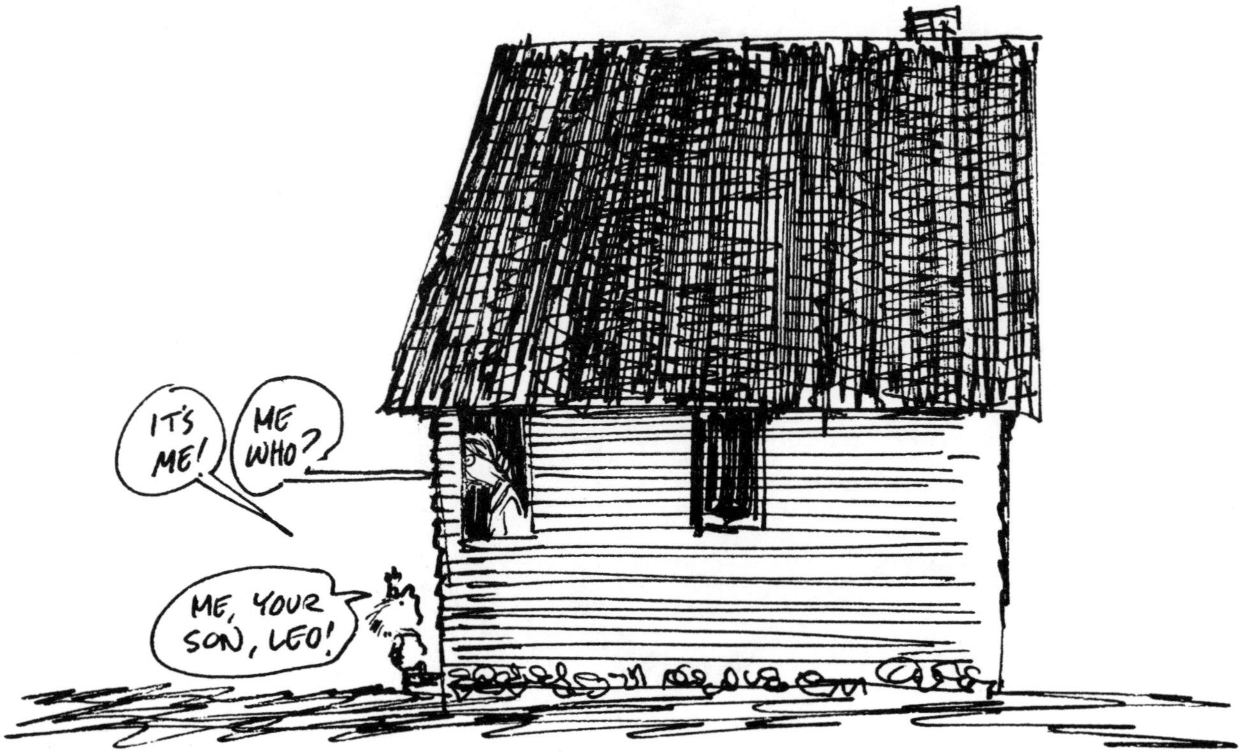
IT'S ME!
ME WHO?
ME, YOUR SON, LEO!

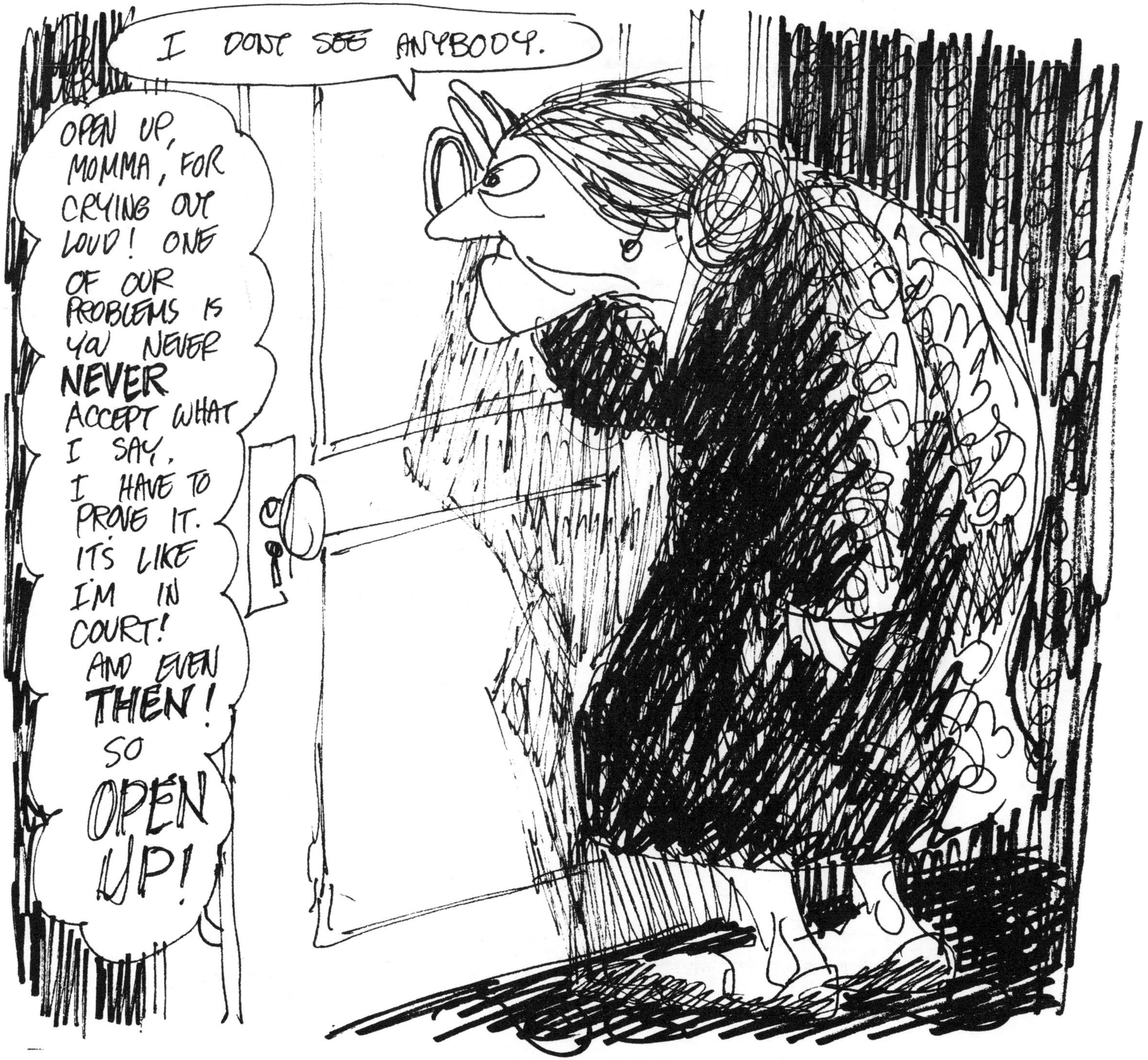
I DONT SEE ANYBODY.
OPEN UP, MOMMA, FOR CRYING OUT LOUD! ONE OF OUR PROBLEMS IS YOU NEVER NEVER ACCEPT WHAT I SAY. I HAVE TO PROVE IT. ITS LIKE I'M IN COURT! AND EVEN THEN! SO OPEN UP!

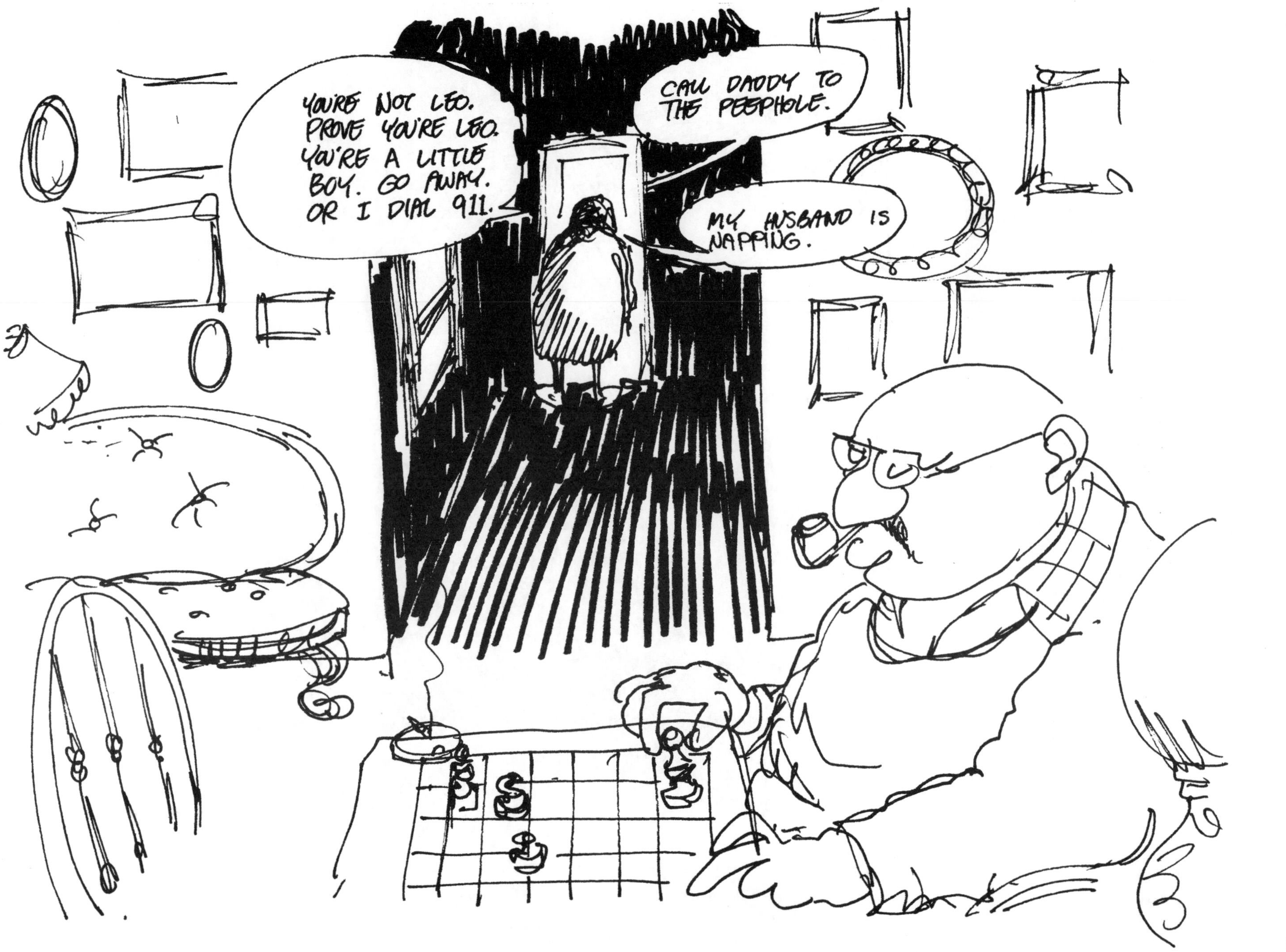
YOU'RE NOT LEO. PROVE YOU'RE LEO. YOU'RE A LITTLE BOY. GO AWAY. OR I DIAL 911.
CALL DADDY TO THE PEEPHOLE.
MY HUSBAND IS NAPPING.

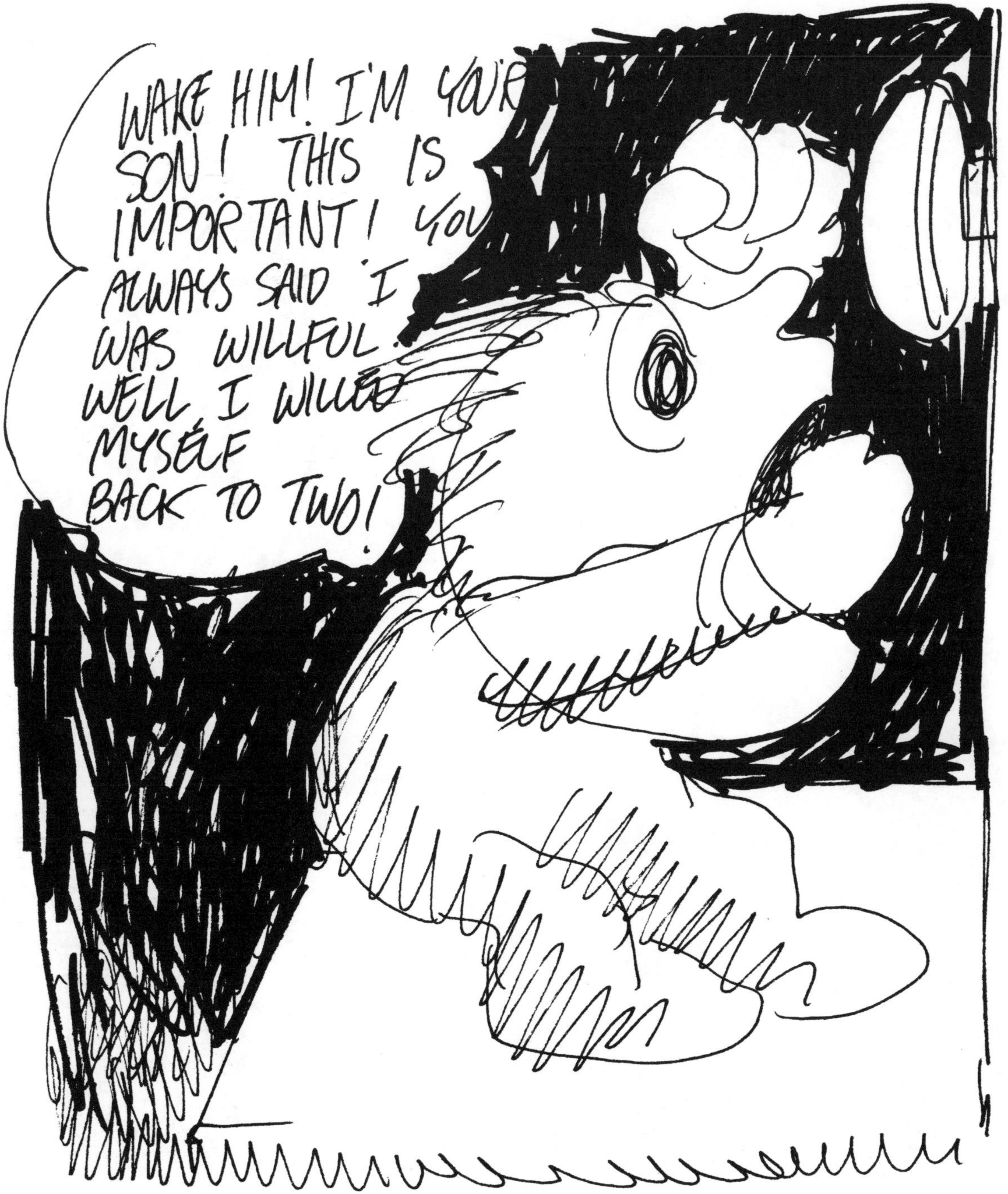
WAKE HIM! I'M YOUR SON! THIS IS IMPORTANT! YOU ALWAYS SAID I WAS WILLFUL. WELL I WILLED MYSELF BACK TO TWO!

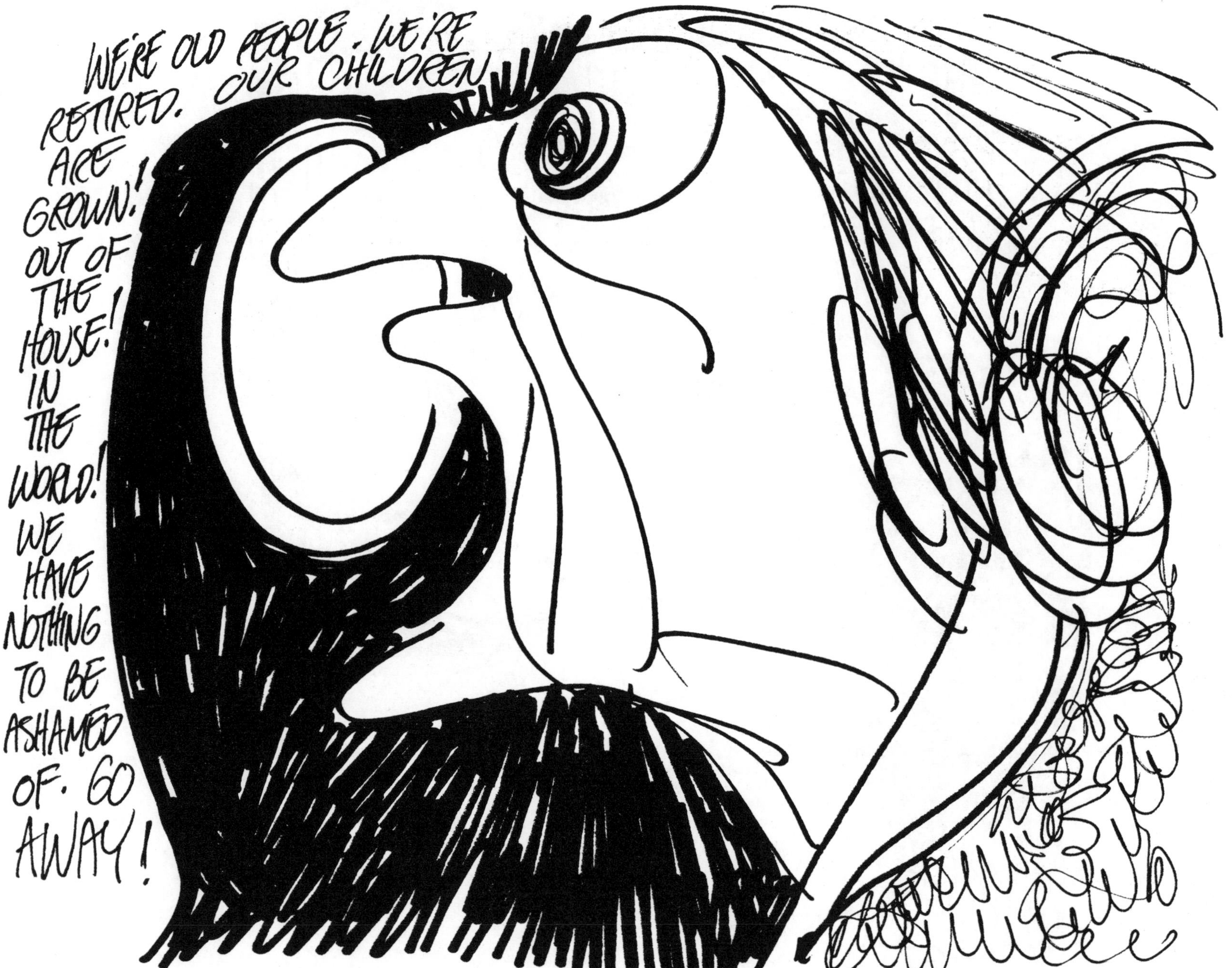
WE'RE OLD PEOPLE. WE'RE RETIRED. OUR CHILDREN ARE GROWN! OUT OF THE HOUSE! IN THE WORLD! WE HAVE NOTHING TO BE ASHAMED OF. GO AWAY!

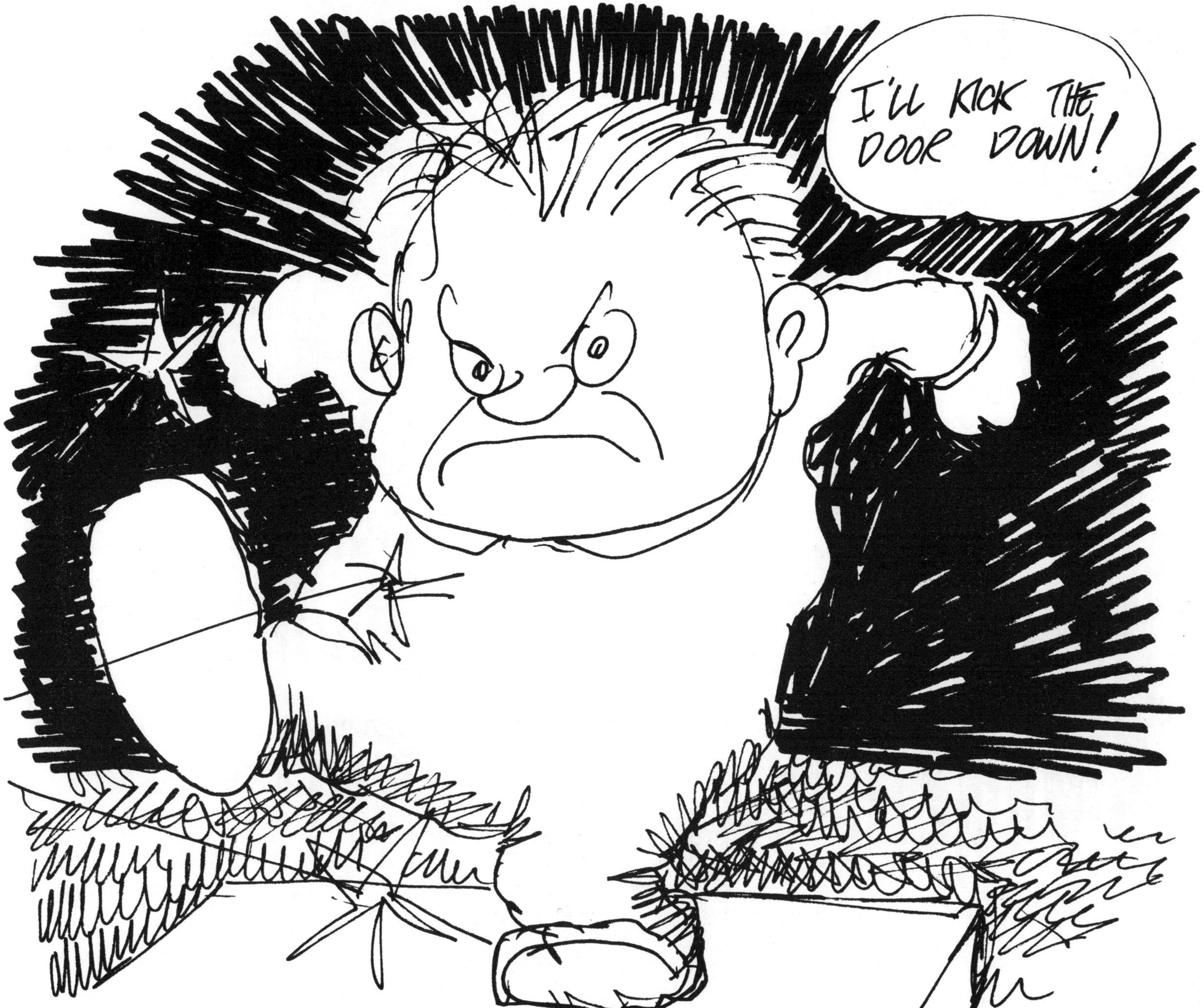
I'LL KICK THE DOOR DOWN!

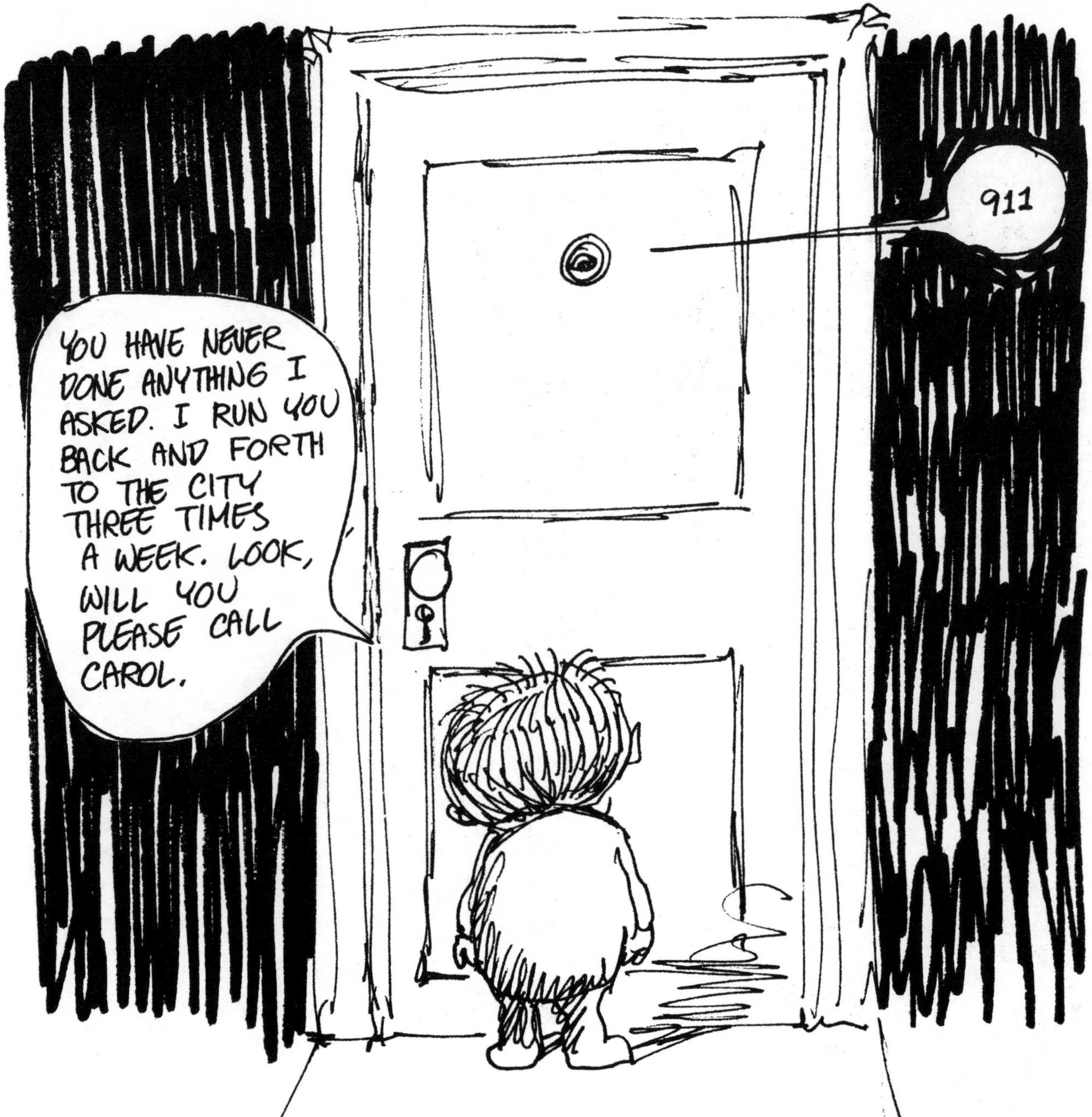
911
YOU HAVE NEVER DONE ANYTHING I ASKED. I RUN YOU BACK AND FORTH TO THE CITY THREE TIMES A WEEK. LOOK, WILL YOU PLEASE CALL CAROL.

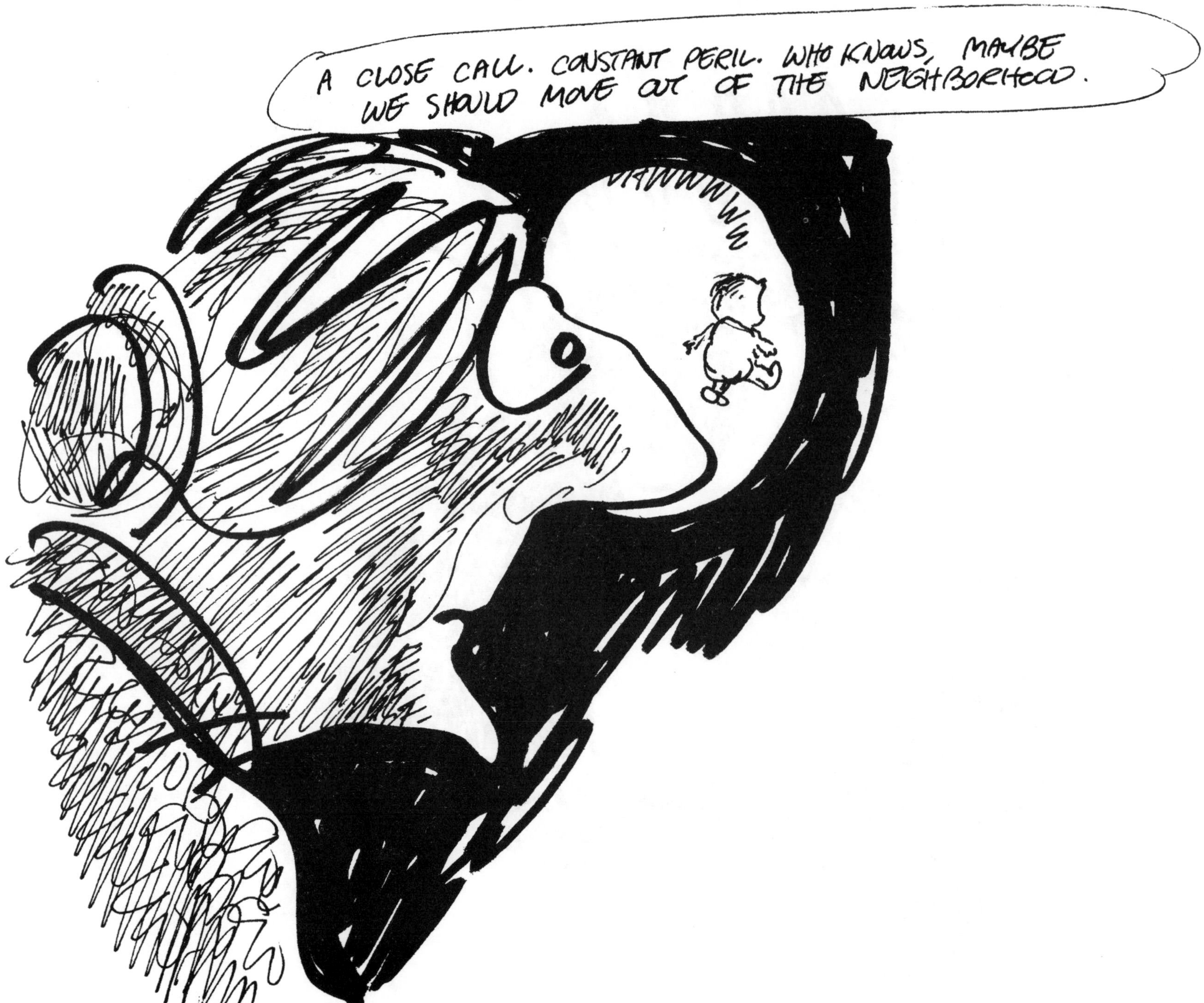
A CLOSE CALL. CONSTANT PERIL. WHO KNOWS, MAYBE WE SHOULD MOVE OUT OF THE NEIGHBORHOOD.

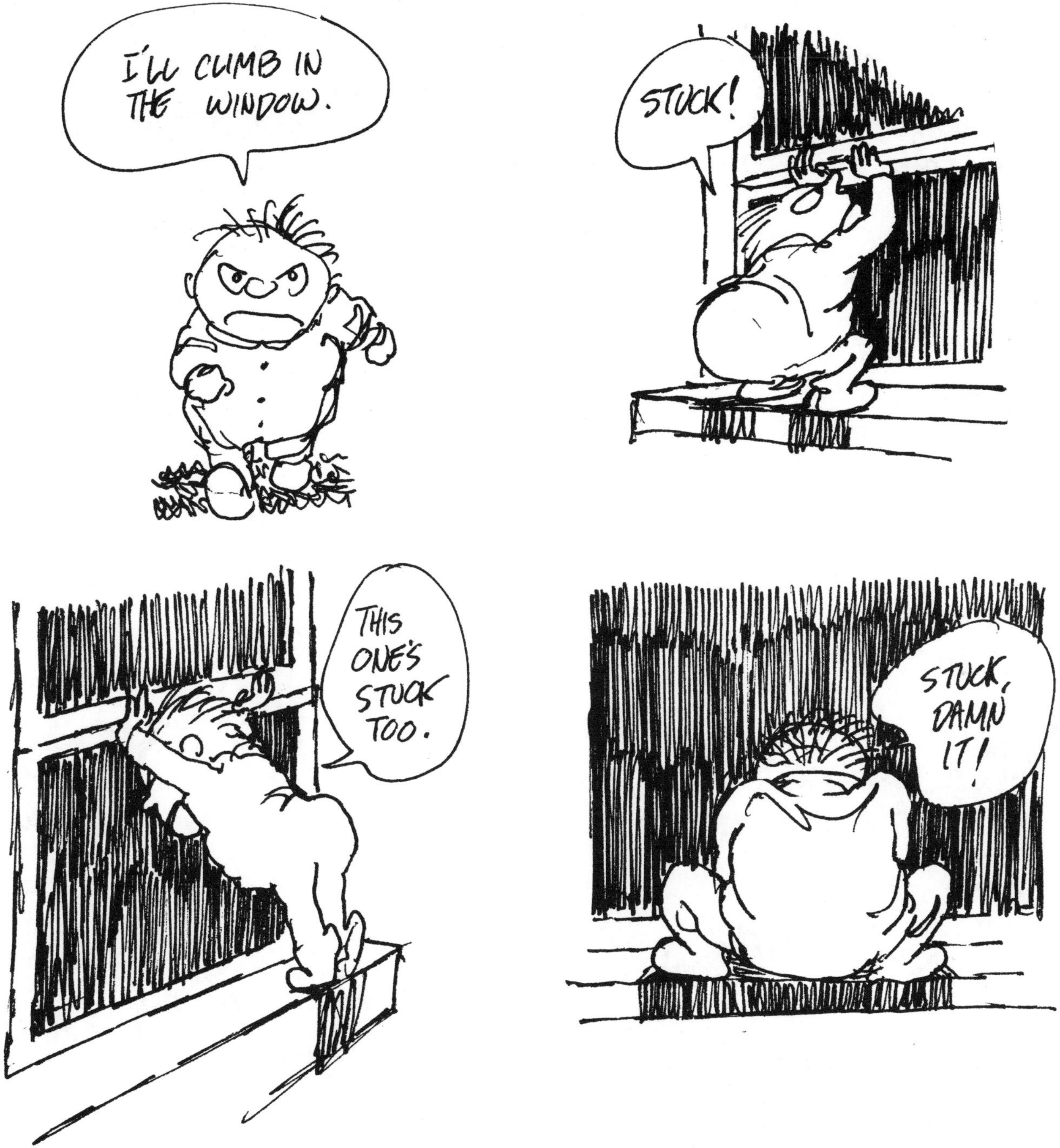
I'LL CLIMB IN THE WINDOW.
STUCK!
THIS ONE'S STUCK TOO.
STUCK, DAMN IT!

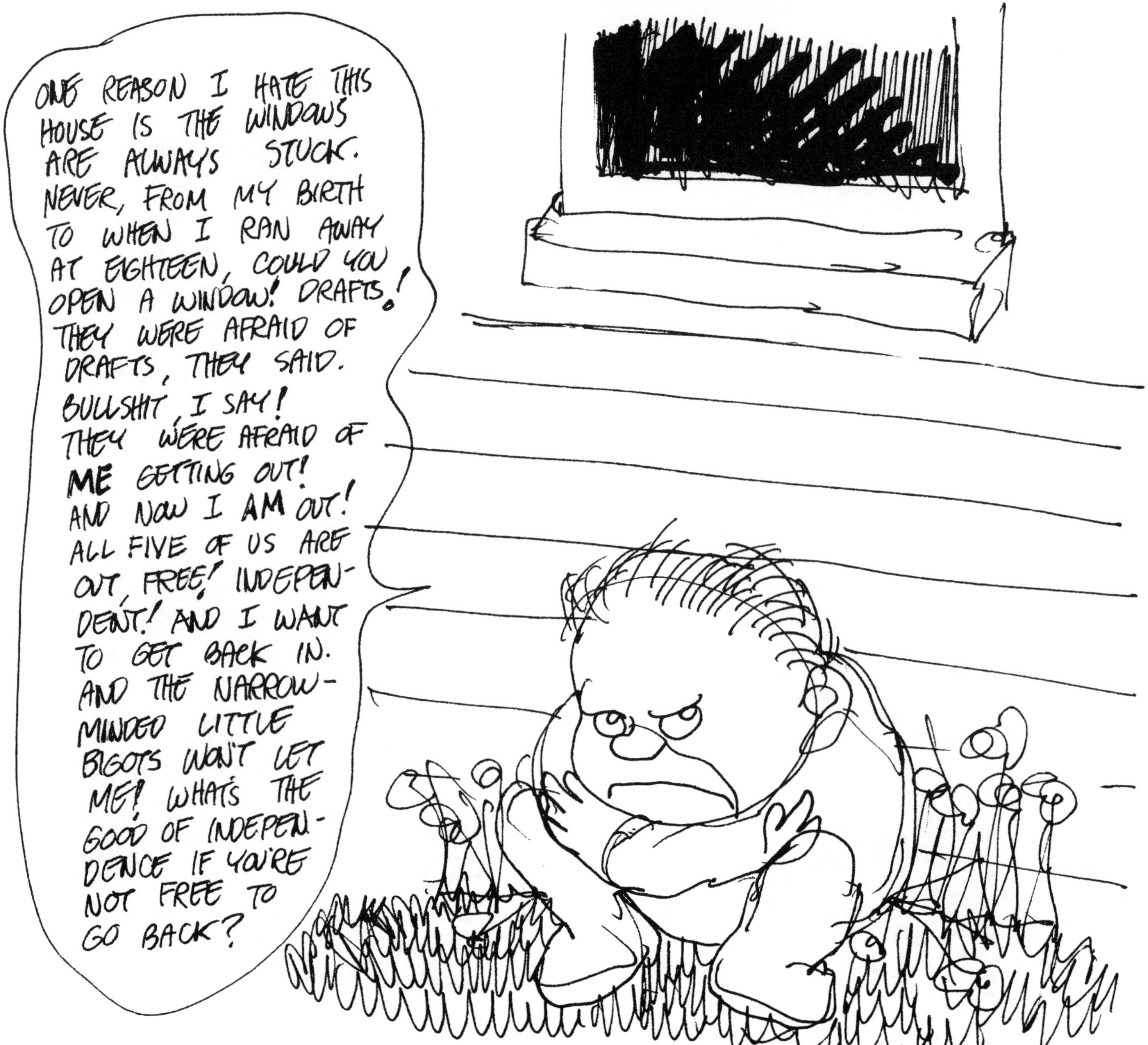
ONE REASON I HATE THIS HOUSE IS THE WINDOWS ARE ALWAYS STUCK. NEVER, FROM MY BIRTH TO WHEN I RAN AWAY AT EIGHTEEN, COULD YOU OPEN A WINDOW! DRAFTS! THEY WERE AFRAID OF DRAFTS, THEY SAID. BULLSHIT, I SAY! THEY WERE AFRAID OF **ME** GETTING OUT! AND NOW I **AM** OUT! ALL FIVE OF US ARE OUT, FREE! INDEPEN-DENT! AND I WANT TO GET BACK IN. AND THE NARROW-MINDED LITTLE BIGOTS WON'T LET ME! WHAT'S THE GOOD OF INDEPEN-DENCE IF YOU'RE NOT FREE TO GO BACK?

I'LL THROW A ROCK THROUGH THE WINDOW.
NO. IT WILL WAKE MY FATHER. I NEED HIM ON MY SIDE.
SHE ALWAYS CAME BETWEEN US!
HE TRIED HIS BEST. NOT A BRILLIANT MAN. BUT HE RAISED FIVE KIDS. BEFORE HE GOT DRUNK ONE CHRISTMAS AND TRIED TO BURN DOWN THE HOUSE.
THAT WOULD FLUSH THEM OUT!

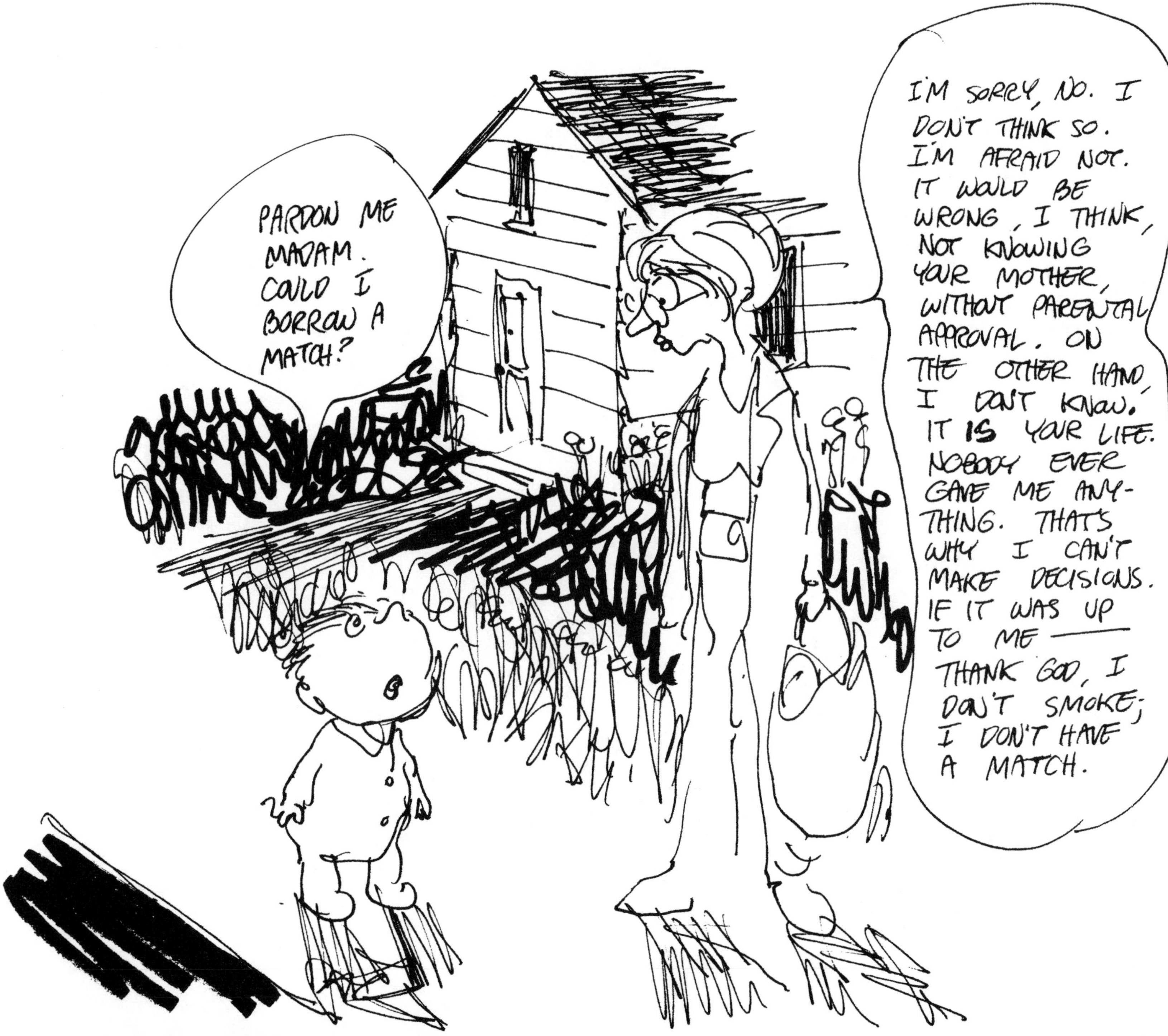
PARDON ME MADAM. COULD I BORROW A MATCH?
I'M SORRY, NO. I DON'T THINK SO. I'M AFRAID NOT. IT WOULD BE WRONG, I THINK, NOT KNOWING YOUR MOTHER, WITHOUT PARENTAL APPROVAL. ON THE OTHER HAND, I DON'T KNOW. IT IS YOUR LIFE. NOBODY EVER GAVE ME ANYTHING. THAT'S WHY I CAN'T MAKE DECISIONS. IF IT WAS UP TO ME — THANK GOD, I DON'T SMOKE; I DON'T HAVE A MATCH.

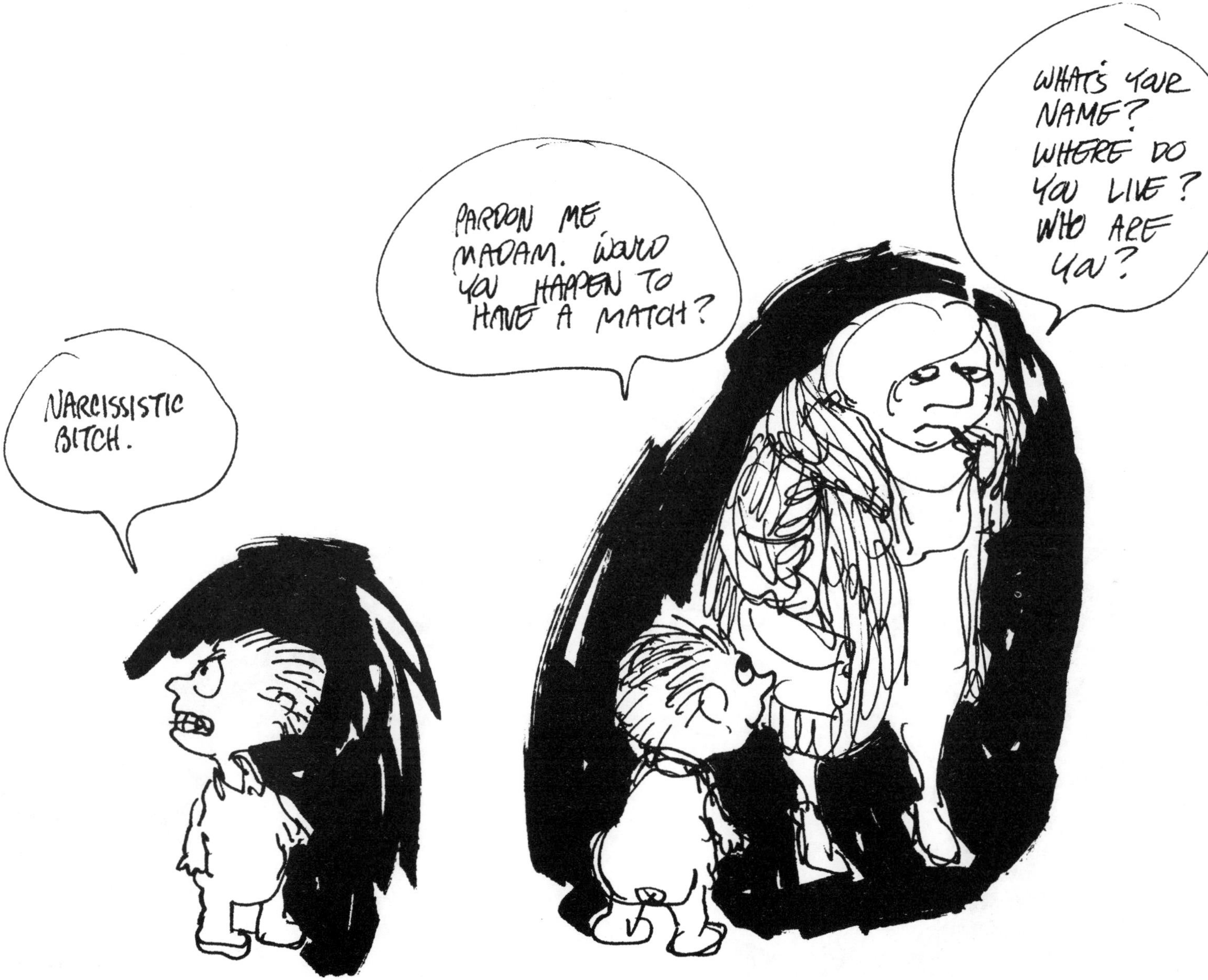
NARCISSISTIC BITCH.
PARDON ME MADAM. WOULD YOU HAPPEN TO HAVE A MATCH?
WHAT'S YOUR NAME? WHERE DO YOU LIVE? WHO ARE YOU?

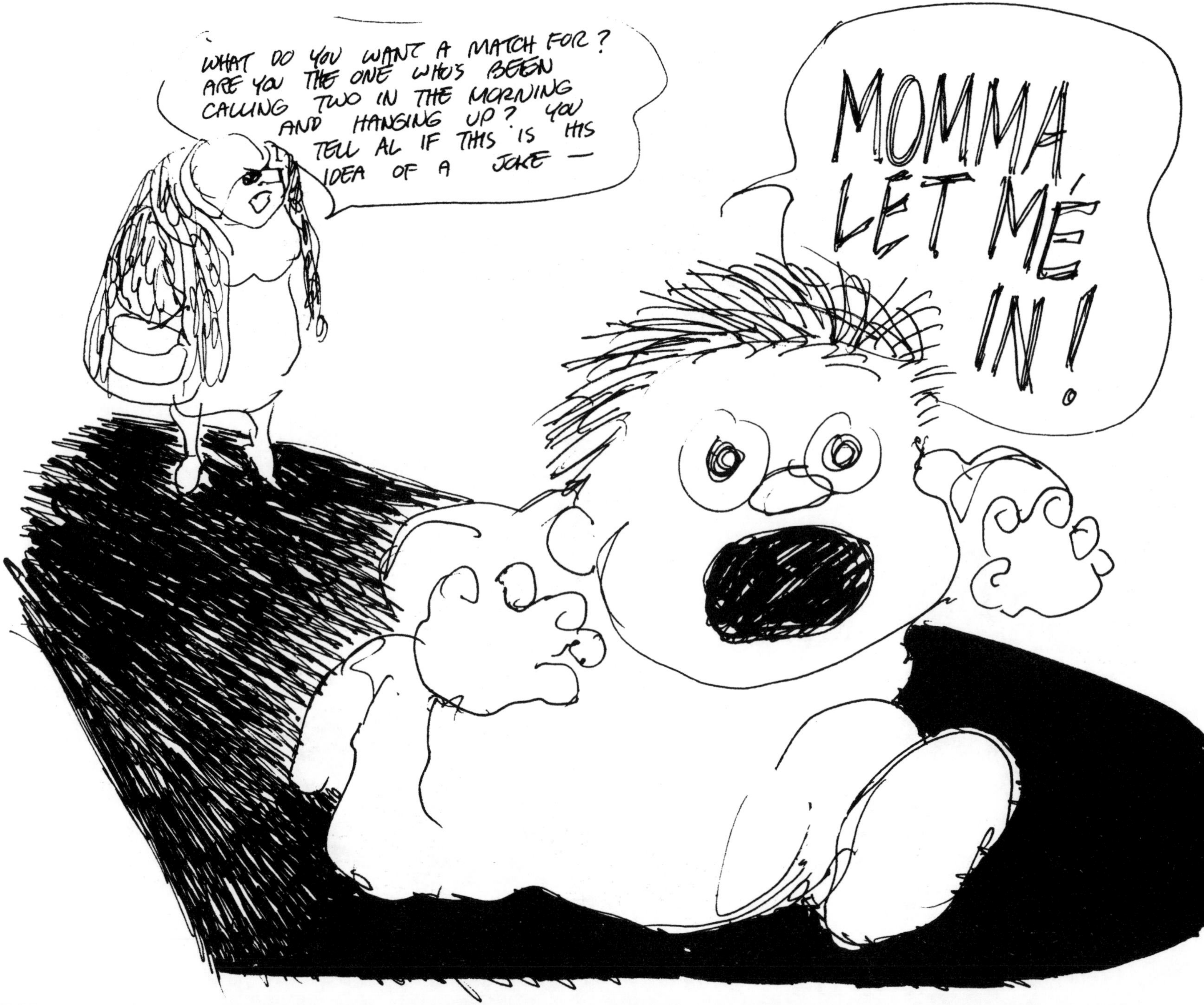
WHAT DO YOU WANT A MATCH FOR? ARE YOU THE ONE WHO'S BEEN CALLING TWO IN THE MORNING AND HANGING UP? YOU TELL AL IF THIS IS HIS IDEA OF A JOKE —
MOMMA LET ME IN!

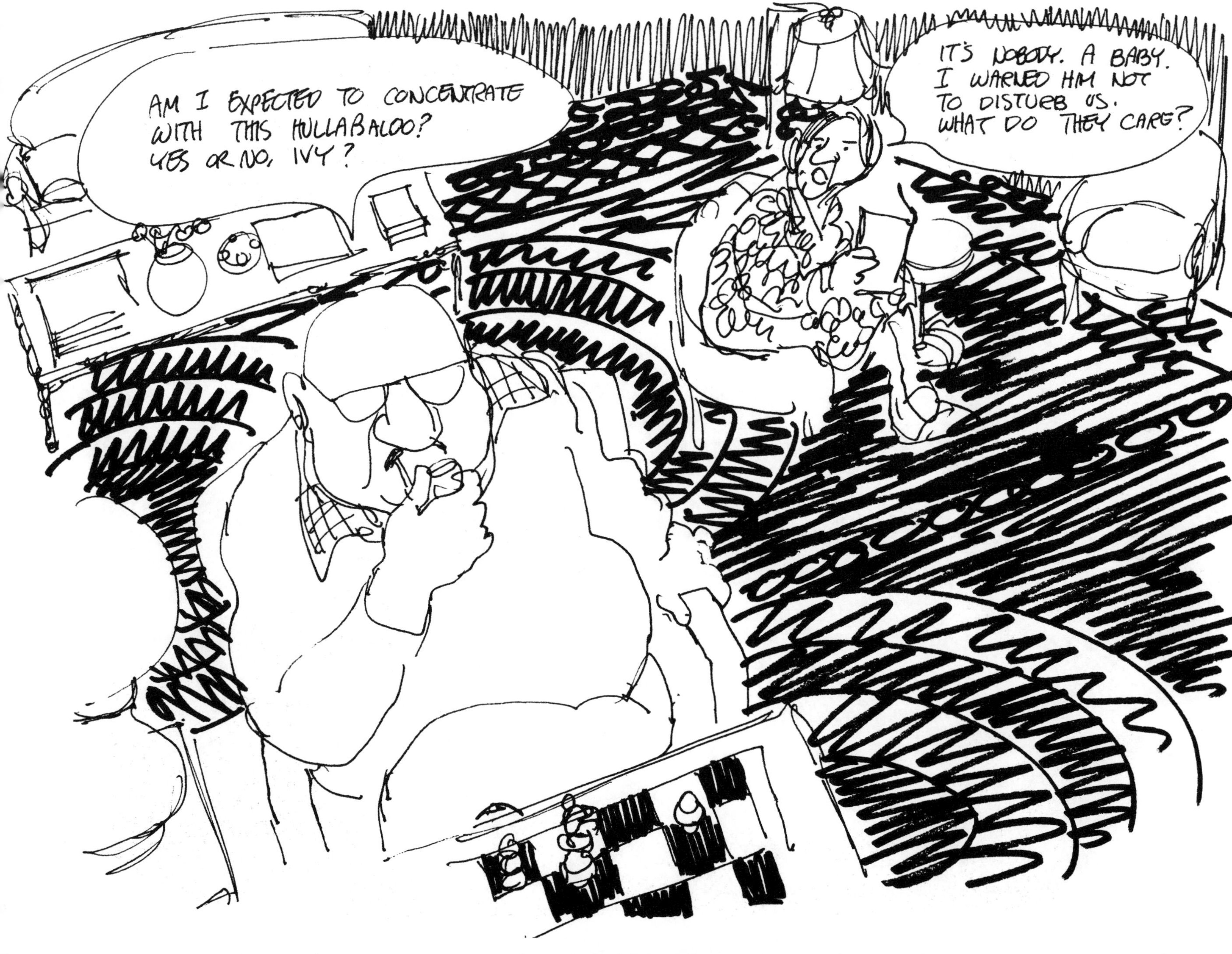
AM I EXPECTED TO CONCENTRATE WITH THIS HULLABALOO? YES OR NO, IVY?
IT'S NOBODY. A BABY. I WARNED HIM NOT TO DISTURB US. WHAT DO THEY CARE?

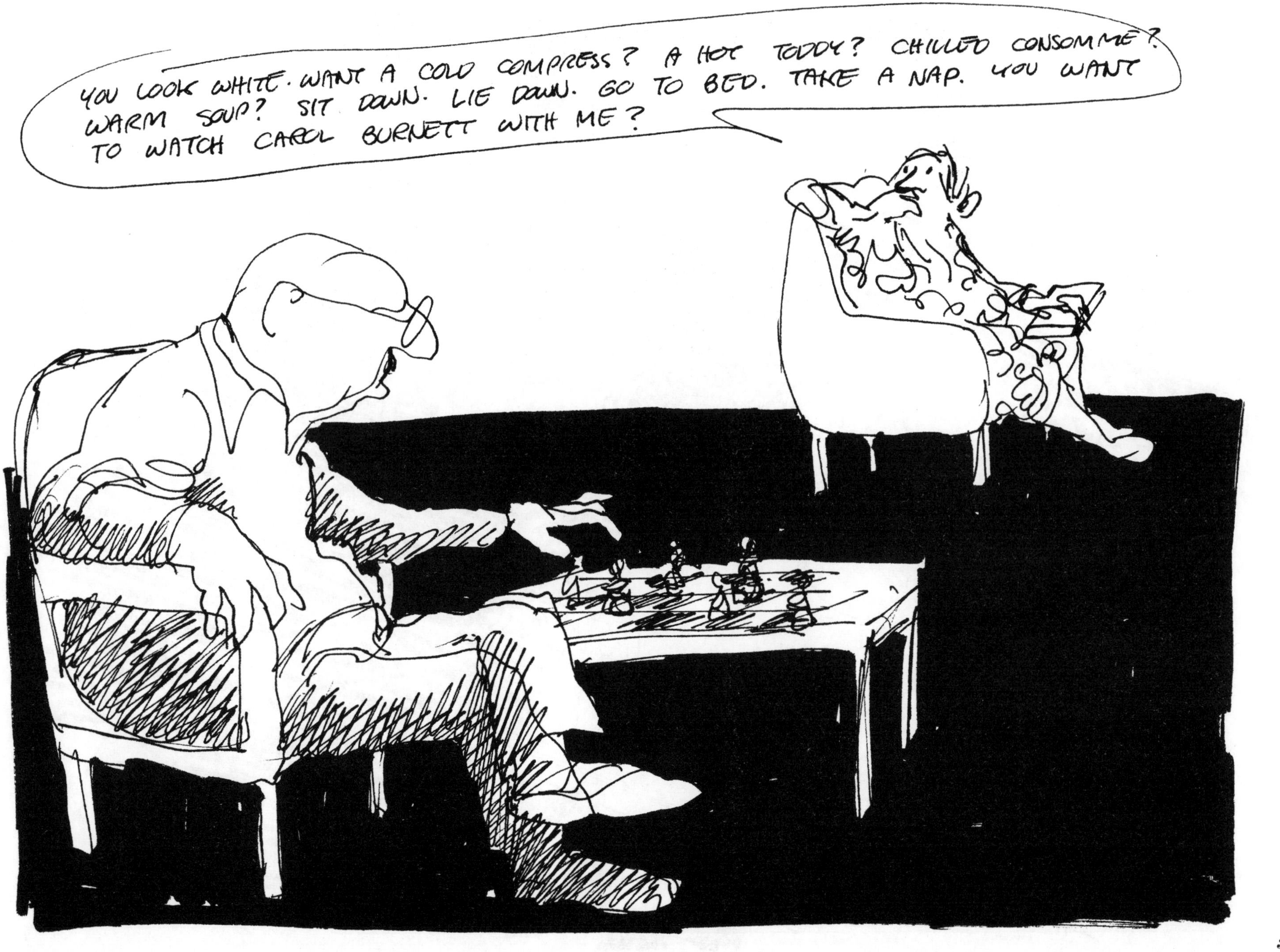
YOU LOOK WHITE. WANT A COLD COMPRESS? A HOT TODDY? CHILLED CONSOMME? WARM SOUP? SIT DOWN. LIE DOWN. GO TO BED. TAKE A NAP. YOU WANT TO WATCH CAROL BURNETT WITH ME?

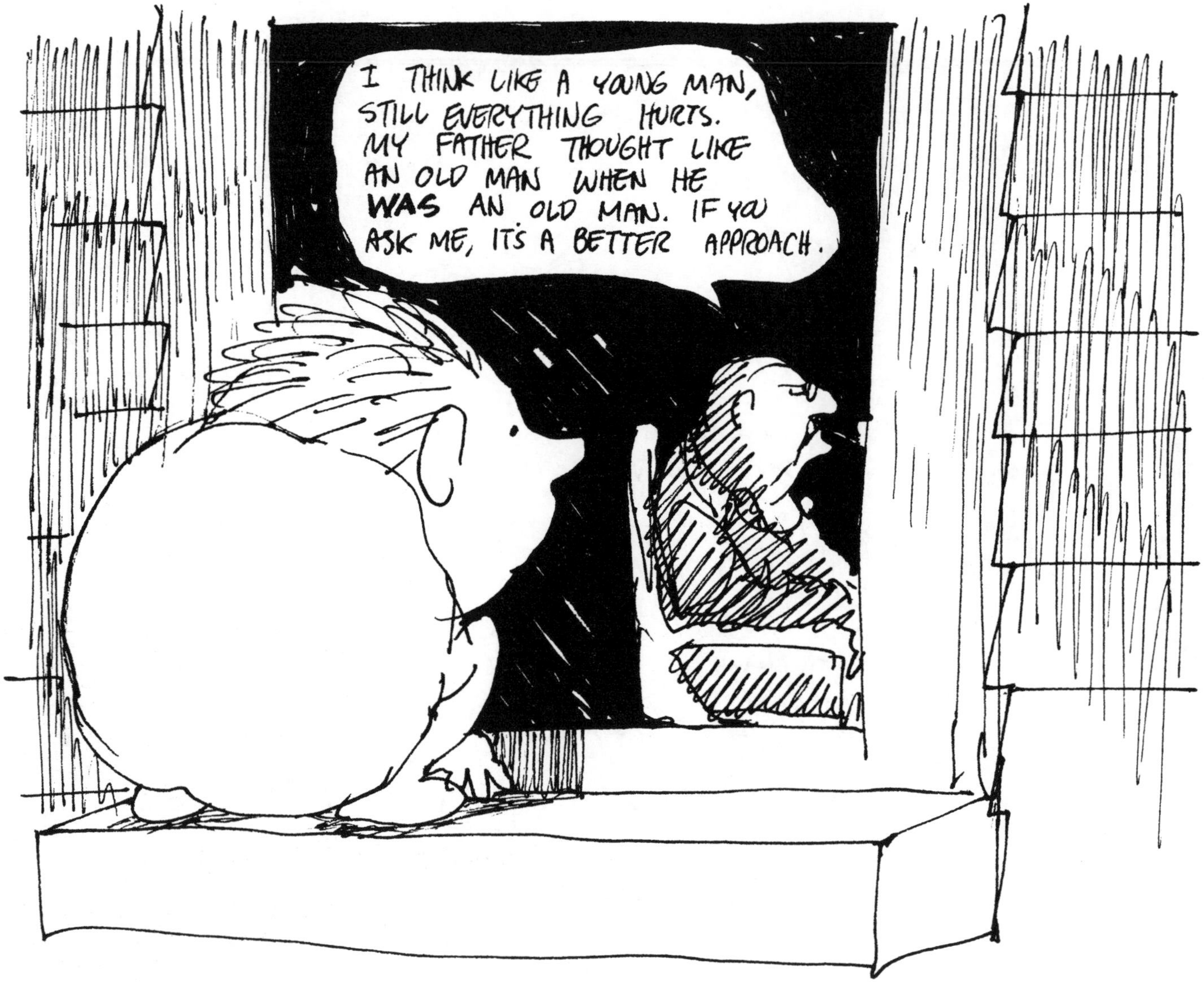
I THINK LIKE A YOUNG MAN, STILL EVERYTHING HURTS. MY FATHER THOUGHT LIKE AN OLD MAN WHEN HE **WAS** AN OLD MAN. IF YOU ASK ME, IT'S A BETTER APPROACH.

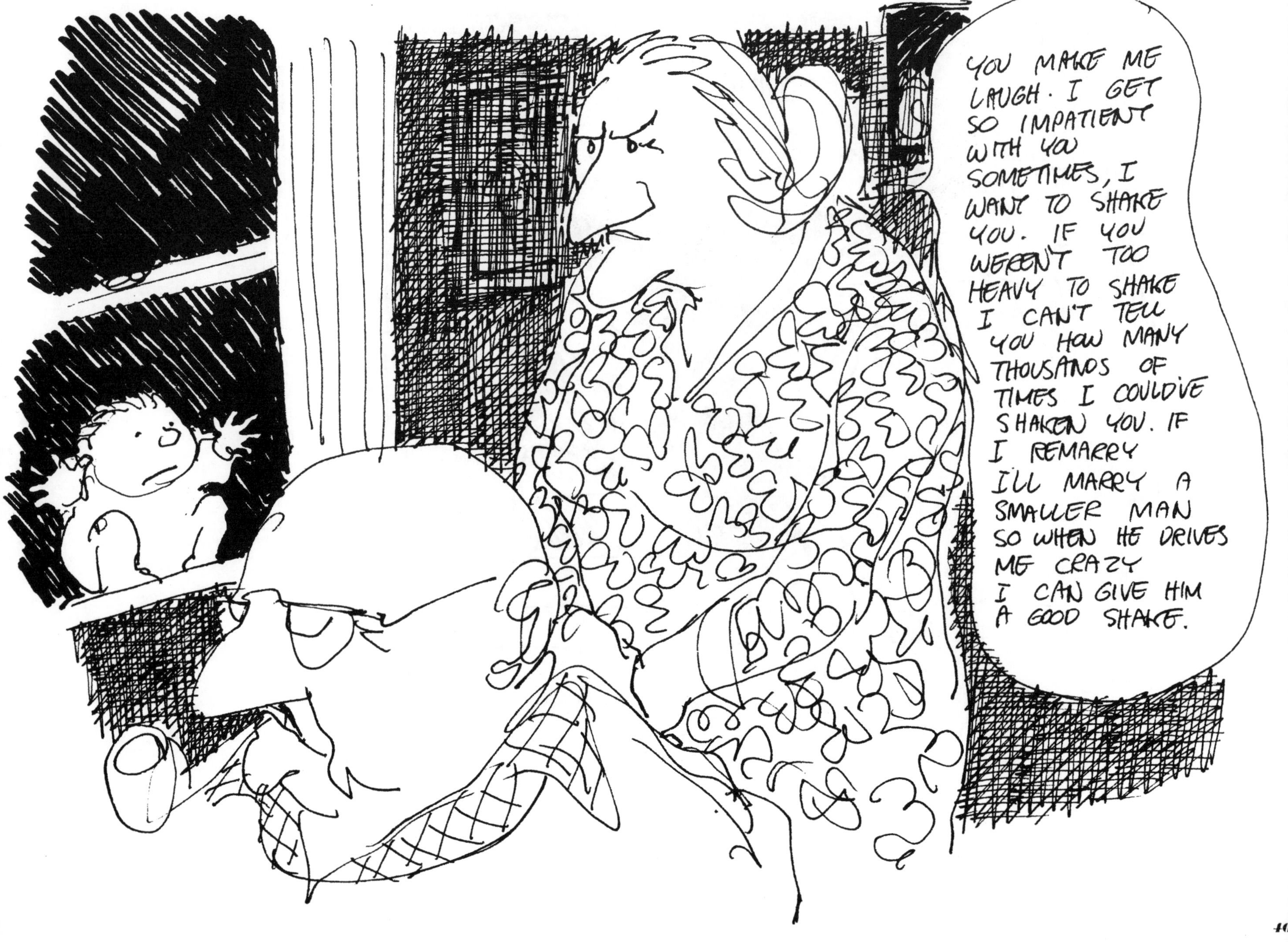
YOU MAKE ME LAUGH. I GET SO IMPATIENT WITH YOU SOMETIMES, I WANT TO SHAKE YOU. IF YOU WEREN'T TOO HEAVY TO SHAKE I CAN'T TELL YOU HOW MANY THOUSANDS OF TIMES I COULD'VE SHAKEN YOU. IF I REMARRY I'LL MARRY A SMALLER MAN SO WHEN HE DRIVES ME CRAZY I CAN GIVE HIM A GOOD SHAKE.

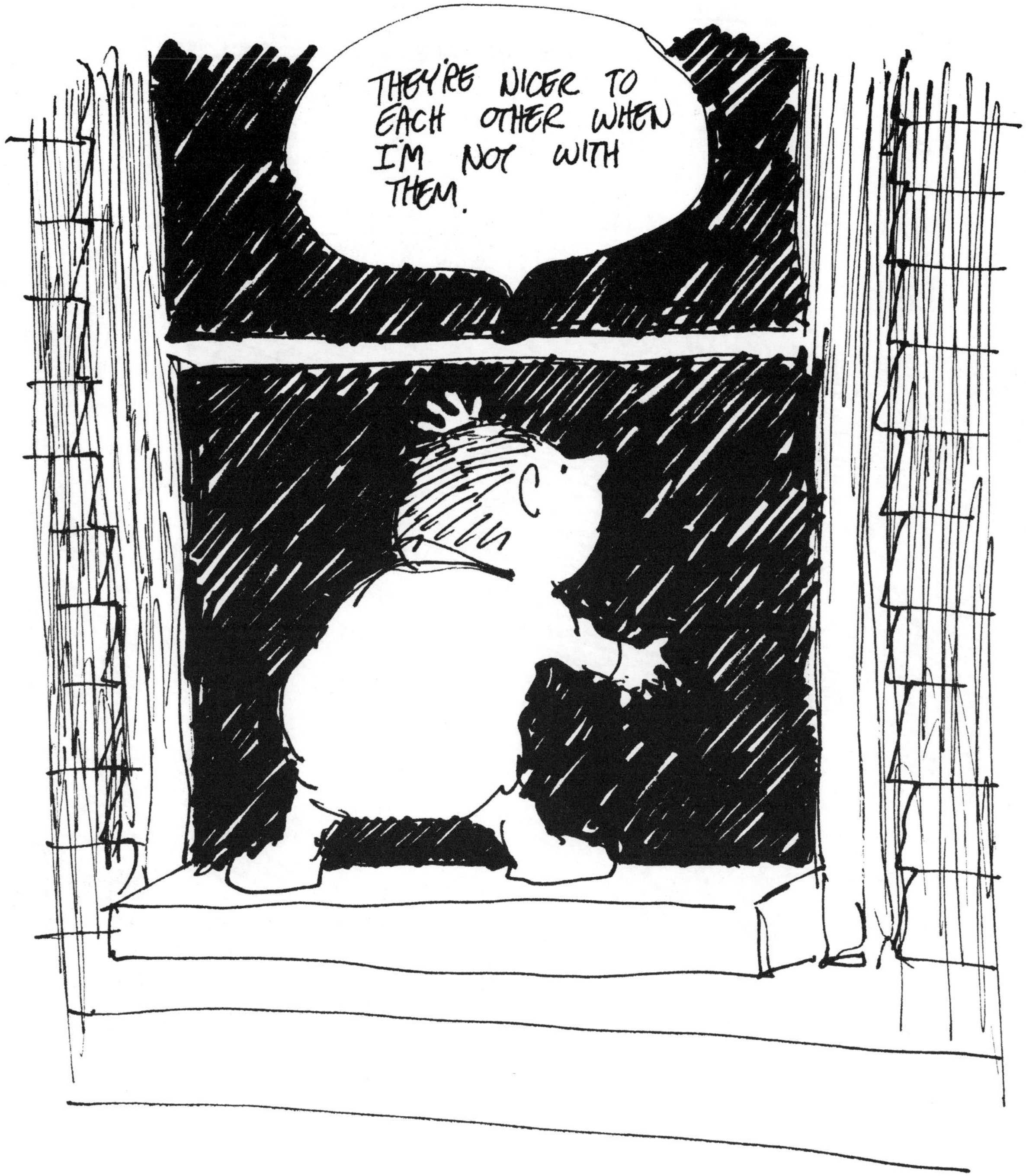
THEY'RE NICER TO EACH OTHER WHEN I'M NOT WITH THEM.

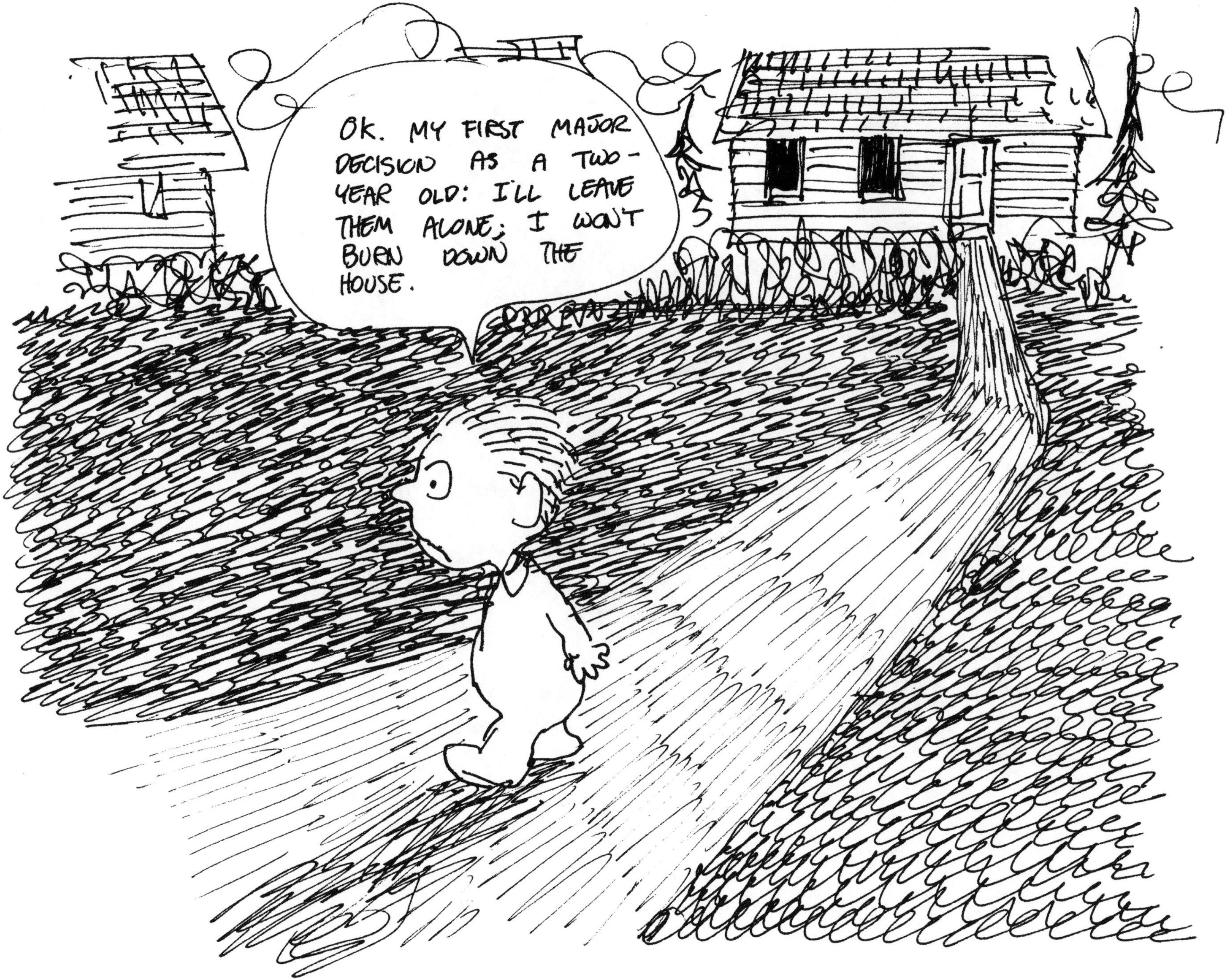
OK. MY FIRST MAJOR DECISION AS A TWO-YEAR OLD: I'LL LEAVE THEM ALONE; I WON'T BURN DOWN THE HOUSE.

Plans

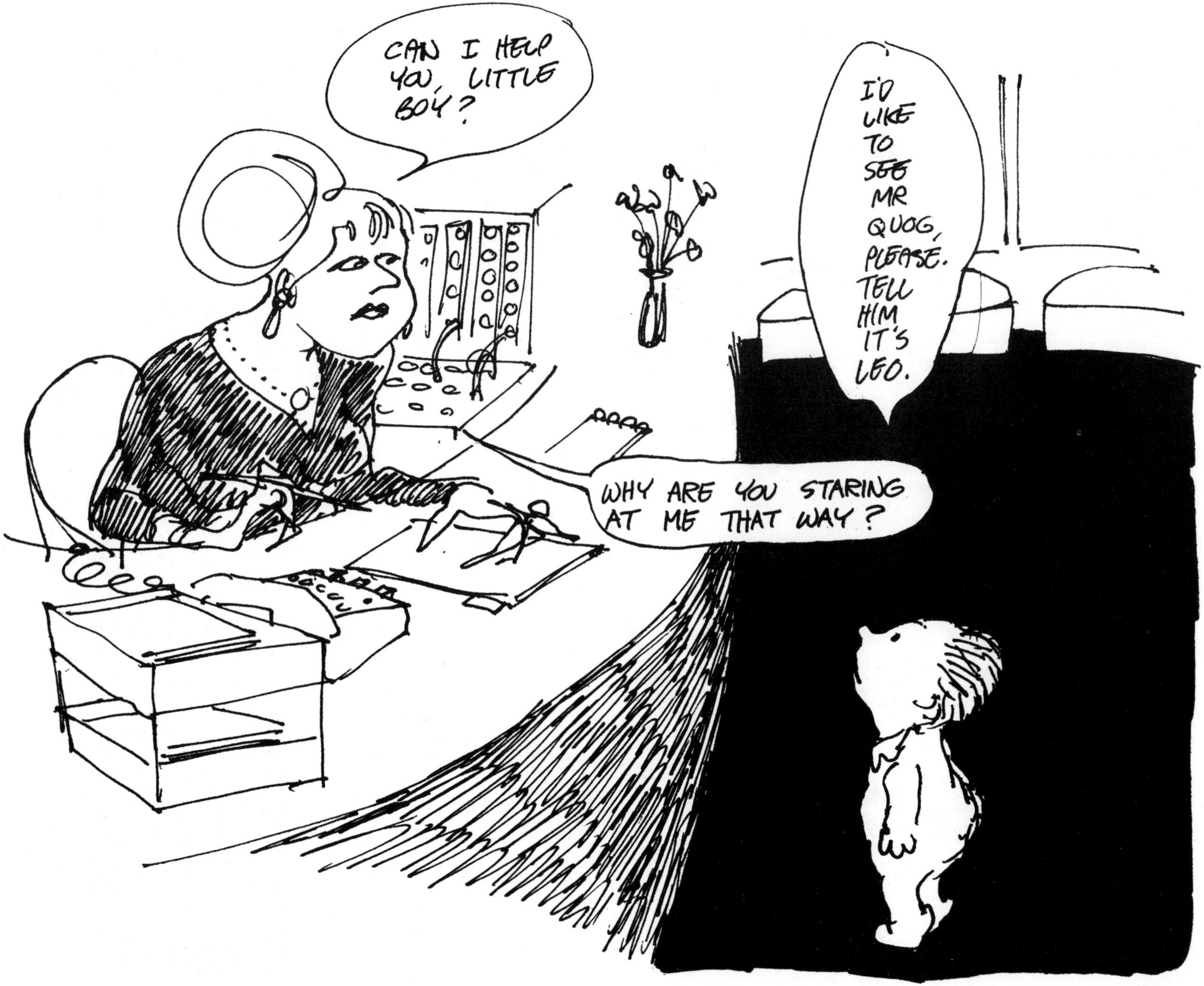
CAN I HELP YOU, LITTLE BOY?
I'D LIKE TO SEE MR QUOG, PLEASE. TELL HIM IT'S LEO.
WHY ARE YOU STARING AT ME THAT WAY?

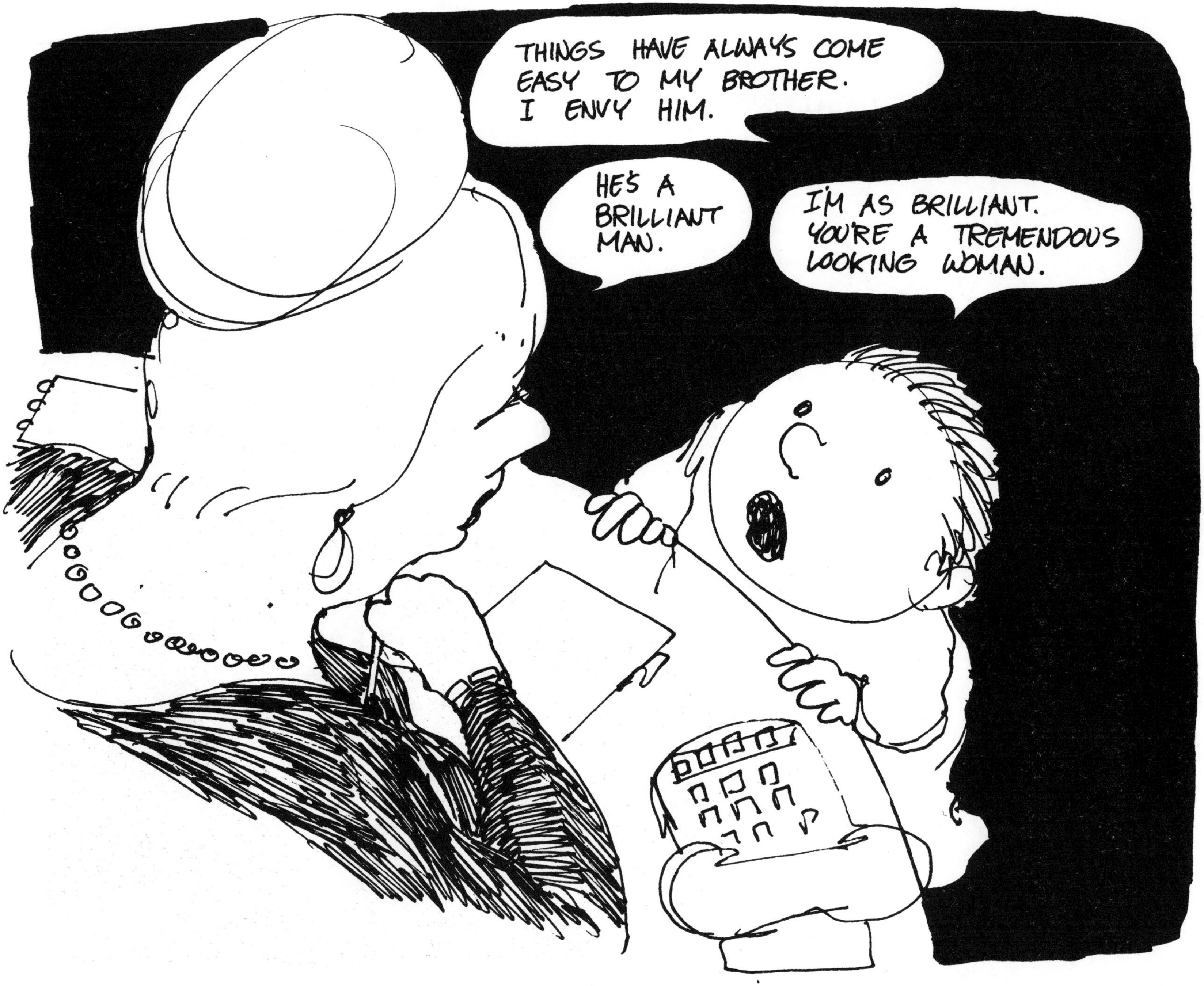
THINGS HAVE ALWAYS COME EASY TO MY BROTHER. I ENVY HIM.
HE'S A BRILLIANT MAN.
I'M AS BRILLIANT. YOU'RE A TREMENDOUS LOOKING WOMAN.

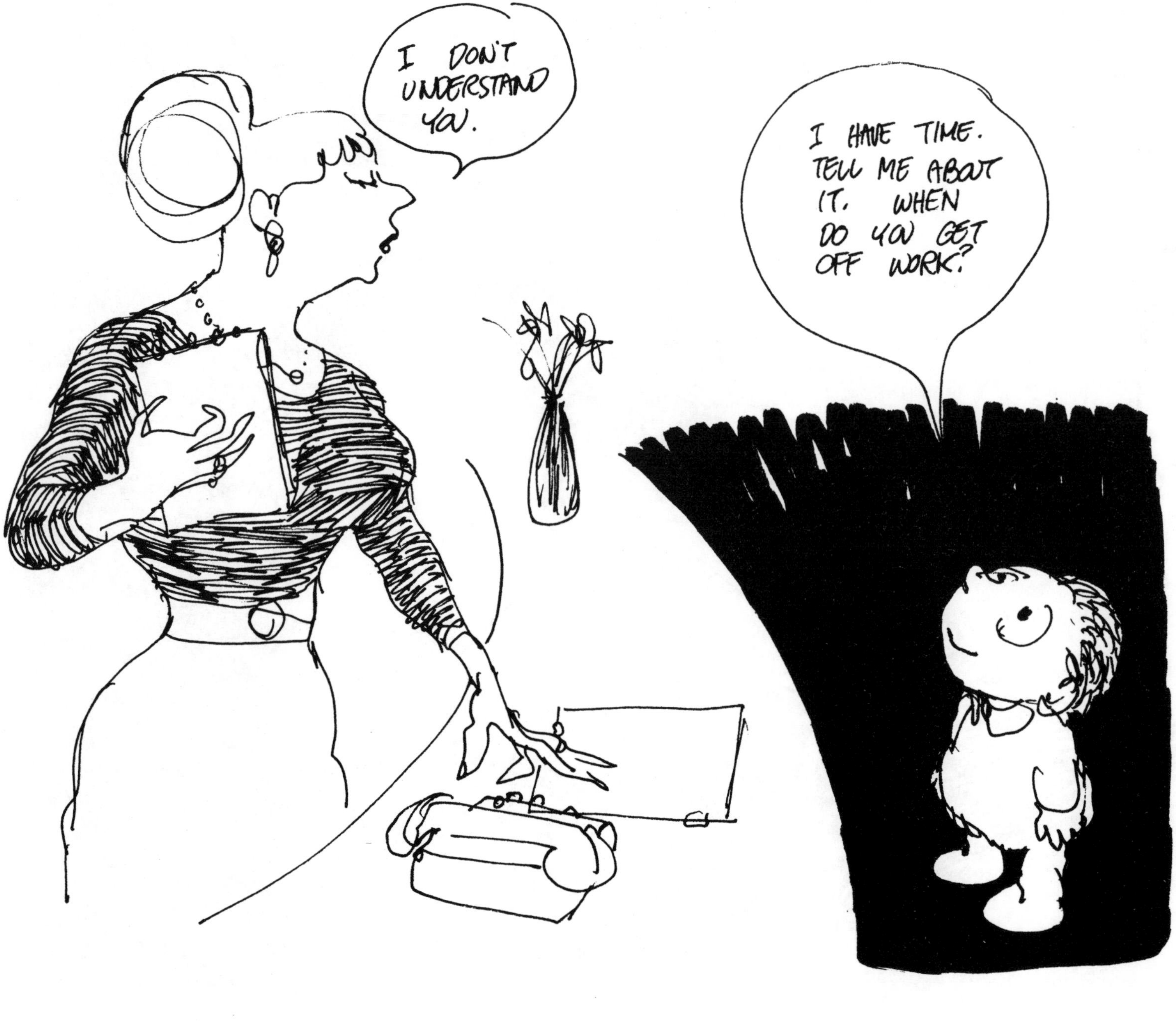
I DON'T UNDERSTAND YOU.
I HAVE TIME. TELL ME ABOUT IT. WHEN DO YOU GET OFF WORK?

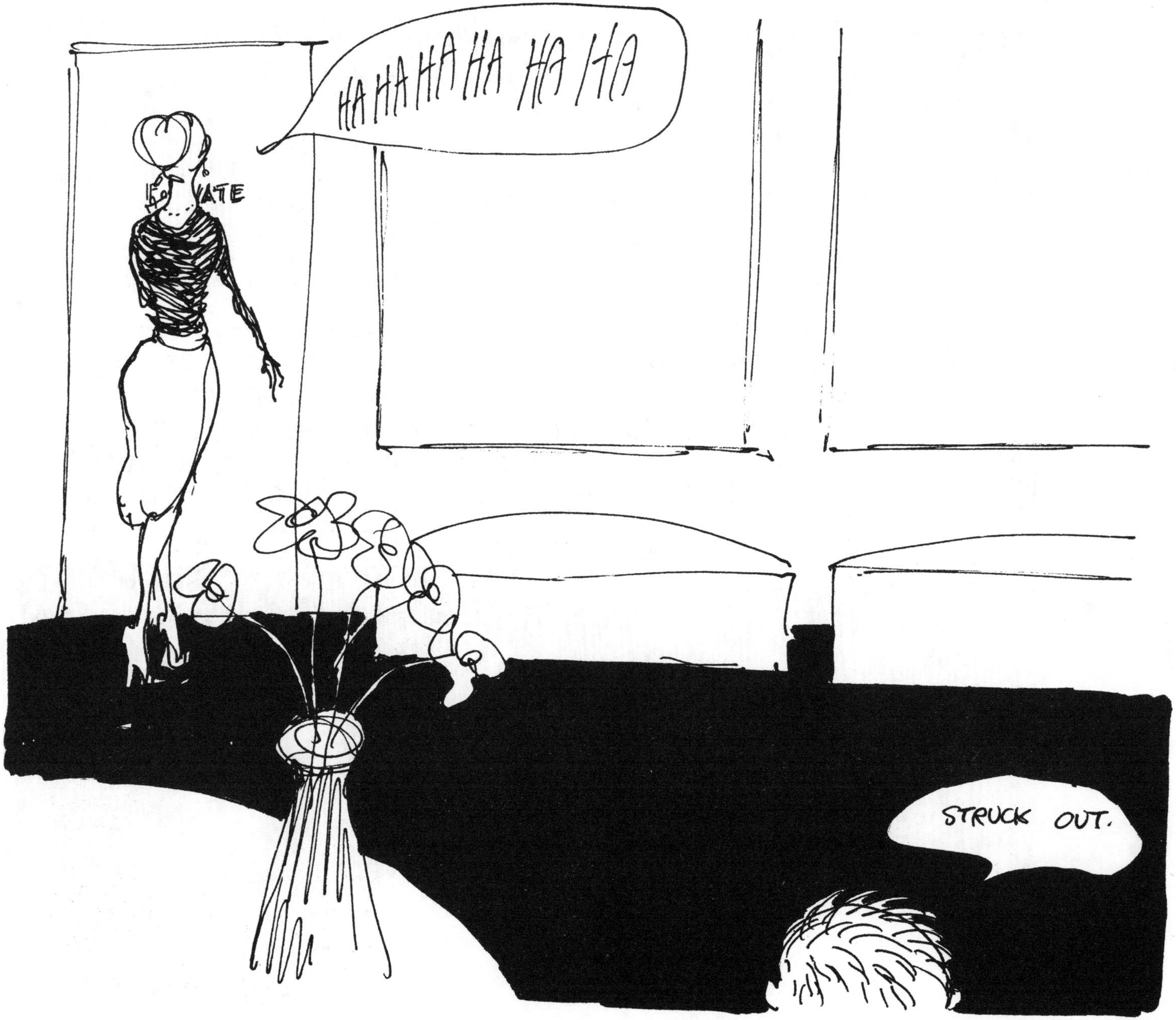
HA HA HA HA HA HA
STRUCK OUT.

PRIVATE
SHE'S NOT THE FIRST. WHEN I WAS FORTY-TWO I WOULD HAVE GIVEN UP. BUT NOW I'M MORE STUBBORN. SHE'LL GIVE IN TO ME OR I'LL MAKE HER LIFE MISERABLE. I'LL CALL HER AT ALL HOURS. I'LL SIT ON HER DOORSTEP. I'LL FOLLOW HER TO WORK. I MUST HAVE HER! CHARLIE HAS HER AND HE DOESN'T EVEN NEED HER. HIS WIFE IN A BIKINI; AN INCREDIBLE SIGHT TO BEHOLD! HE CAN'T HAVE BOTH!

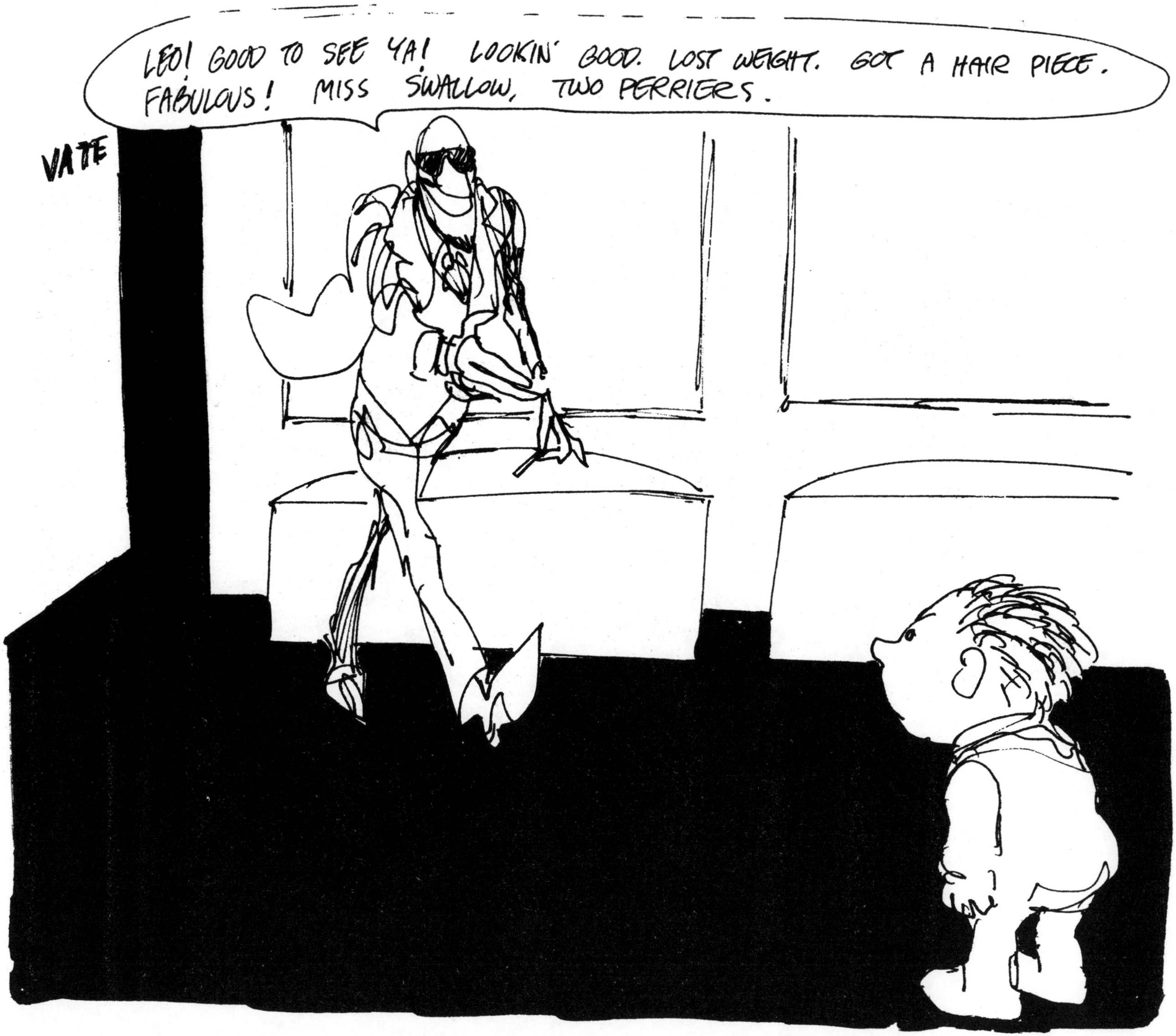
LEO! GOOD TO SEE YA! LOOKIN' GOOD. LOST WEIGHT. GOT A HAIR PIECE. FABULOUS! MISS SWALLOW, TWO PERRIERS.
VATE

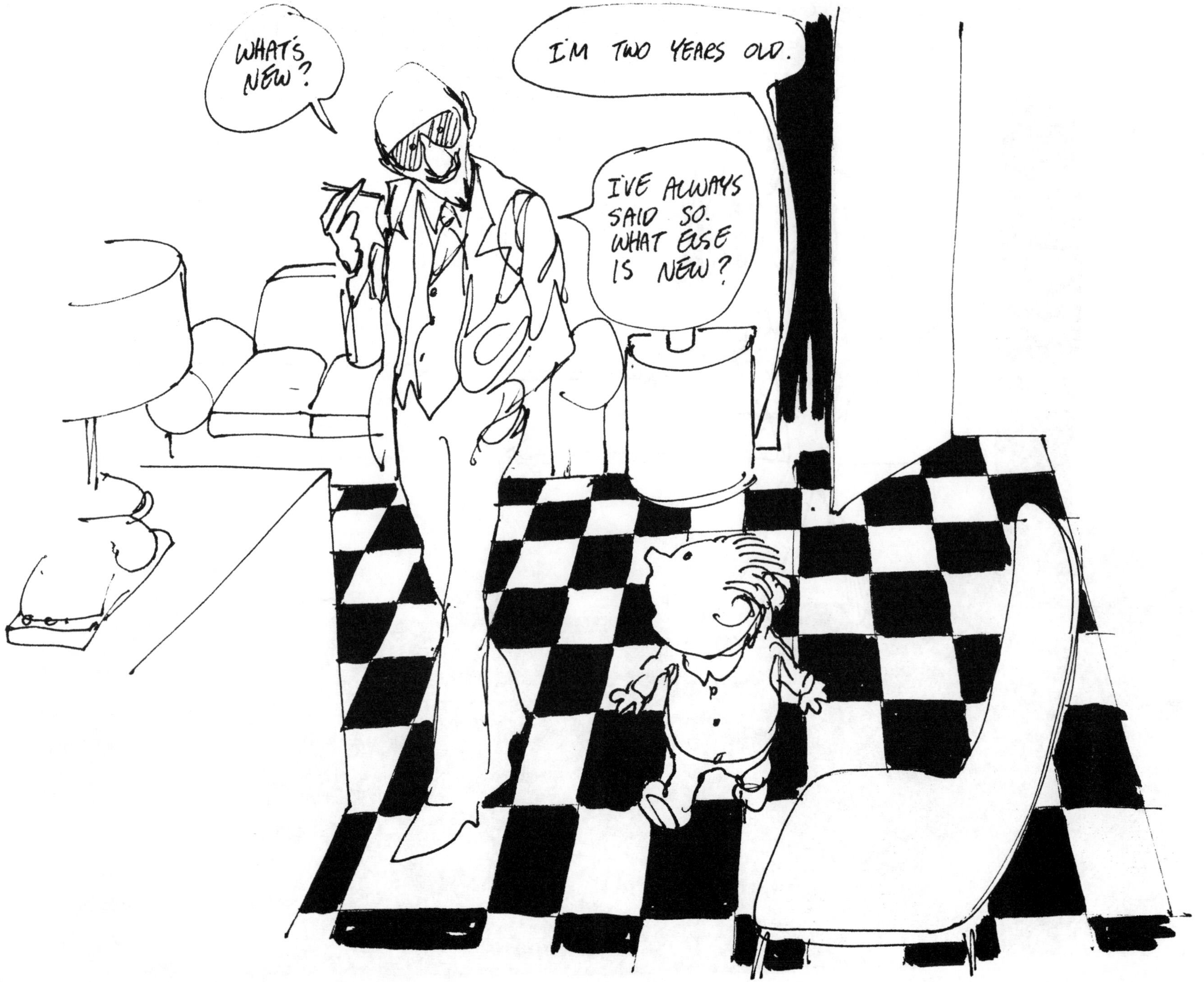
WHAT'S NEW?
I'M TWO YEARS OLD.
I'VE ALWAYS SAID SO. WHAT ELSE IS NEW?

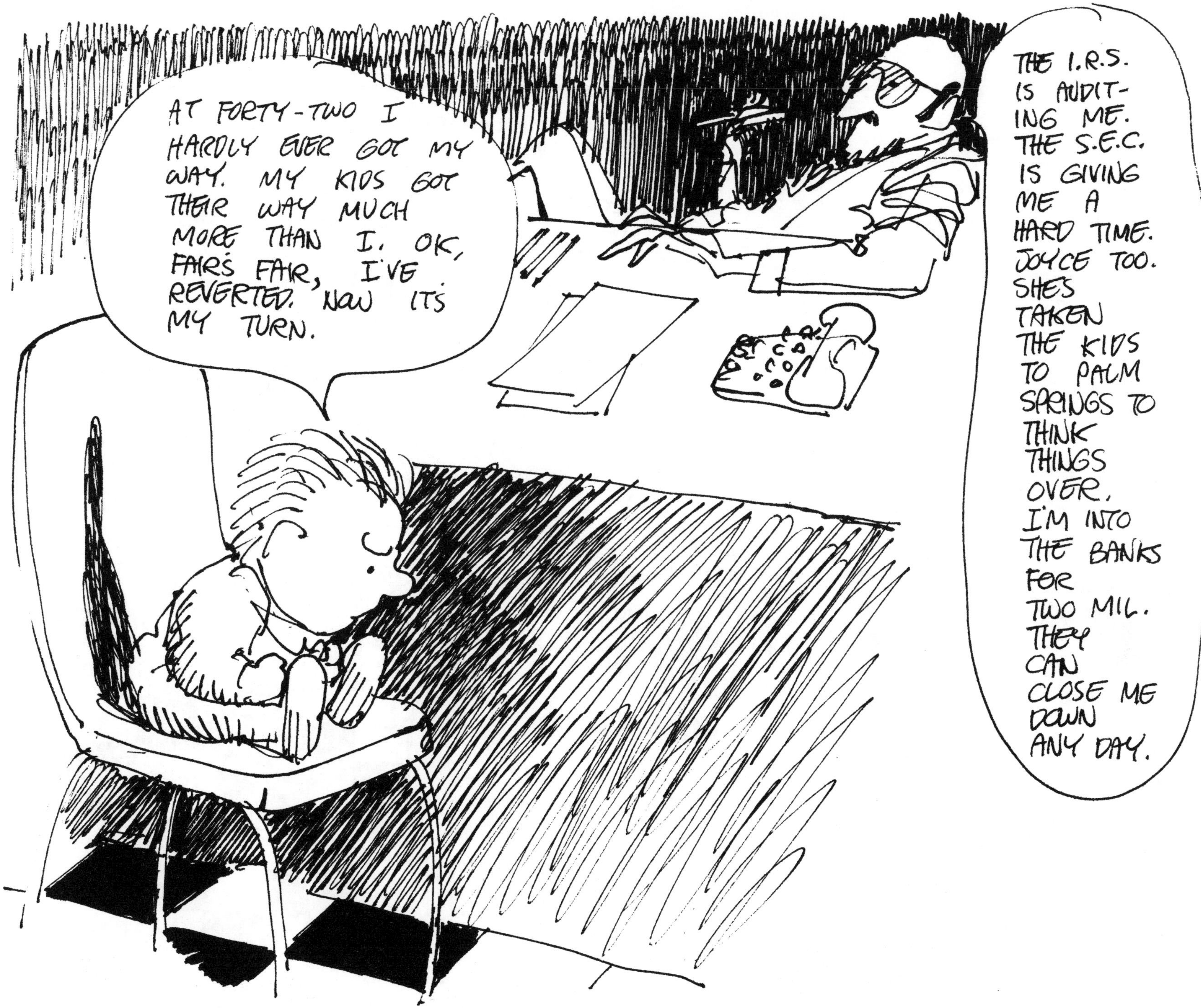
AT FORTY-TWO I HARDLY EVER GOT MY WAY. MY KIDS GOT THEIR WAY MUCH MORE THAN I. OK, FAIR'S FAIR, I'VE REVERTED. NOW IT'S MY TURN.
THE I.R.S. IS AUDITING ME. THE S.E.C. IS GIVING ME A HARD TIME. JOYCE TOO. SHE'S TAKEN THE KIDS TO PALM SPRINGS TO THINK THINGS OVER. I'M INTO THE BANKS FOR TWO MIL. THEY CAN CLOSE ME DOWN ANY DAY.

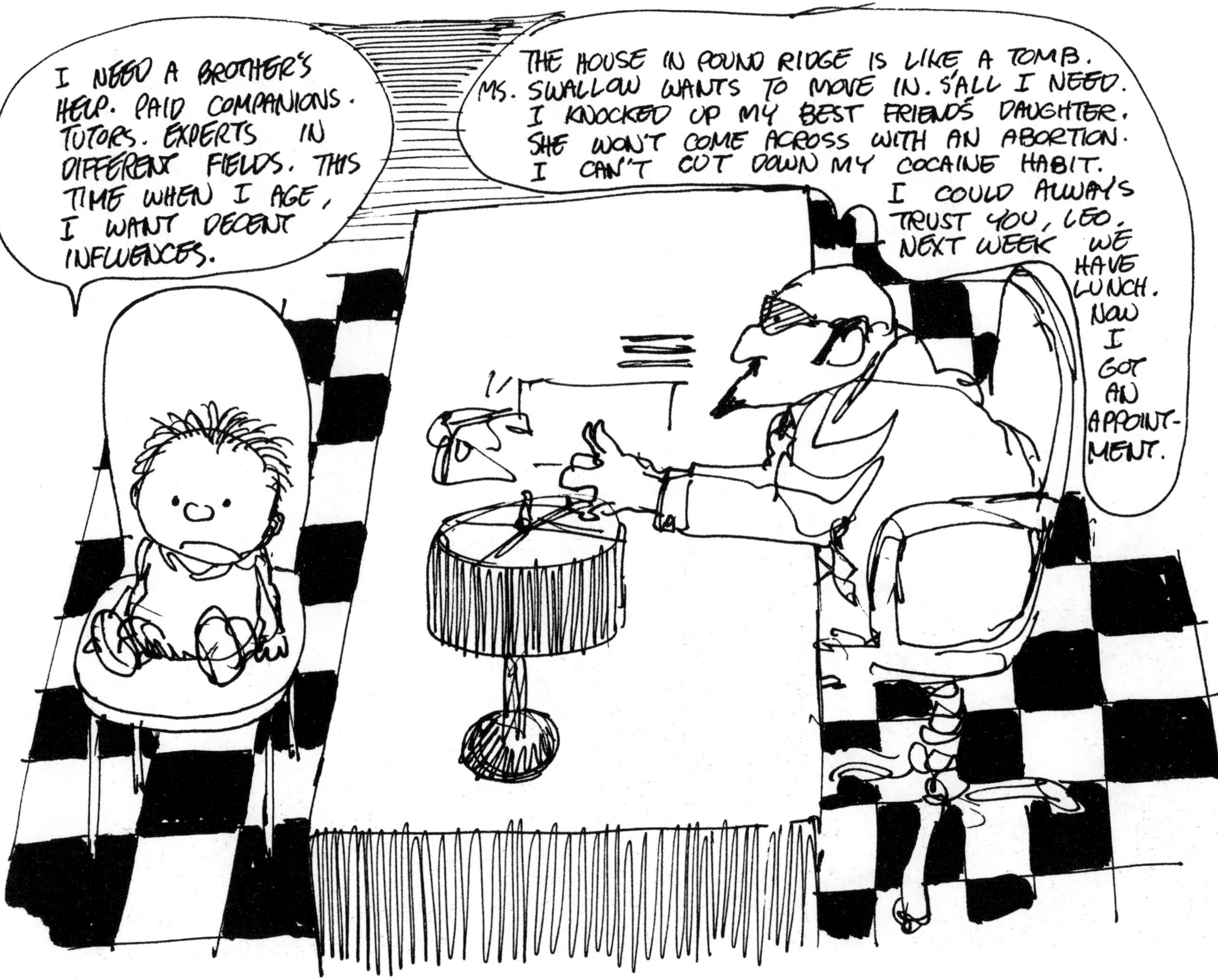
I NEED A BROTHER'S HELP. PAID COMPANIONS. TUTORS. EXPERTS IN DIFFERENT FIELDS. THIS TIME WHEN I AGE, I WANT DECENT INFLUENCES.
THE HOUSE IN POUND RIDGE IS LIKE A TOMB. MS. SWALLOW WANTS TO MOVE IN. S'ALL I NEED. I KNOCKED UP MY BEST FRIEND'S DAUGHTER. SHE WON'T COME ACROSS WITH AN ABORTION. I CAN'T CUT DOWN MY COCAINE HABIT. I COULD ALWAYS TRUST YOU, LEO. NEXT WEEK WE HAVE LUNCH. NOW I GOT AN APPOINTMENT.

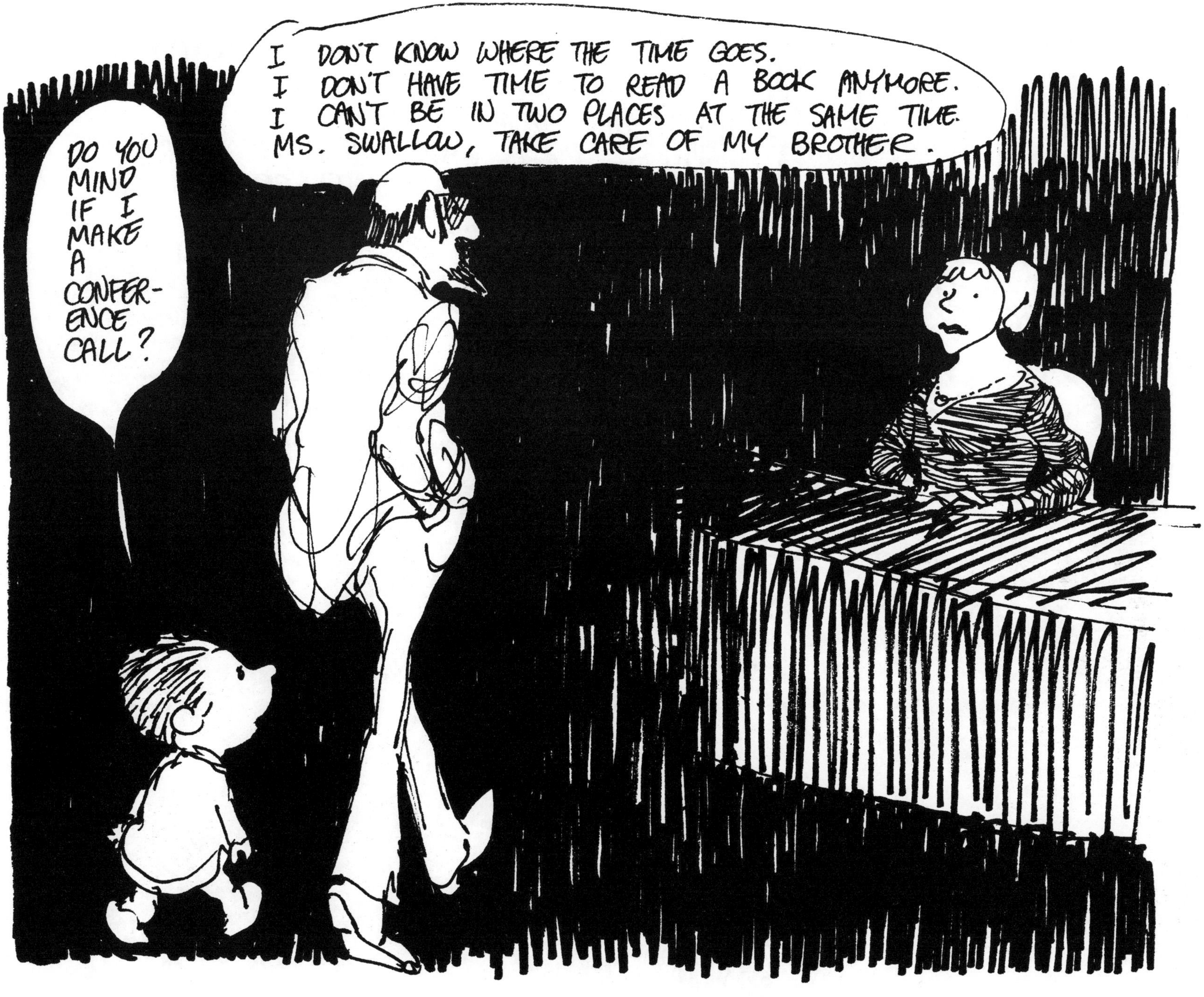
I DON'T KNOW WHERE THE TIME GOES. I DON'T HAVE TIME TO READ A BOOK ANYMORE. I CAN'T BE IN TWO PLACES AT THE SAME TIME. MS. SWALLOW, TAKE CARE OF MY BROTHER.
DO YOU MIND IF I MAKE A CONFERENCE CALL?

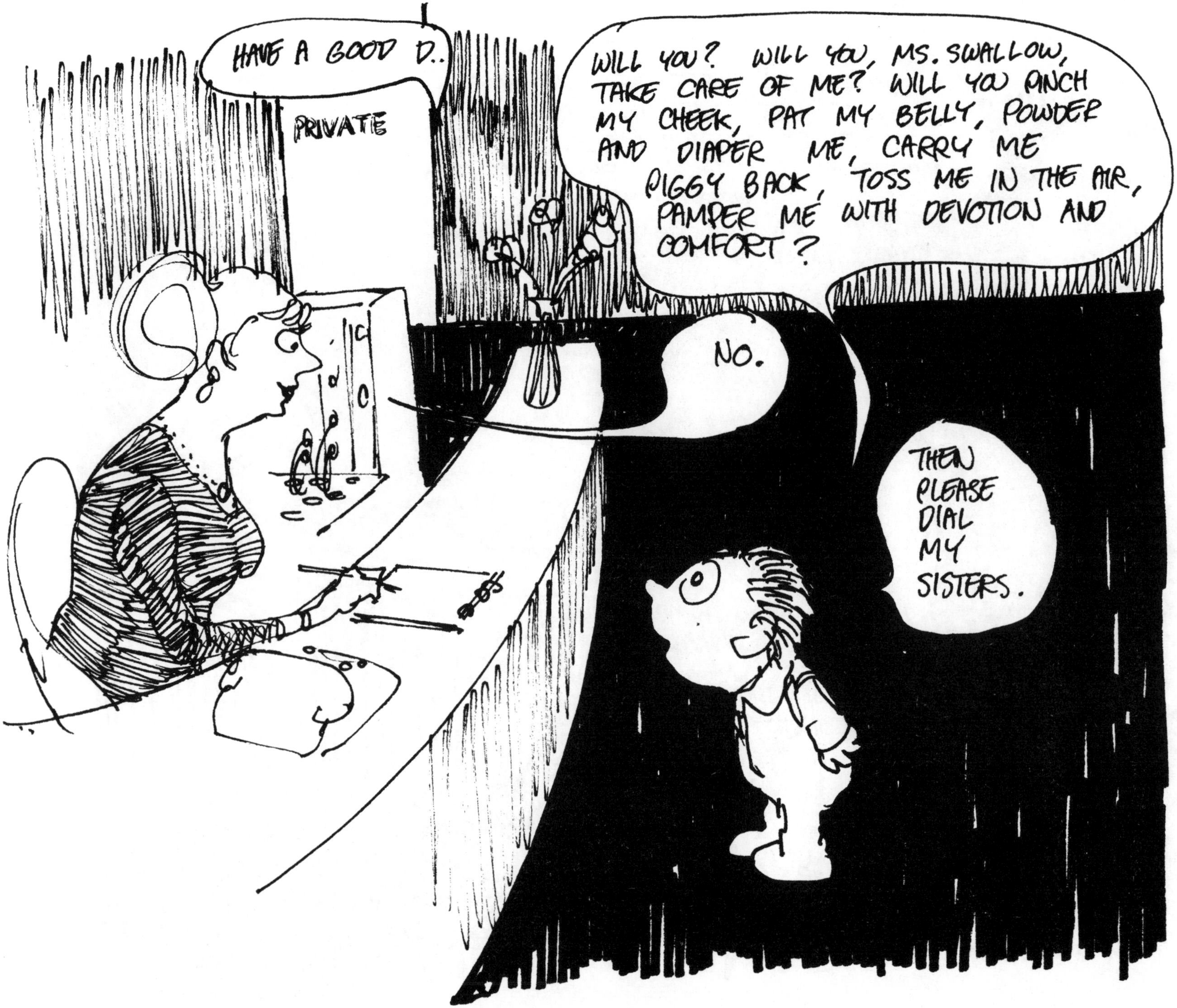
HAVE A GOOD D..
PRIVATE
WILL YOU? WILL YOU, MS. SWALLOW, TAKE CARE OF ME? WILL YOU PINCH MY CHEEK, PAT MY BELLY, POWDER AND DIAPER ME, CARRY ME PIGGY BACK, TOSS ME IN THE AIR, PAMPER ME WITH DEVOTION AND COMFORT?
NO.
THEN PLEASE DIAL MY SISTERS.

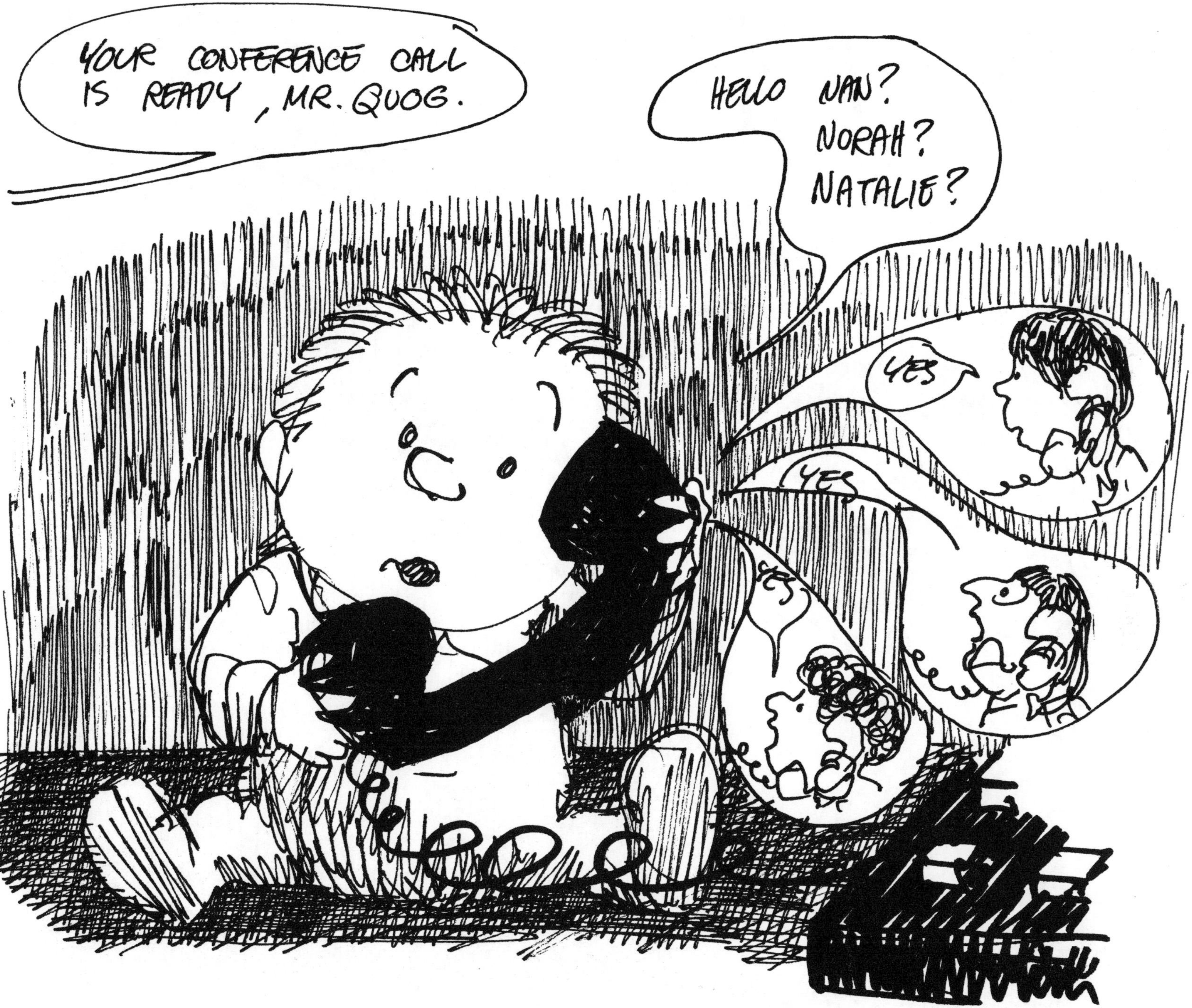
YOUR CONFERENCE CALL IS READY, MR. QUOG.
HELLO NAN? NORAH? NATALIE?
YES
YES
YES

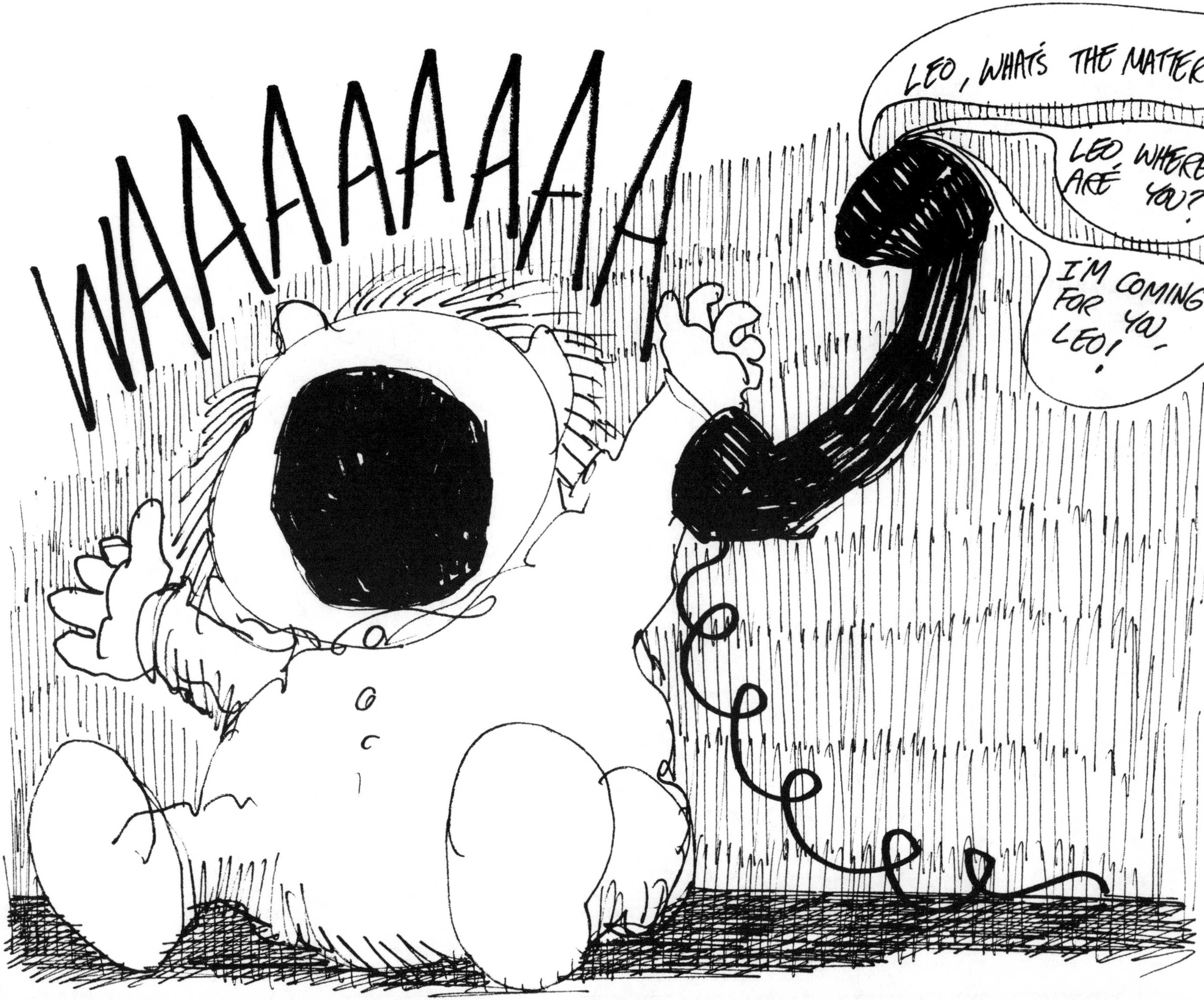
WAAAAAAAA
LEO, WHAT'S THE MATTER?
LEO, WHERE ARE YOU?
I'M COMING FOR YOU LEO!

RESCUE

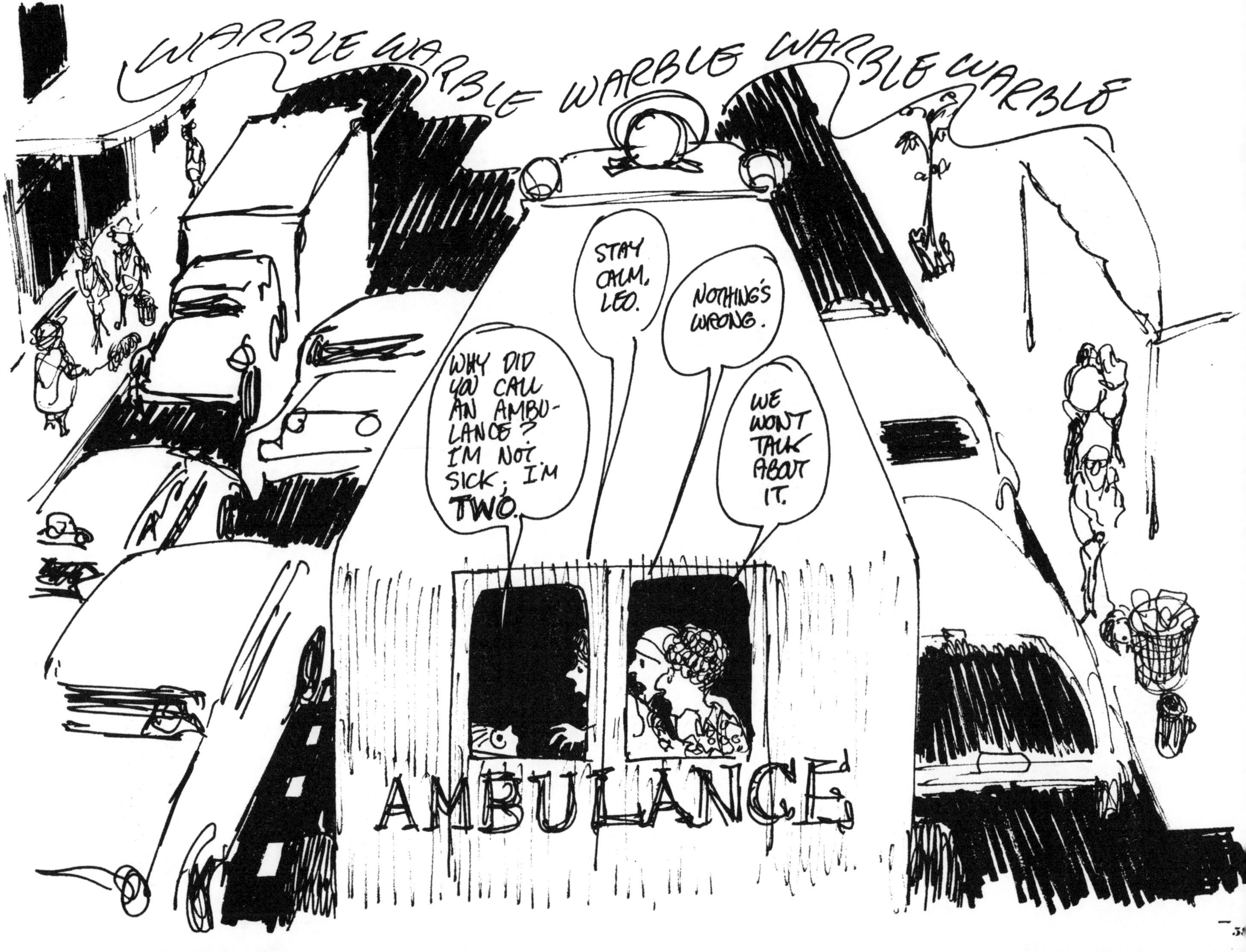
WARBLE WARBLE WARBLE WARBLE WARBLE WARBLE
WHY DID YOU CALL AN AMBULANCE? I'M NOT SICK. I'M TWO.
STAY CALM, LEO.
NOTHING'S WRONG.
WE WONT TALK ABOUT IT.
AMBULANCE

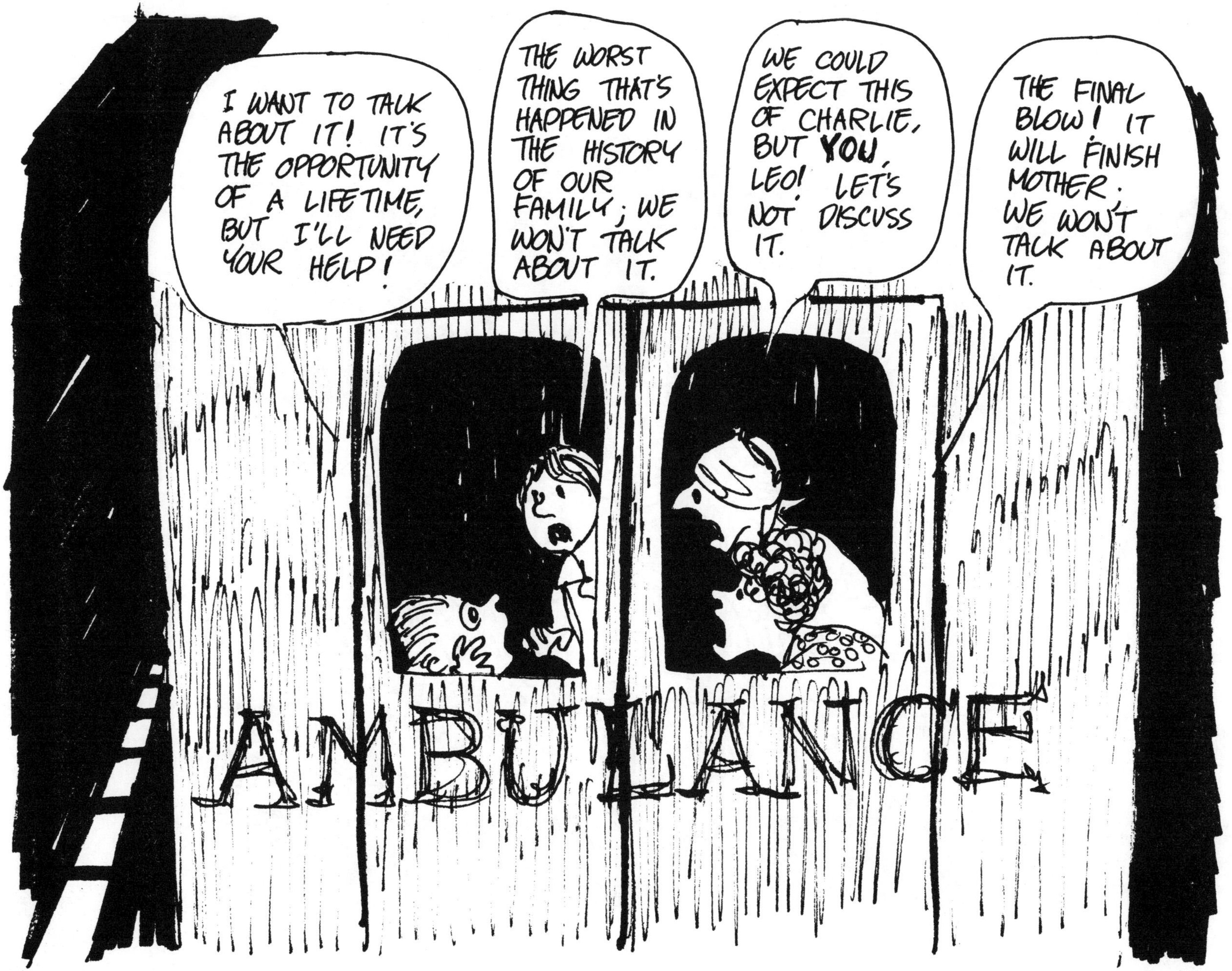
I WANT TO TALK ABOUT IT! IT'S THE OPPORTUNITY OF A LIFETIME, BUT I'LL NEED YOUR HELP!
THE WORST THING THAT'S HAPPENED IN THE HISTORY OF OUR FAMILY; WE WON'T TALK ABOUT IT.
WE COULD EXPECT THIS OF CHARLIE, BUT YOU, LEO! LET'S NOT DISCUSS IT.
THE FINAL BLOW! IT WILL FINISH MOTHER. WE WON'T TALK ABOUT IT.
AMBULANCE

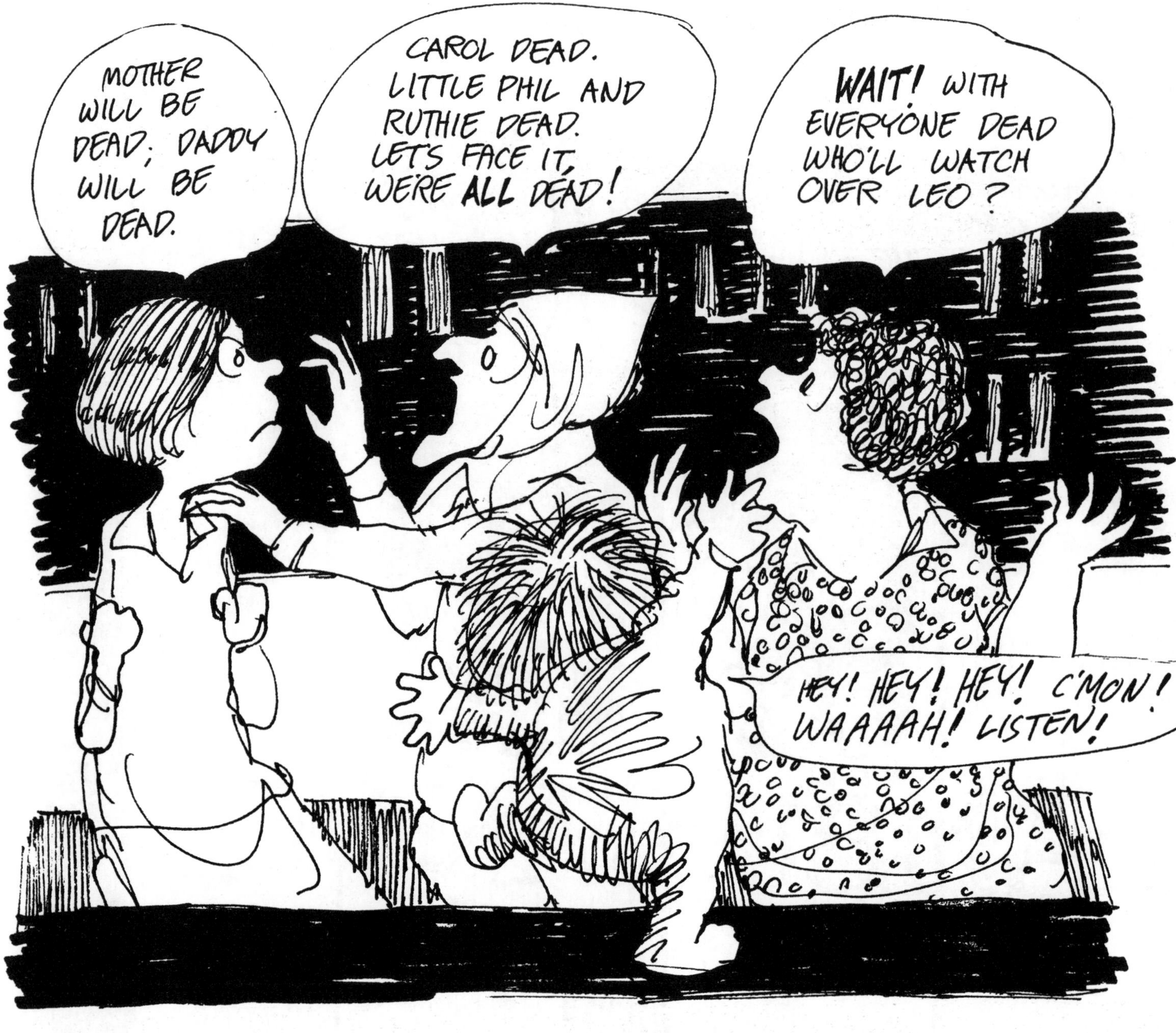
MOTHER WILL BE DEAD; DADDY WILL BE DEAD.
CAROL DEAD. LITTLE PHIL AND RUTHIE DEAD. LET'S FACE IT, WE'RE ALL DEAD!
WAIT! WITH EVERYONE DEAD WHO'LL WATCH OVER LEO?
HEY! HEY! HEY! C'MON! WAAAAH! LISTEN!

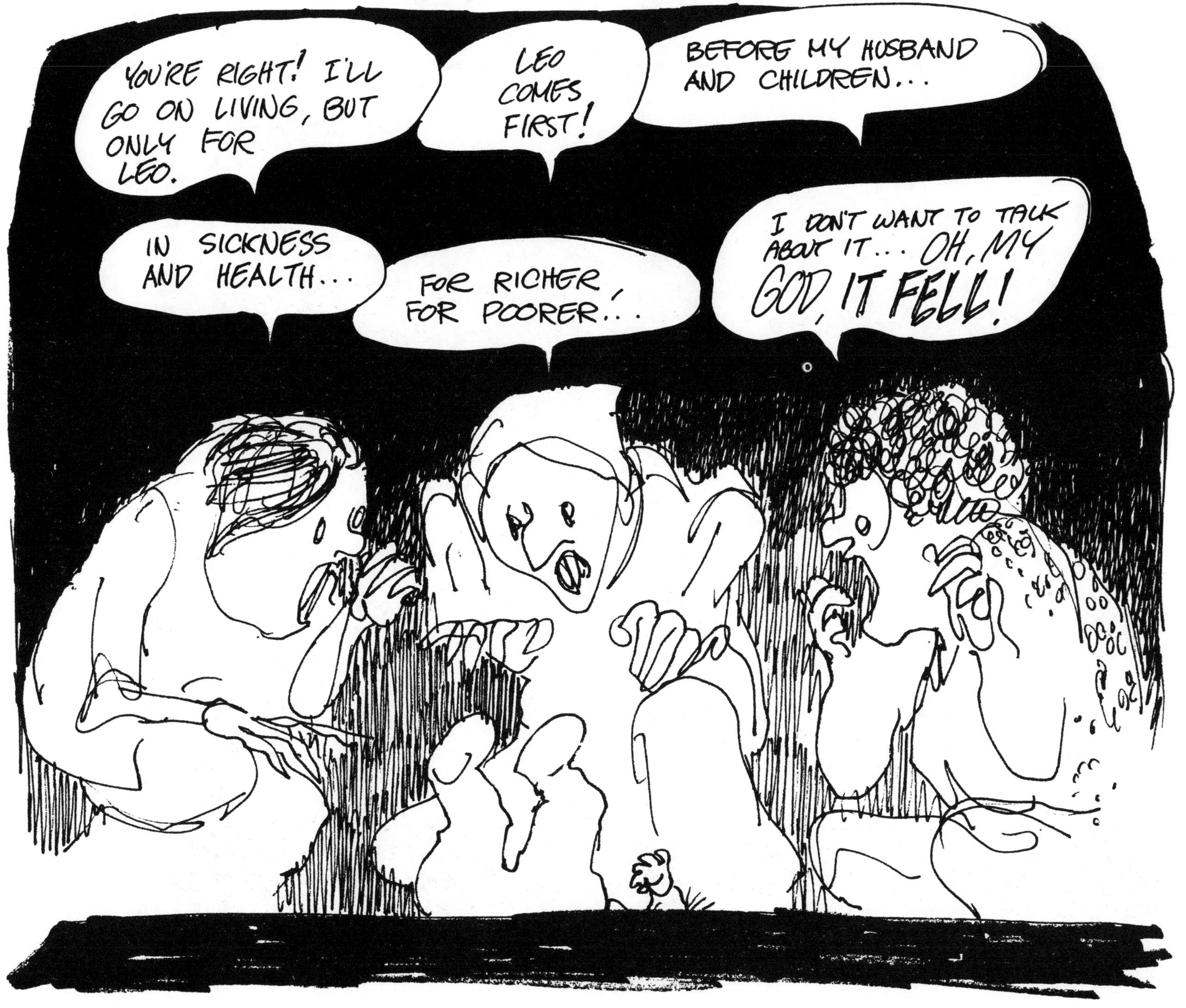
YOU'RE RIGHT! I'LL GO ON LIVING, BUT ONLY FOR LEO.
LEO COMES FIRST!
BEFORE MY HUSBAND AND CHILDREN...
IN SICKNESS AND HEALTH...
FOR RICHER, FOR POORER...
I DON'T WANT TO TALK ABOUT IT... OH, MY GOD, IT FELL!

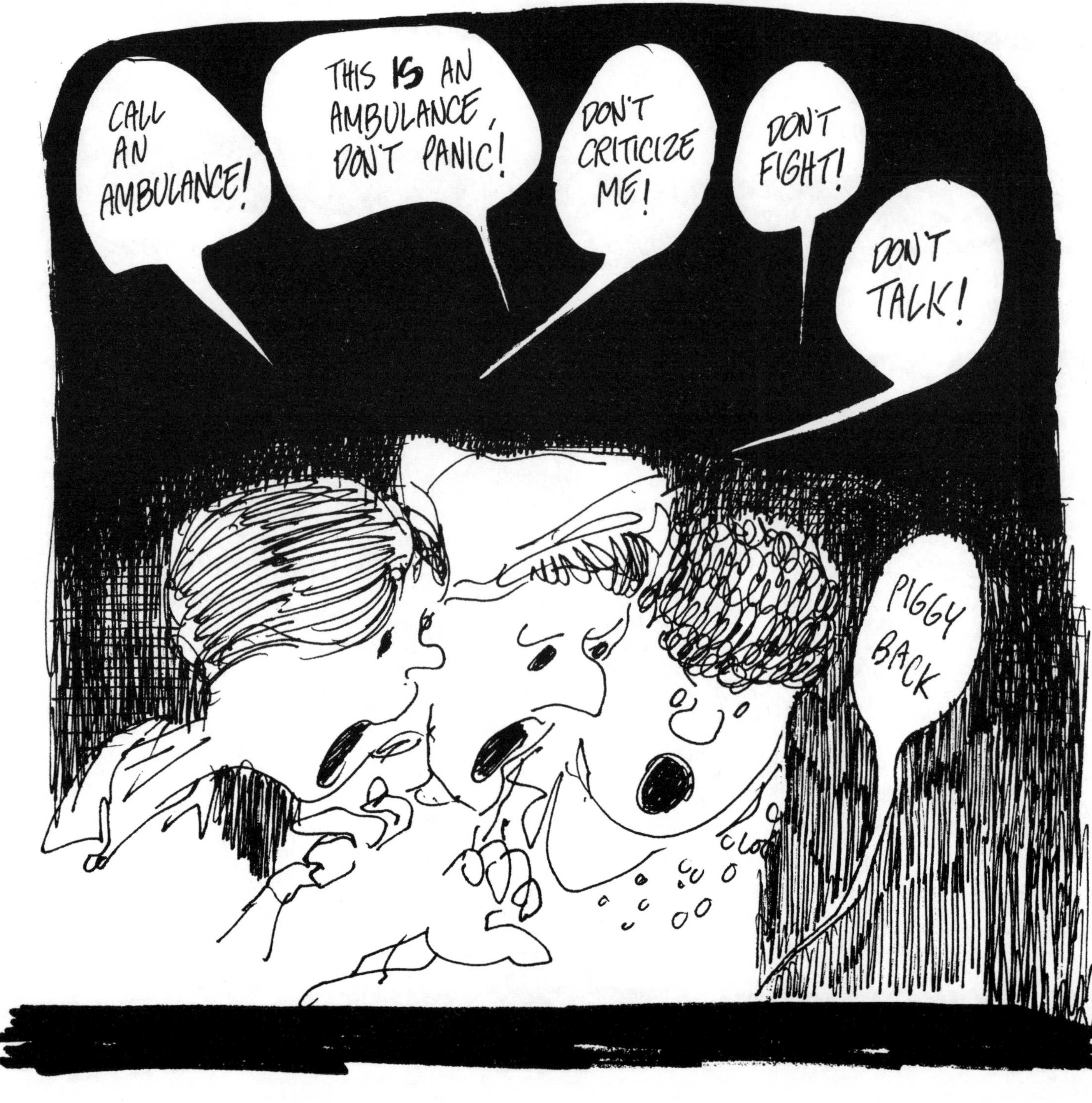
CALL AN AMBULANCE!
THIS IS AN AMBULANCE, DON'T PANIC!
DON'T CRITICIZE ME!
DON'T FIGHT!
DON'T TALK!
PIGGY BACK

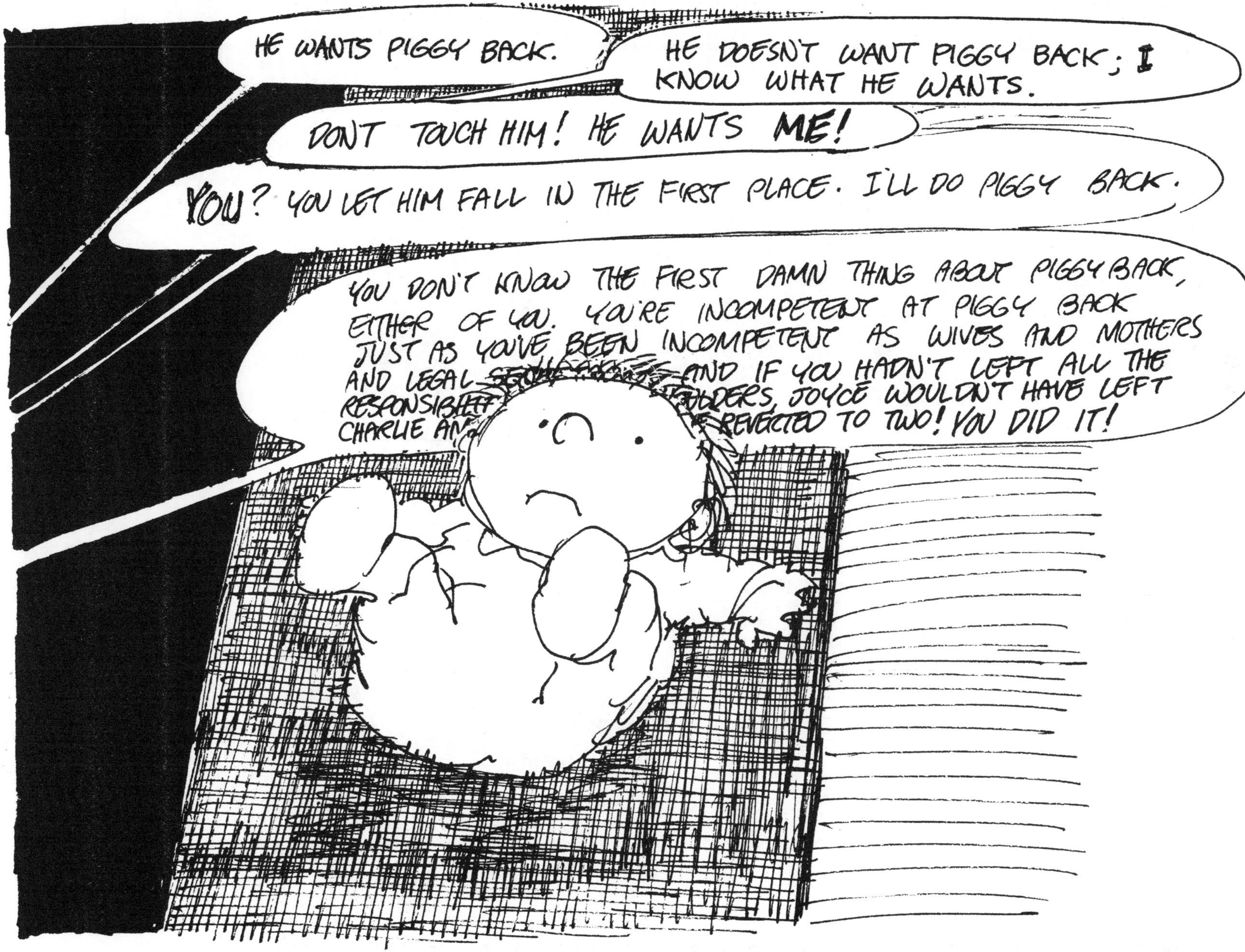

HE WANTS PIGGY BACK.
HE DOESN'T WANT PIGGY BACK; I KNOW WHAT HE WANTS.
DONT TOUCH HIM! HE WANTS ME!
YOU? YOU LET HIM FALL IN THE FIRST PLACE. I'LL DO PIGGY BACK.
YOU DON'T KNOW THE FIRST DAMN THING ABOUT PIGGY BACK, EITHER OF YOU. YOU'RE INCOMPETENT AT PIGGY BACK JUST AS YOU'VE BEEN INCOMPETENT AS WIVES AND MOTHERS AND LEGAL AND IF YOU HADN'T LEFT ALL THE RESPONSIB DERS, JOYCE WOULDN'T HAVE LEFT CHARLIE AN REVERTED TO TWO! YOU DID IT!

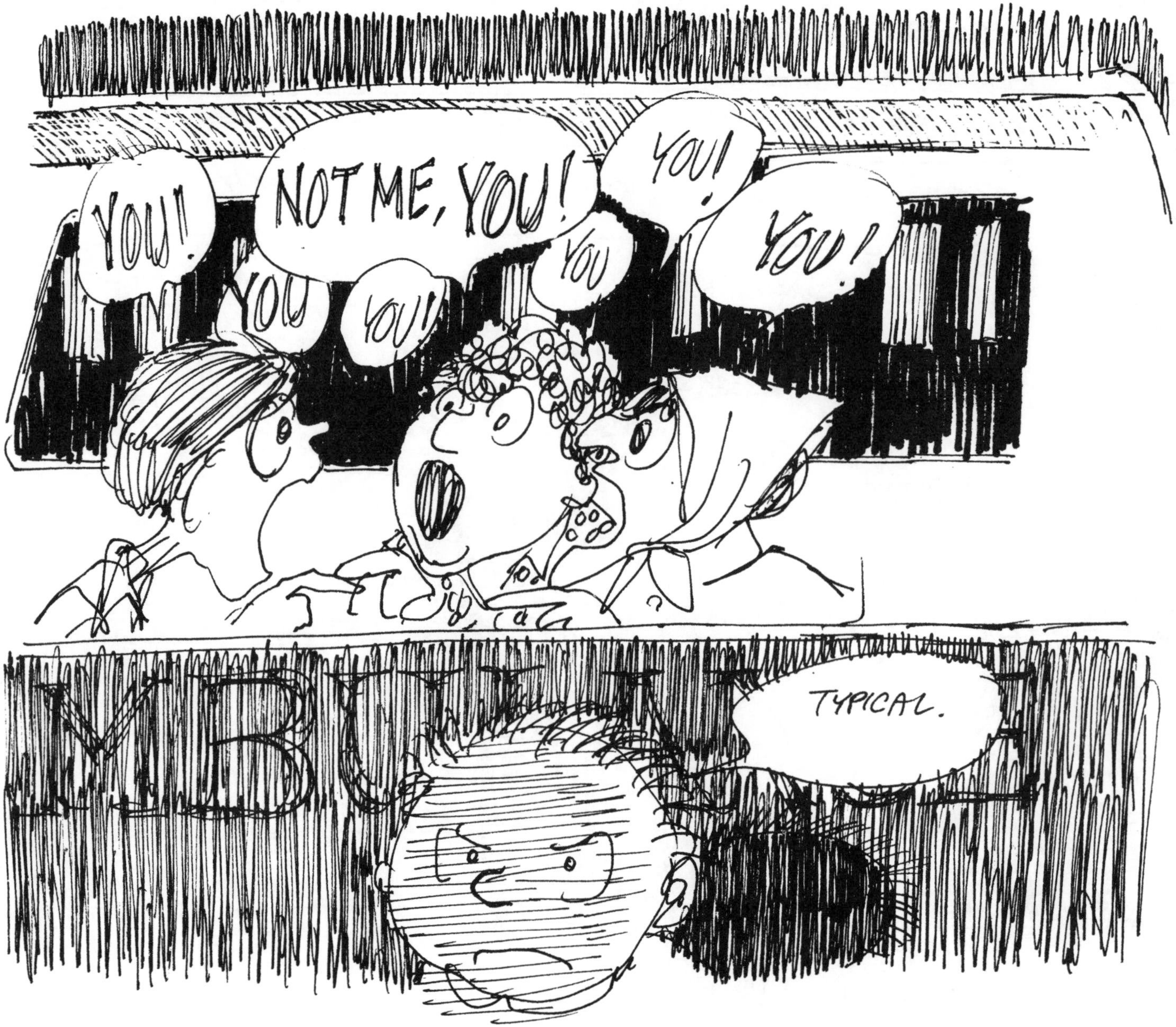
YOU!
YOU
NOT ME, YOU!
YOU!
YOU
YOU!
YOU!
TYPICAL.

THE LAW

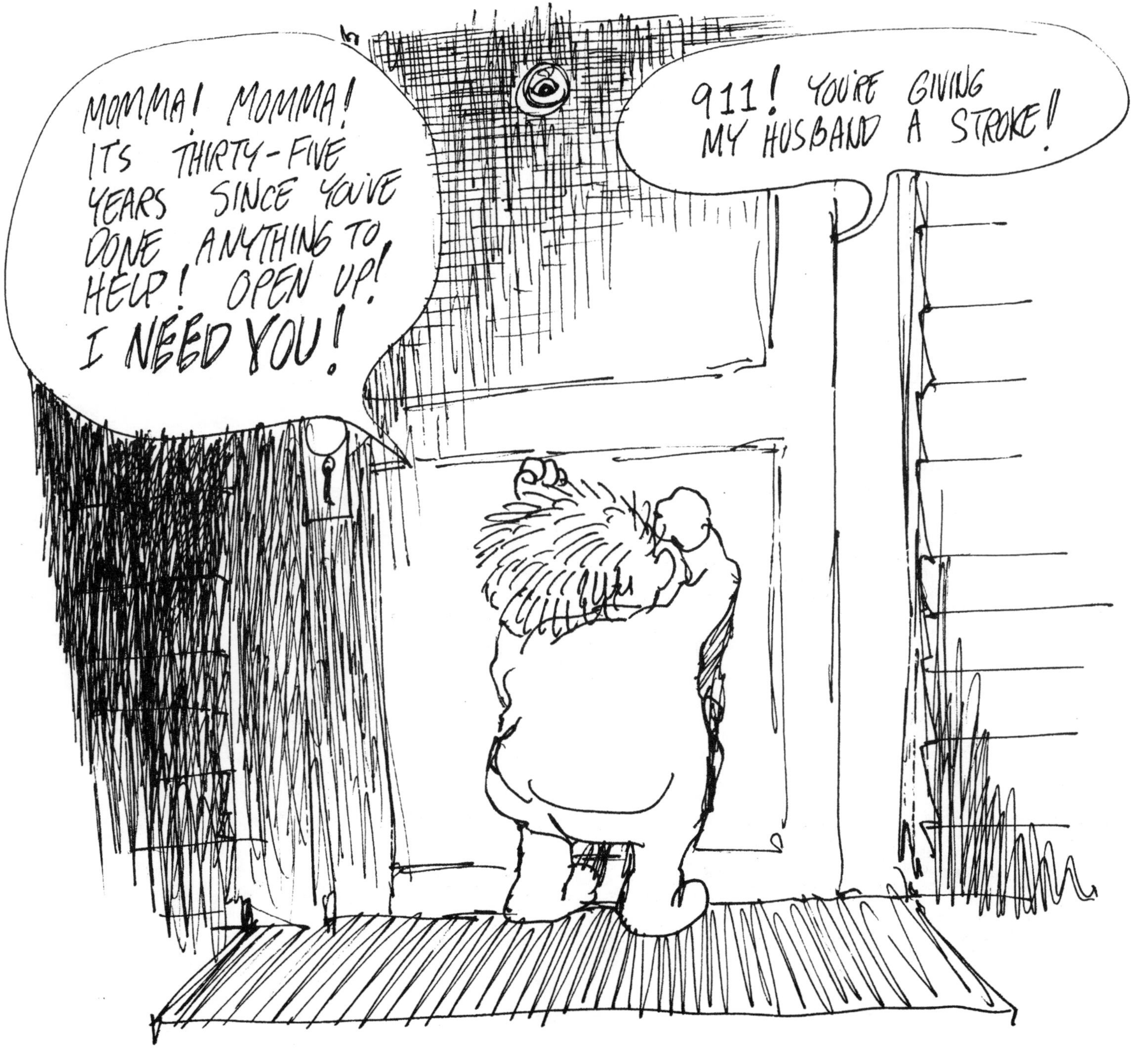
MOMMA! MOMMA! ITS THIRTY-FIVE YEARS SINCE YOU'VE DONE ANYTHING TO HELP! OPEN UP! I NEED YOU!
911! YOU'RE GIVING MY HUSBAND A STROKE!

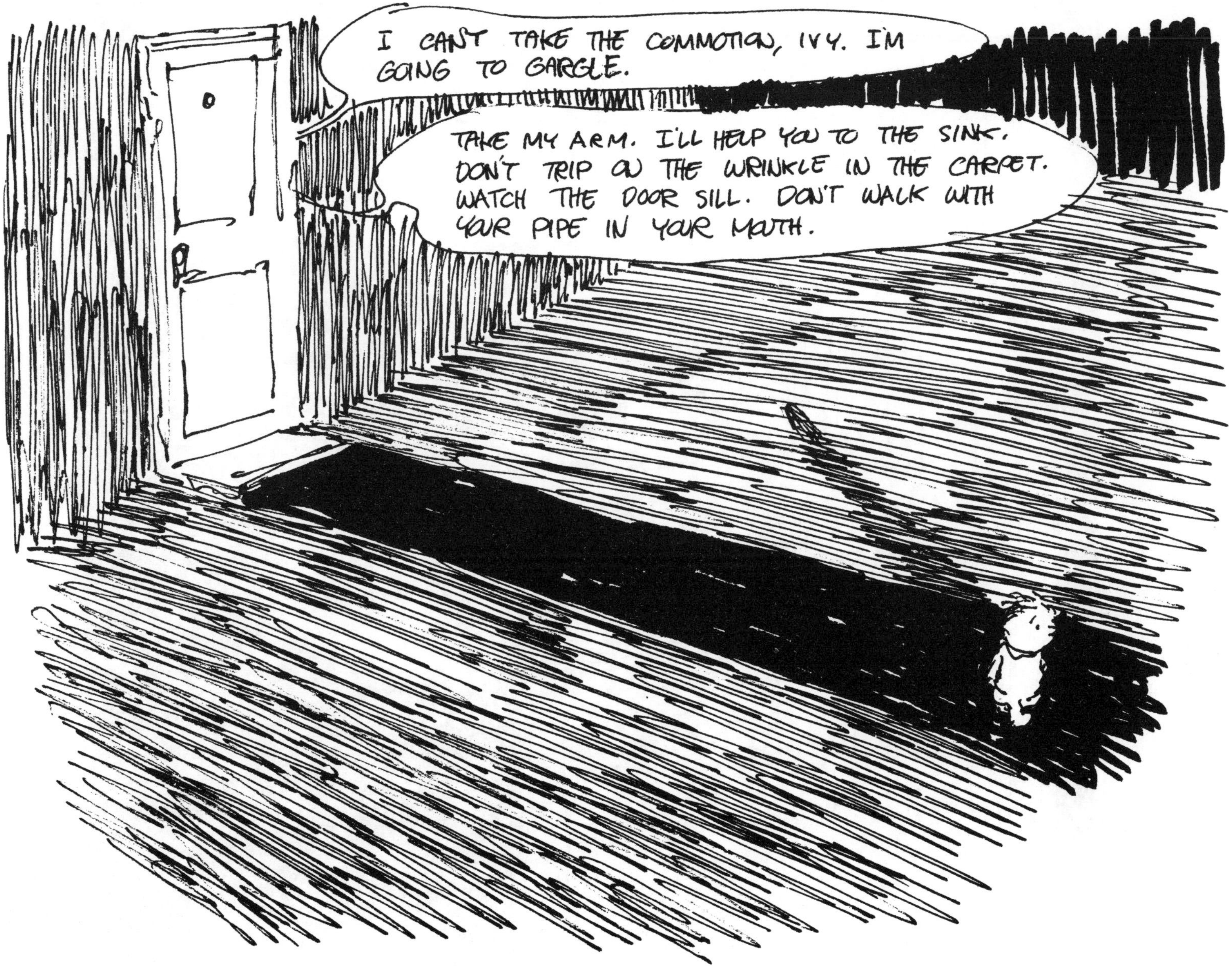
I CAN'T TAKE THE COMMOTION, IVY. I'M GOING TO GARGLE.
TAKE MY ARM. I'LL HELP YOU TO THE SINK. DON'T TRIP ON THE WRINKLE IN THE CARPET. WATCH THE DOOR SILL. DON'T WALK WITH YOUR PIPE IN YOUR MOUTH.

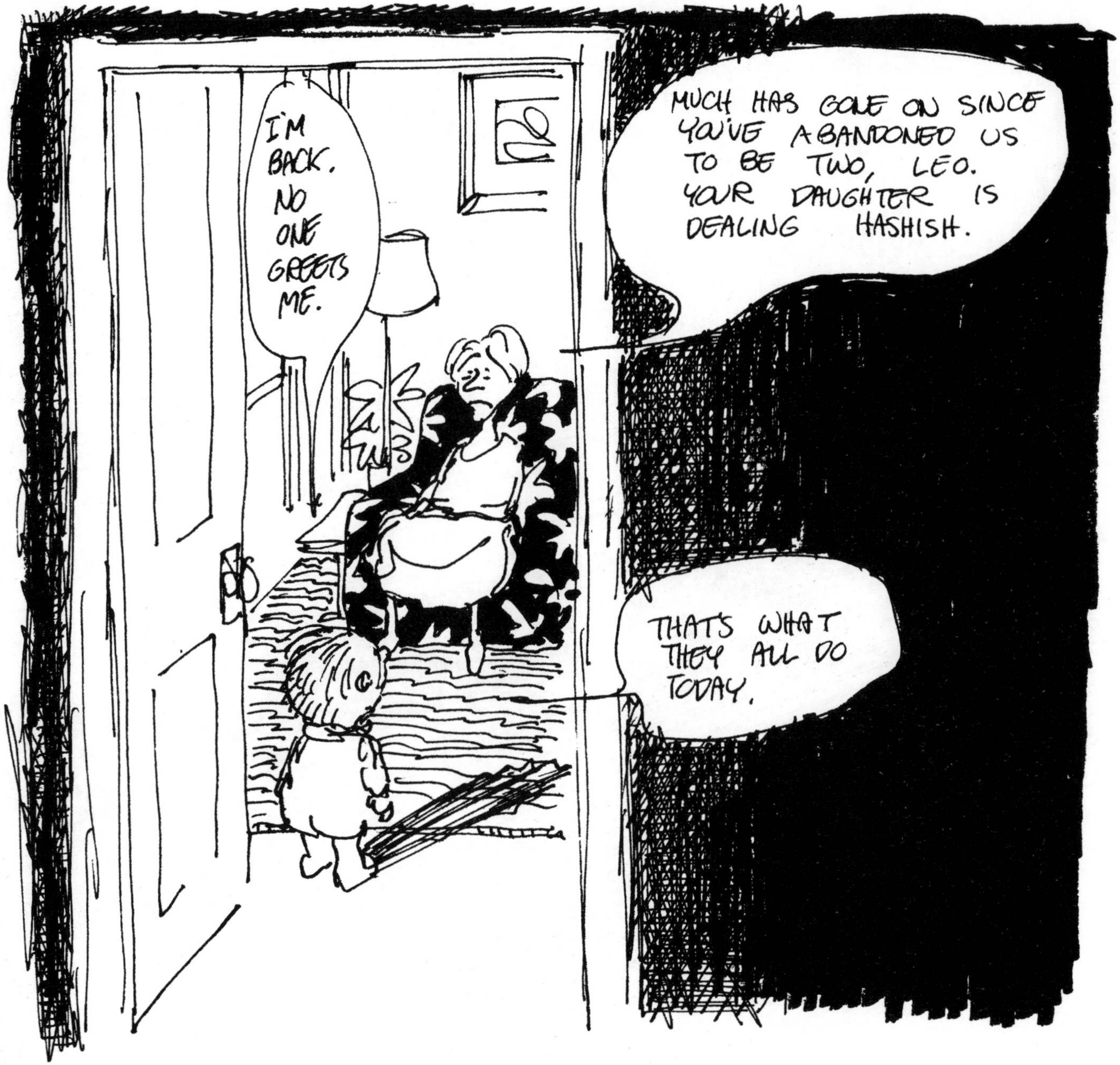
I'M BACK. NO ONE GREETS ME.
MUCH HAS GONE ON SINCE YOU'VE ABANDONED US TO BE TWO, LEO. YOUR DAUGHTER IS DEALING HASHISH.
THAT'S WHAT THEY ALL DO TODAY.

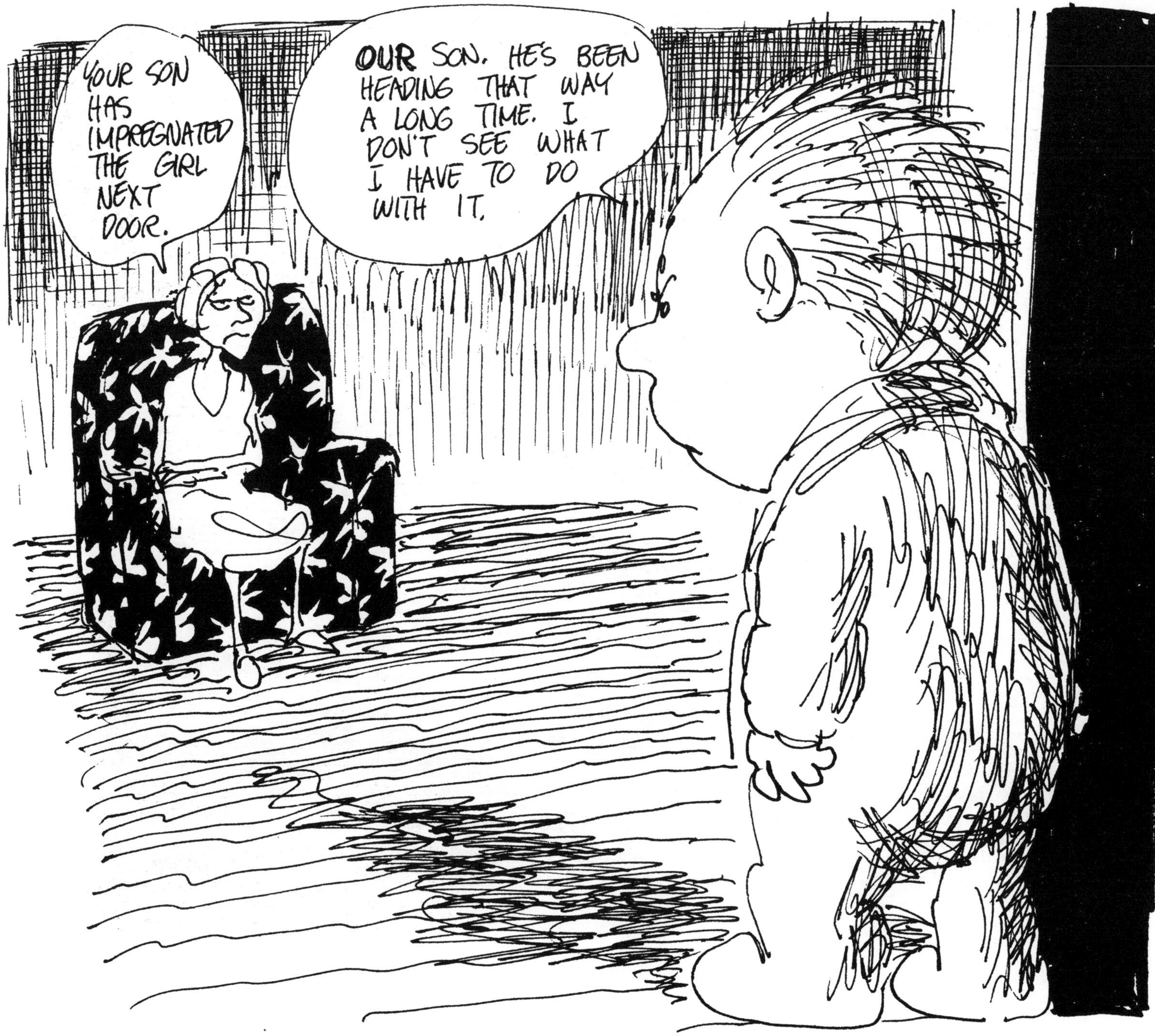
YOUR SON HAS IMPREGNATED THE GIRL NEXT DOOR.
OUR SON. HE'S BEEN HEADING THAT WAY A LONG TIME. I DON'T SEE WHAT I HAVE TO DO WITH IT.

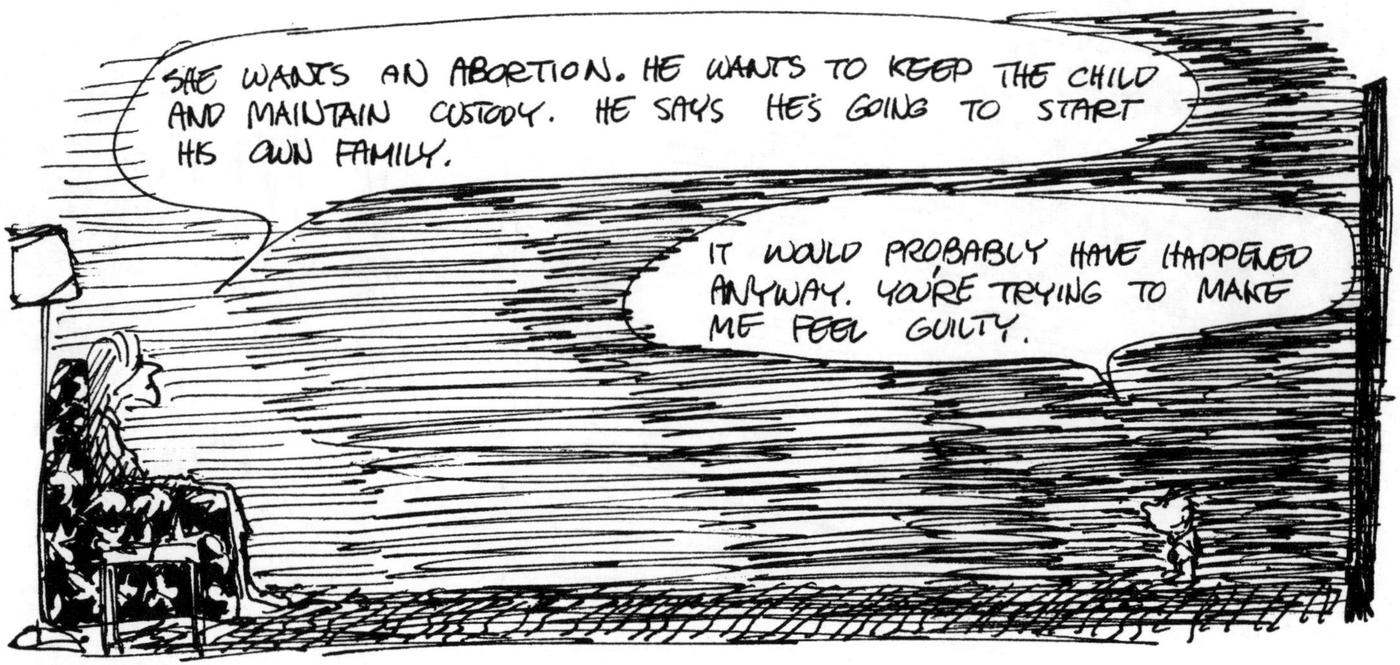
SHE WANTS AN ABORTION. HE WANTS TO KEEP THE CHILD AND MAINTAIN CUSTODY. HE SAYS HE'S GOING TO START HIS OWN FAMILY.
IT WOULD PROBABLY HAVE HAPPENED ANYWAY. YOU'RE TRYING TO MAKE ME FEEL GUILTY.

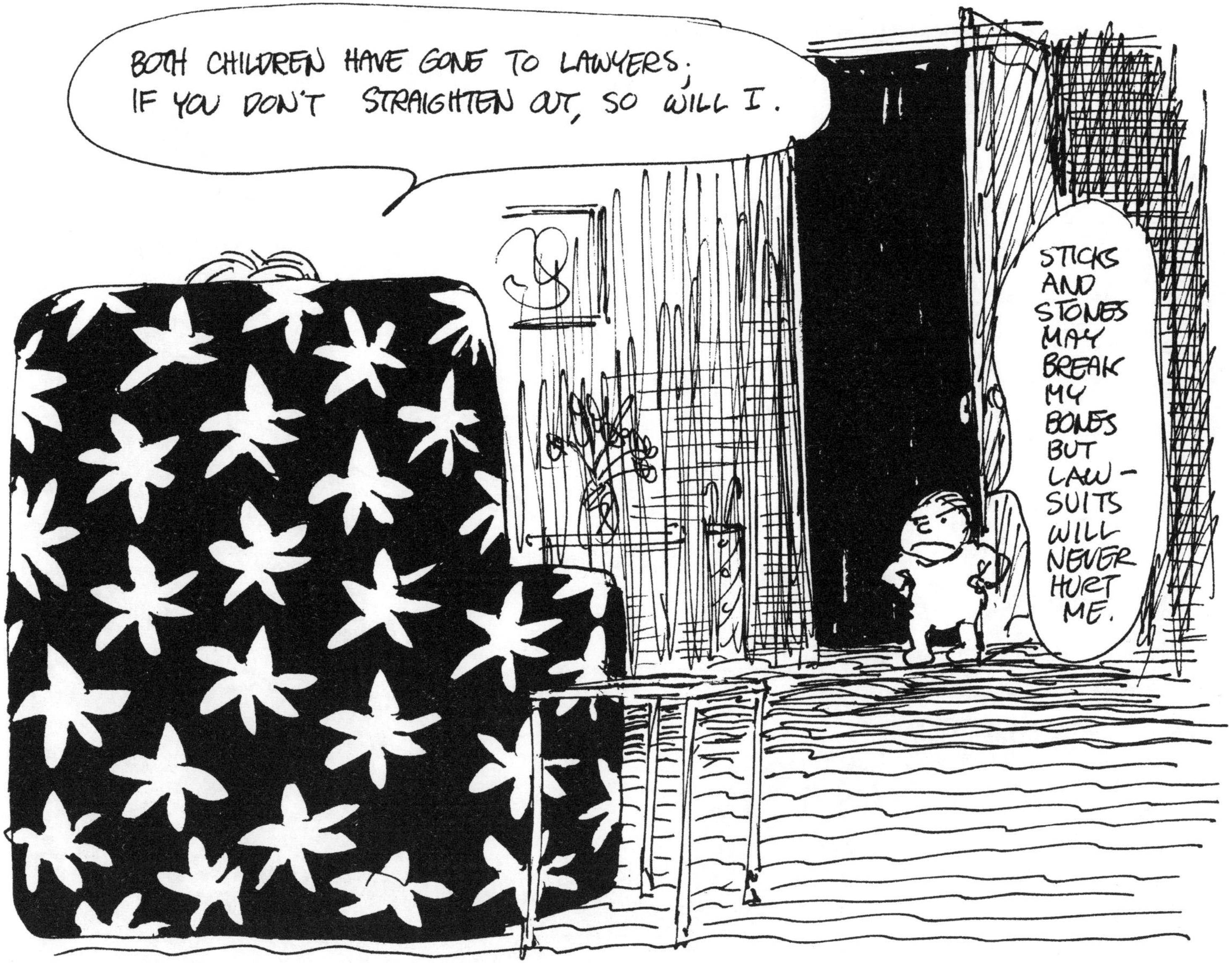
BOTH CHILDREN HAVE GONE TO LAWYERS;
IF YOU DON'T STRAIGHTEN OUT, SO WILL I.
STICKS AND STONES MAY BREAK MY BONES BUT LAW-SUITS WILL NEVER HURT ME.

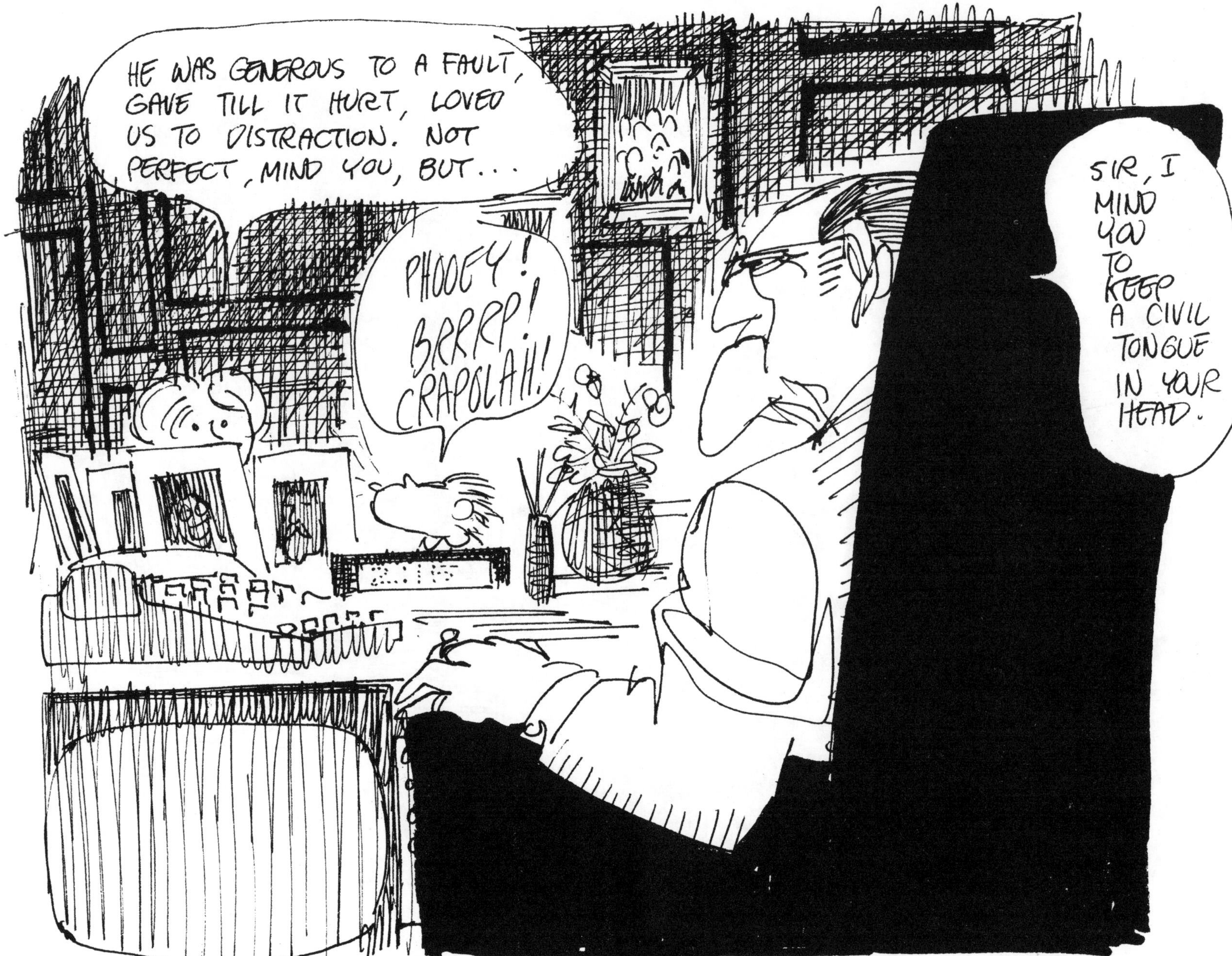
HE WAS GENEROUS TO A FAULT, GAVE TILL IT HURT, LOVED US TO DISTRACTION. NOT PERFECT, MIND YOU, BUT...
PHOOEY! BRRRP! CRAPOLAH!
SIR, I MIND YOU TO KEEP A CIVIL TONGUE IN YOUR HEAD.

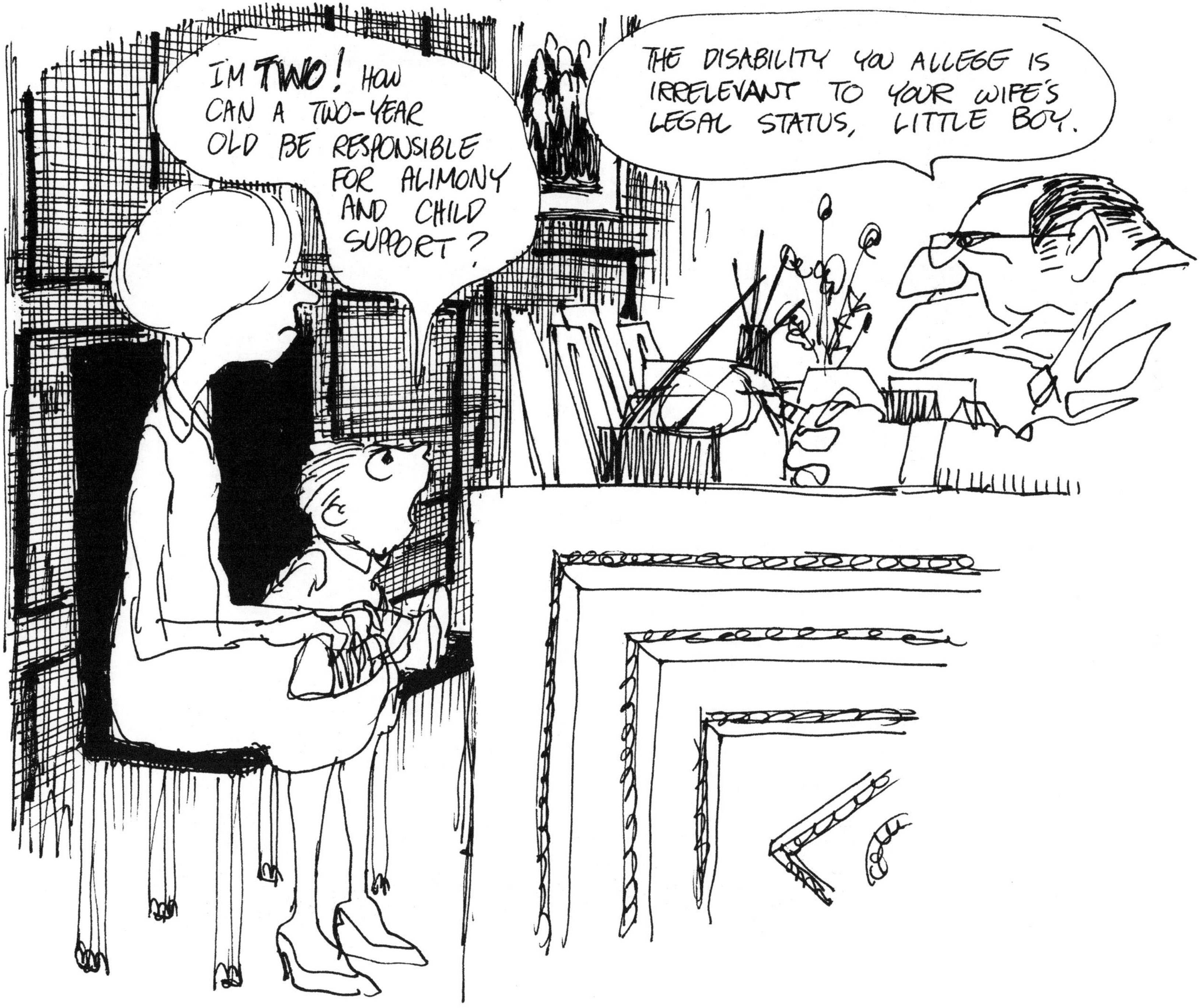
I'M TWO! HOW CAN A TWO-YEAR OLD BE RESPONSIBLE FOR ALIMONY AND CHILD SUPPORT?
THE DISABILITY YOU ALLEGE IS IRRELEVANT TO YOUR WIFE'S LEGAL STATUS, LITTLE BOY.

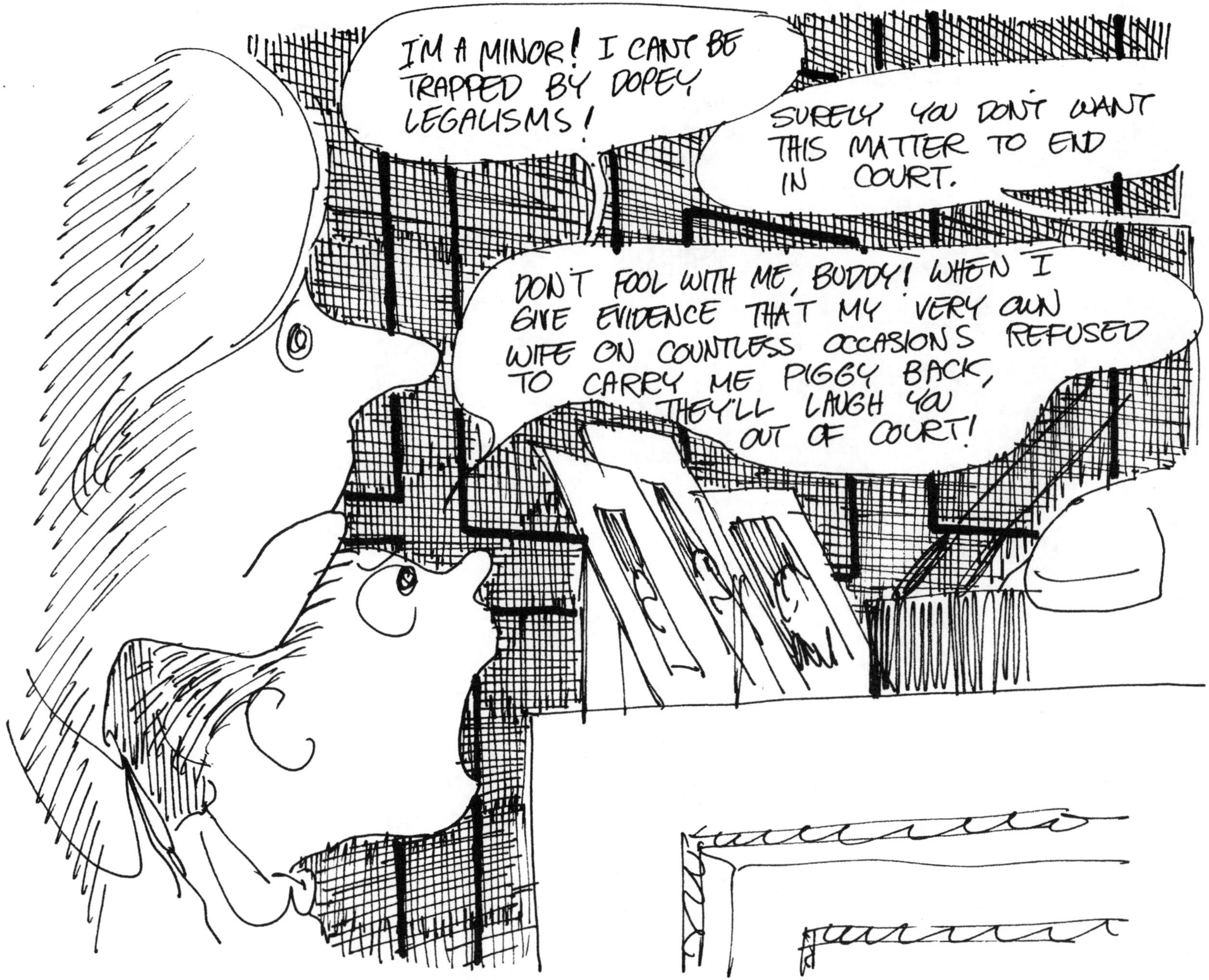
I'M A MINOR! I CAN'T BE TRAPPED BY DOPEY LEGALISMS!
SURELY YOU DON'T WANT THIS MATTER TO END IN COURT.
DON'T FOOL WITH ME, BUDDY! WHEN I GIVE EVIDENCE THAT MY VERY OWN WIFE ON COUNTLESS OCCASIONS REFUSED TO CARRY ME PIGGY BACK, THEY'LL LAUGH YOU OUT OF COURT!

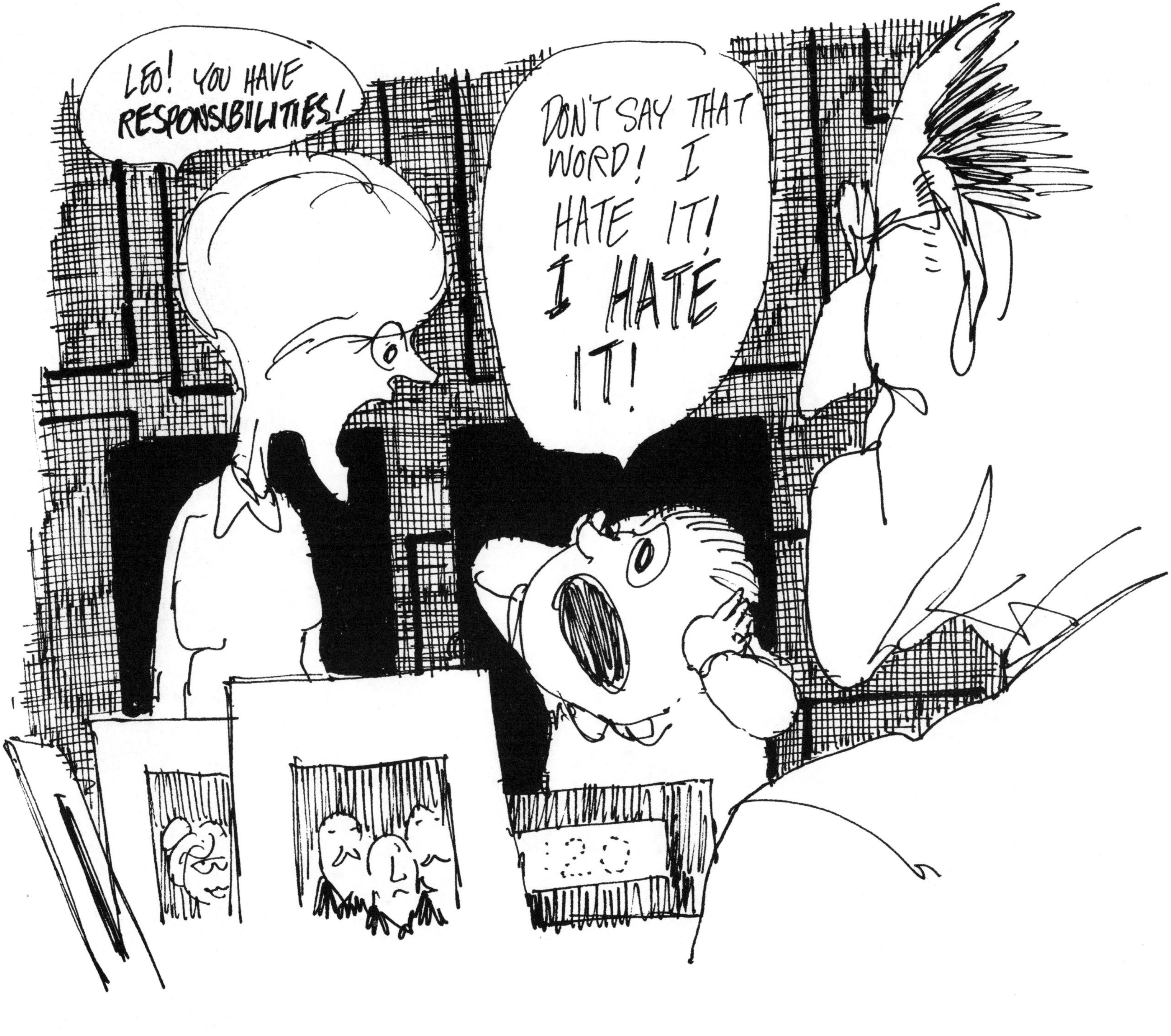
LEO! YOU HAVE RESPONSIBILITIES!
DON'T SAY THAT WORD! I HATE IT! I HATE IT!

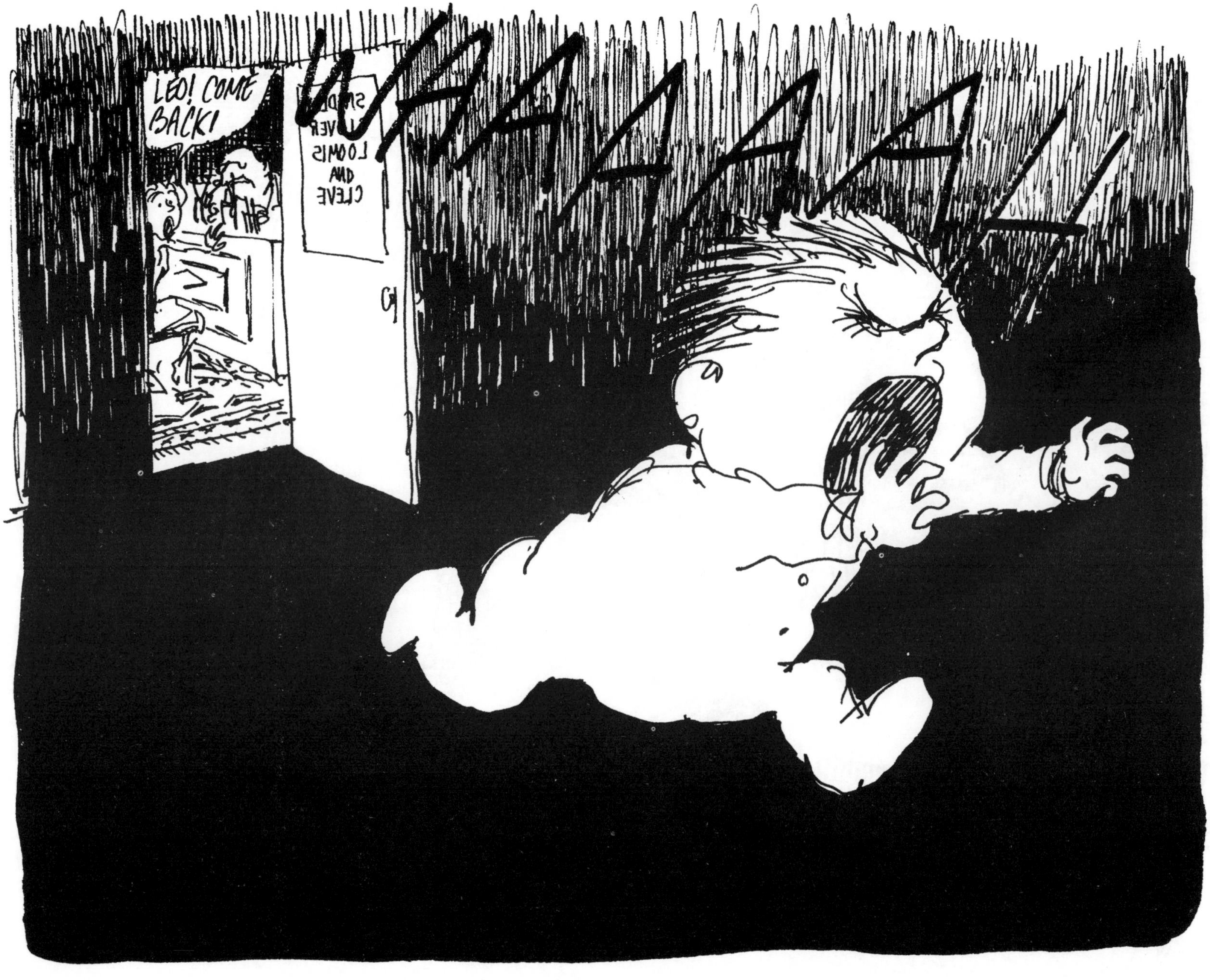
LEO! COME BACK!
WAAAAAH

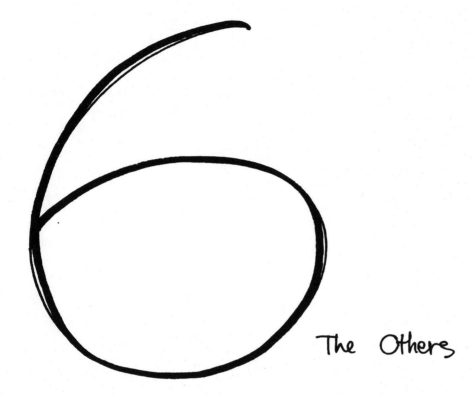

The Others

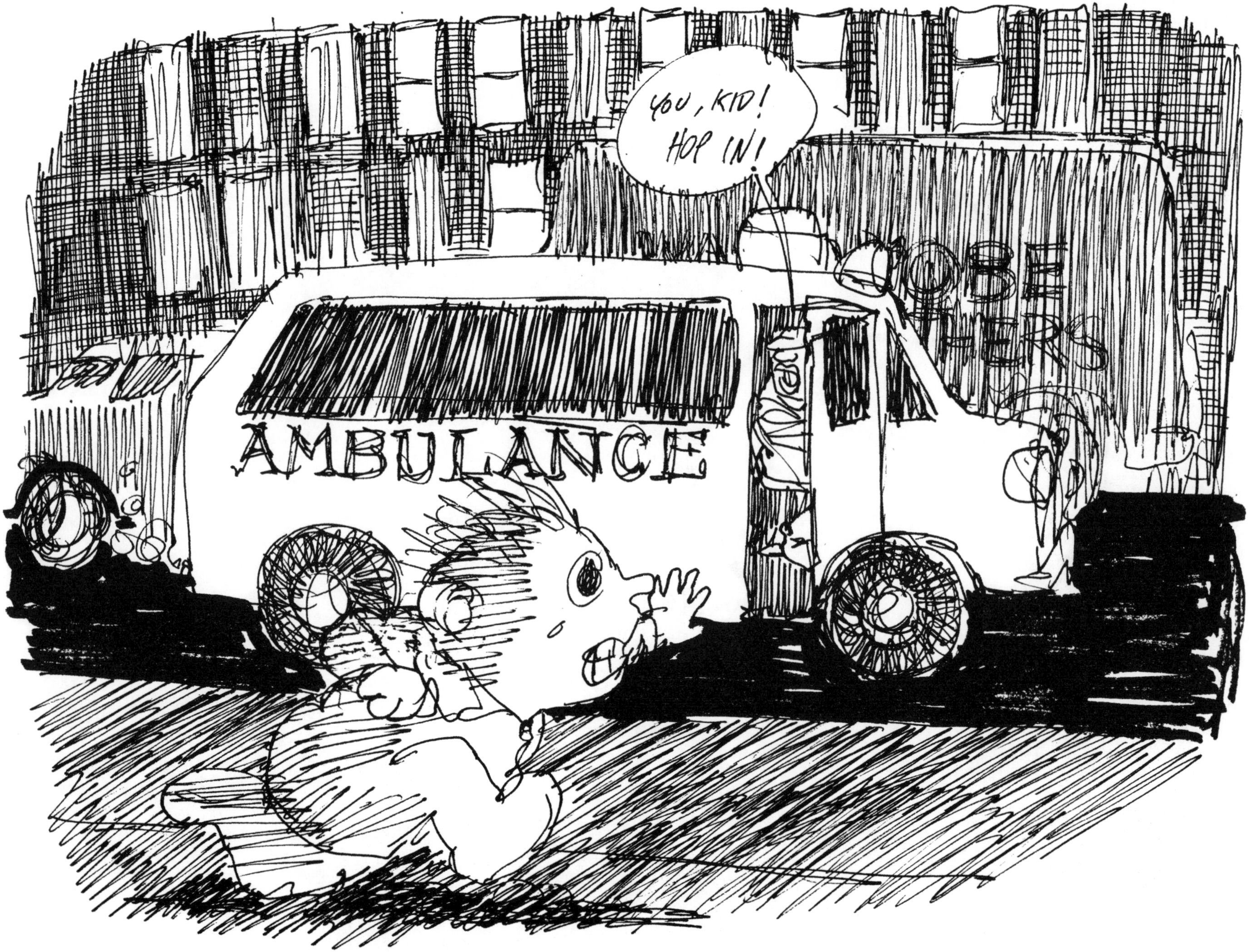
YOU, KID! HOP IN!
AMBULANCE

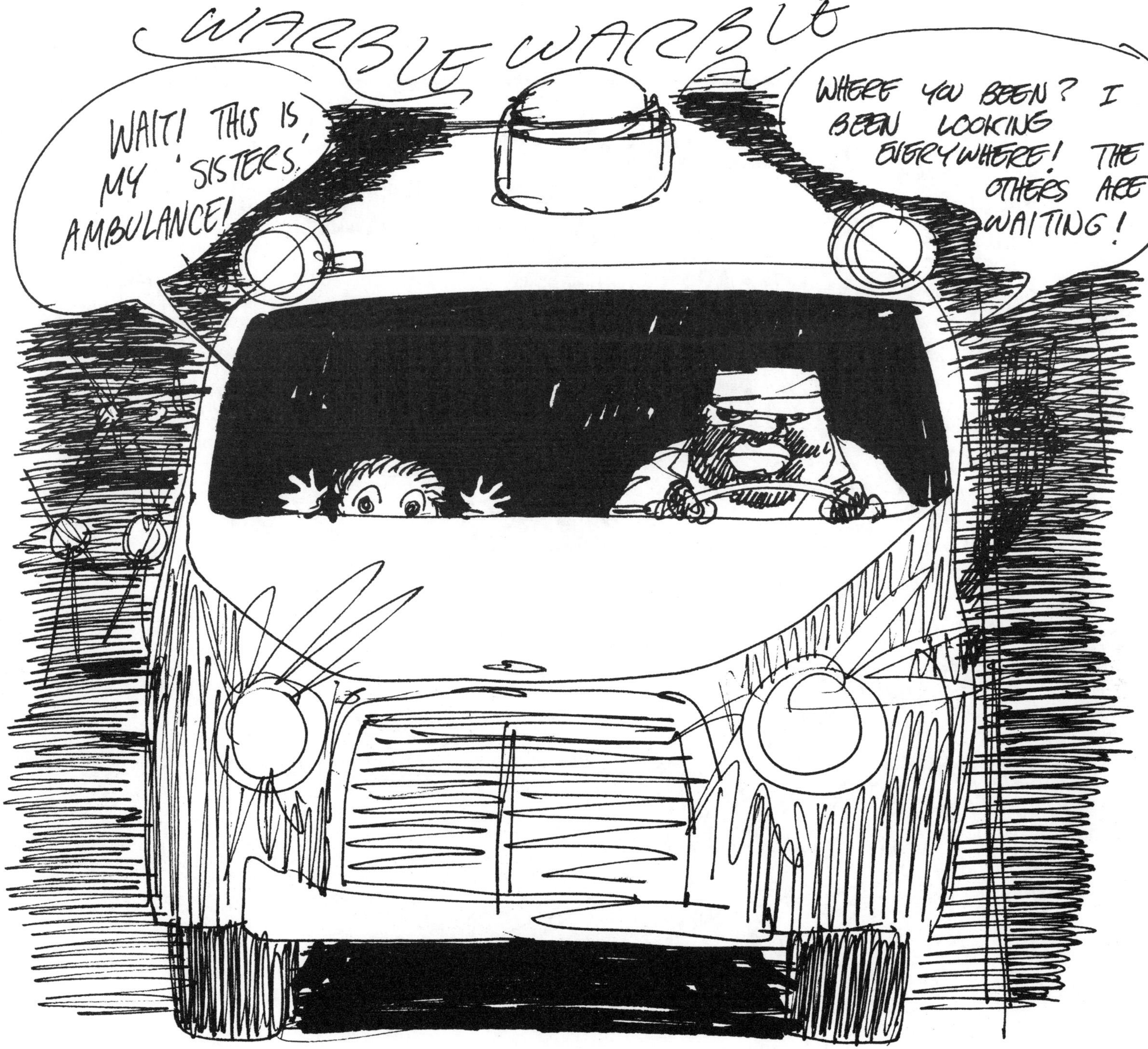
WARBLE WARBLE
WAIT! THIS IS, MY 'SISTERS' AMBULANCE!
WHERE YOU BEEN? I BEEN LOOKING EVERYWHERE! THE OTHERS ARE WAITING!

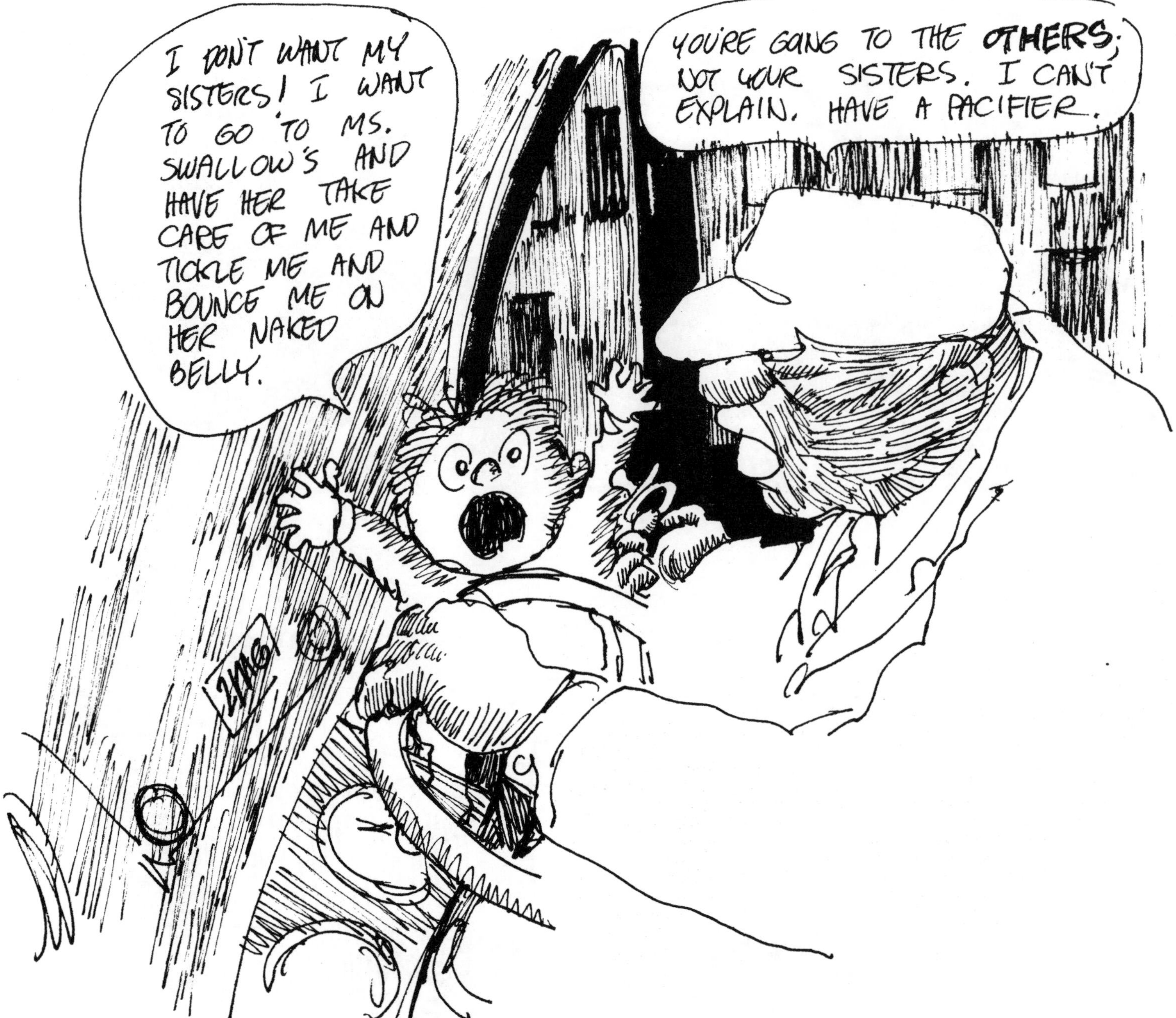
I DON'T WANT MY SISTERS! I WANT TO GO TO MS. SWALLOW'S AND HAVE HER TAKE CARE OF ME AND TICKLE ME AND BOUNCE ME ON HER NAKED BELLY.
YOU'RE GOING TO THE **OTHERS**; NOT YOUR SISTERS. I CAN'T EXPLAIN. HAVE A PACIFIER.
2YNG

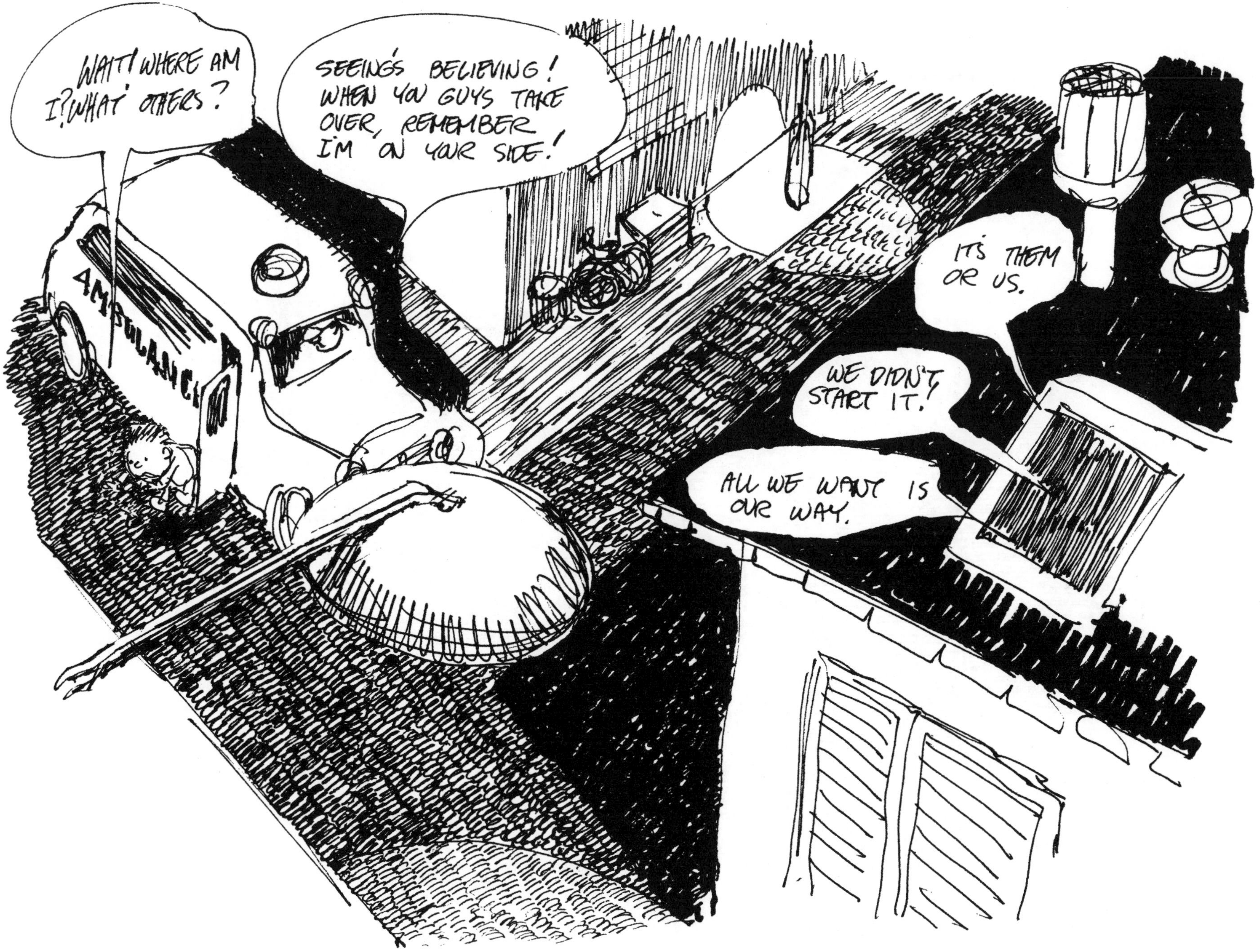
WAIT! WHERE AM I? WHAT OTHERS?
SEEING'S BELIEVING! WHEN YOU GUYS TAKE OVER, REMEMBER I'M ON YOUR SIDE!
AMBULANCE
IT'S THEM OR US.
WE DIDN'T START IT.
ALL WE WANT IS OUR WAY.

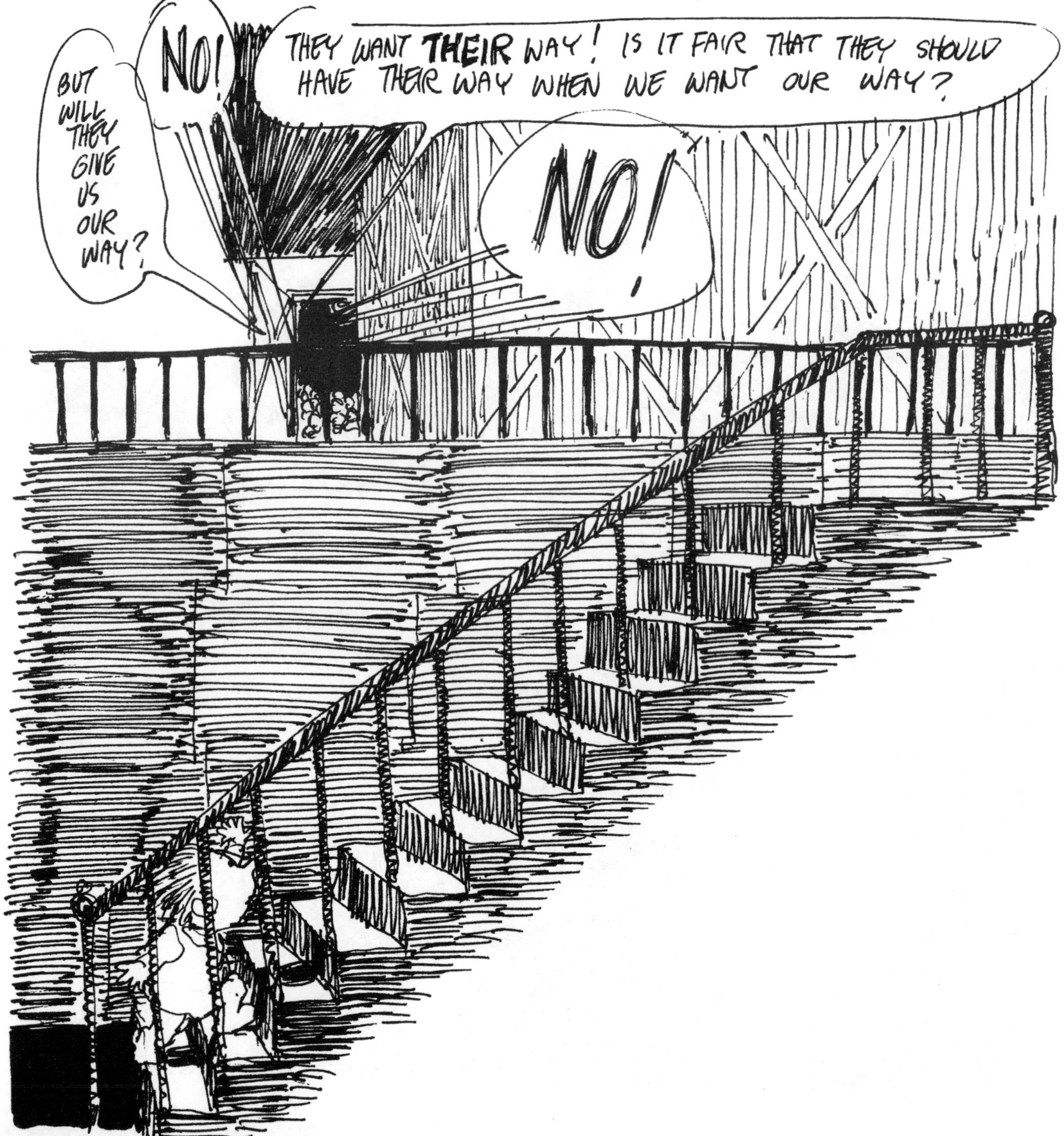
BUT WILL THEY GIVE US OUR WAY?
NO!
THEY WANT THEIR WAY! IS IT FAIR THAT THEY SHOULD HAVE THEIR WAY WHEN WE WANT OUR WAY?
NO!

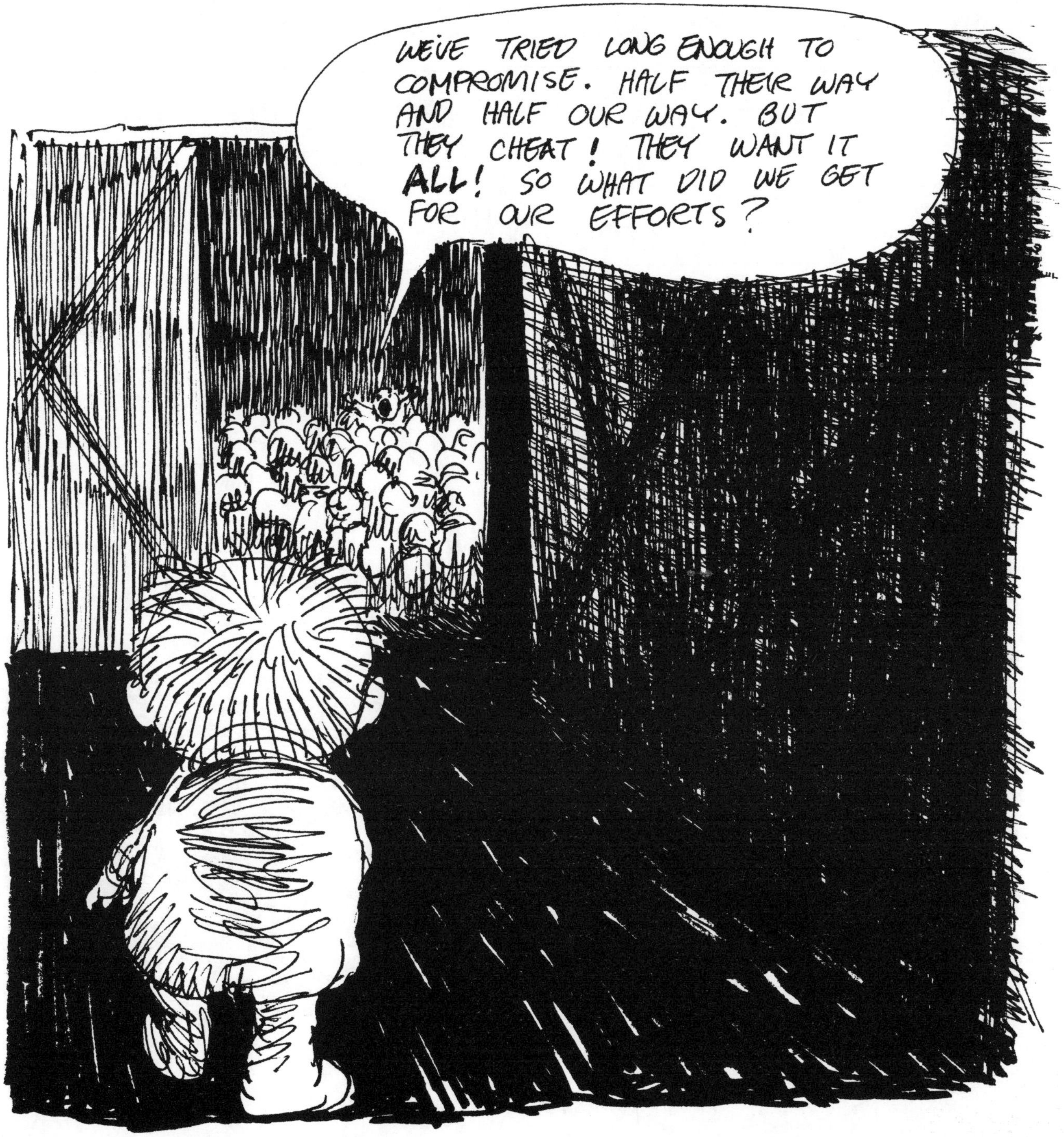
WE'VE TRIED LONG ENOUGH TO COMPROMISE. HALF THEIR WAY AND HALF OUR WAY. BUT THEY CHEAT! THEY WANT IT **ALL**! SO WHAT DID WE GET FOR OUR EFFORTS?

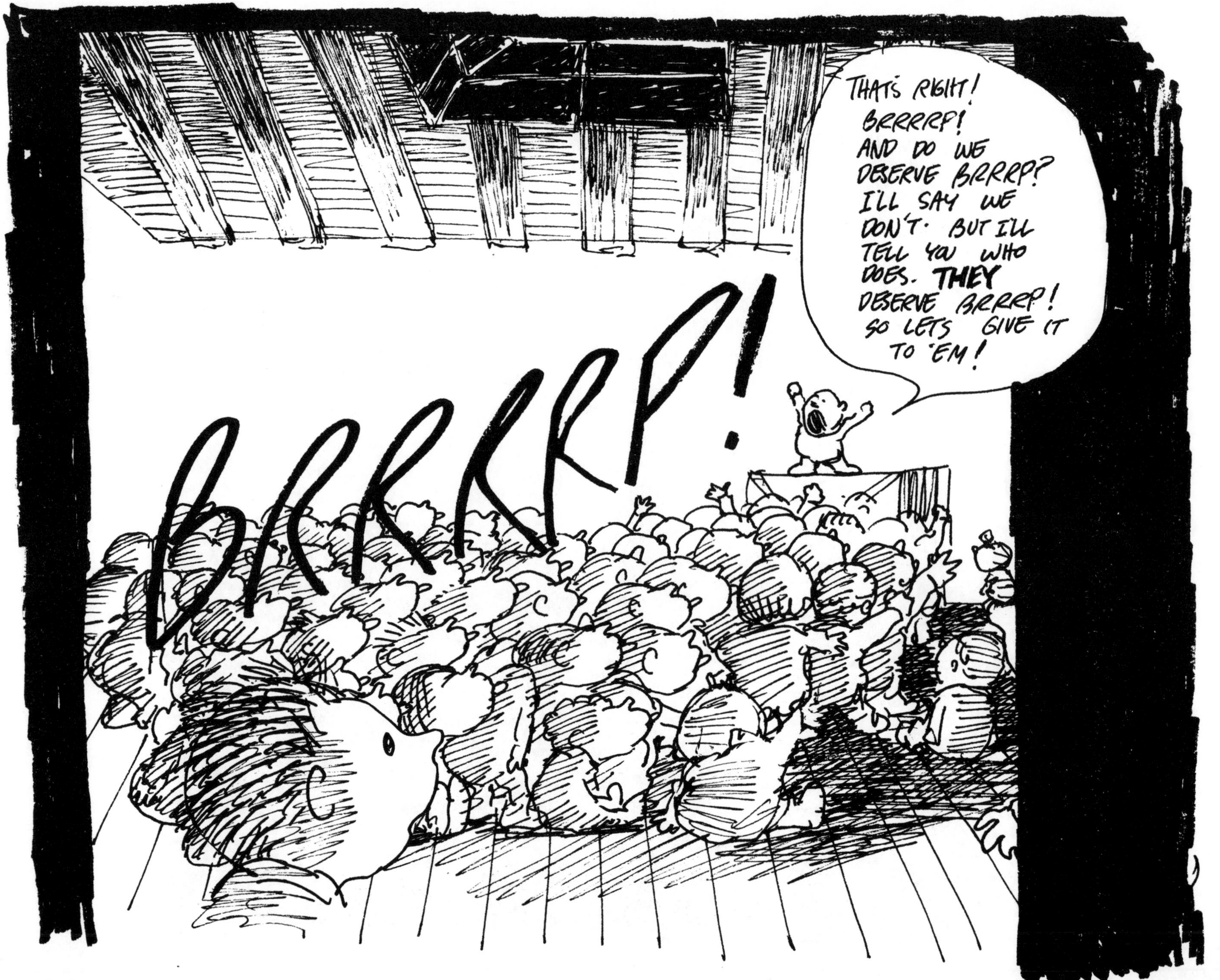
THAT'S RIGHT! BRRRRP! AND DO WE DESERVE BRRRP? I'LL SAY WE DON'T. BUT I'LL TELL YOU WHO DOES. THEY DESERVE BRRRP! SO LETS GIVE IT TO 'EM!
BRRRRP!

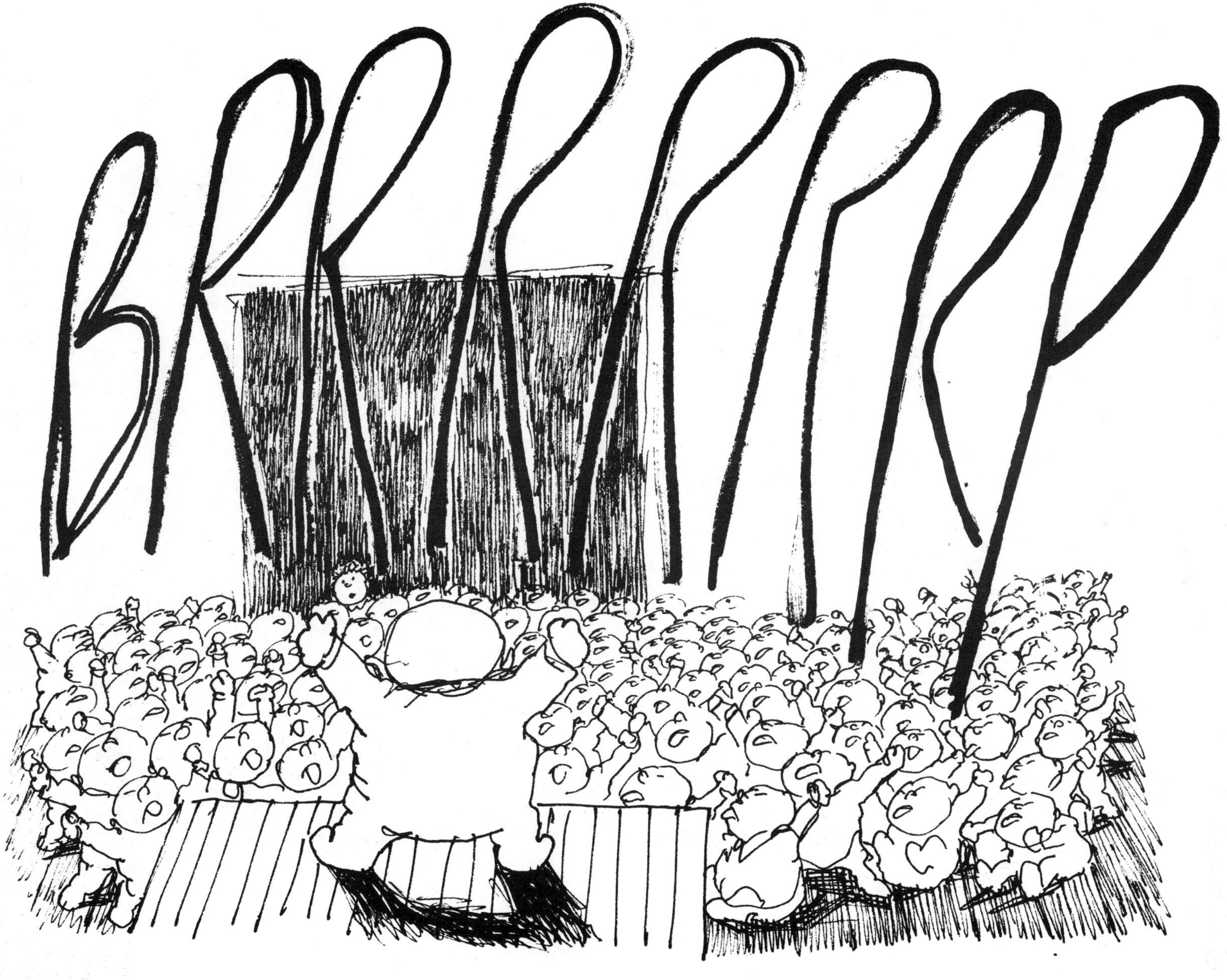
BRRRRRRRP

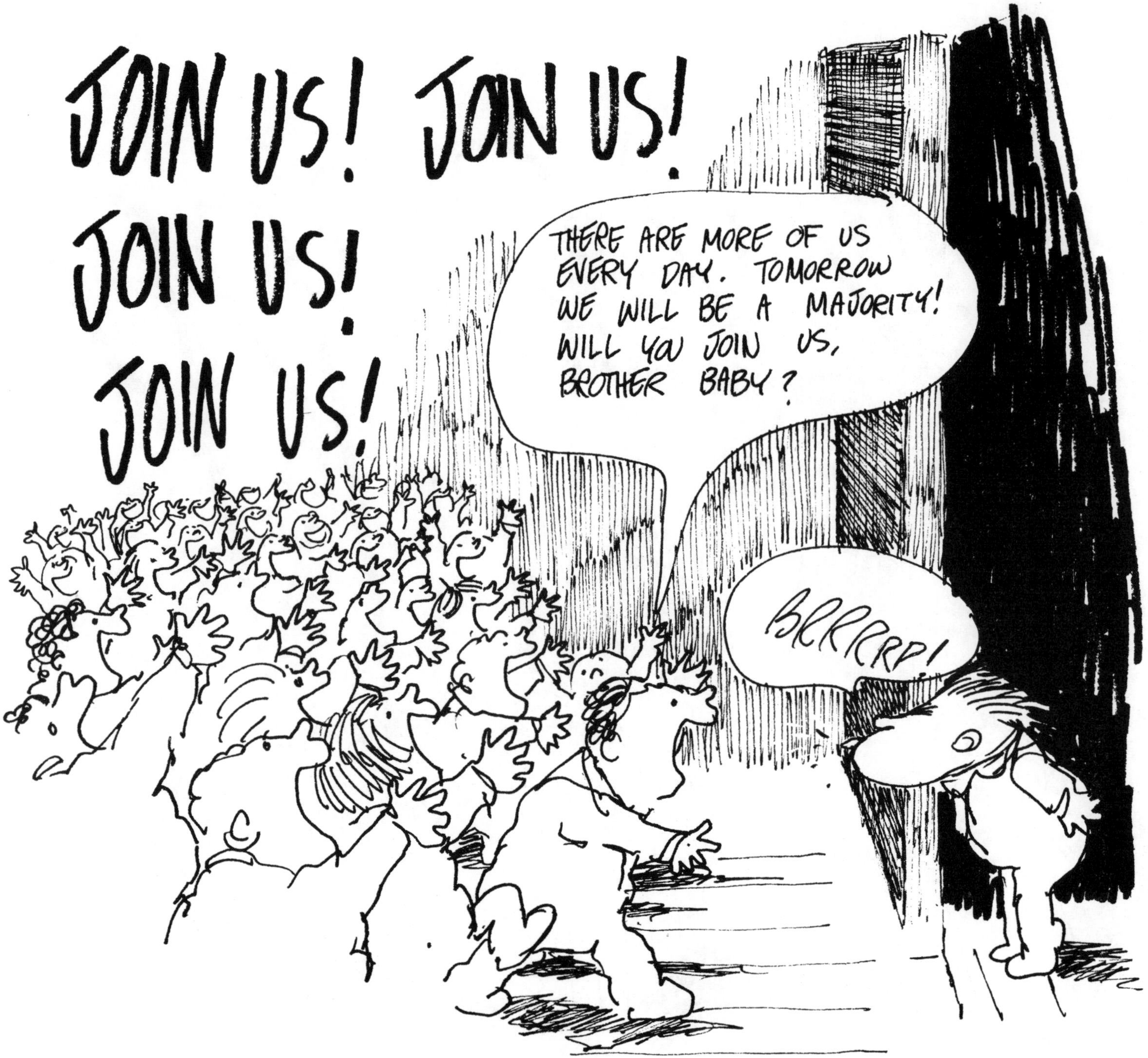
JOIN US! JOIN US!
JOIN US!
JOIN US!
THERE ARE MORE OF US EVERY DAY. TOMORROW WE WILL BE A MAJORITY! WILL YOU JOIN US, BROTHER BABY?
BRRRRRP!

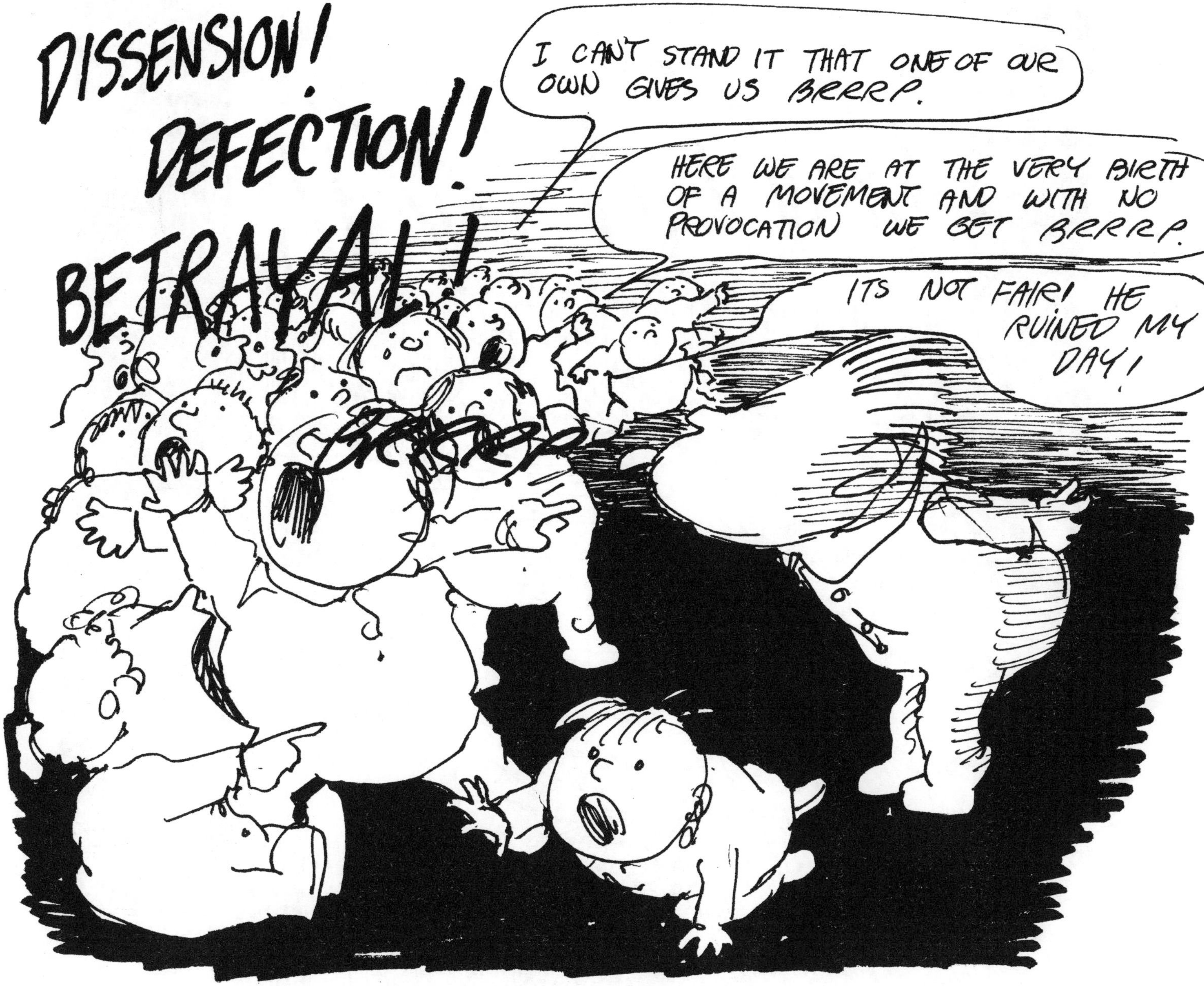
DISSENSION!
DEFECTION!
BETRAYAL!
I CAN'T STAND IT THAT ONE OF OUR OWN GIVES US BRRRP.
HERE WE ARE AT THE VERY BIRTH OF A MOVEMENT AND WITH NO PROVOCATION WE GET BRRRP.
ITS NOT FAIR! HE RUINED MY DAY!

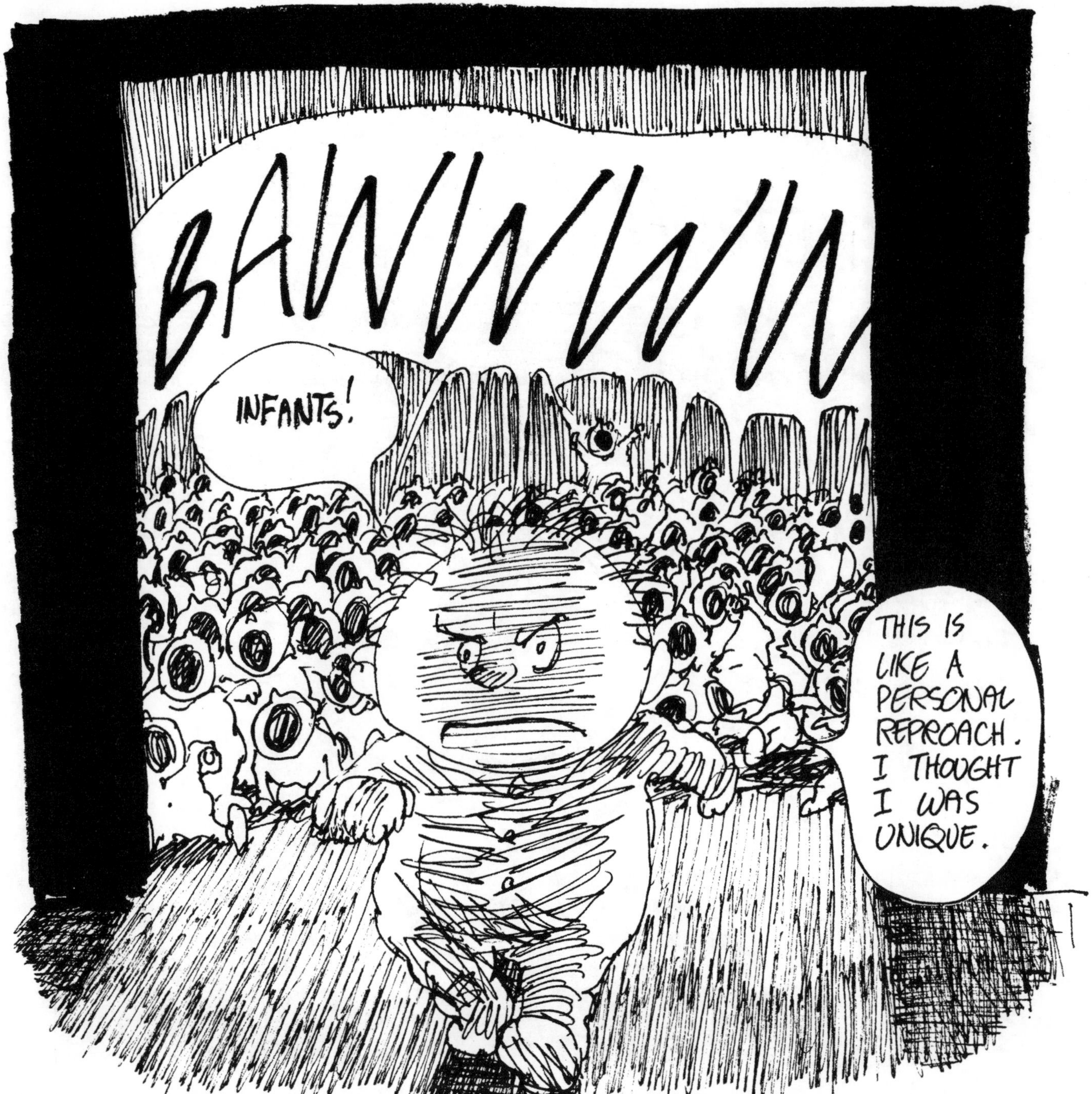
BAWWWW
INFANTS!
THIS IS LIKE A PERSONAL REPROACH. I THOUGHT I WAS UNIQUE.

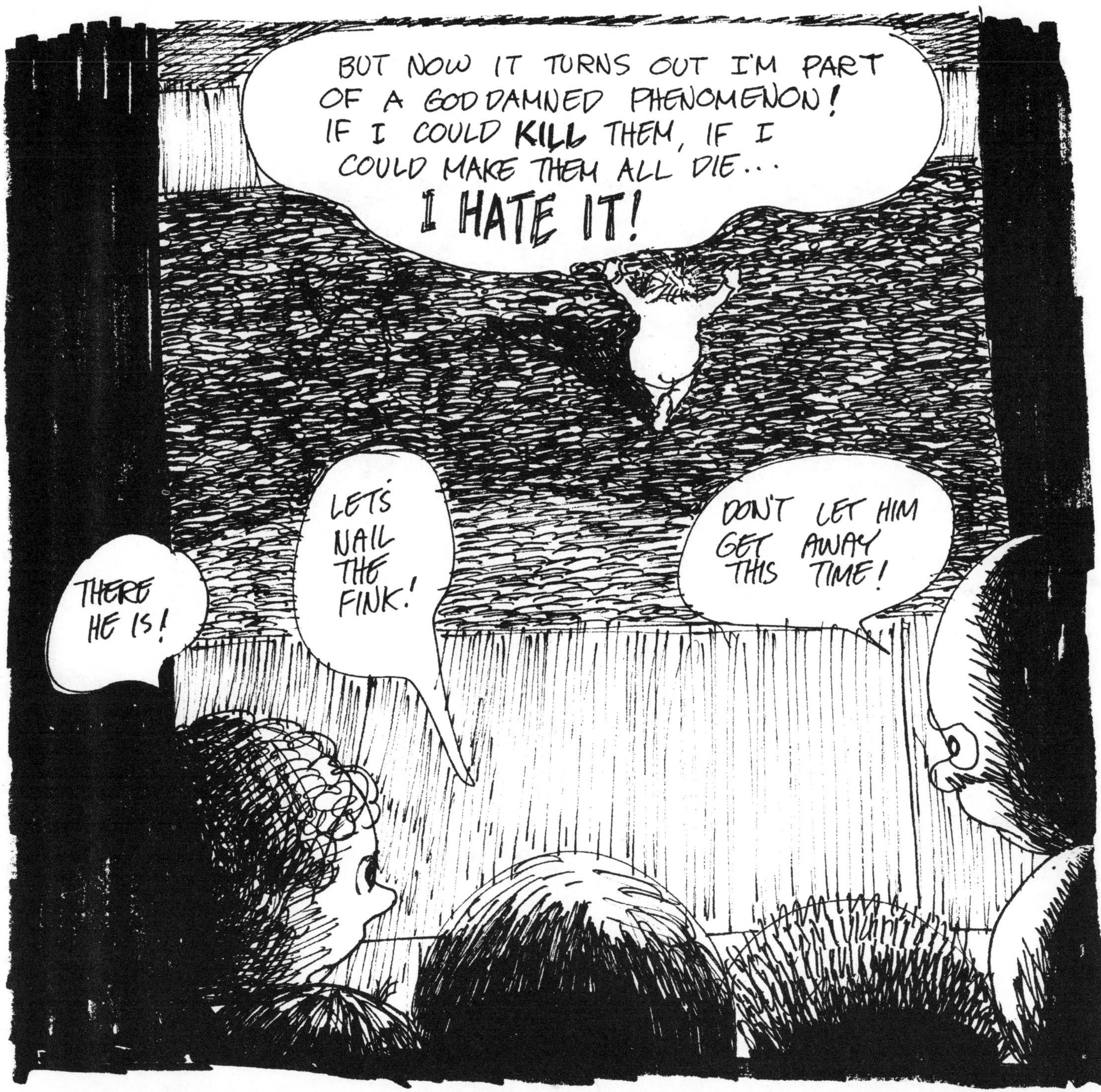
BUT NOW IT TURNS OUT I'M PART OF A GODDAMNED PHENOMENON! IF I COULD KILL THEM, IF I COULD MAKE THEM ALL DIE... I HATE IT!
THERE HE IS!
LETS NAIL THE FINK!
DON'T LET HIM GET AWAY THIS TIME!

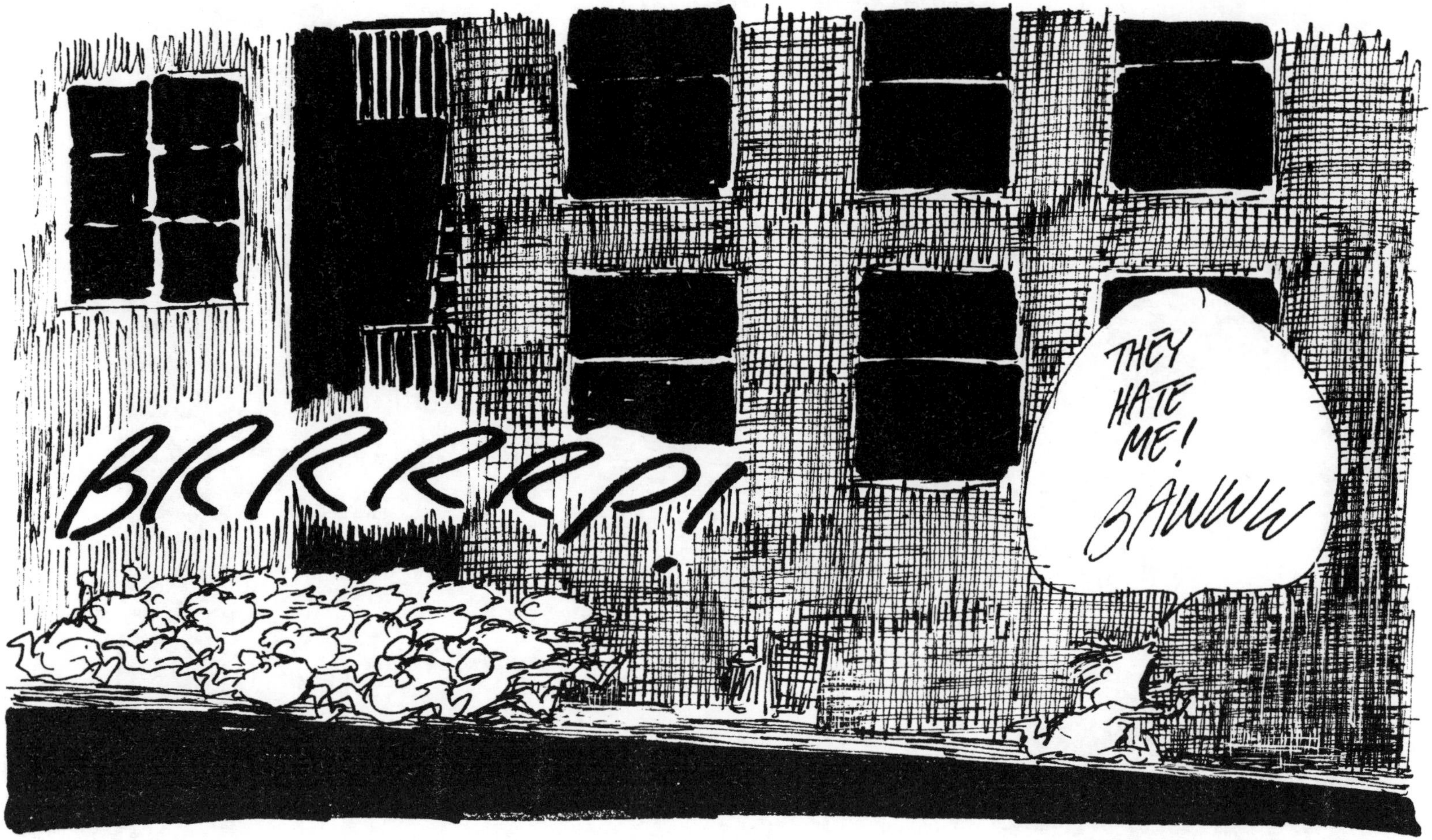
BRRRRP!
THEY HATE ME! BAWWW

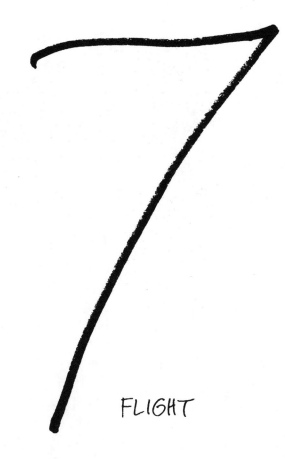

FLIGHT

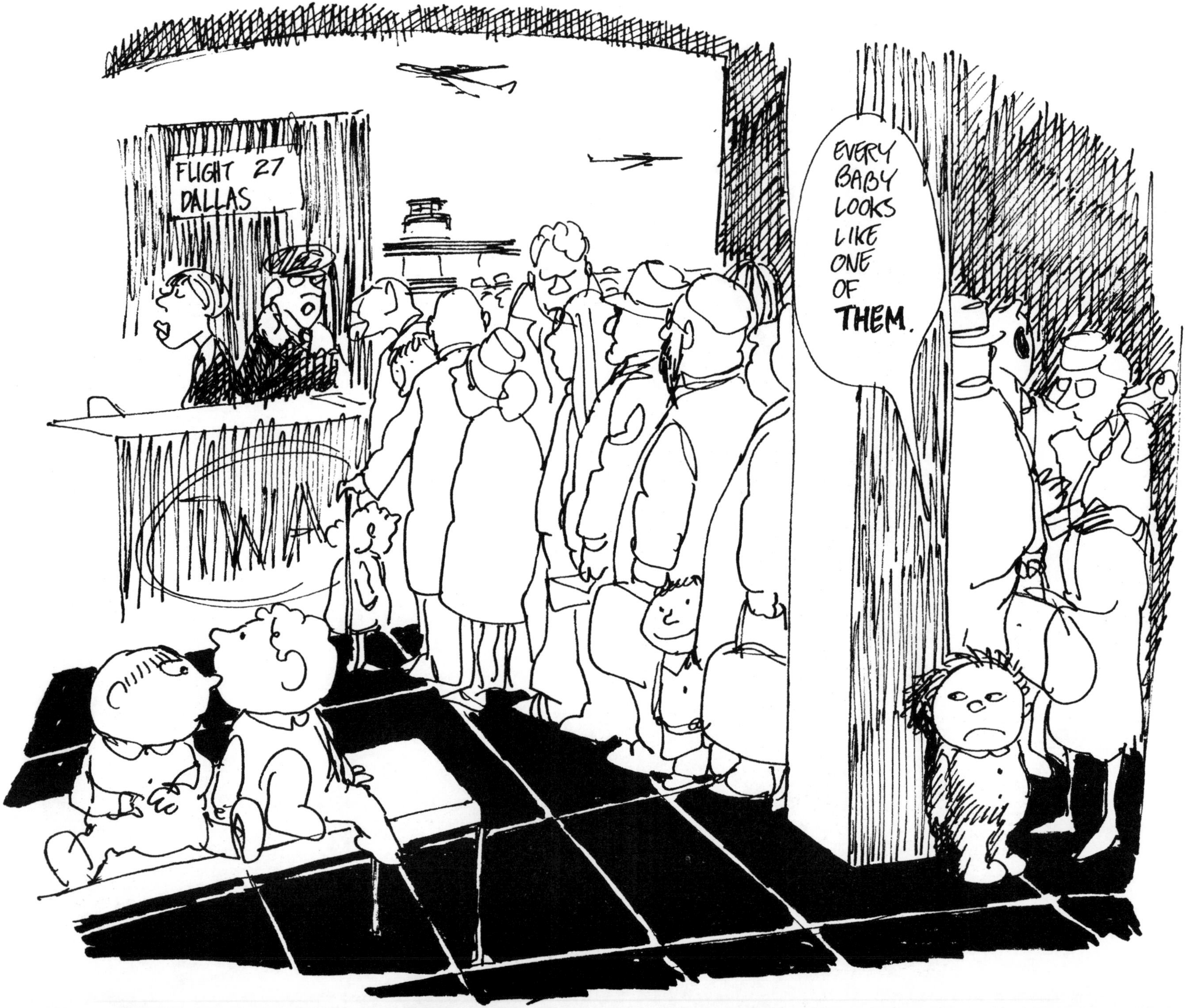
FLIGHT 27
DALLAS
TWA
EVERY BABY LOOKS LIKE ONE OF **THEM**.

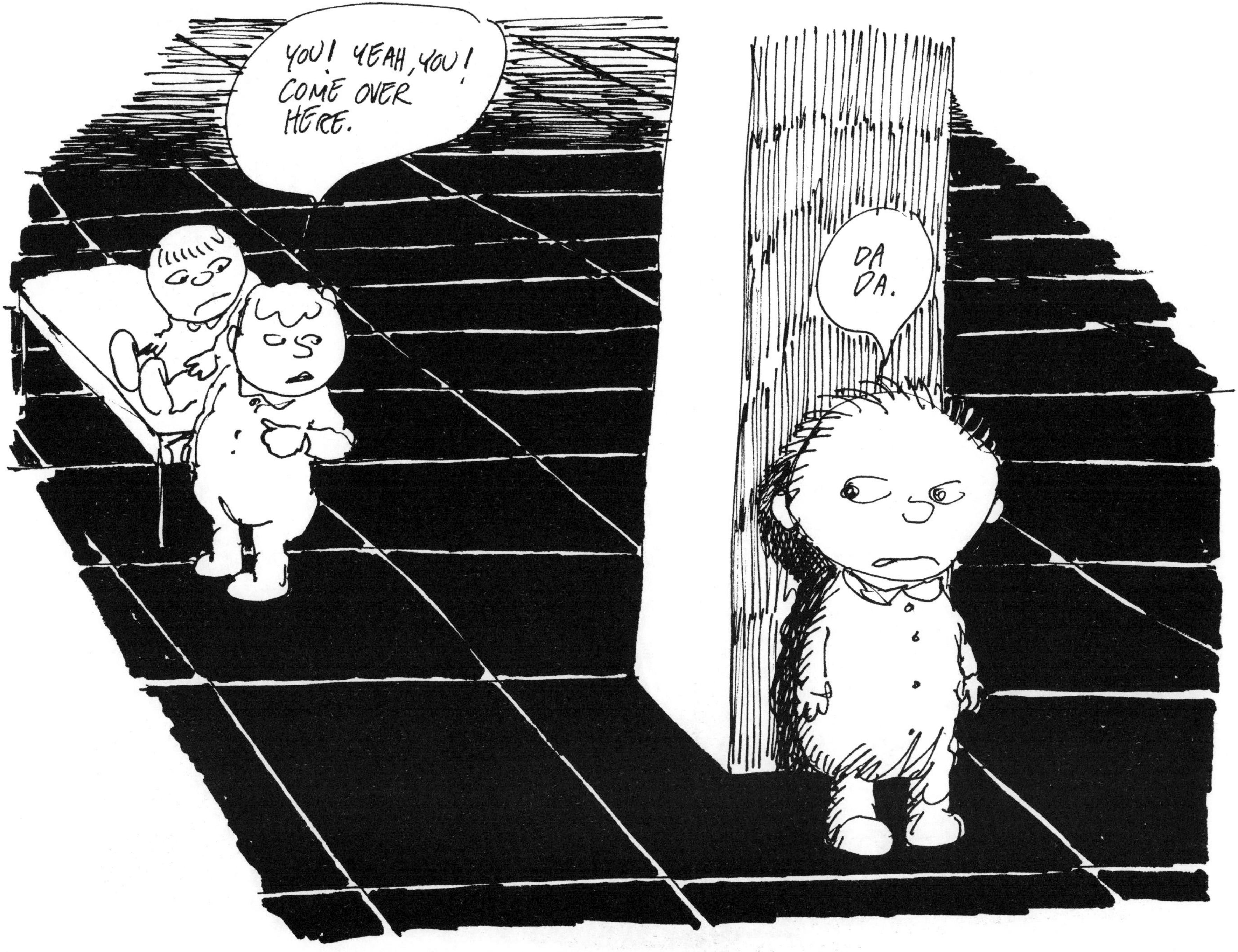
YOU! YEAH, YOU! COME OVER HERE.
DA DA.

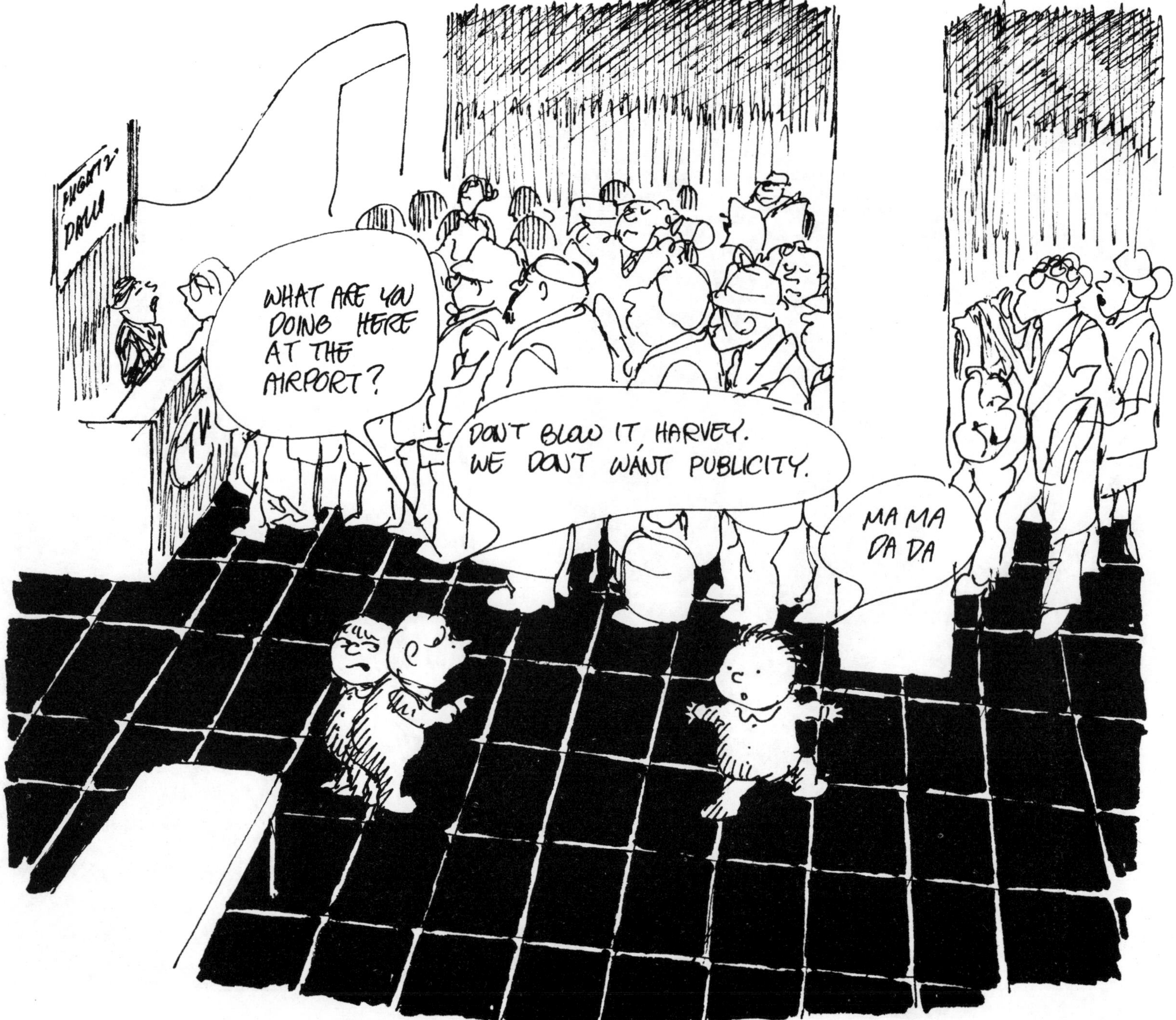
WHAT ARE YOU DOING HERE AT THE AIRPORT?
DON'T BLOW IT, HARVEY. WE DON'T WANT PUBLICITY.
MA MA DA DA

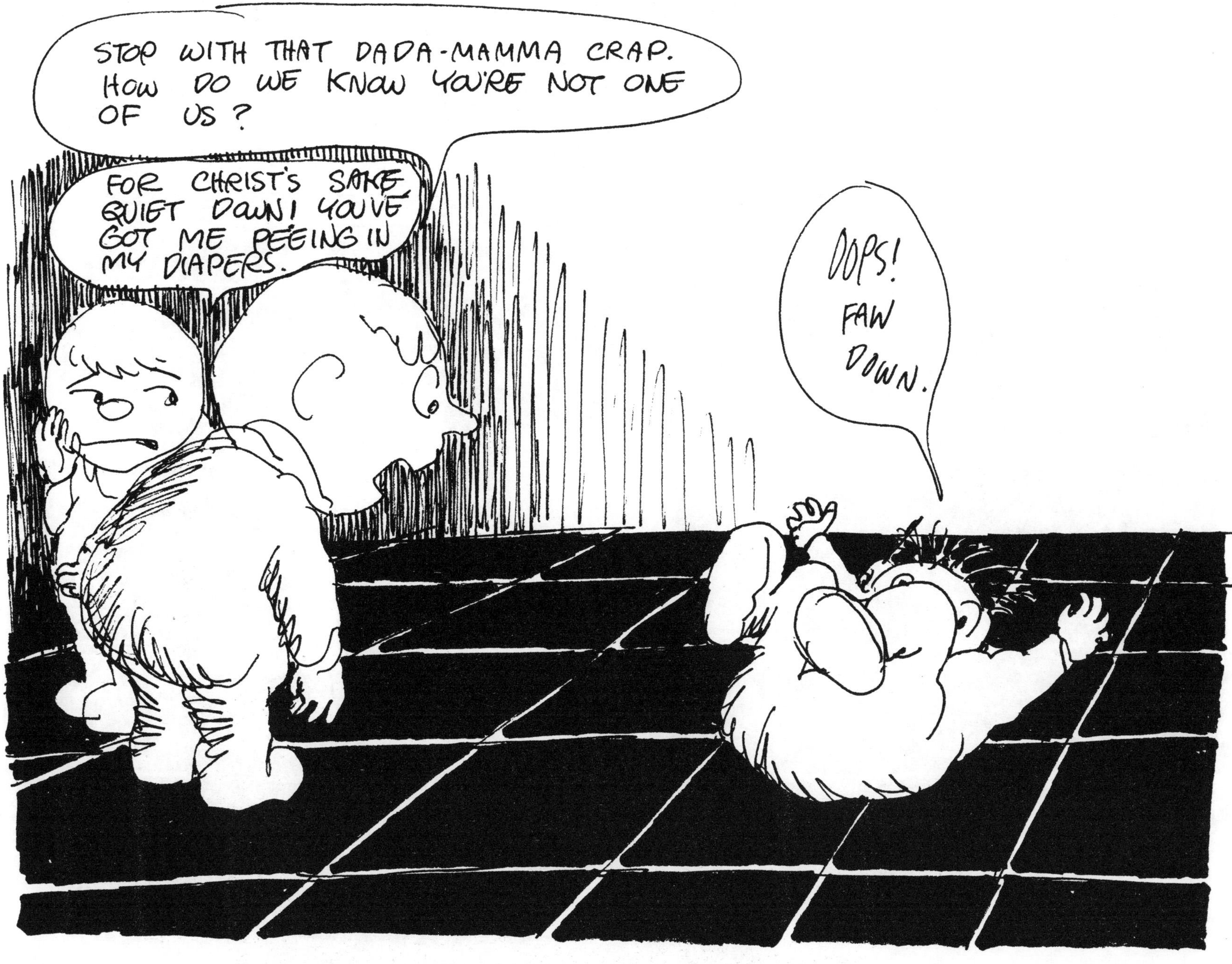
STOP WITH THAT DADA-MAMMA CRAP. HOW DO WE KNOW YOU'RE NOT ONE OF US?
FOR CHRIST'S SAKE, QUIET DOWN! YOU'VE GOT ME PEEING IN MY DIAPERS.
OOPS! FAW DOWN.

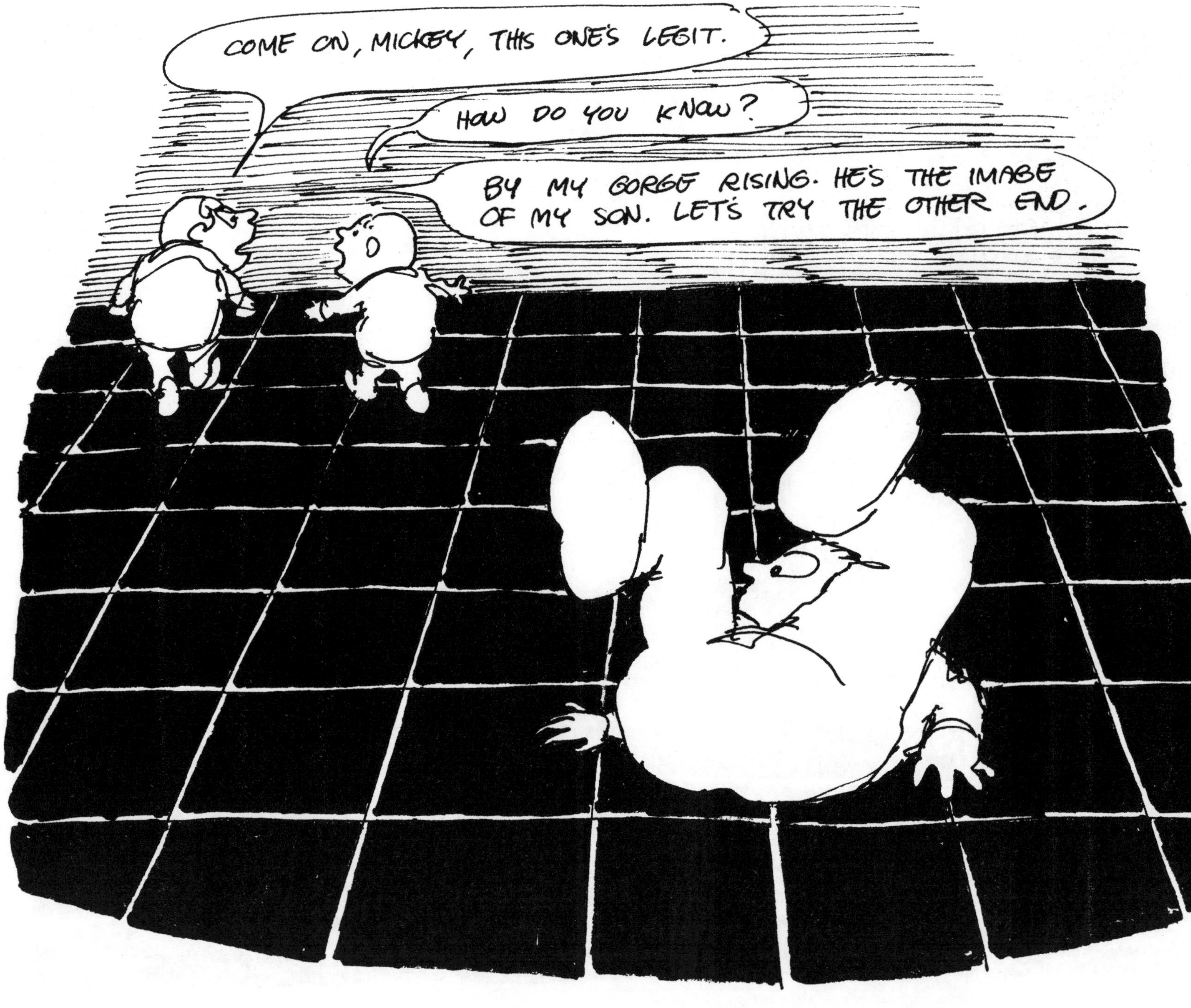
COME ON, MICKEY, THIS ONE'S LEGIT.
HOW DO YOU KNOW?
BY MY GORGE RISING. HE'S THE IMAGE OF MY SON. LET'S TRY THE OTHER END.

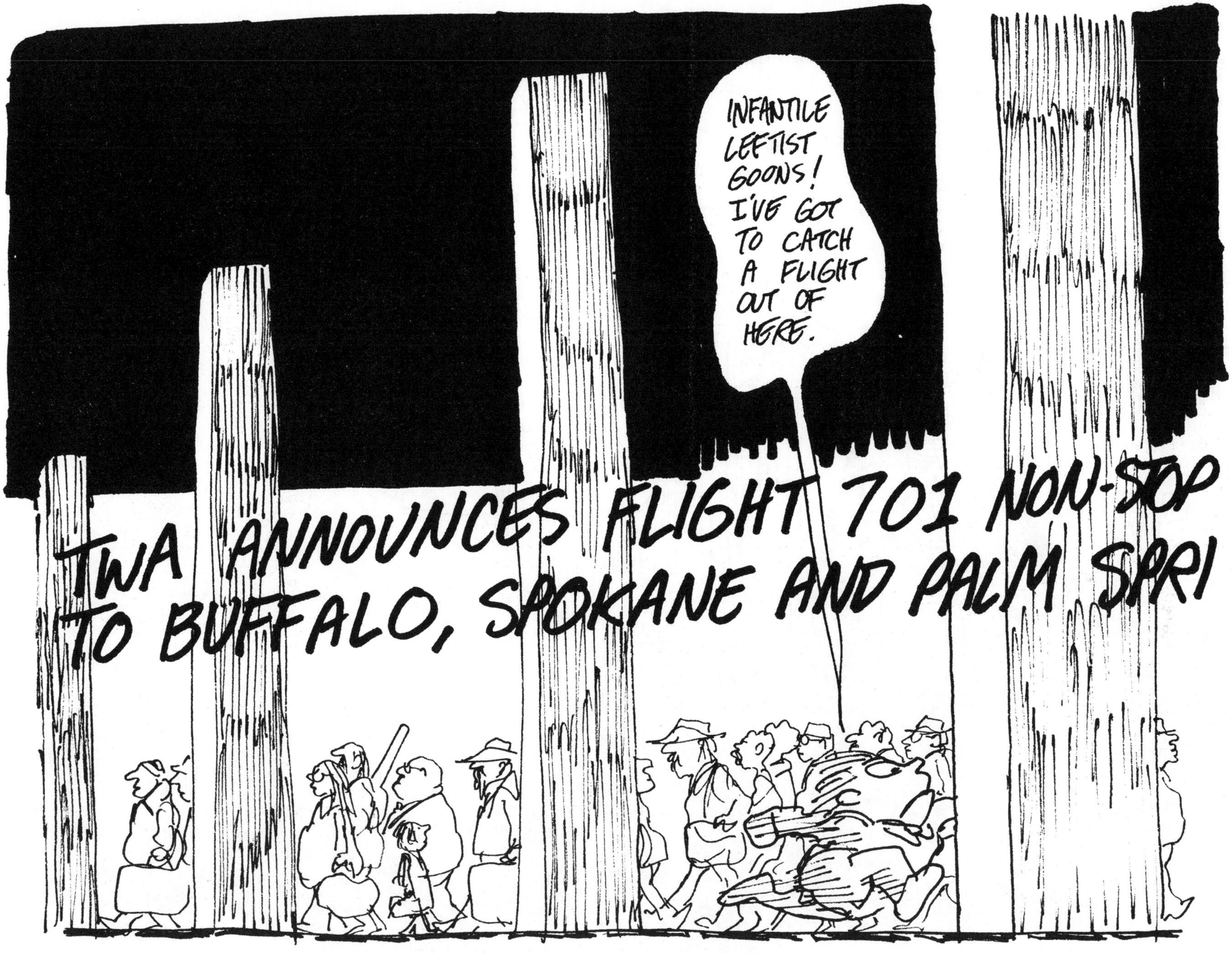
INFANTILE LEFTIST GOONS! I'VE GOT TO CATCH A FLIGHT OUT OF HERE.
TWA ANNOUNCES FLIGHT 701 NON-STOP TO BUFFALO, SPOKANE AND PALM SPRI

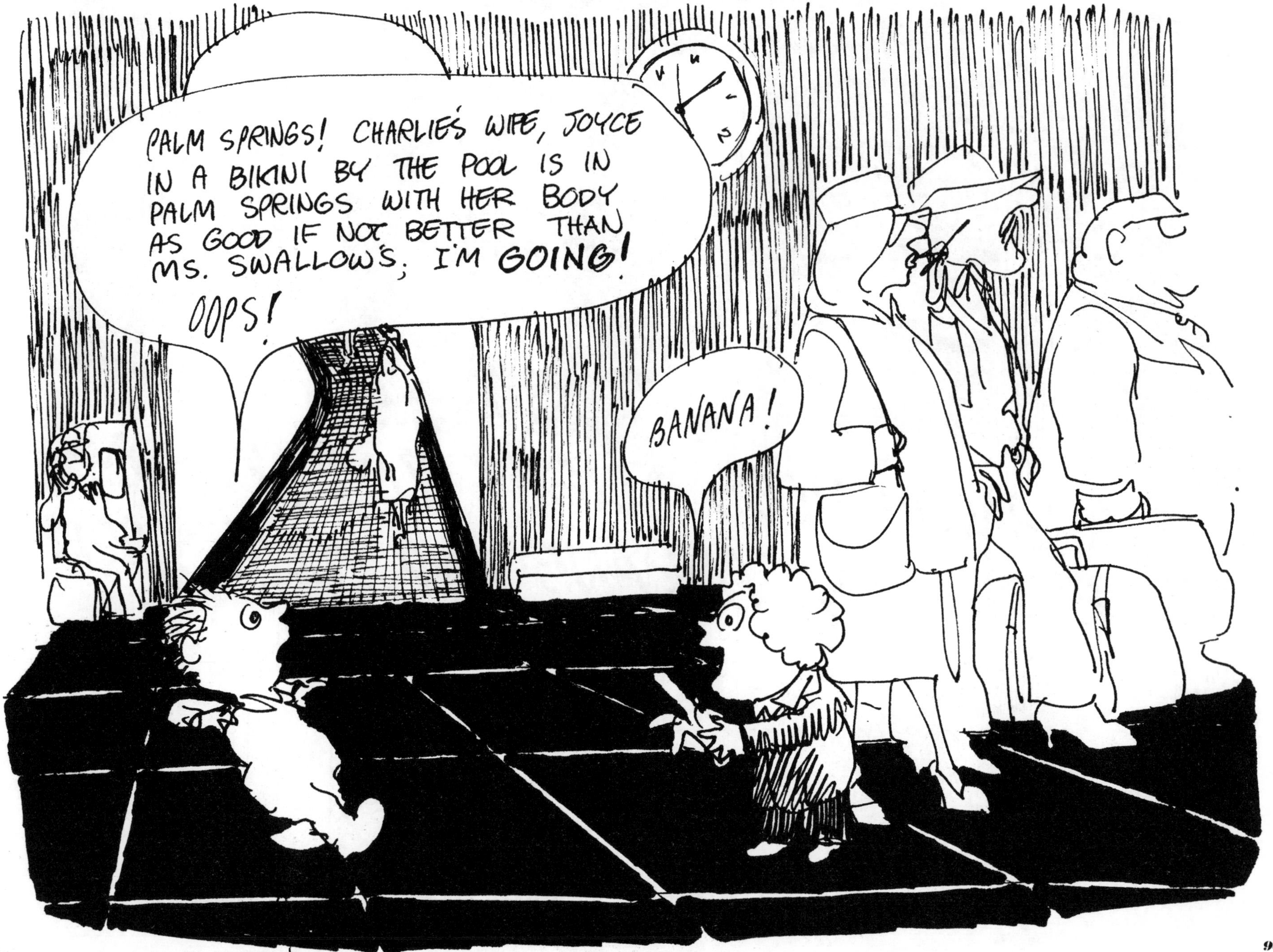
PALM SPRINGS! CHARLIE'S WIFE, JOYCE IN A BIKINI BY THE POOL IS IN PALM SPRINGS WITH HER BODY AS GOOD IF NOT BETTER THAN MS. SWALLOW'S; I'M GOING!
OOPS!
BANANA!

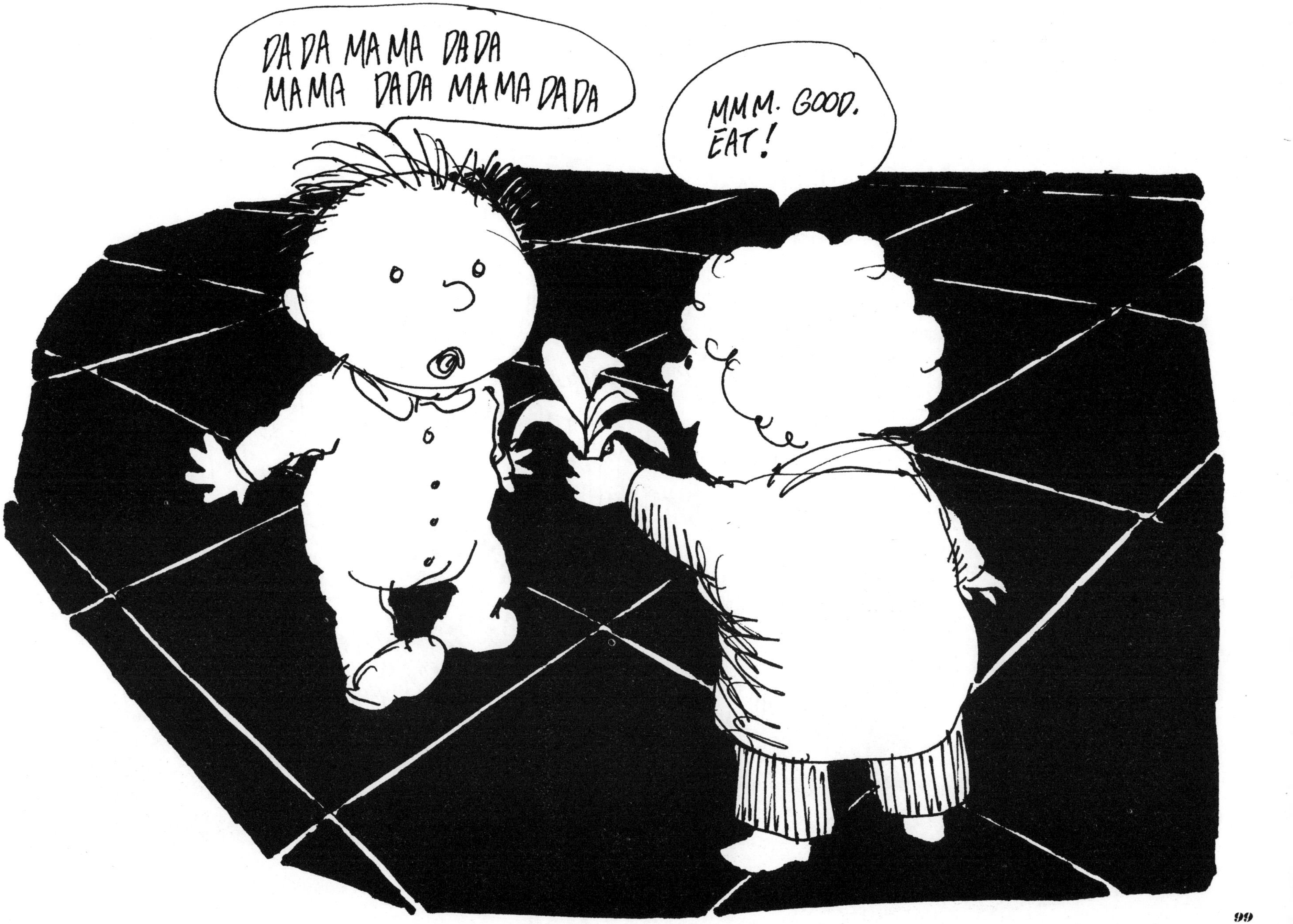
DA DA MA MA DA DA
MA MA DA DA MA MA DA DA
MMM. GOOD.
EAT!

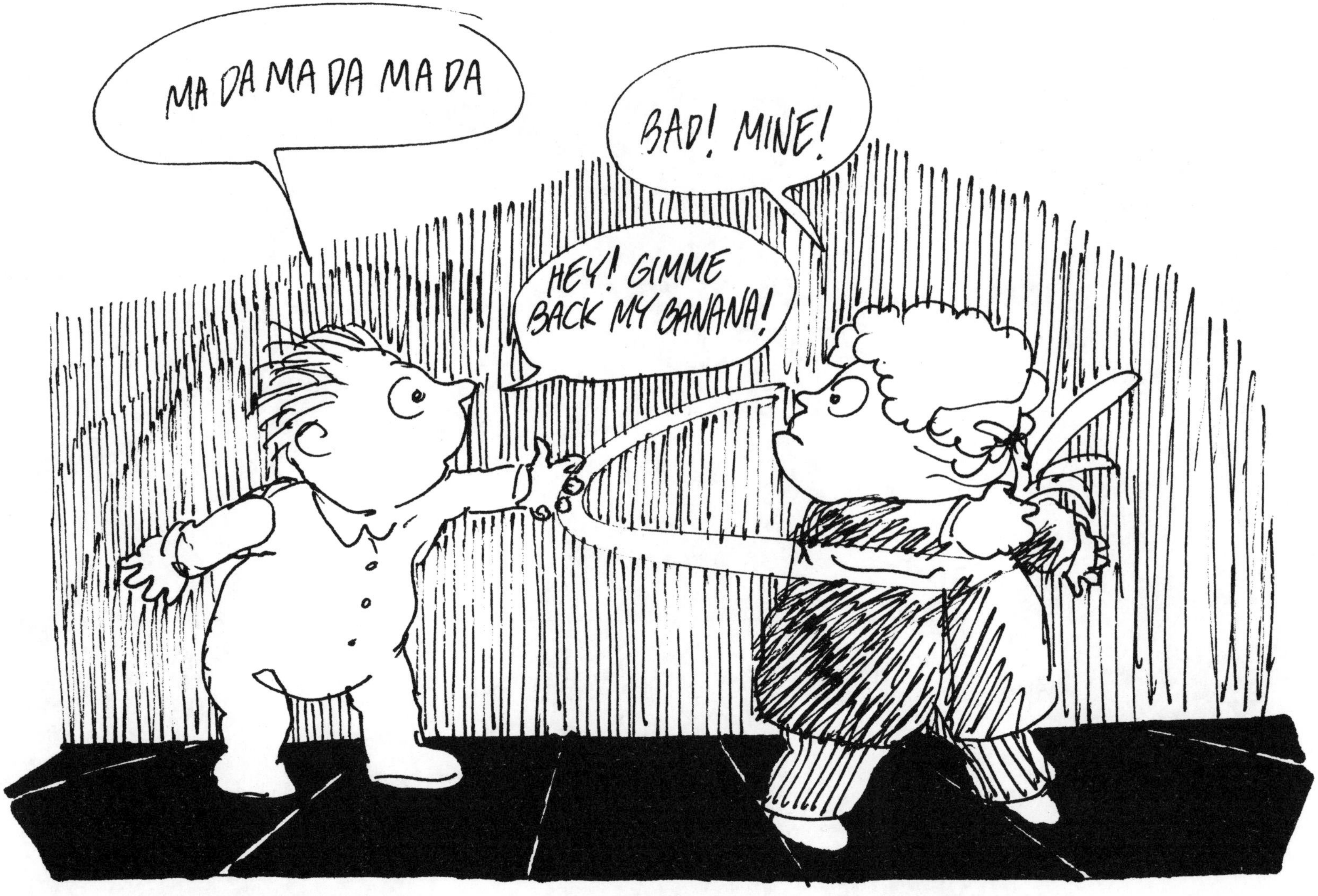
MA DA MA DA MA DA
HEY! GIMME BACK MY BANANA!
BAD! MINE!

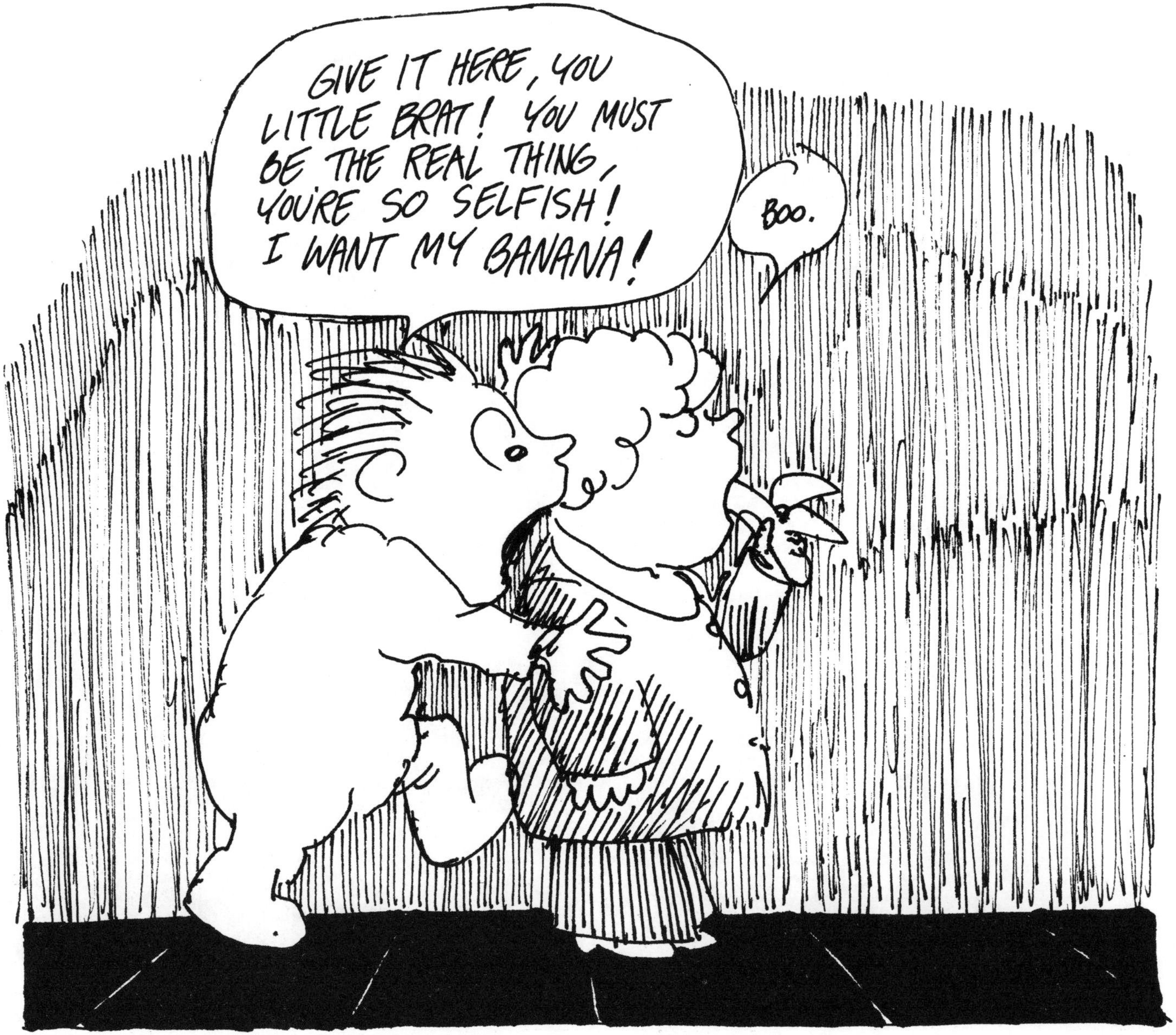
GIVE IT HERE, YOU LITTLE BRAT! YOU MUST BE THE REAL THING, YOU'RE SO SELFISH! I WANT MY BANANA!
BOO.

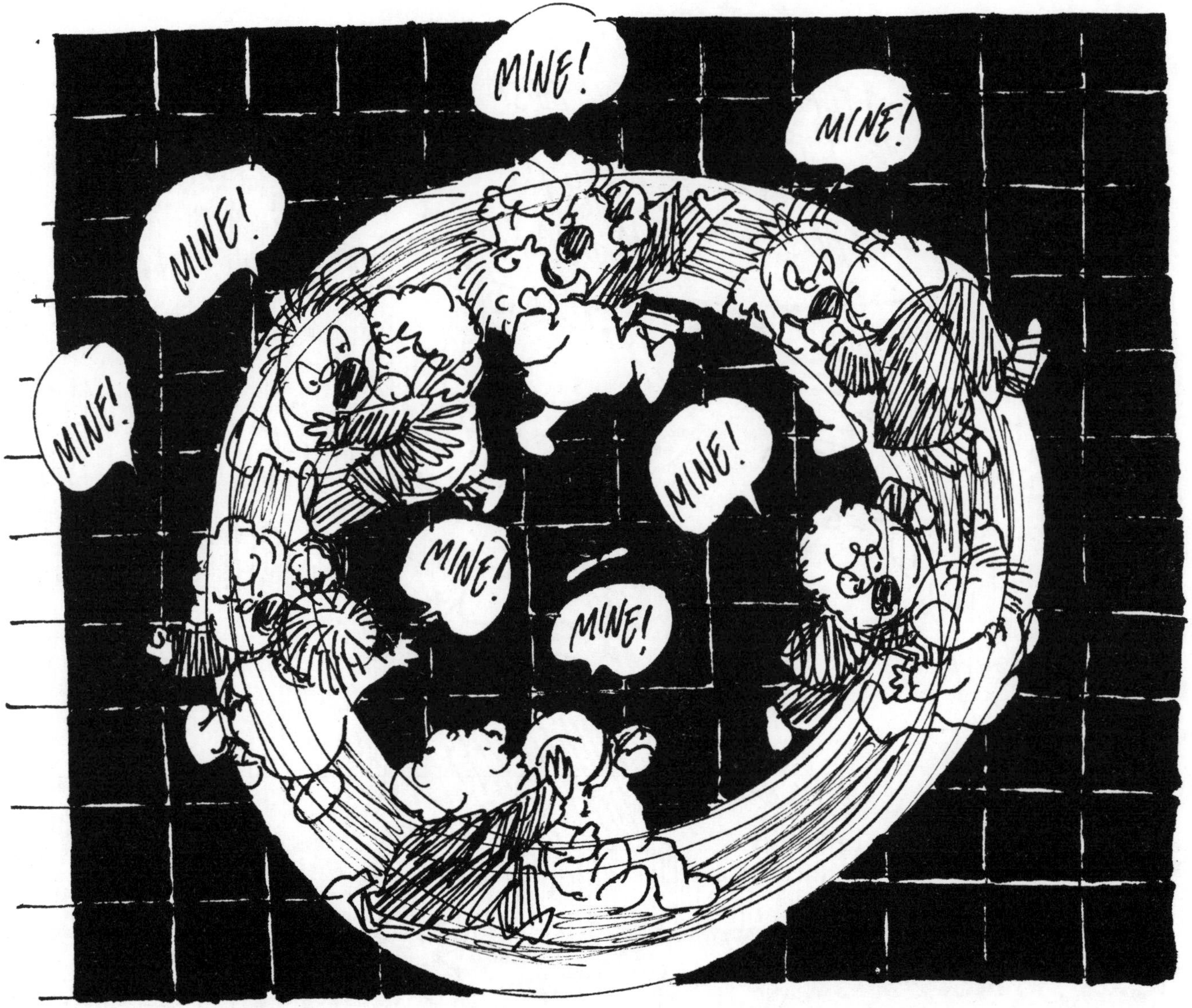
MINE!
MINE!
MINE!
MINE!
MINE!
MINE!
MINE!

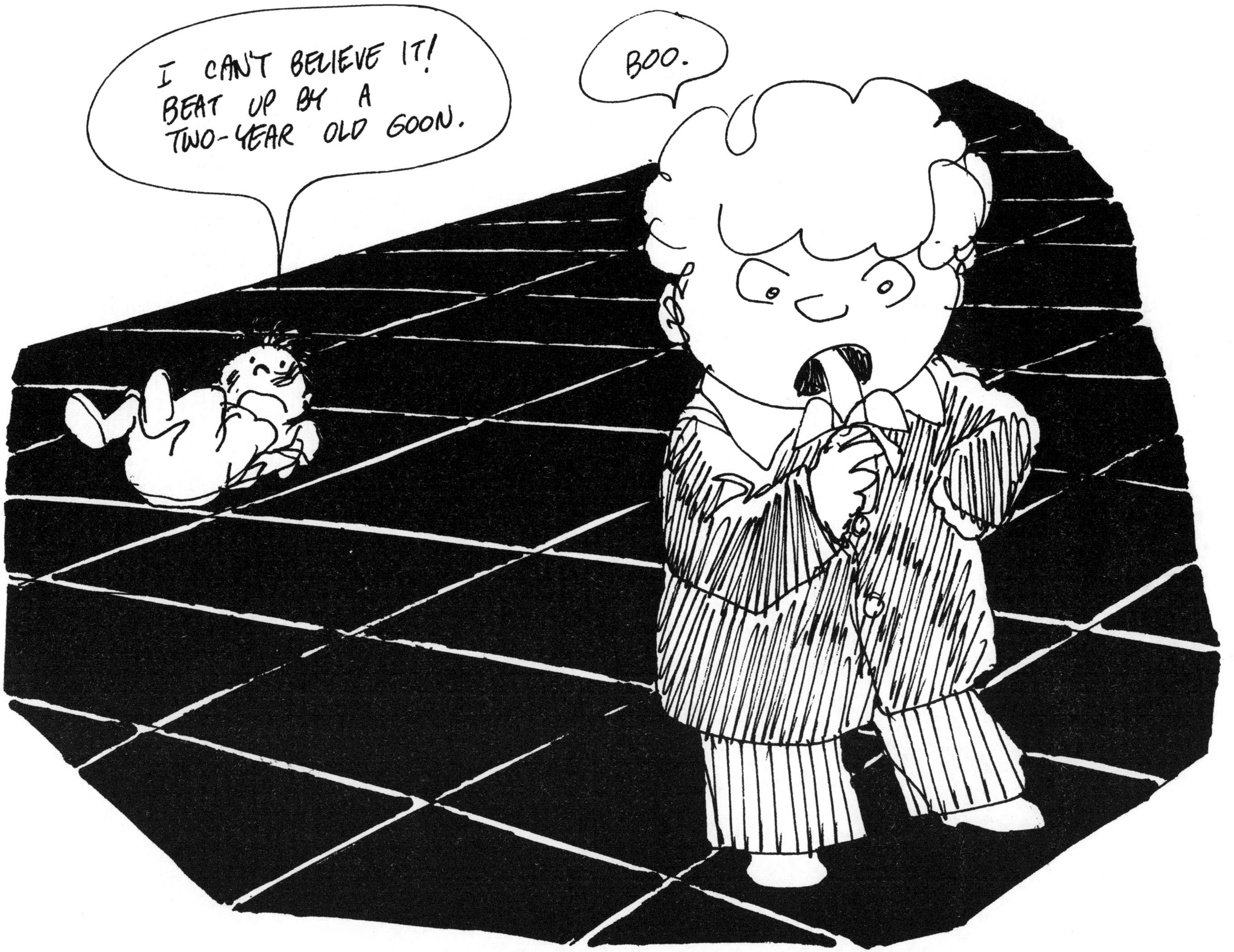
I CAN'T BELIEVE IT! BEAT UP BY A TWO-YEAR OLD GOON.
BOO.

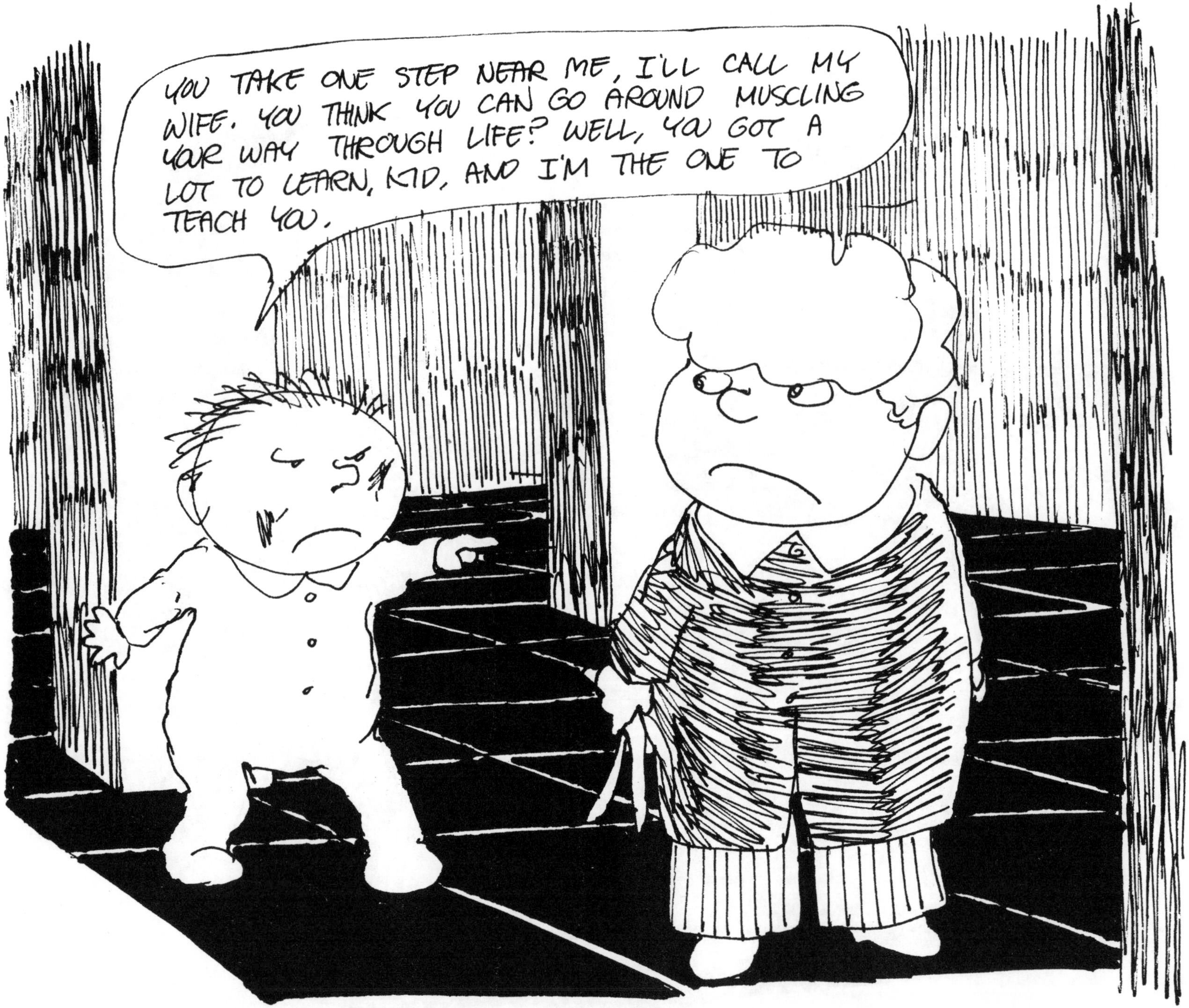
YOU TAKE ONE STEP NEAR ME, I'LL CALL MY WIFE. YOU THINK YOU CAN GO AROUND MUSCLING YOUR WAY THROUGH LIFE? WELL, YOU GOT A LOT TO LEARN, KID, AND I'M THE ONE TO TEACH YOU.

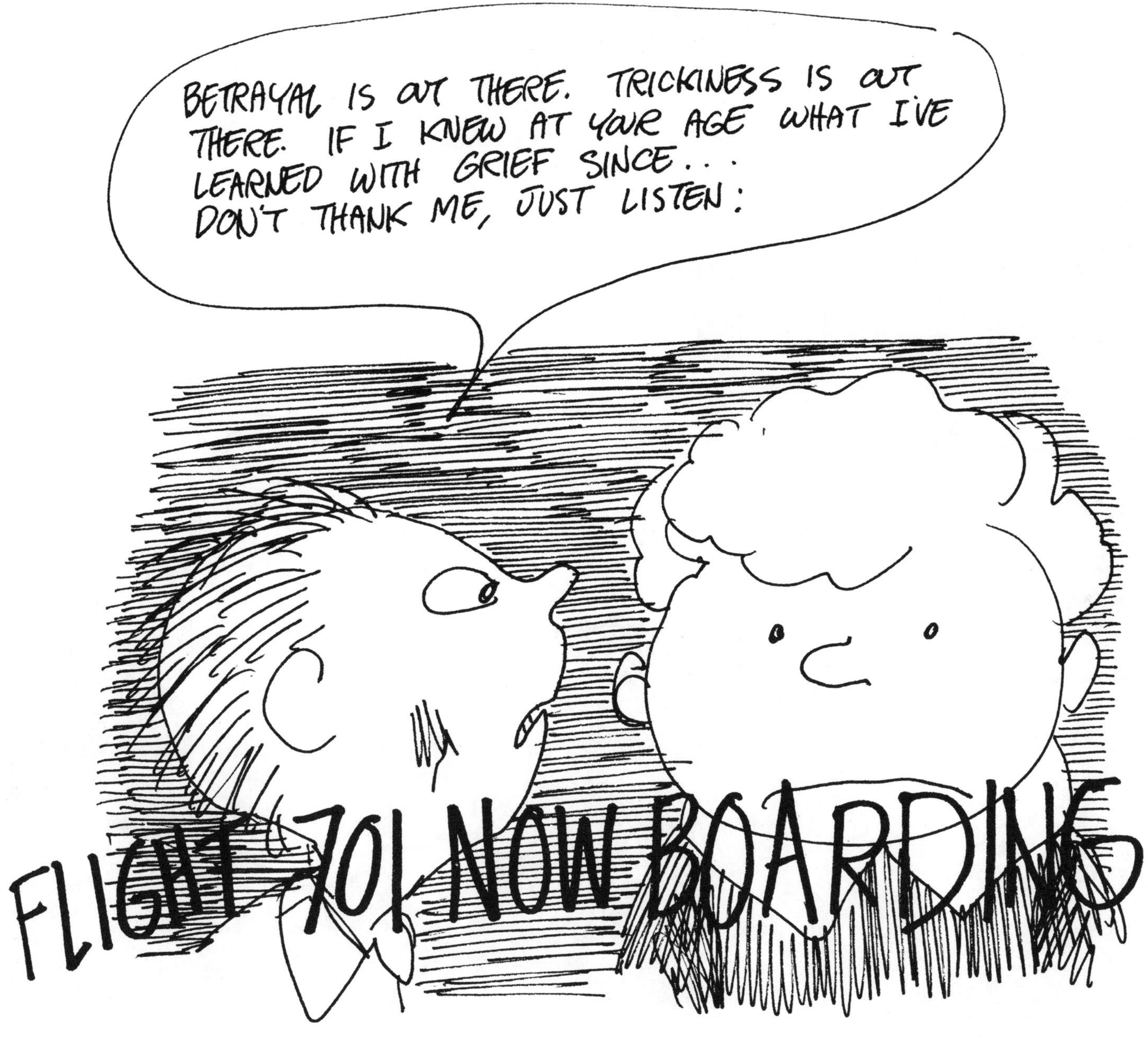
BETRAYAL IS OUT THERE. TRICKINESS IS OUT THERE. IF I KNEW AT YOUR AGE WHAT I'VE LEARNED WITH GRIEF SINCE... DON'T THANK ME, JUST LISTEN:
FLIGHT 701 NOW BOARDING

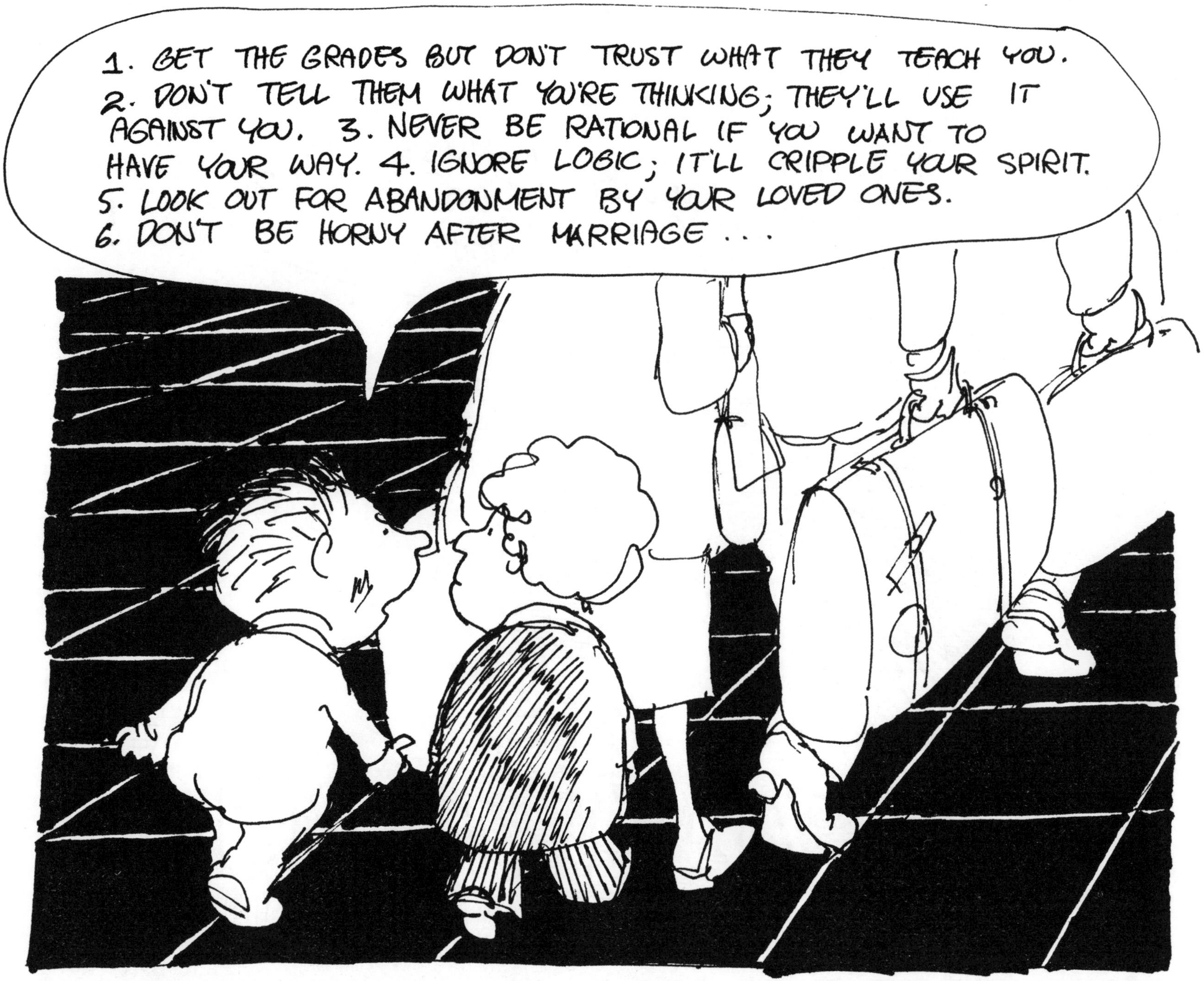
1. GET THE GRADES BUT DON'T TRUST WHAT THEY TEACH YOU. 2. DON'T TELL THEM WHAT YOU'RE THINKING; THEY'LL USE IT AGAINST YOU. 3. NEVER BE RATIONAL IF YOU WANT TO HAVE YOUR WAY. 4. IGNORE LOGIC; IT'LL CRIPPLE YOUR SPIRIT. 5. LOOK OUT FOR ABANDONMENT BY YOUR LOVED ONES. 6. DON'T BE HORNY AFTER MARRIAGE . . .

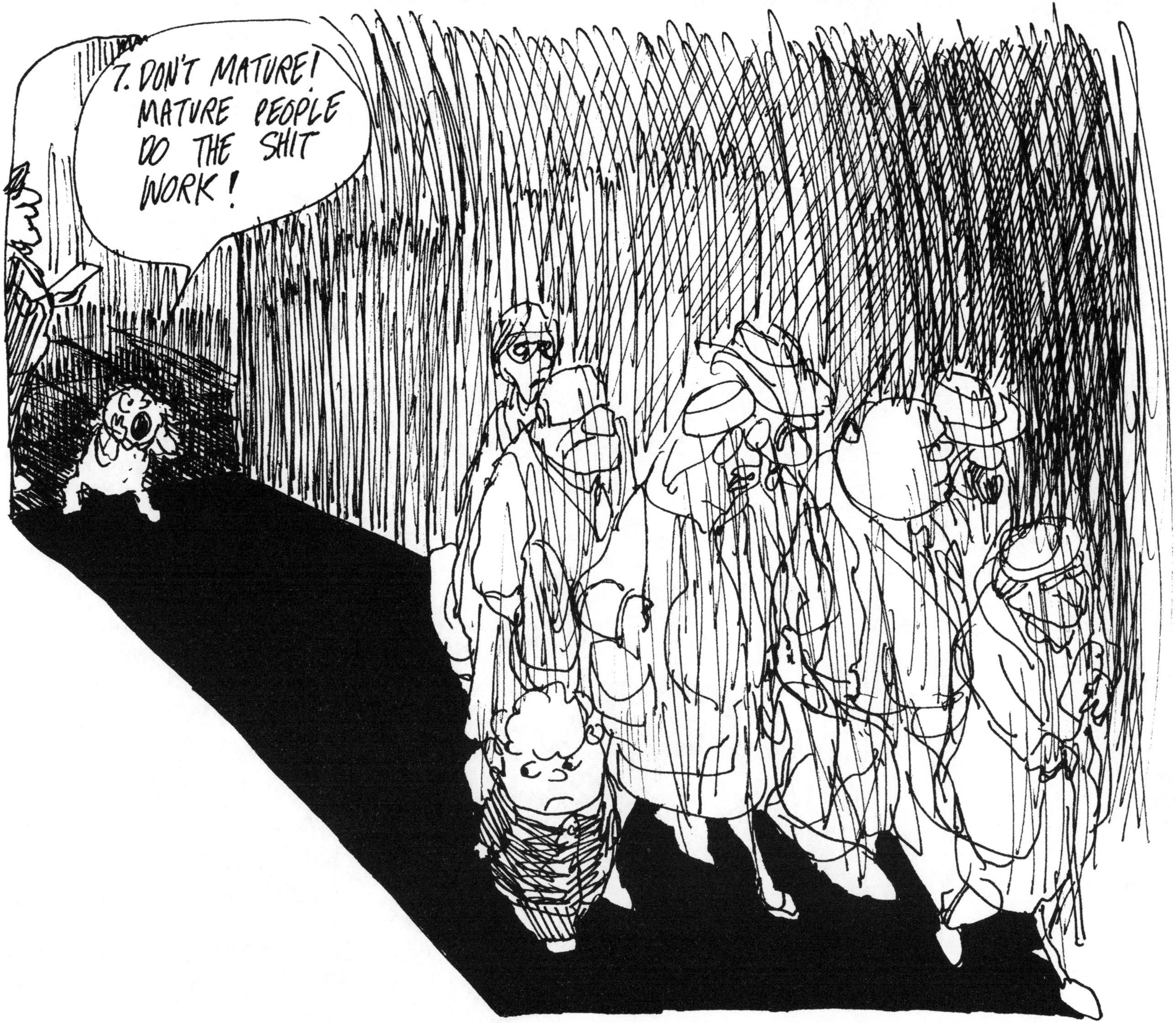
7. DON'T MATURE! MATURE PEOPLE DO THE SHIT WORK!

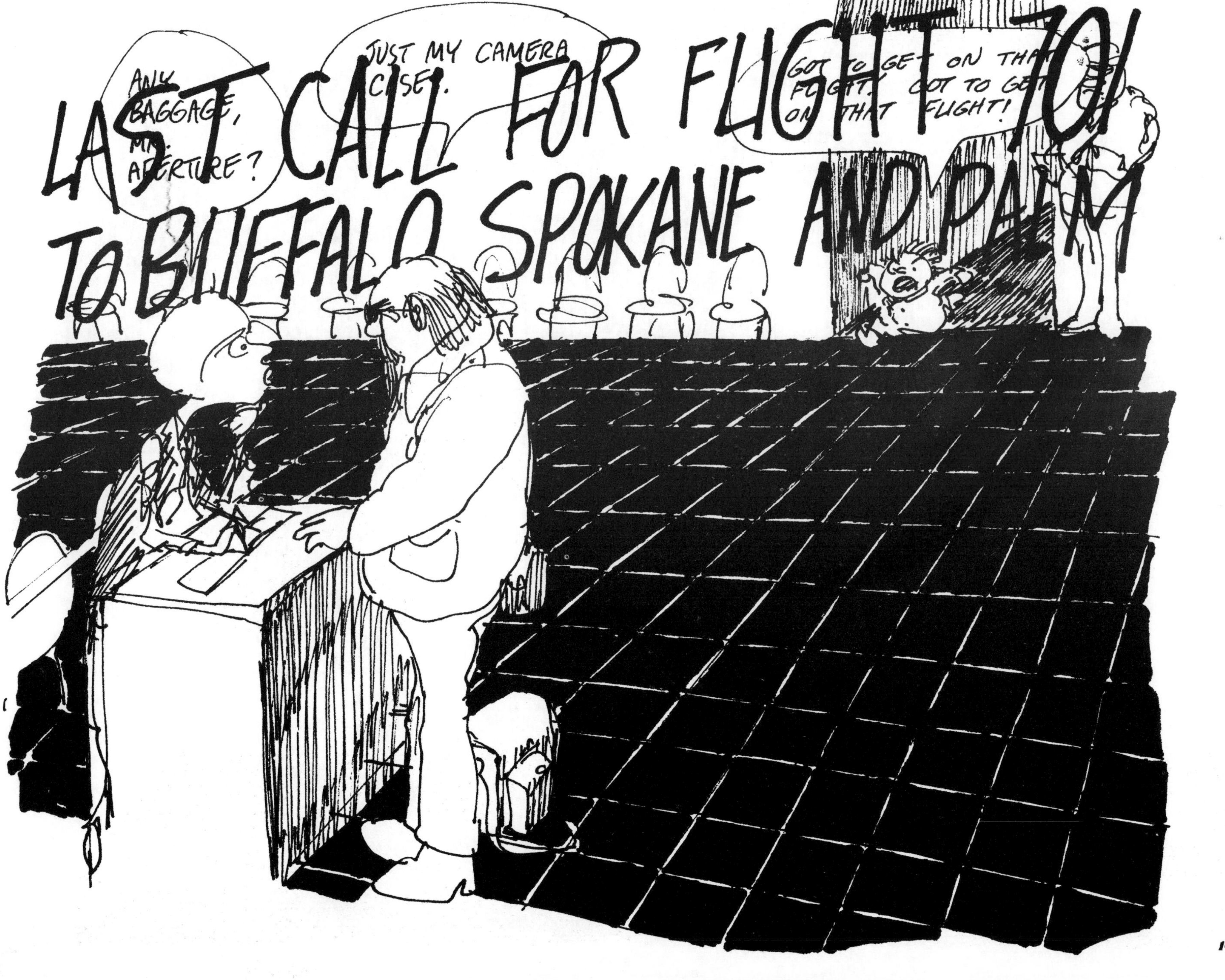
LAST CALL FOR FLIGHT 701 TO BUFFALO SPOKANE AND PALM
ANY BAGGAGE, MR. APERTURE?
JUST MY CAMERA CASE.
GOT TO GET ON THAT FLIGHT, GOT TO GET ON THAT FLIGHT!

GOING TO PALM SPRINGS ON BUSINESS?
PEOPLE IS DOING A SPREAD ON JERRY FORD. GREAT GUY. GOOD FRIEND. GET IN SOME GOLF.

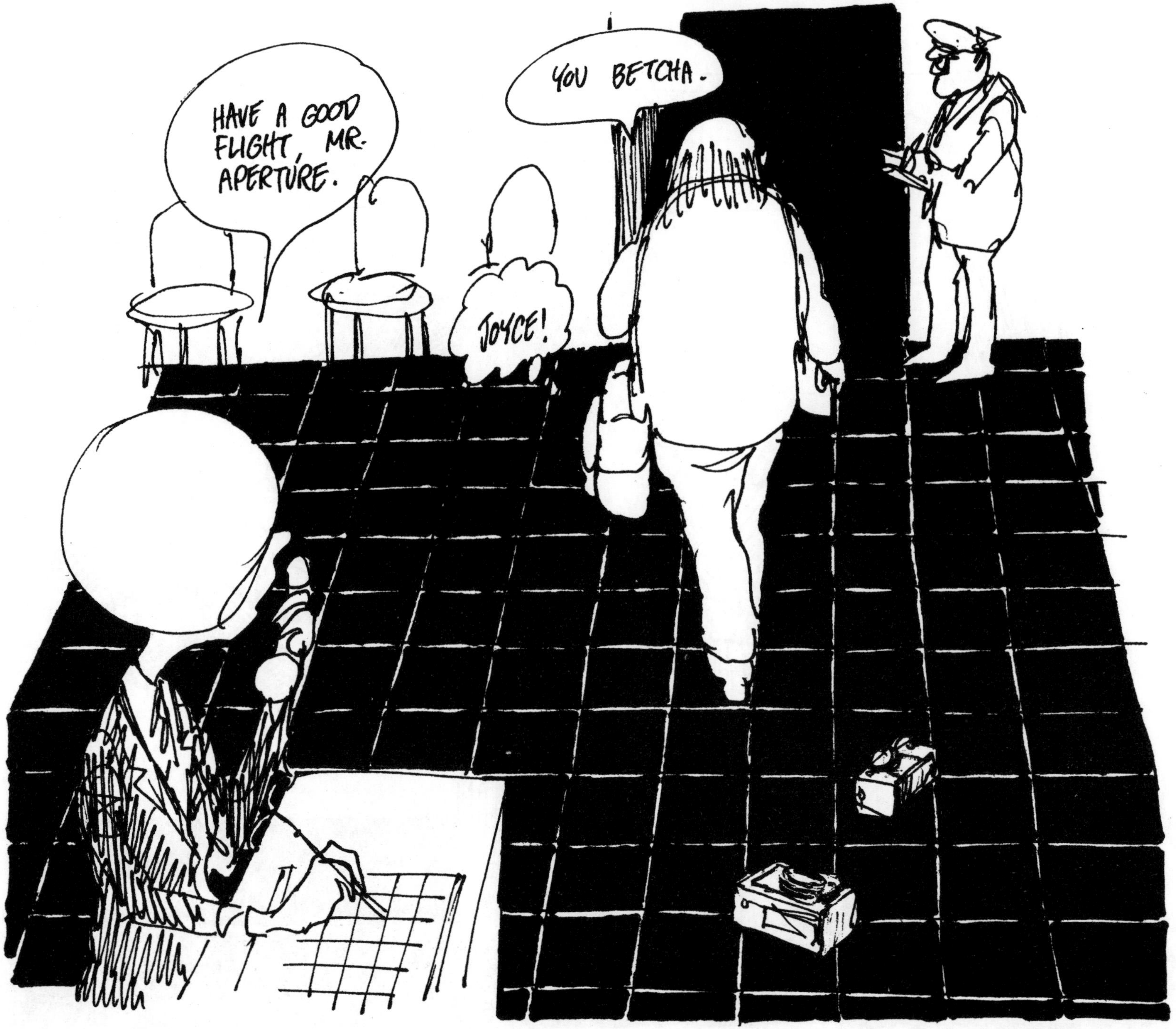
HAVE A GOOD FLIGHT, MR. APERTURE.
JOYCE!
YOU BETCHA.

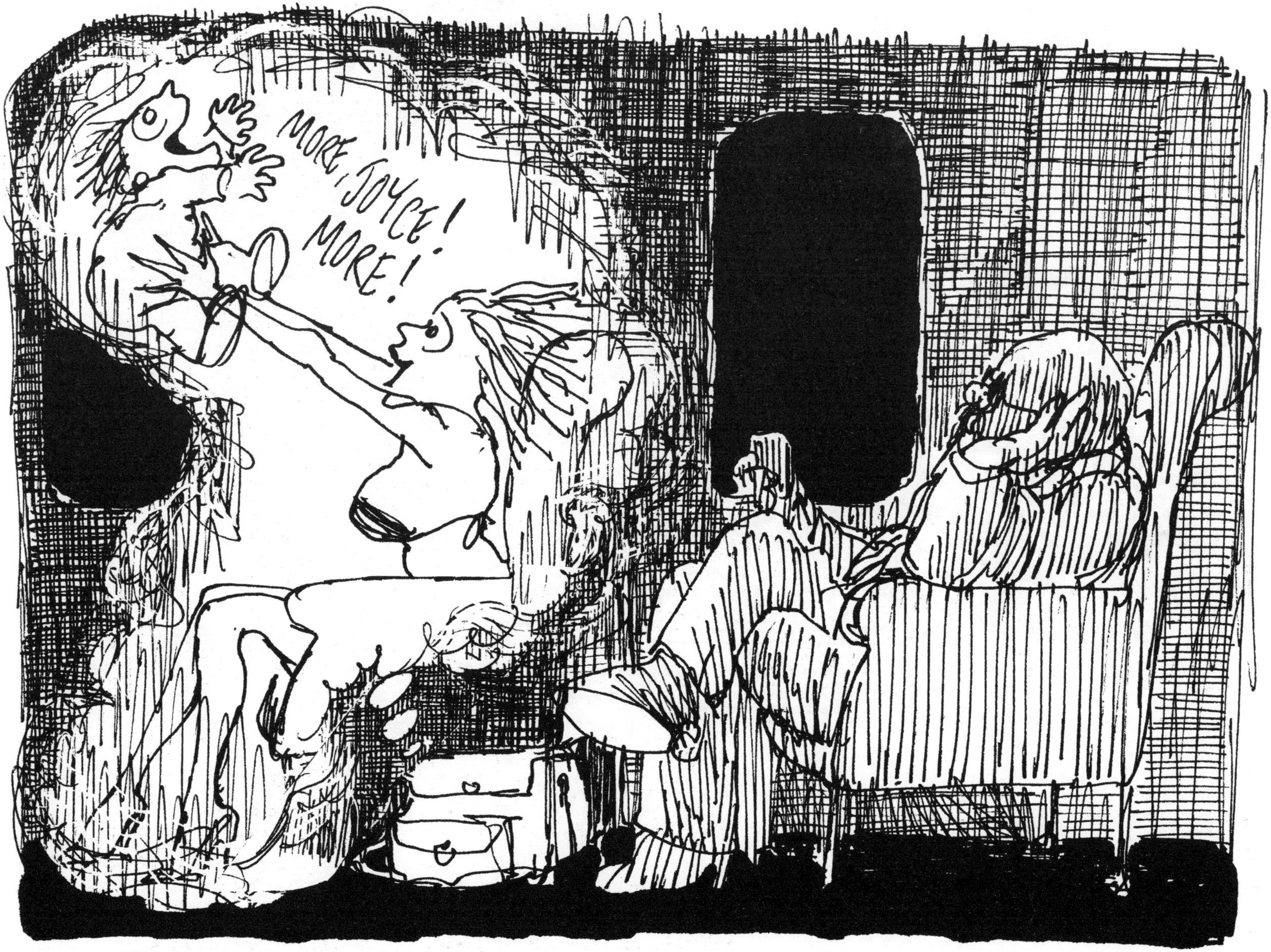
MORE, JOYCE! MORE!

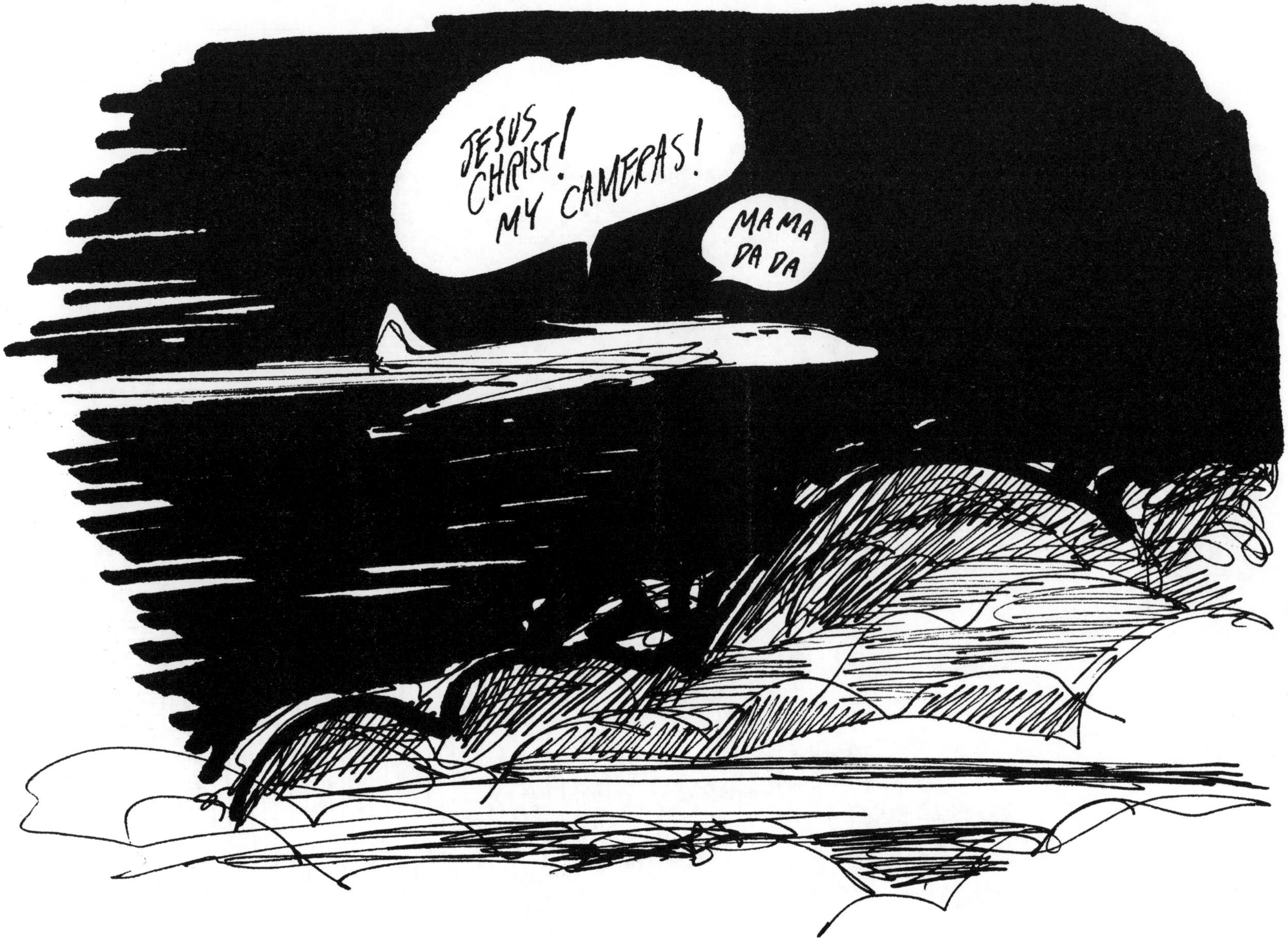
JESUS CHRIST! MY CAMERAS!
MAMA DA DA

DREAM'S END

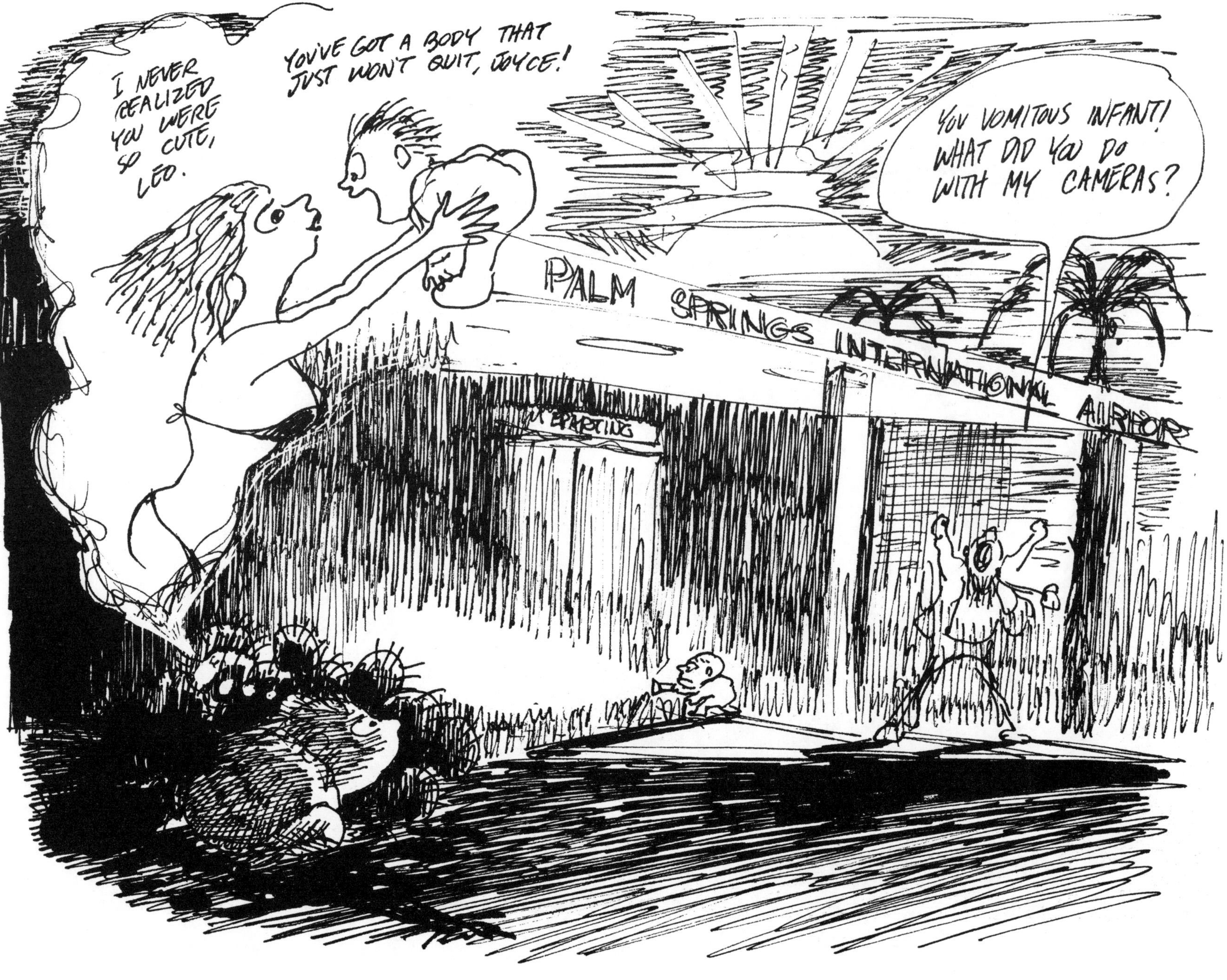
I NEVER REALIZED YOU WERE SO CUTE, LEO.
YOU'VE GOT A BODY THAT JUST WON'T QUIT, JOYCE!
YOU VOMITOUS INFANT! WHAT DID YOU DO WITH MY CAMERAS?
PALM SPRINGS INTERNATIONAL AIRPOR
DEPARTING

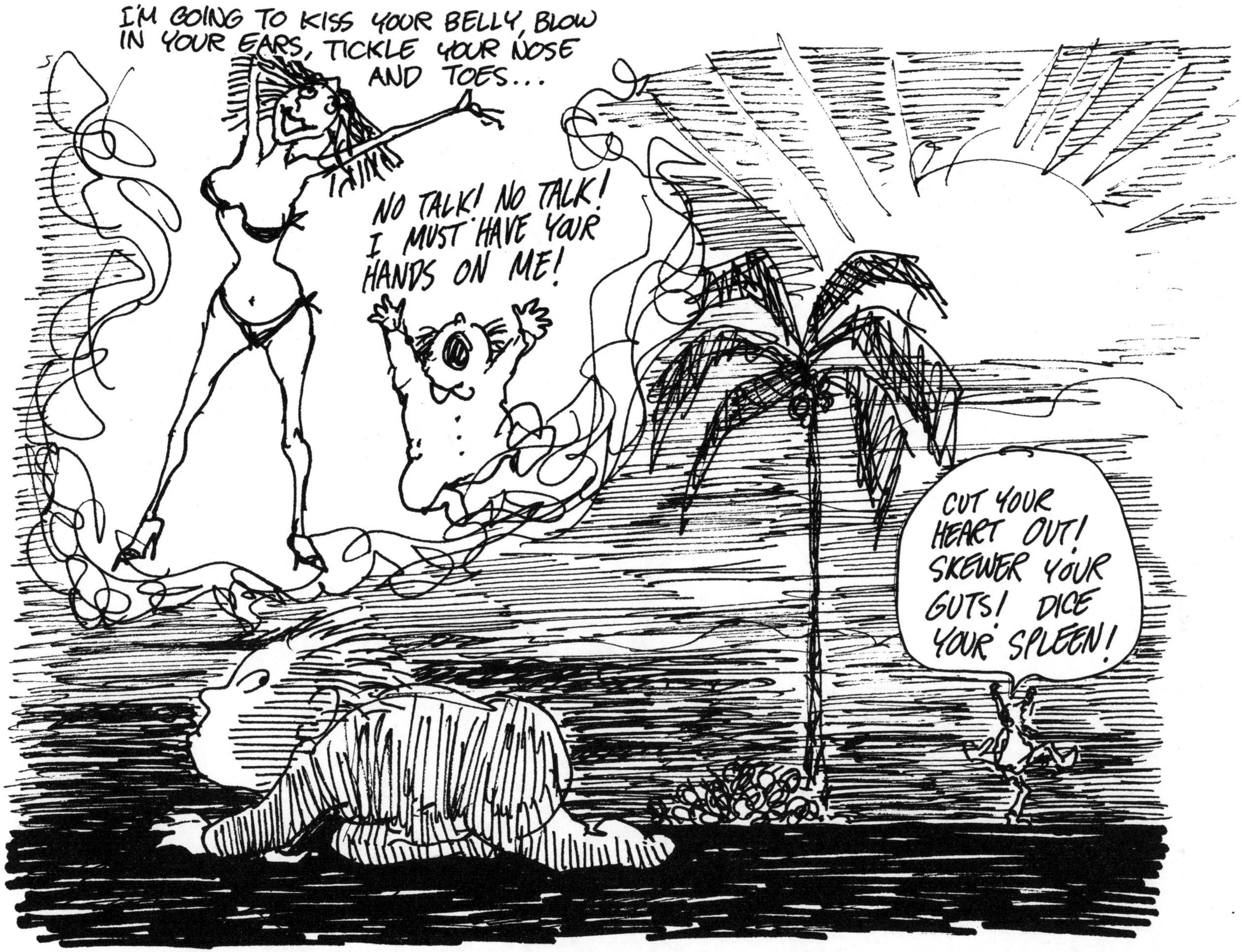
I'M GOING TO KISS YOUR BELLY, BLOW IN YOUR EARS, TICKLE YOUR NOSE AND TOES...
NO TALK! NO TALK! I MUST HAVE YOUR HANDS ON ME!
CUT YOUR HEART OUT! SKEWER YOUR GUTS! DICE YOUR SPLEEN!

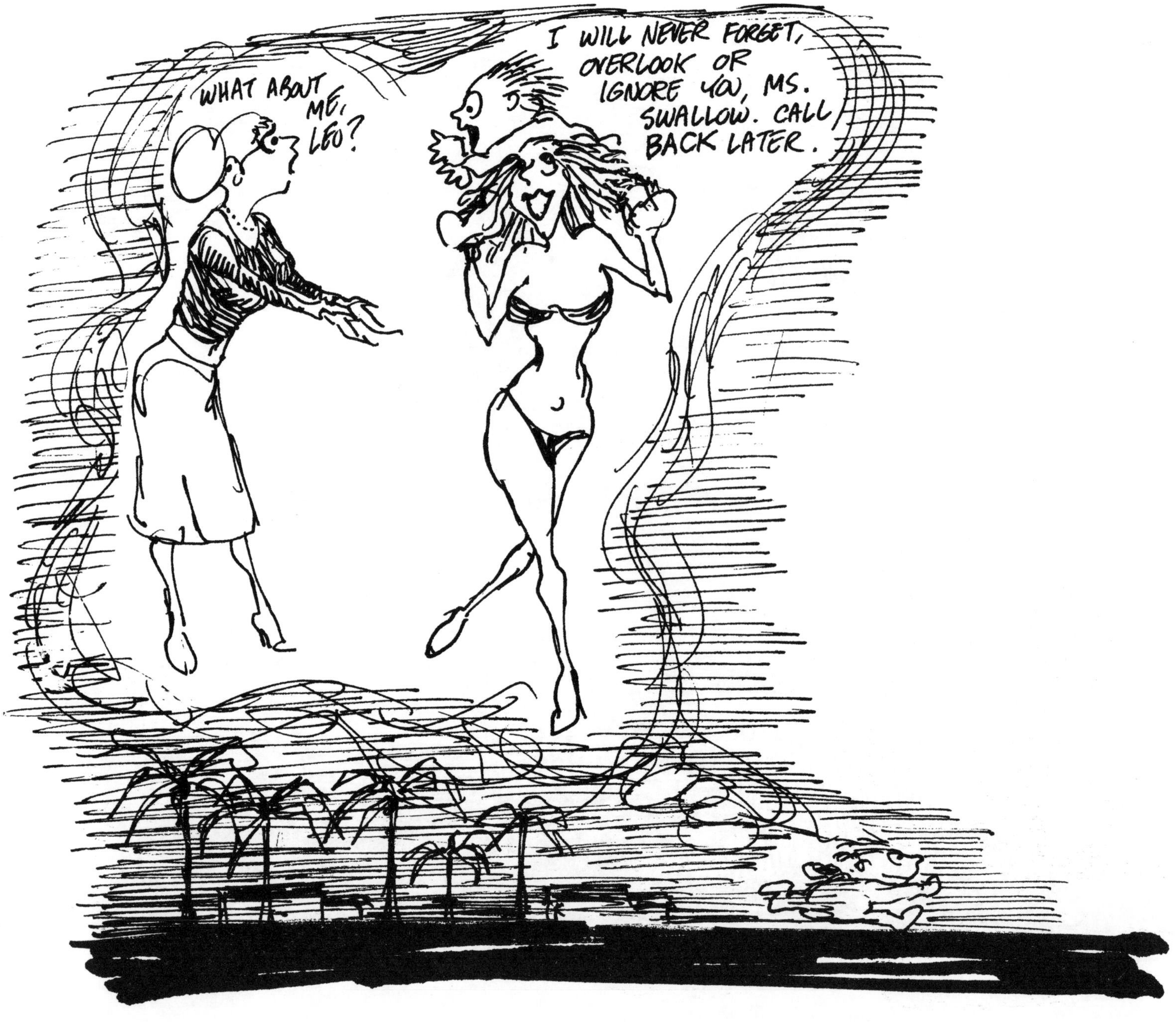
WHAT ABOUT ME, LEO?
I WILL NEVER FORGET, OVERLOOK OR IGNORE YOU, MS. SWALLOW. CALL BACK LATER.

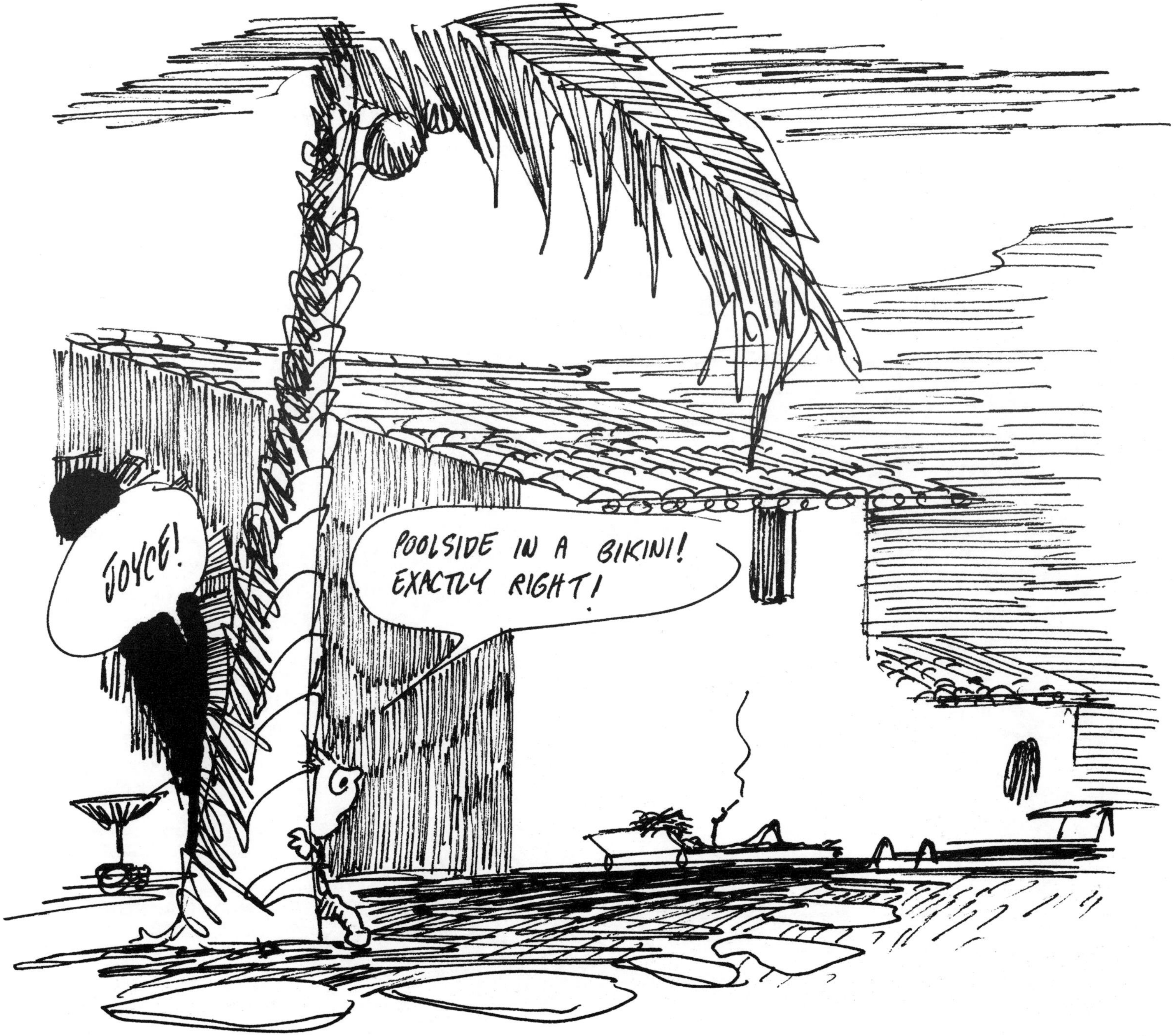
JOYCE!
POOLSIDE IN A BIKINI! EXACTLY RIGHT!

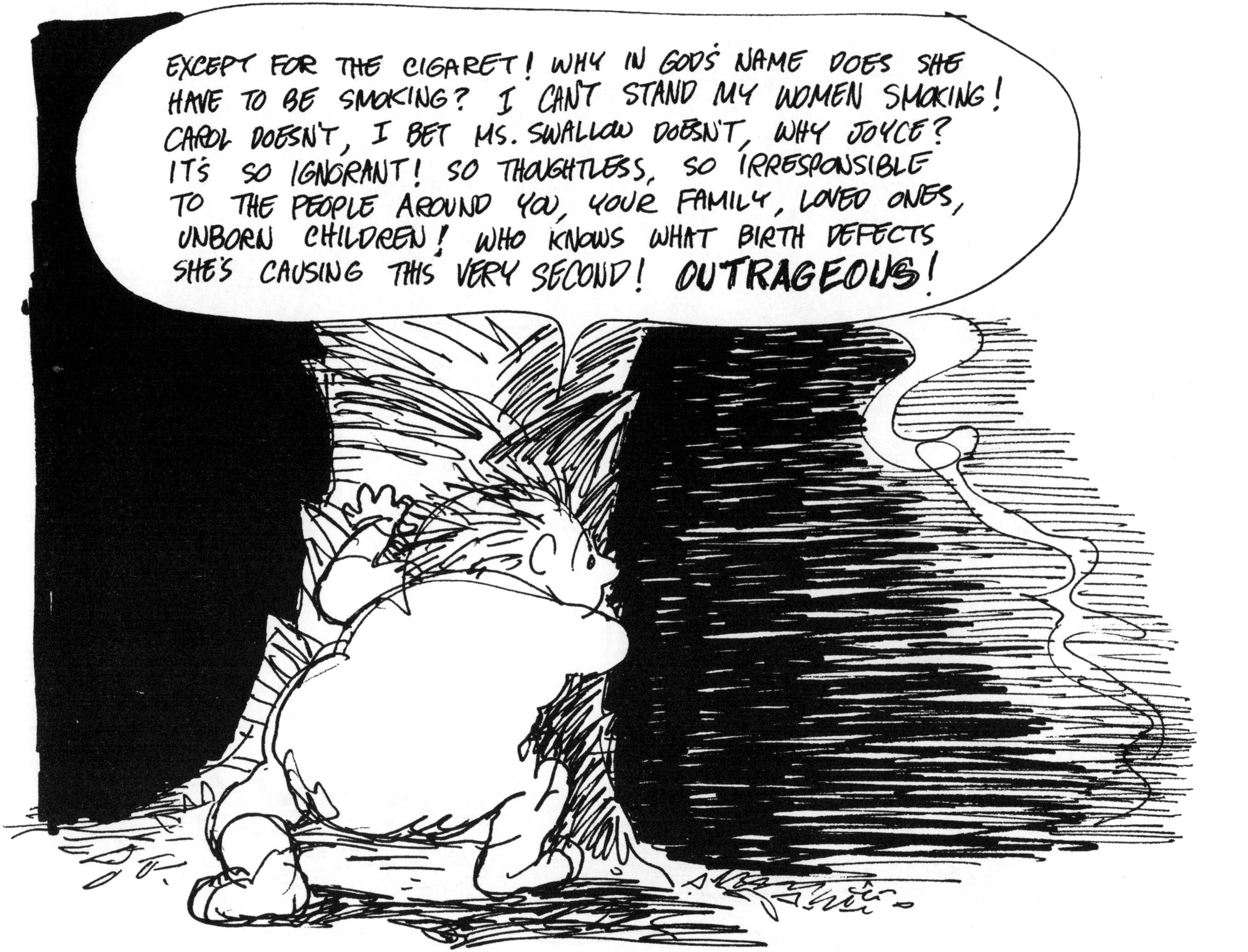
EXCEPT FOR THE CIGARET! WHY IN GOD'S NAME DOES SHE HAVE TO BE SMOKING? I CAN'T STAND MY WOMEN SMOKING! CAROL DOESN'T, I BET MS. SWALLOW DOESN'T, WHY JOYCE? IT'S SO IGNORANT! SO THOUGHTLESS, SO IRRESPONSIBLE TO THE PEOPLE AROUND YOU, YOUR FAMILY, LOVED ONES, UNBORN CHILDREN! WHO KNOWS WHAT BIRTH DEFECTS SHE'S CAUSING THIS VERY SECOND! OUTRAGEOUS!

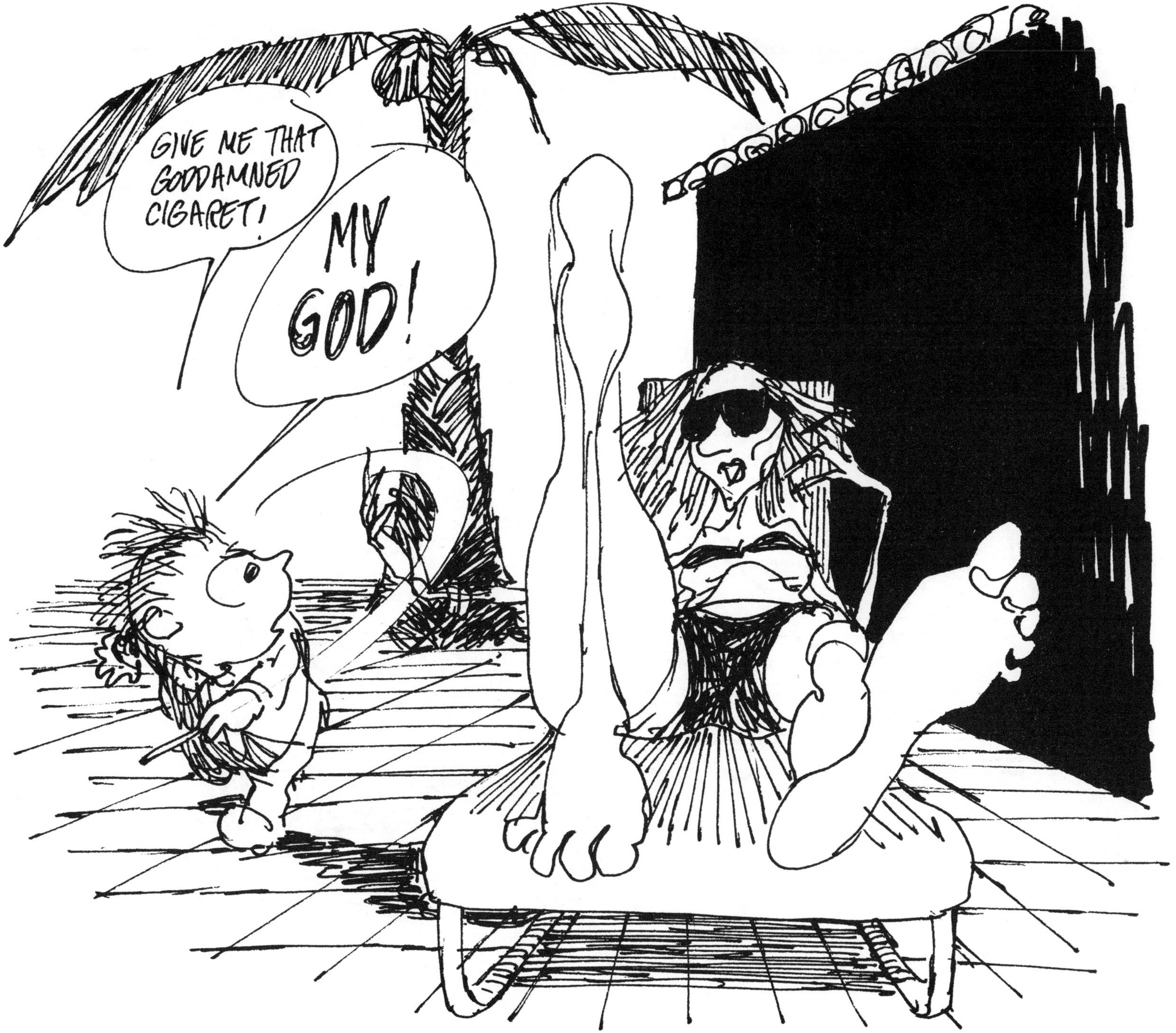
GIVE ME THAT GODDAMNED CIGARET!
MY GOD!

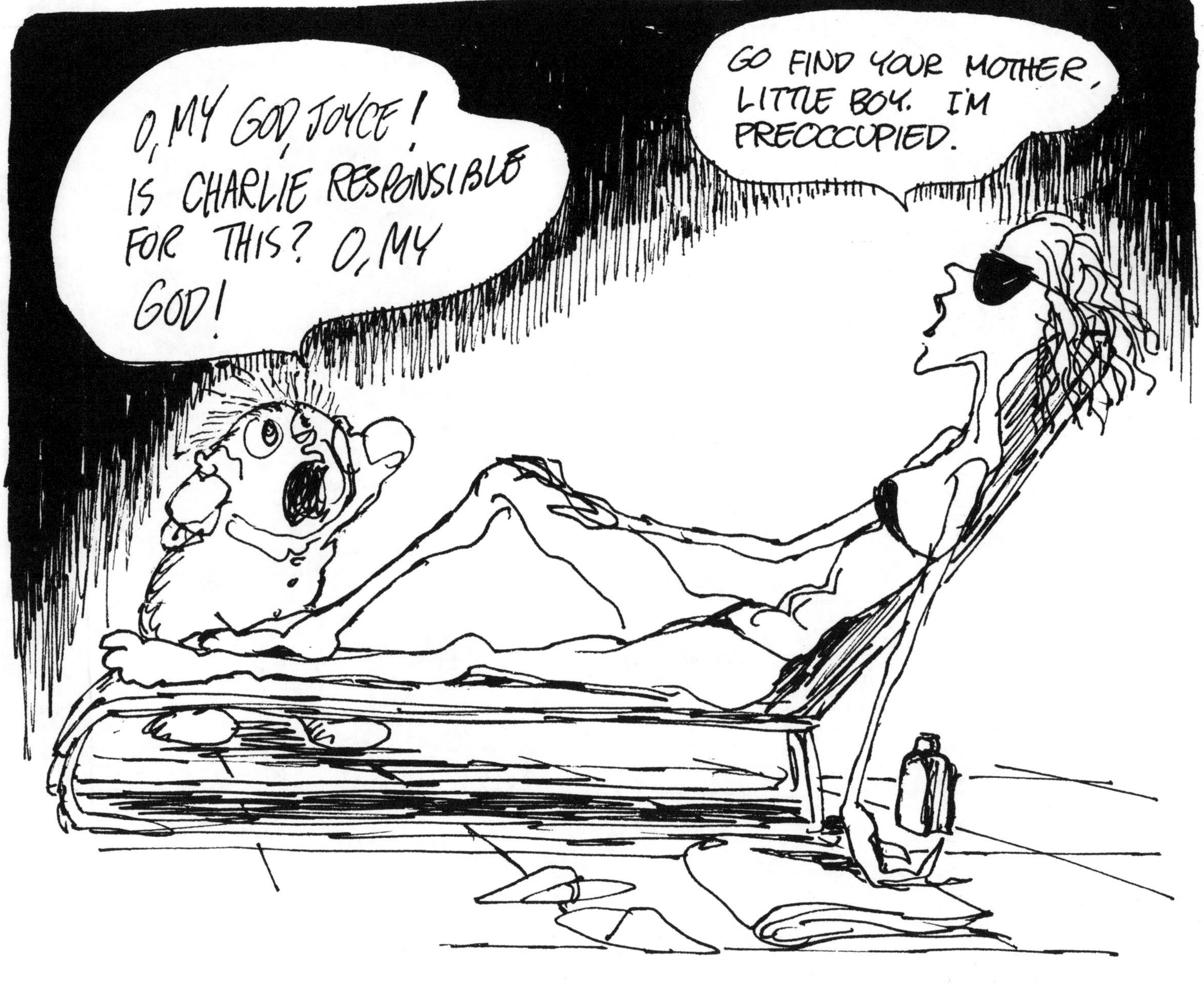
O, MY GOD, JOYCE! IS CHARLIE RESPONSIBLE FOR THIS? O, MY GOD!
GO FIND YOUR MOTHER, LITTLE BOY. I'M PREOCCUPIED.

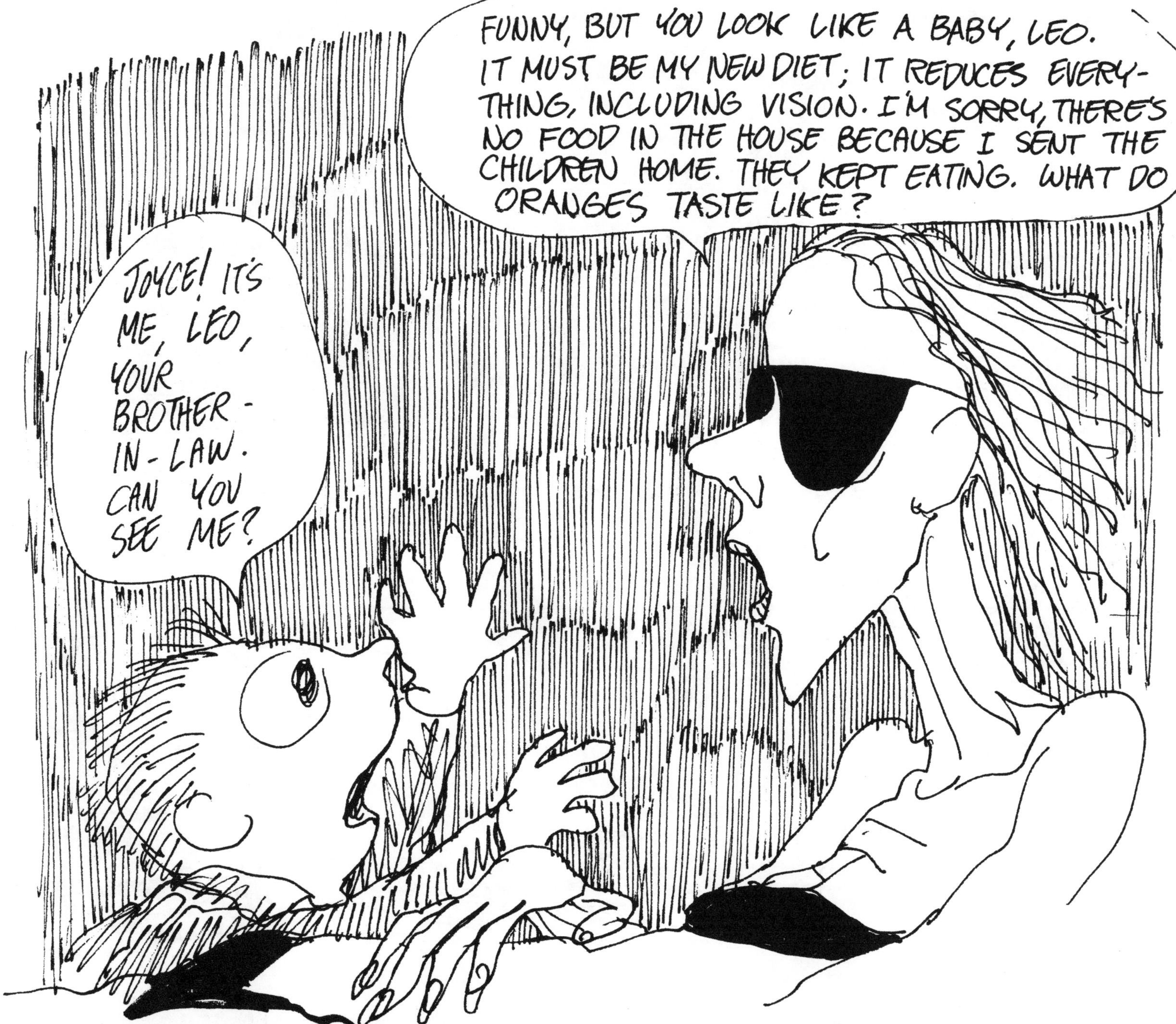
JOYCE! IT'S ME, LEO, YOUR BROTHER-IN-LAW. CAN YOU SEE ME?
FUNNY, BUT YOU LOOK LIKE A BABY, LEO. IT MUST BE MY NEW DIET; IT REDUCES EVERYTHING, INCLUDING VISION. I'M SORRY, THERE'S NO FOOD IN THE HOUSE BECAUSE I SENT THE CHILDREN HOME. THEY KEPT EATING. WHAT DO ORANGES TASTE LIKE?

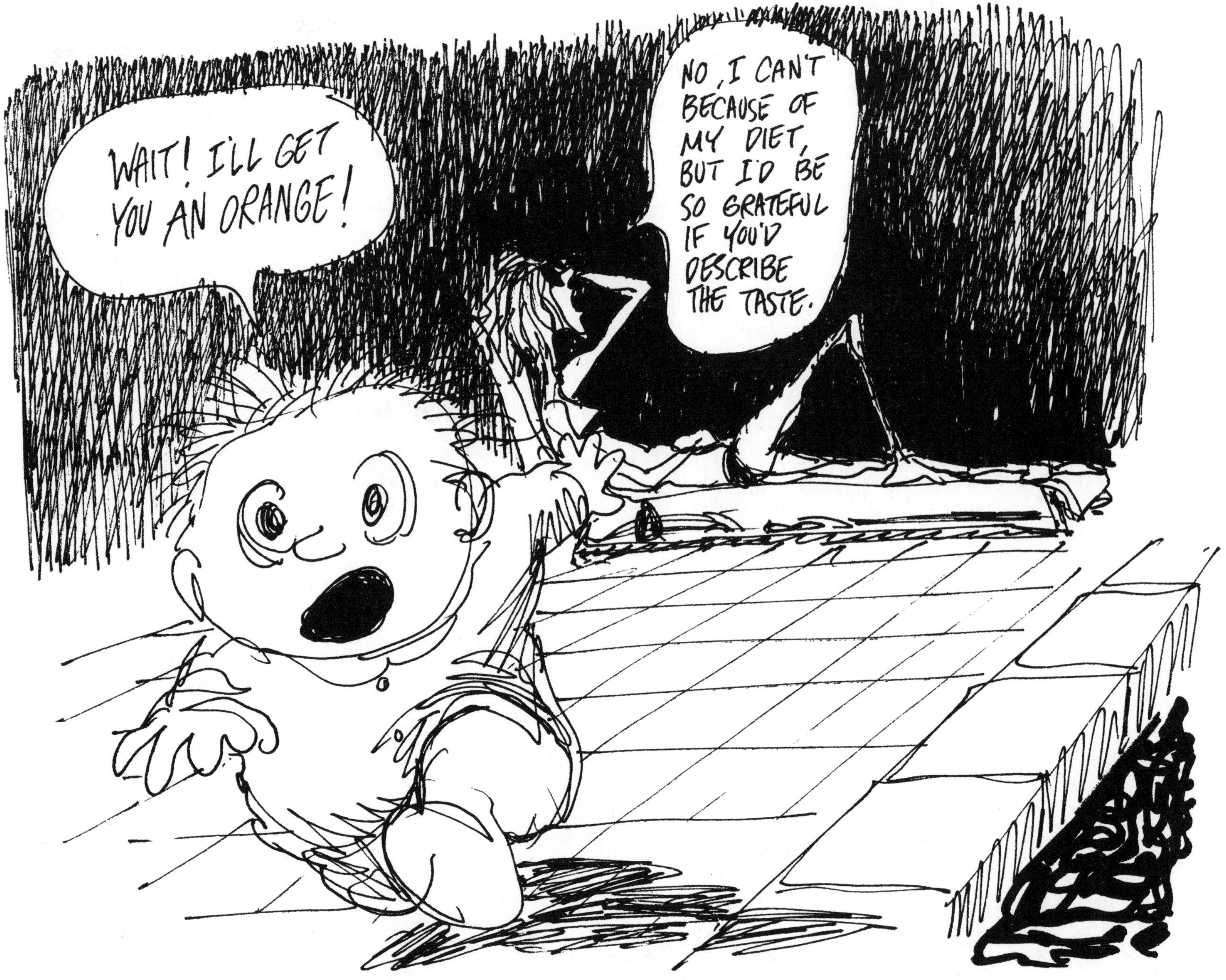
WAIT! I'LL GET YOU AN ORANGE!
NO, I CAN'T BECAUSE OF MY DIET, BUT I'D BE SO GRATEFUL IF YOU'D DESCRIBE THE TASTE.

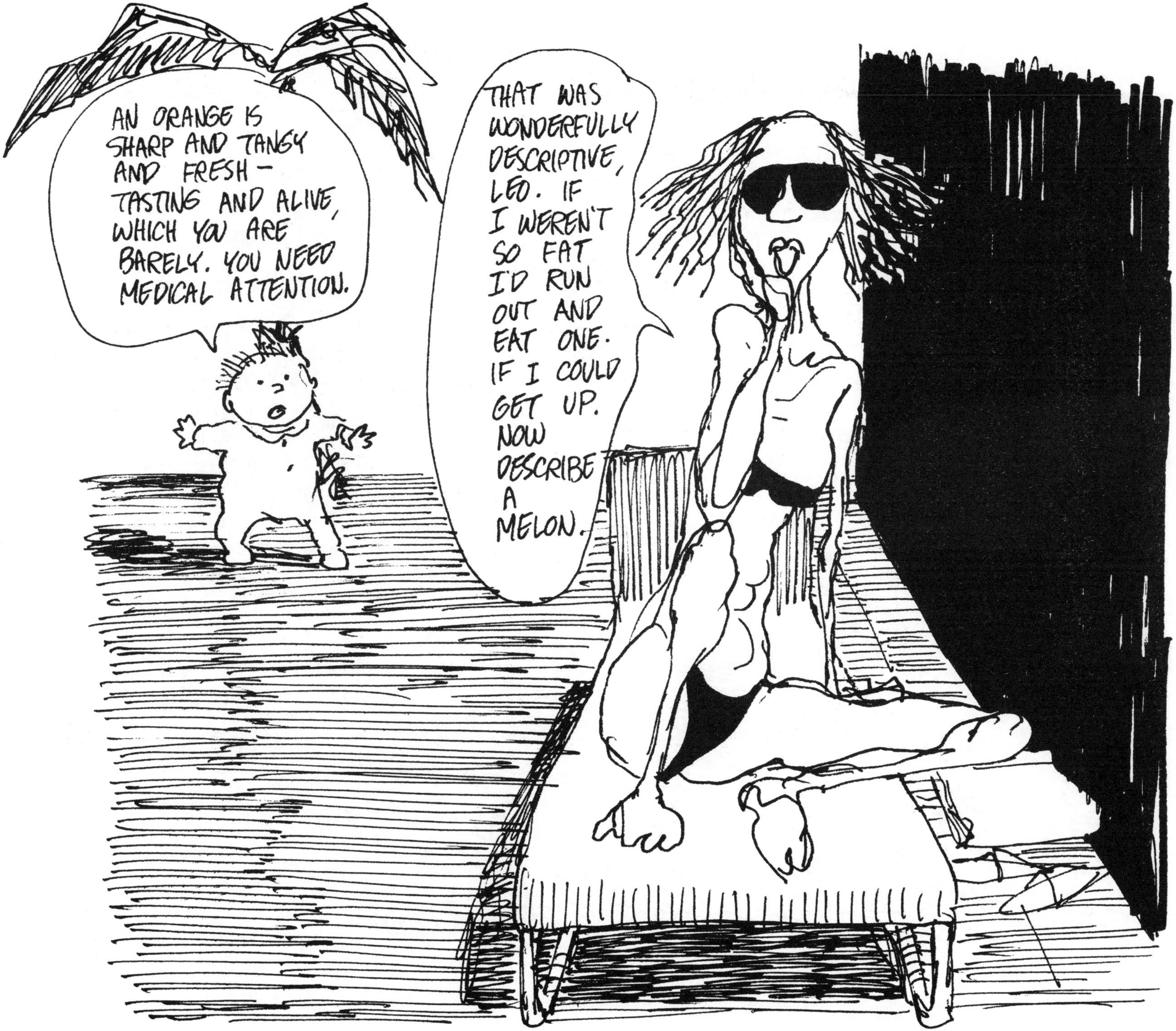
AN ORANGE IS SHARP AND TANGY AND FRESH-TASTING AND ALIVE, WHICH YOU ARE BARELY. YOU NEED MEDICAL ATTENTION.
THAT WAS WONDERFULLY DESCRIPTIVE, LEO. IF I WEREN'T SO FAT I'D RUN OUT AND EAT ONE. IF I COULD GET UP. NOW DESCRIBE A MELON.

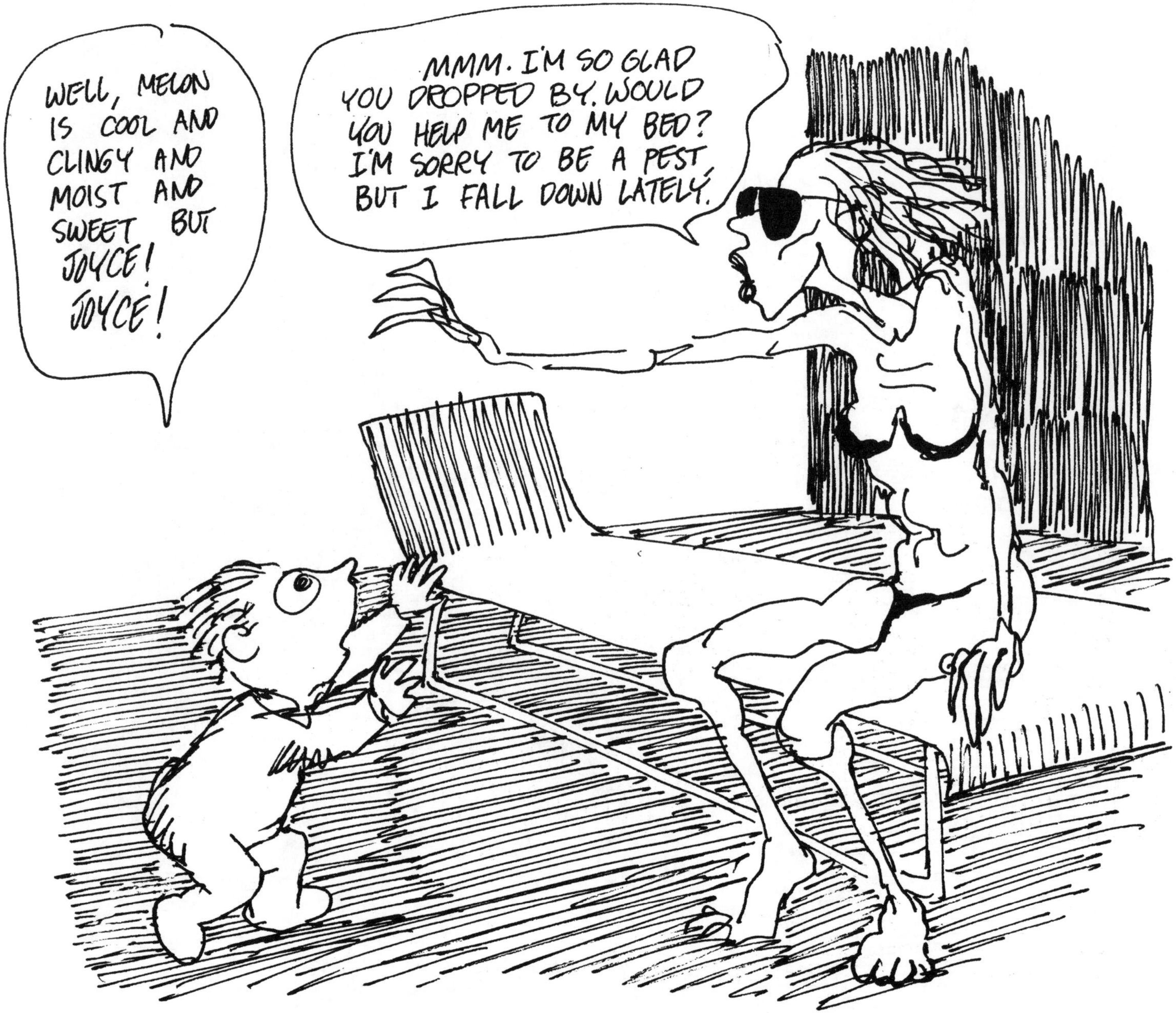
WELL, MELON IS COOL AND CLINGY AND MOIST AND SWEET BUT JOYCE! JOYCE!
MMM. I'M SO GLAD YOU DROPPED BY. WOULD YOU HELP ME TO MY BED? I'M SORRY TO BE A PEST BUT I FALL DOWN LATELY.

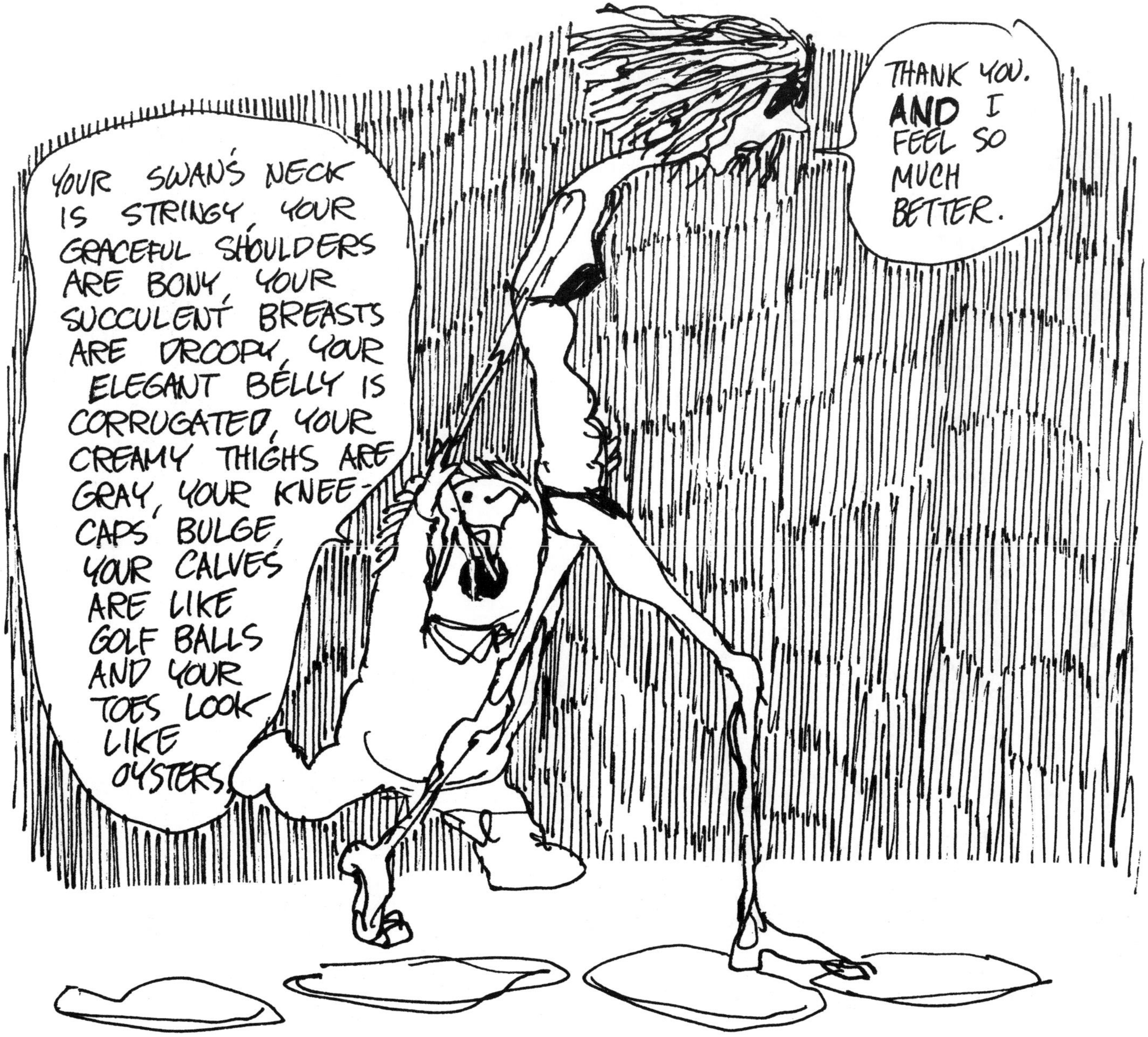
YOUR SWAN'S NECK IS STRINGY, YOUR GRACEFUL SHOULDERS ARE BONY, YOUR SUCCULENT BREASTS ARE DROOPY, YOUR ELEGANT BELLY IS CORRUGATED, YOUR CREAMY THIGHS ARE GRAY, YOUR KNEE-CAPS BULGE, YOUR CALVES ARE LIKE GOLF BALLS AND YOUR TOES LOOK LIKE OYSTERS.
THANK YOU. AND I FEEL SO MUCH BETTER.

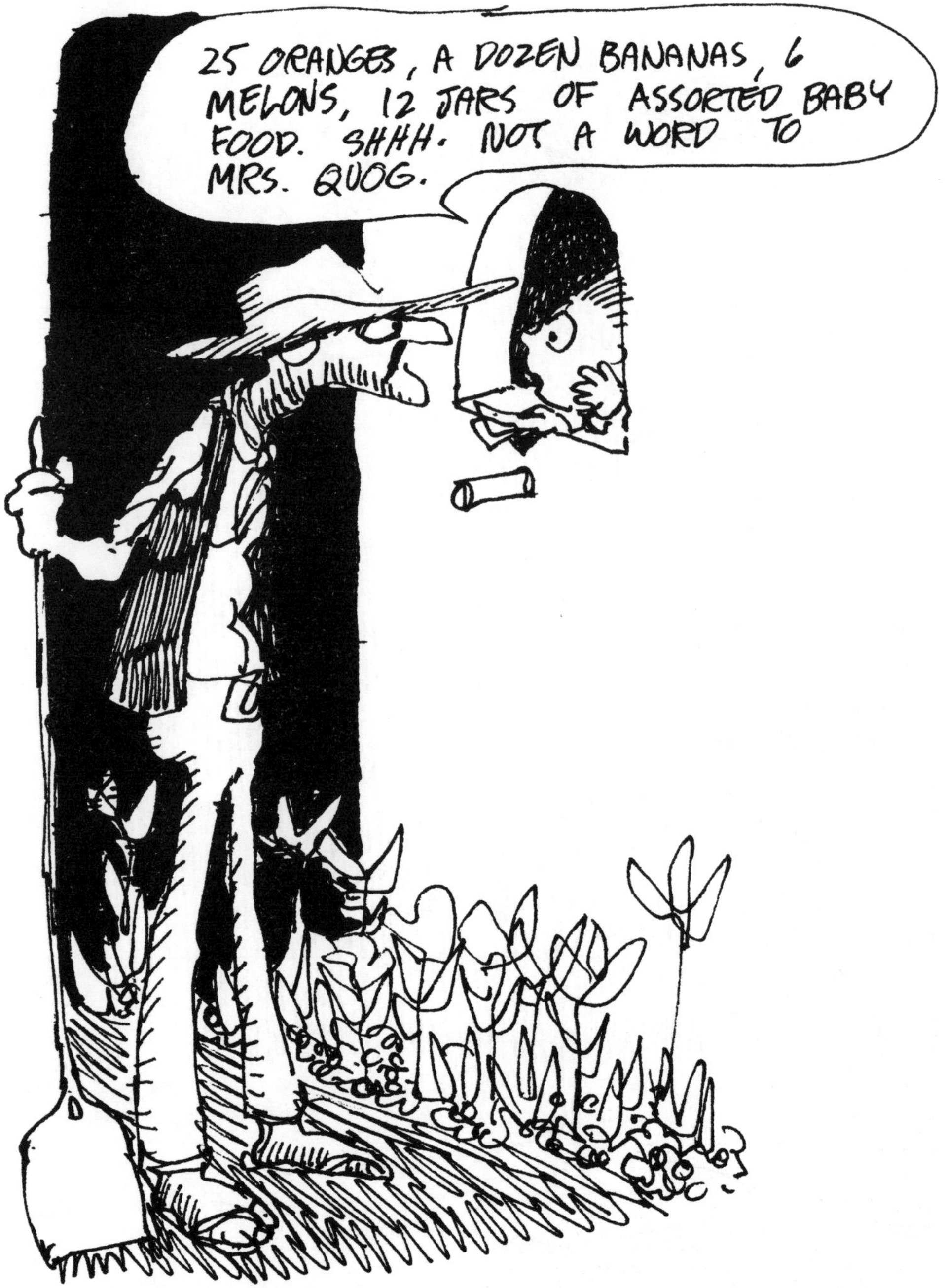
25 ORANGES, A DOZEN BANANAS, 6 MELONS, 12 JARS OF ASSORTED BABY FOOD. SHHH. NOT A WORD TO MRS. QUOG.

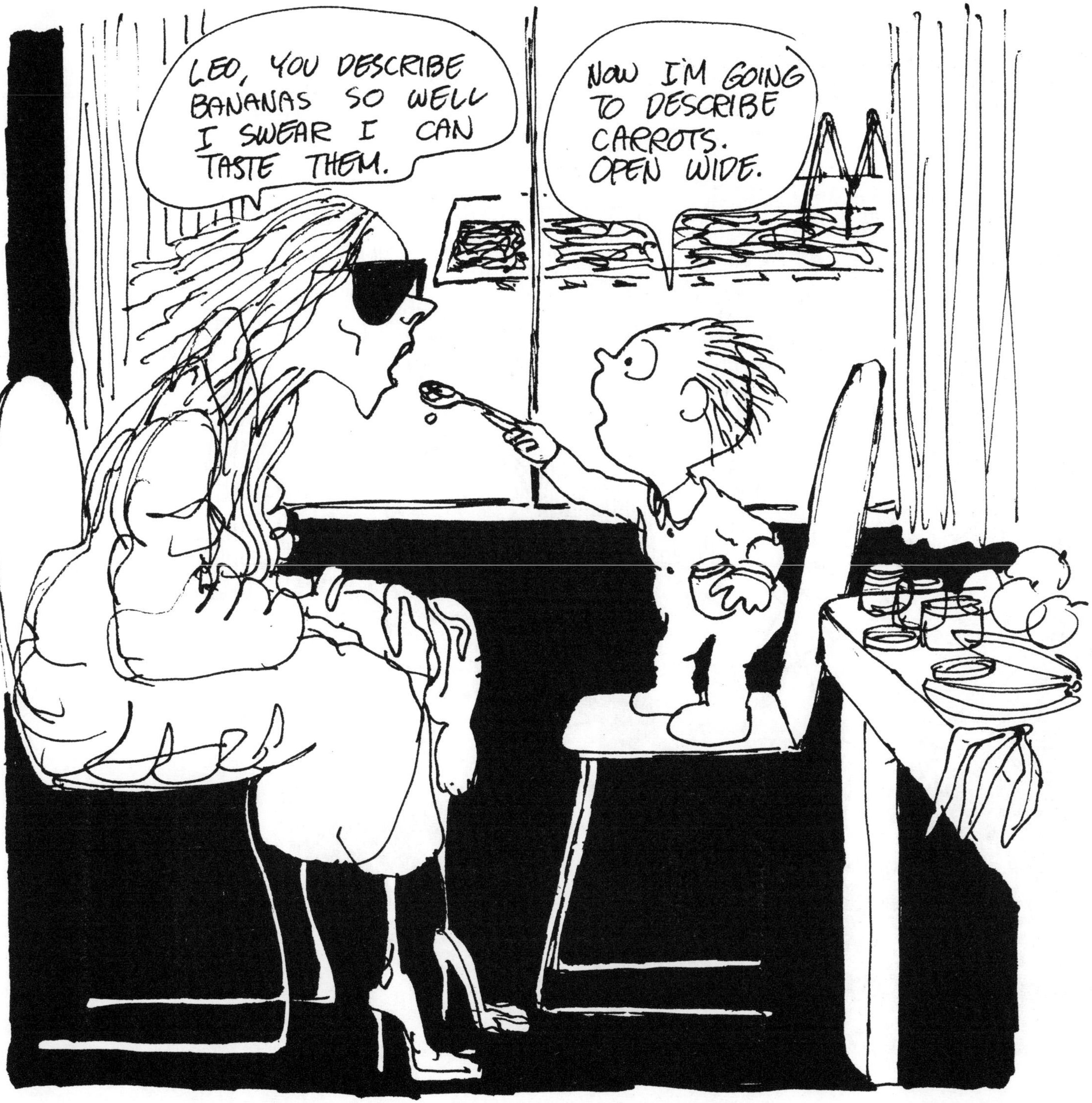
LEO, YOU DESCRIBE BANANAS SO WELL I SWEAR I CAN TASTE THEM.
NOW I'M GOING TO DESCRIBE CARROTS. OPEN WIDE.

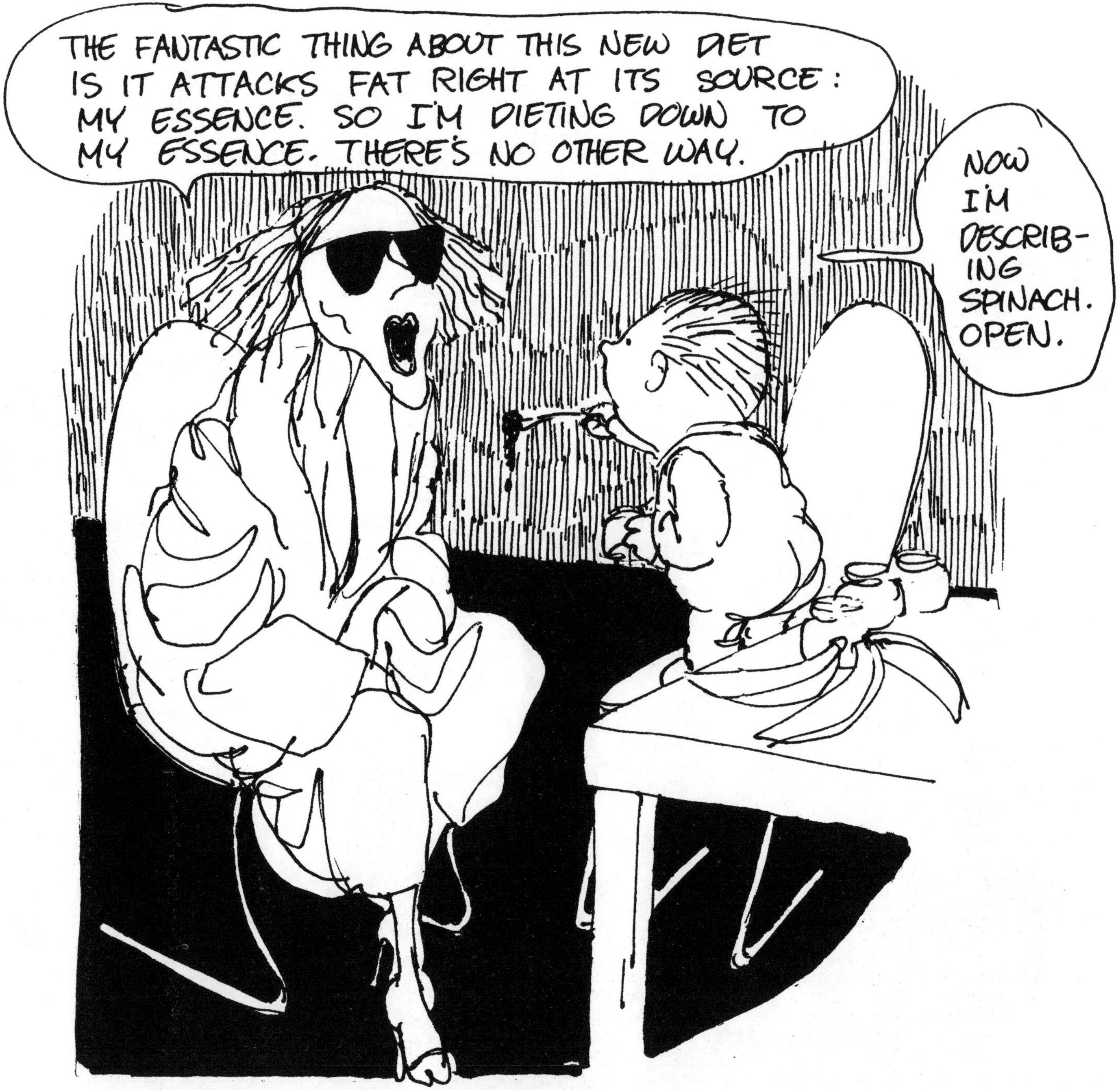
THE FANTASTIC THING ABOUT THIS NEW DIET IS IT ATTACKS FAT RIGHT AT ITS SOURCE: MY ESSENCE. SO I'M DIETING DOWN TO MY ESSENCE. THERE'S NO OTHER WAY.
NOW I'M DESCRIBING SPINACH. OPEN.

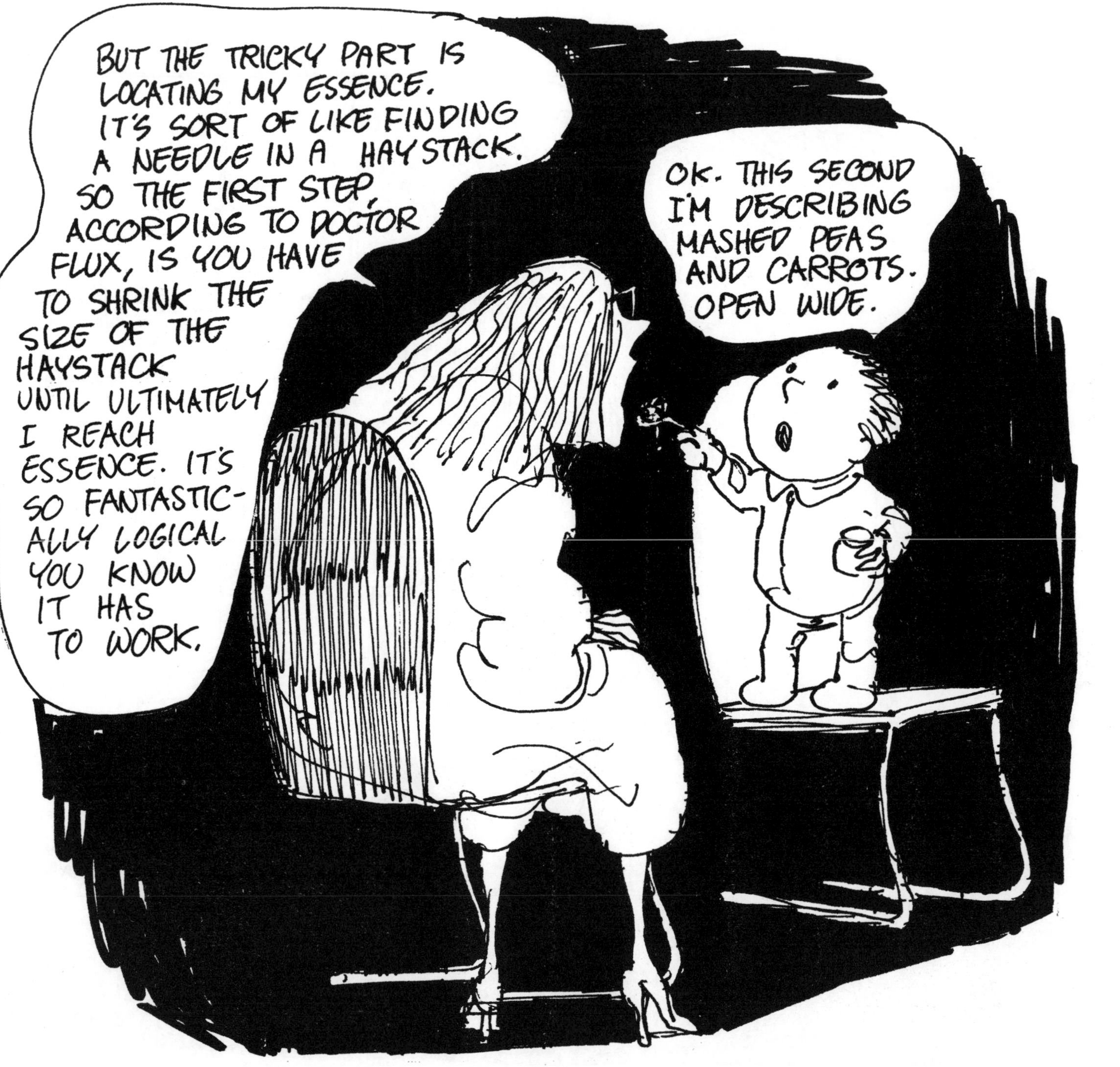
BUT THE TRICKY PART IS LOCATING MY ESSENCE. IT'S SORT OF LIKE FINDING A NEEDLE IN A HAYSTACK. SO THE FIRST STEP, ACCORDING TO DOCTOR FLUX, IS YOU HAVE TO SHRINK THE SIZE OF THE HAYSTACK UNTIL ULTIMATELY I REACH ESSENCE. IT'S SO FANTASTICALLY LOGICAL YOU KNOW IT HAS TO WORK.
OK. THIS SECOND I'M DESCRIBING MASHED PEAS AND CARROTS. OPEN WIDE.

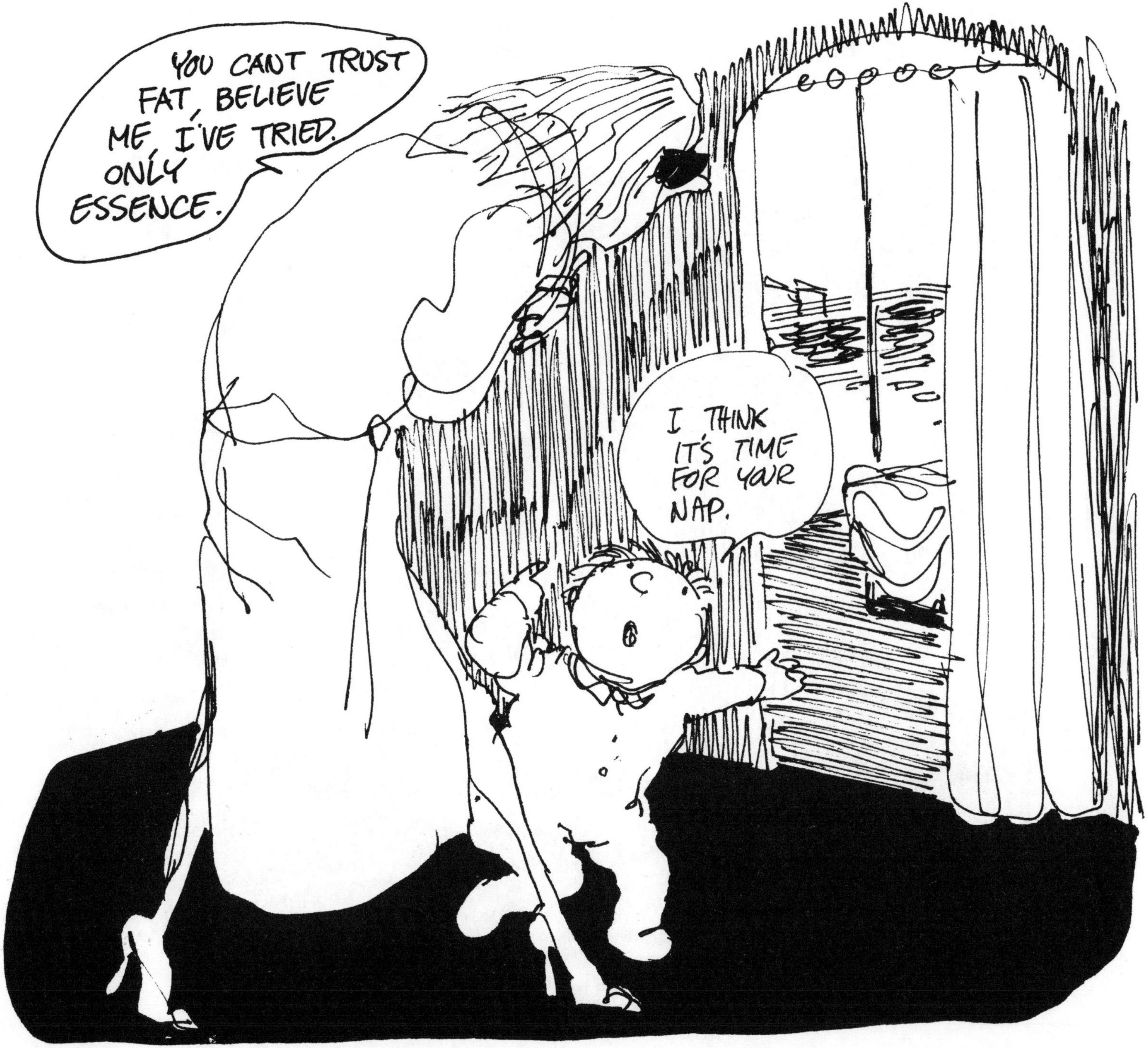
YOU CAN'T TRUST FAT, BELIEVE ME, I'VE TRIED. ONLY ESSENCE.
I THINK IT'S TIME FOR YOUR NAP.

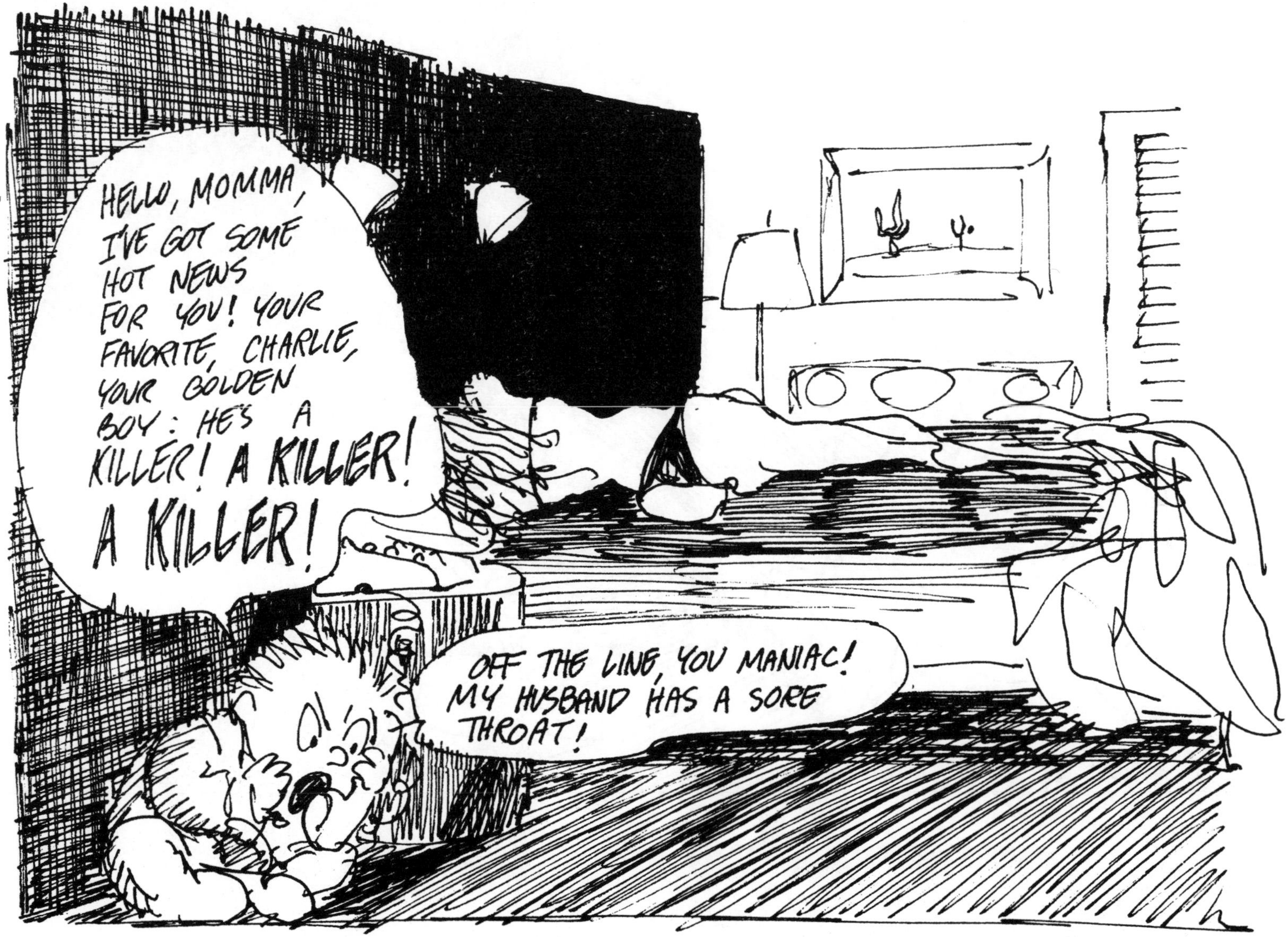
HELLO, MOMMA, I'VE GOT SOME HOT NEWS FOR YOU! YOUR FAVORITE, CHARLIE, YOUR GOLDEN BOY: HE'S A KILLER! A KILLER! A KILLER!
OFF THE LINE, YOU MANIAC! MY HUSBAND HAS A SORE THROAT!

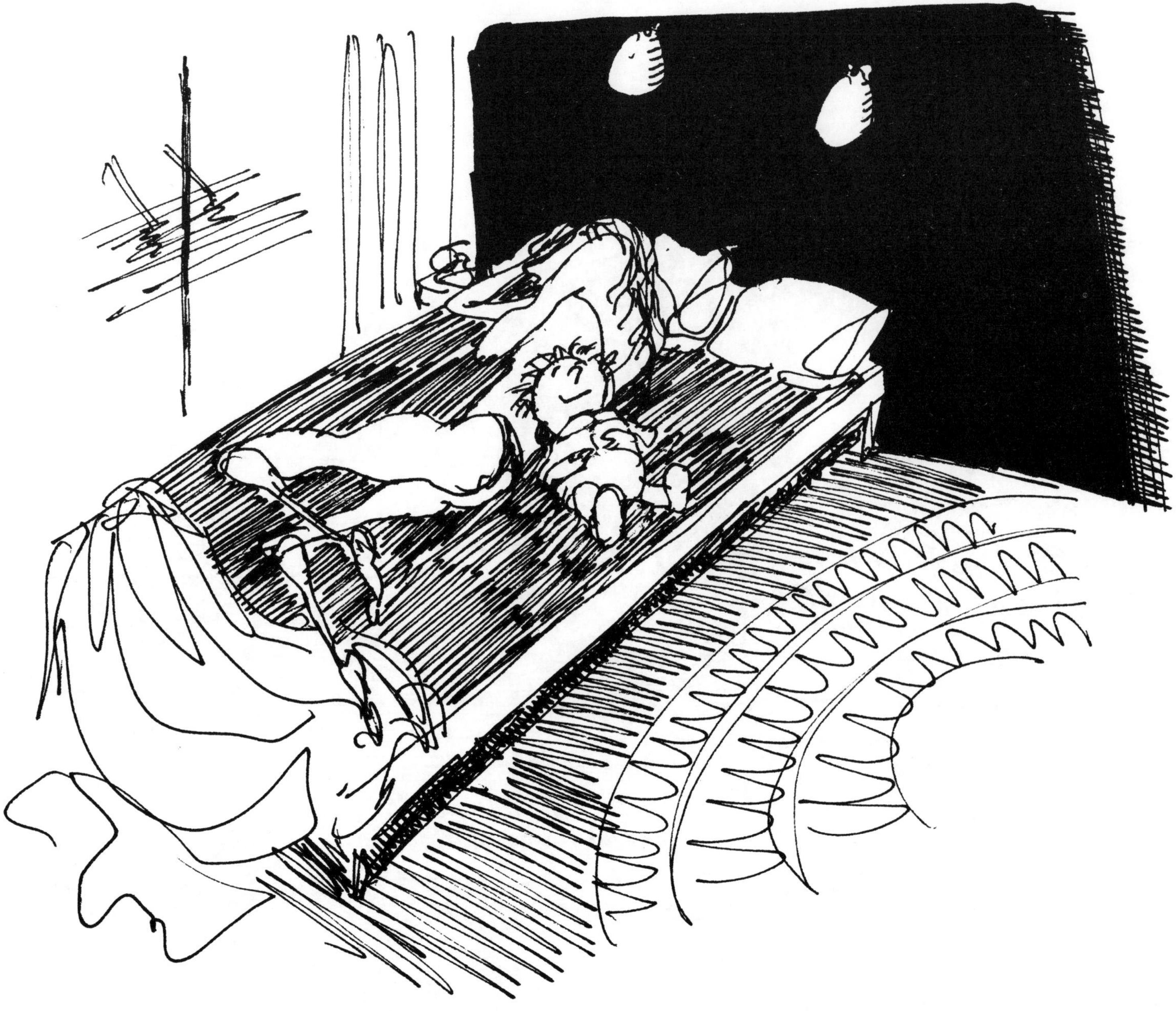

EPIPHANY

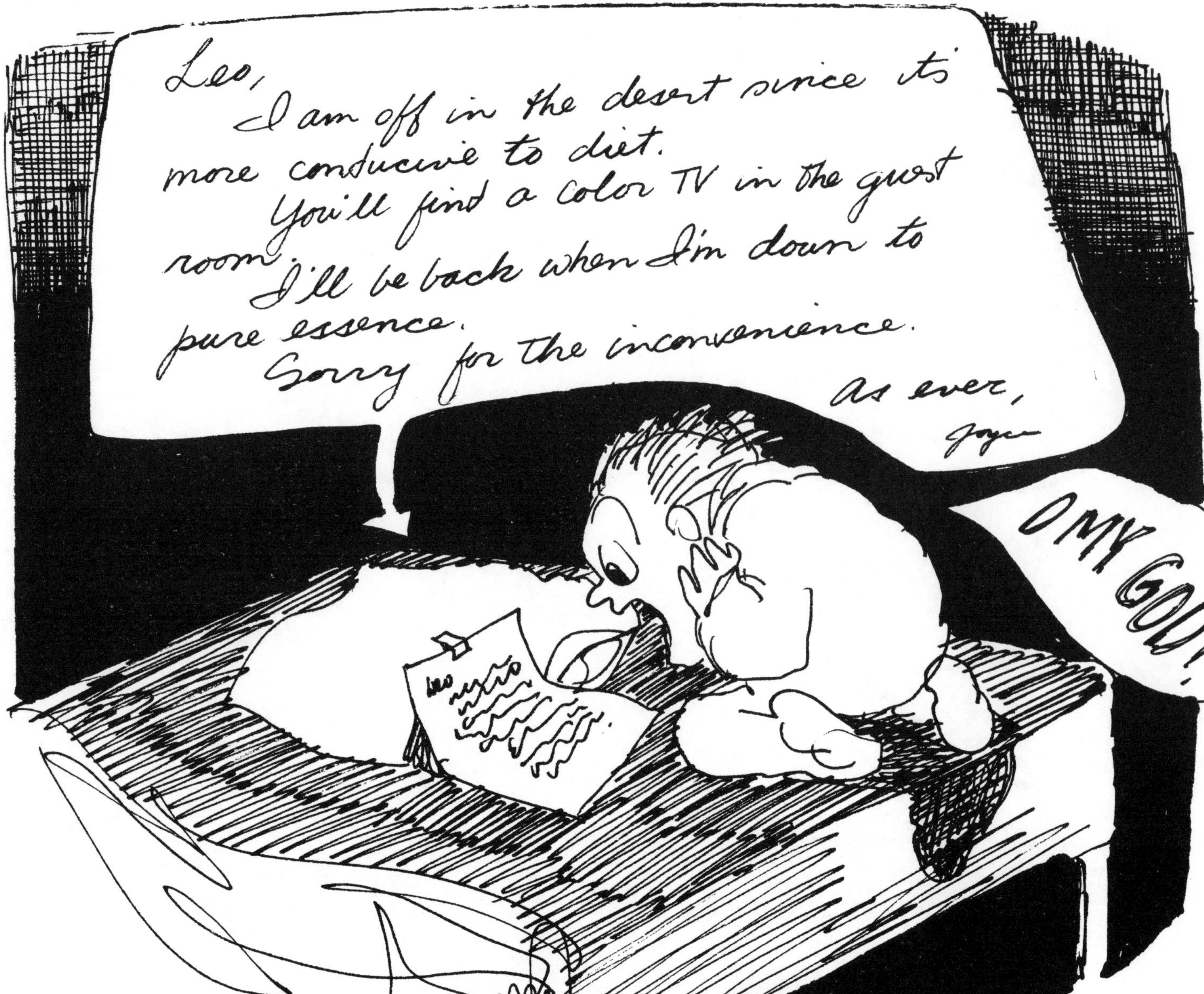
Leo,
I am off in the desert since its more conducive to diet.
You'll find a color TV in the guest room.
I'll be back when I'm down to pure essence.
Sorry for the inconvenience.
As ever,
Joyce
O MY GOD!

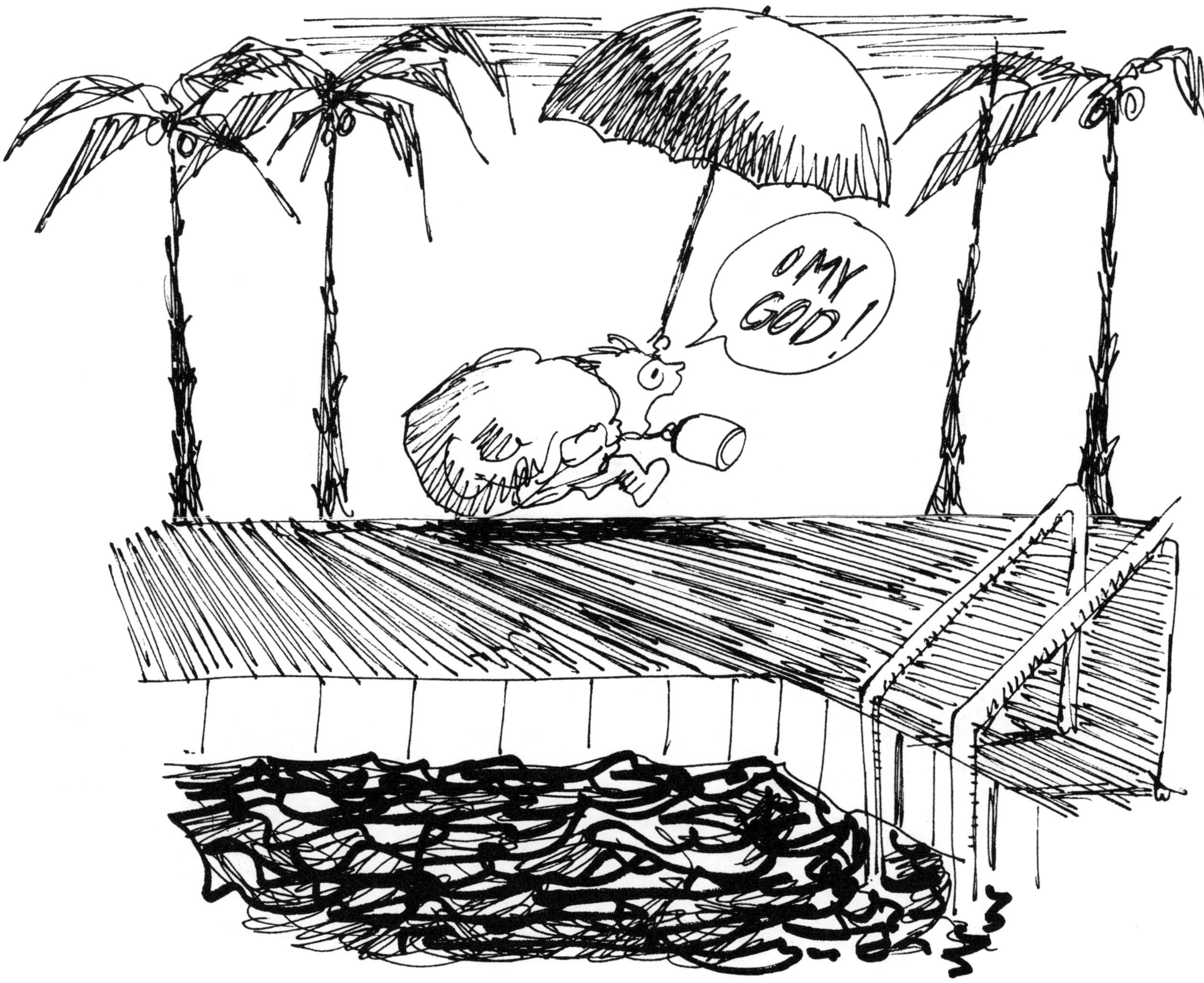
O MY GOD!

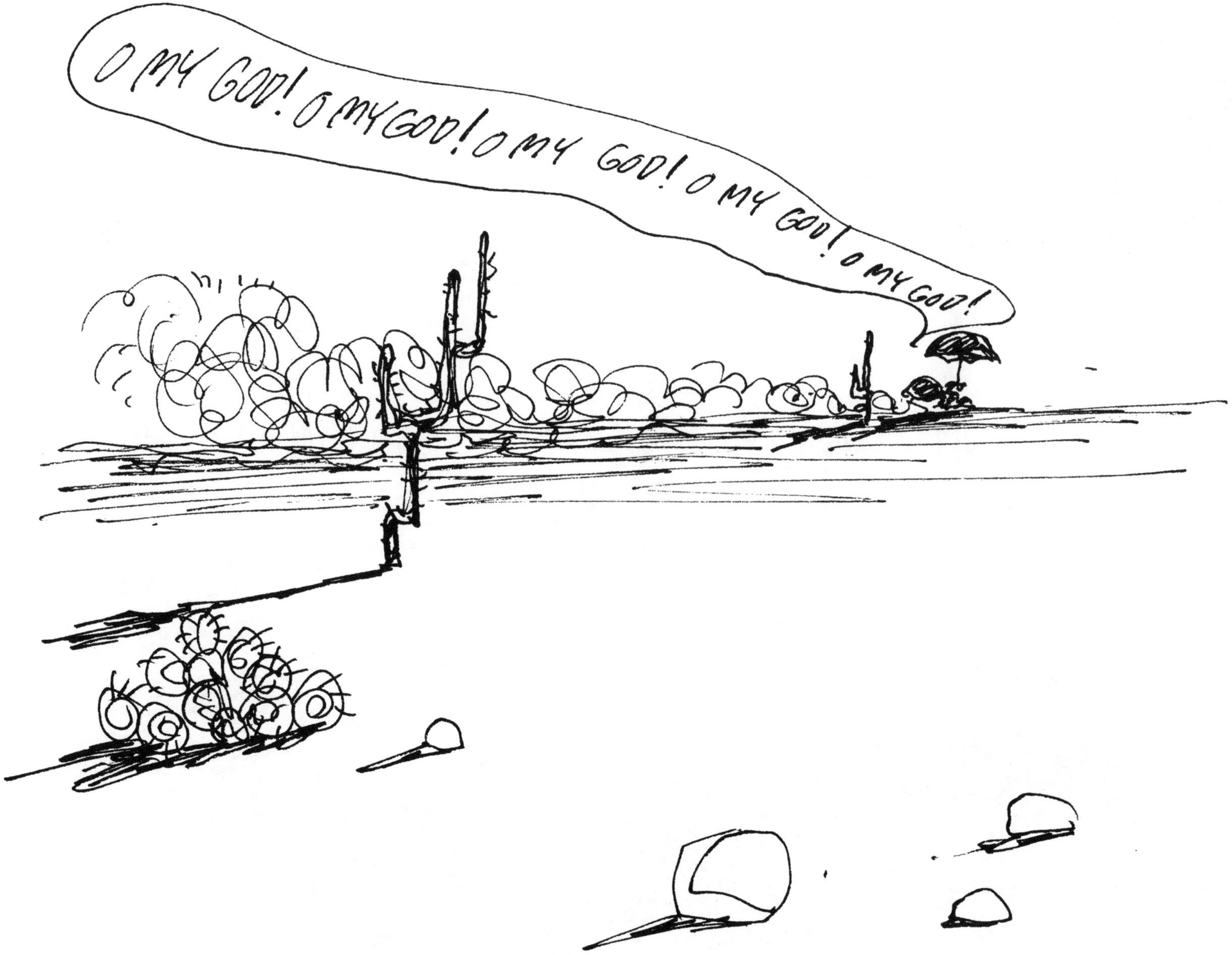
O MY GOD! O MY GOD! O MY GOD! O MY GOD! O MY GOD!

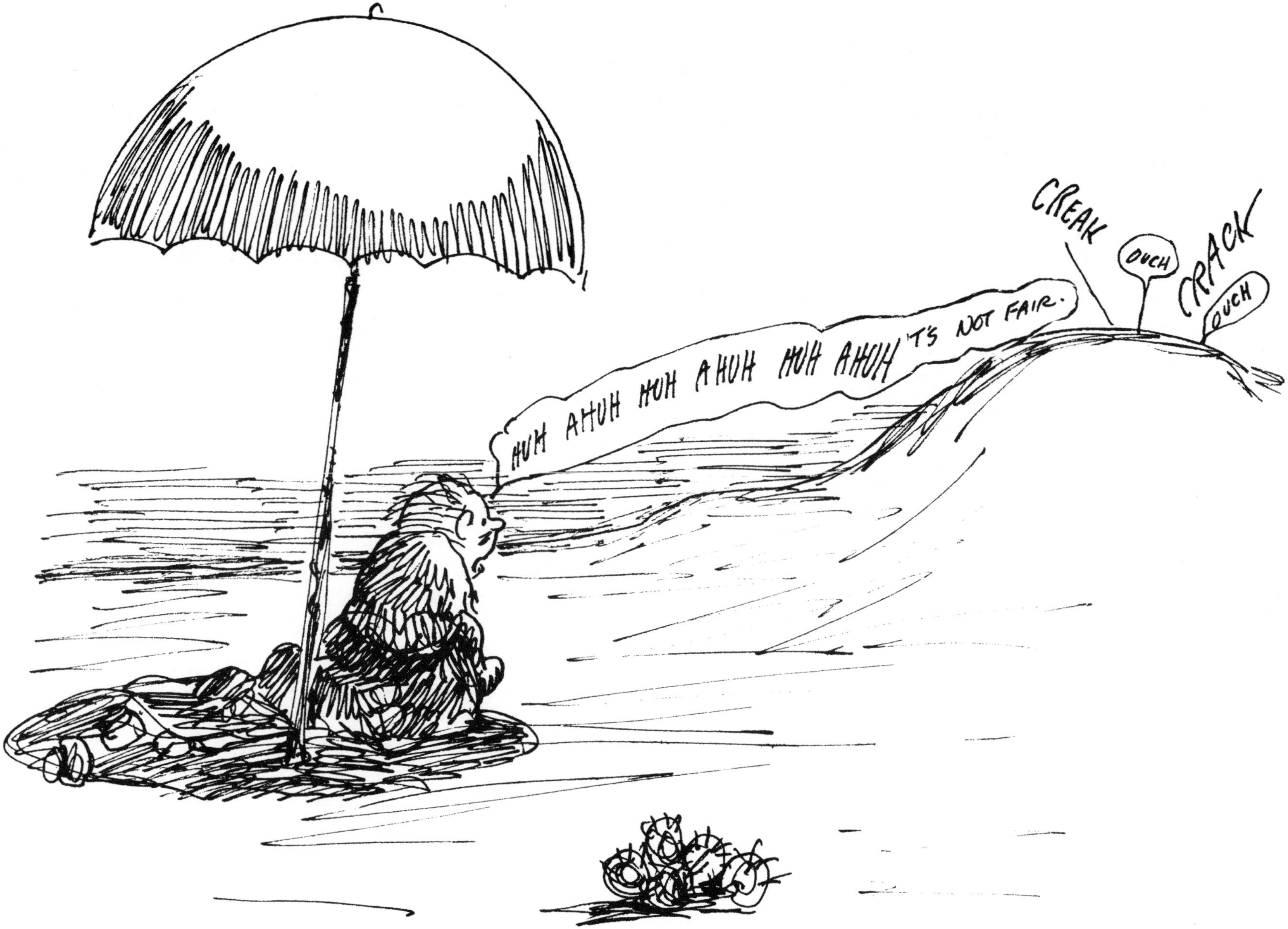
HUH AHUH HUH AHUH HUH AHUH IT'S NOT FAIR.
CREAK
OUCH
CRACK
OUCH

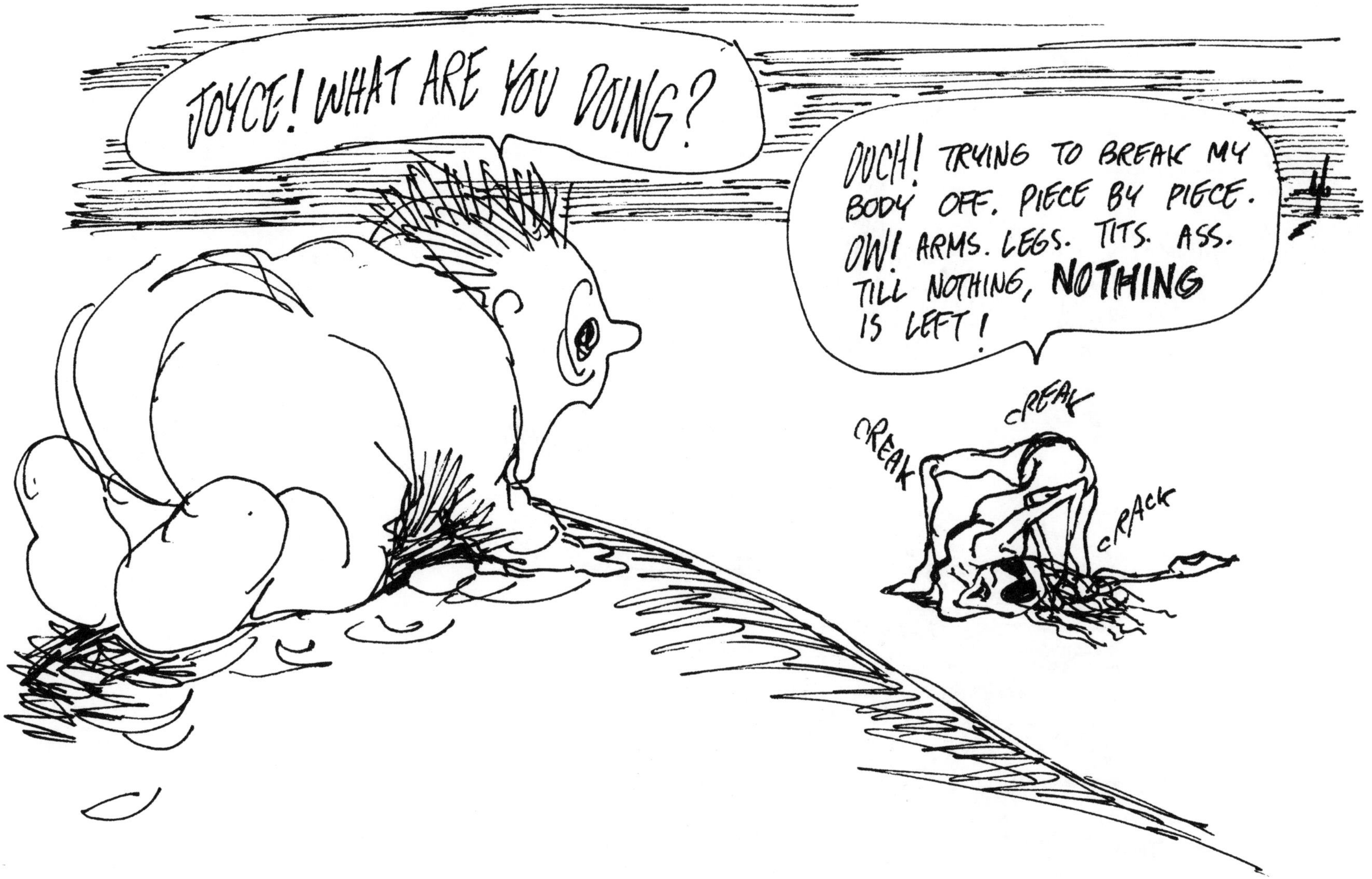
JOYCE! WHAT ARE YOU DOING?
OUCH! TRYING TO BREAK MY BODY OFF. PIECE BY PIECE. OW! ARMS. LEGS. TITS. ASS. TILL NOTHING, **NOTHING** IS LEFT!
CREAK
CREAK
CRACK

BUT ESSENCE. IF I COULD ONLY BE ALL ESSENCE AND NO BODY... BUT I'M ALL BODY! BODY! BODY! BODY!
BODY! BODY! BODY! BODY! BODY!

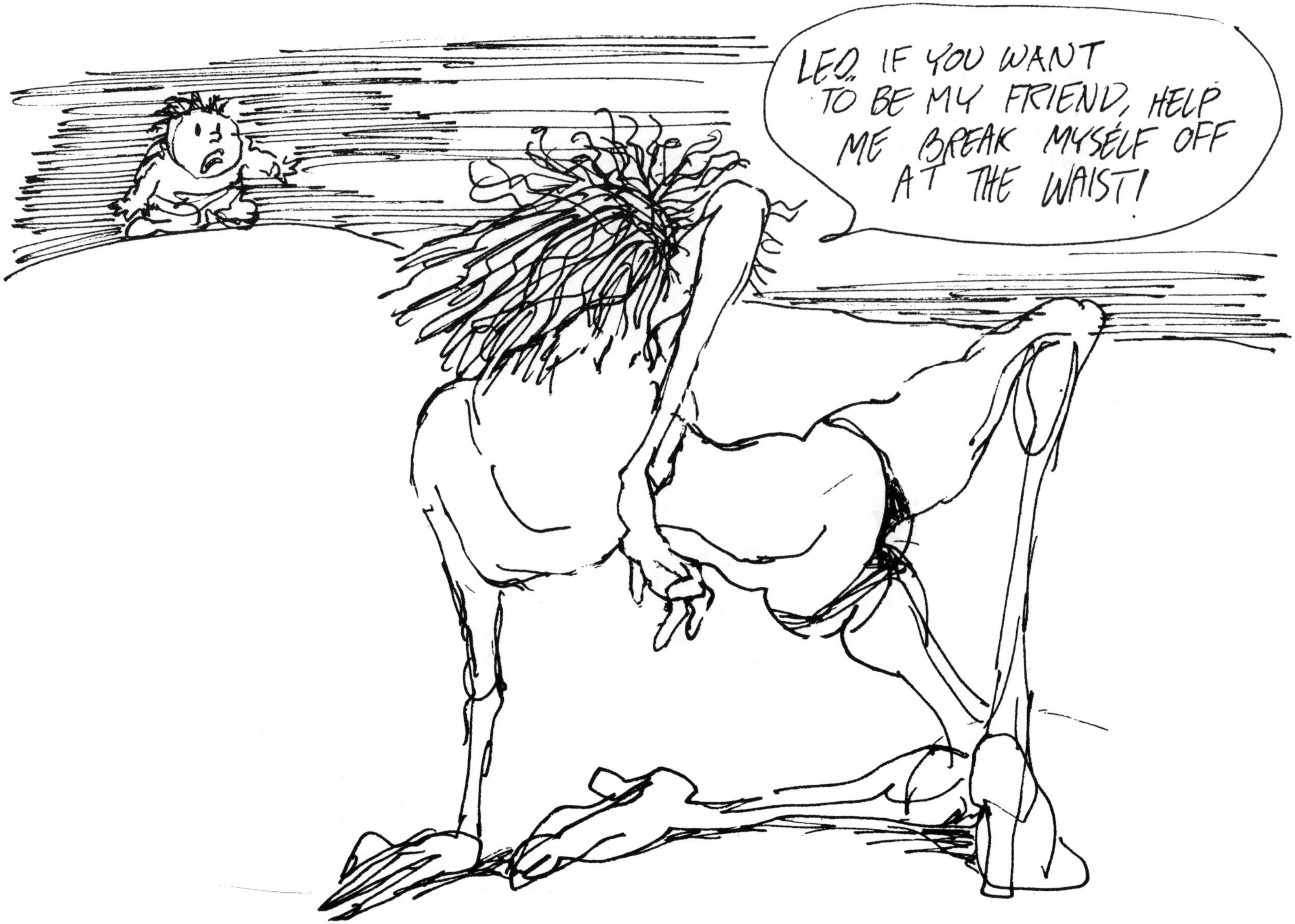
LEO, IF YOU WANT TO BE MY FRIEND, HELP ME BREAK MYSELF OFF AT THE WAIST!

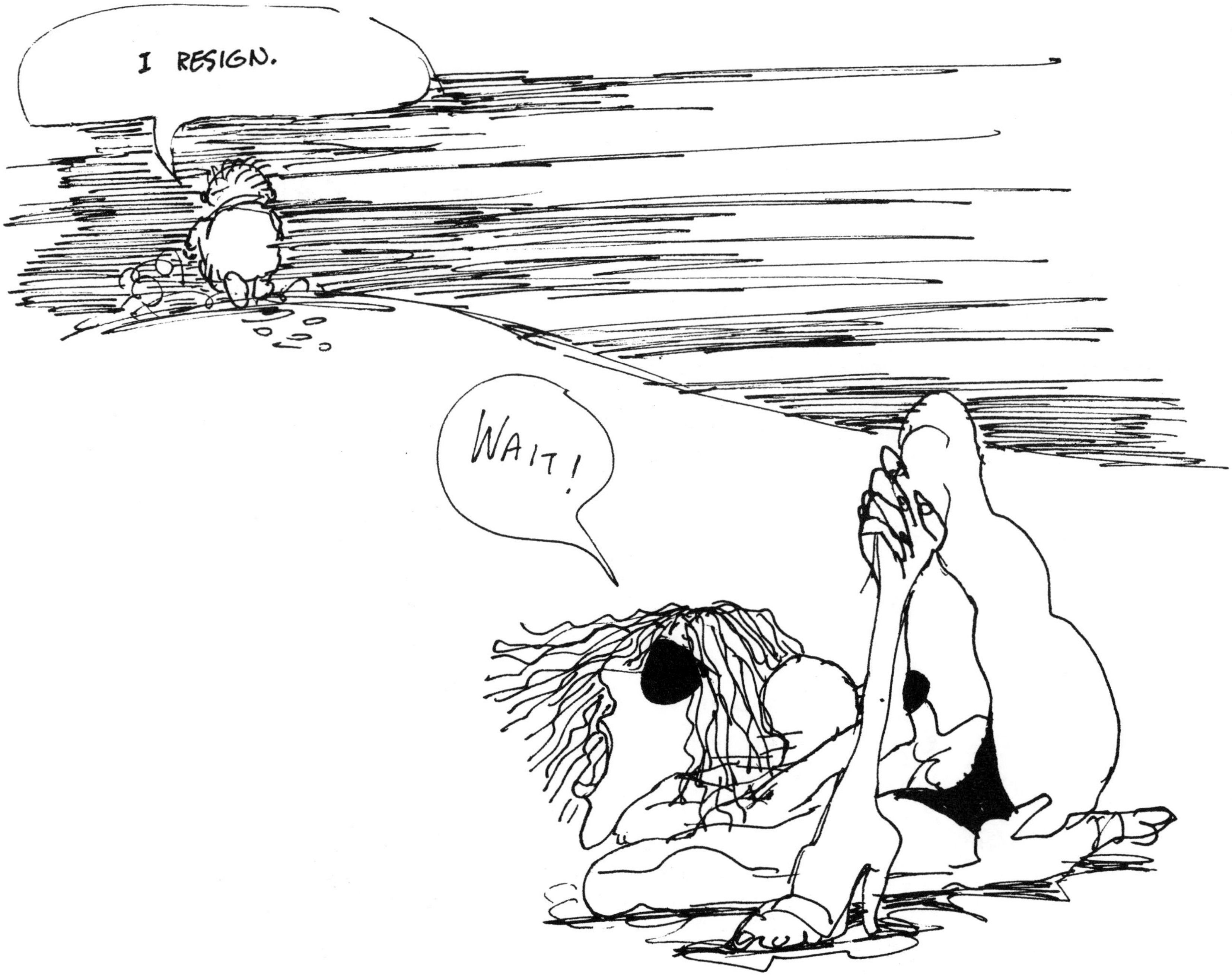
I RESIGN.
WAIT!

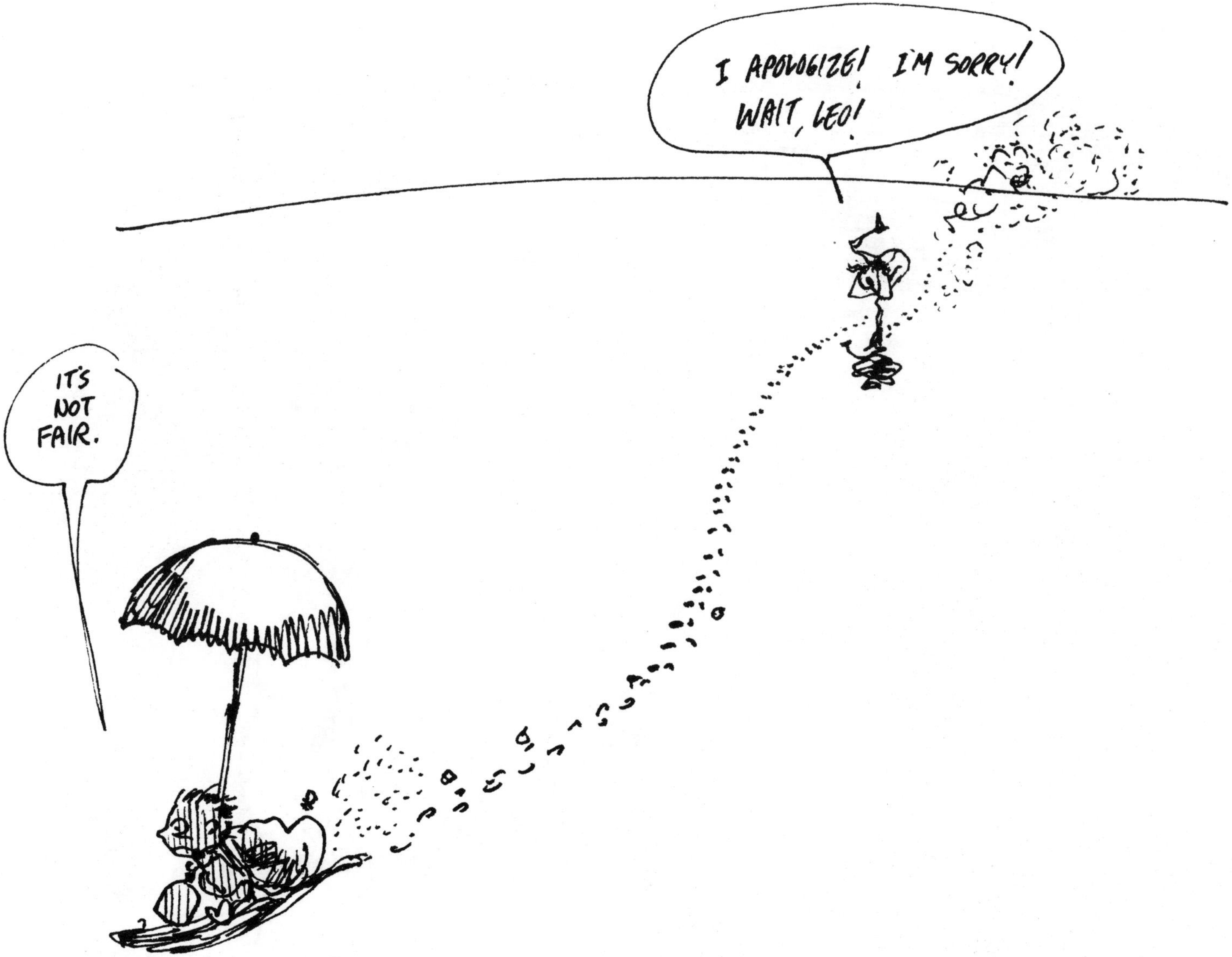
I APOLOGIZE! I'M SORRY!
WAIT, LEO!
IT'S NOT FAIR.

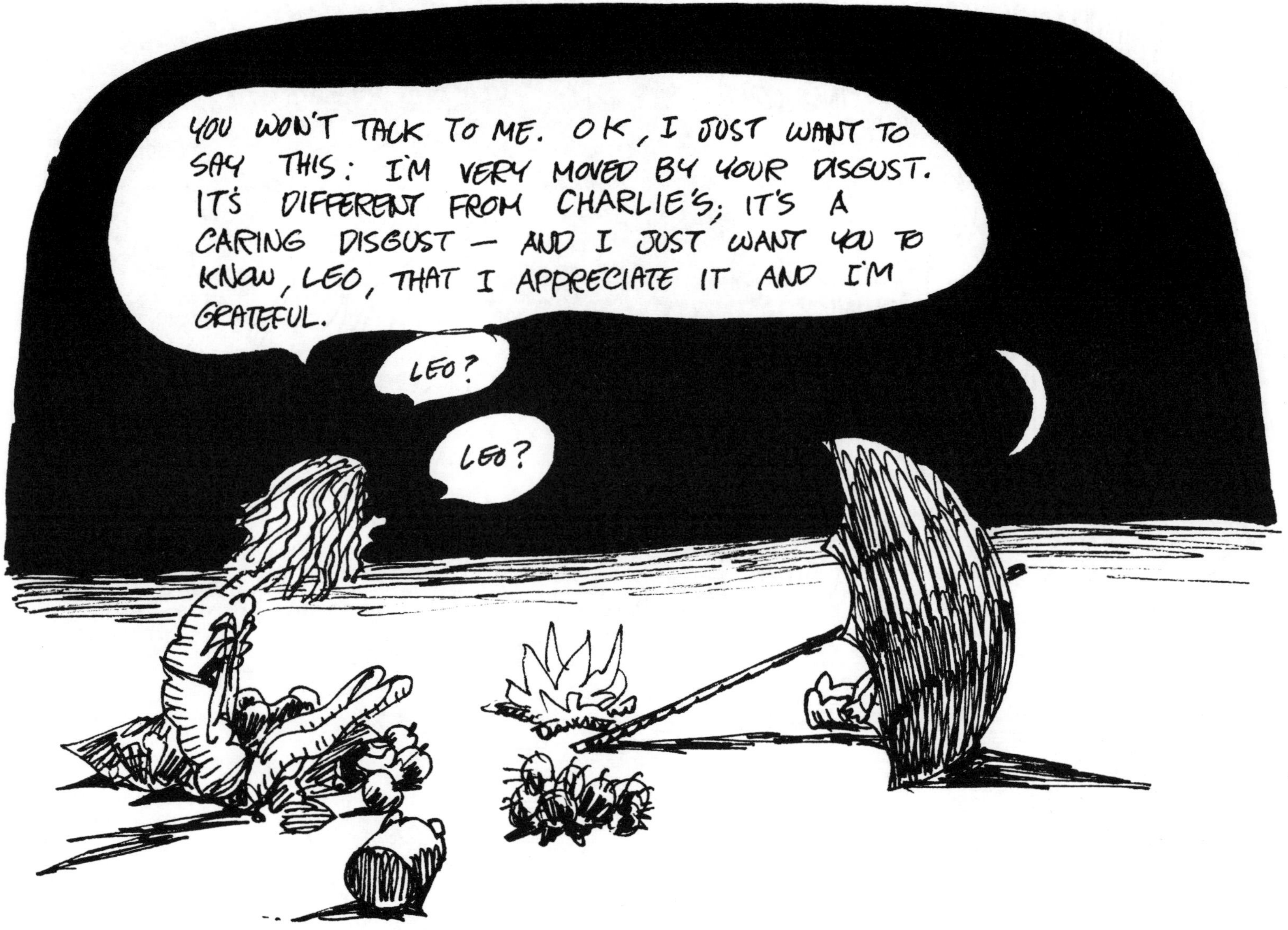
YOU WON'T TALK TO ME. OK, I JUST WANT TO SAY THIS: I'M VERY MOVED BY YOUR DISGUST. IT'S DIFFERENT FROM CHARLIE'S; IT'S A CARING DISGUST — AND I JUST WANT YOU TO KNOW, LEO, THAT I APPRECIATE IT AND I'M GRATEFUL.
LEO?
LEO?

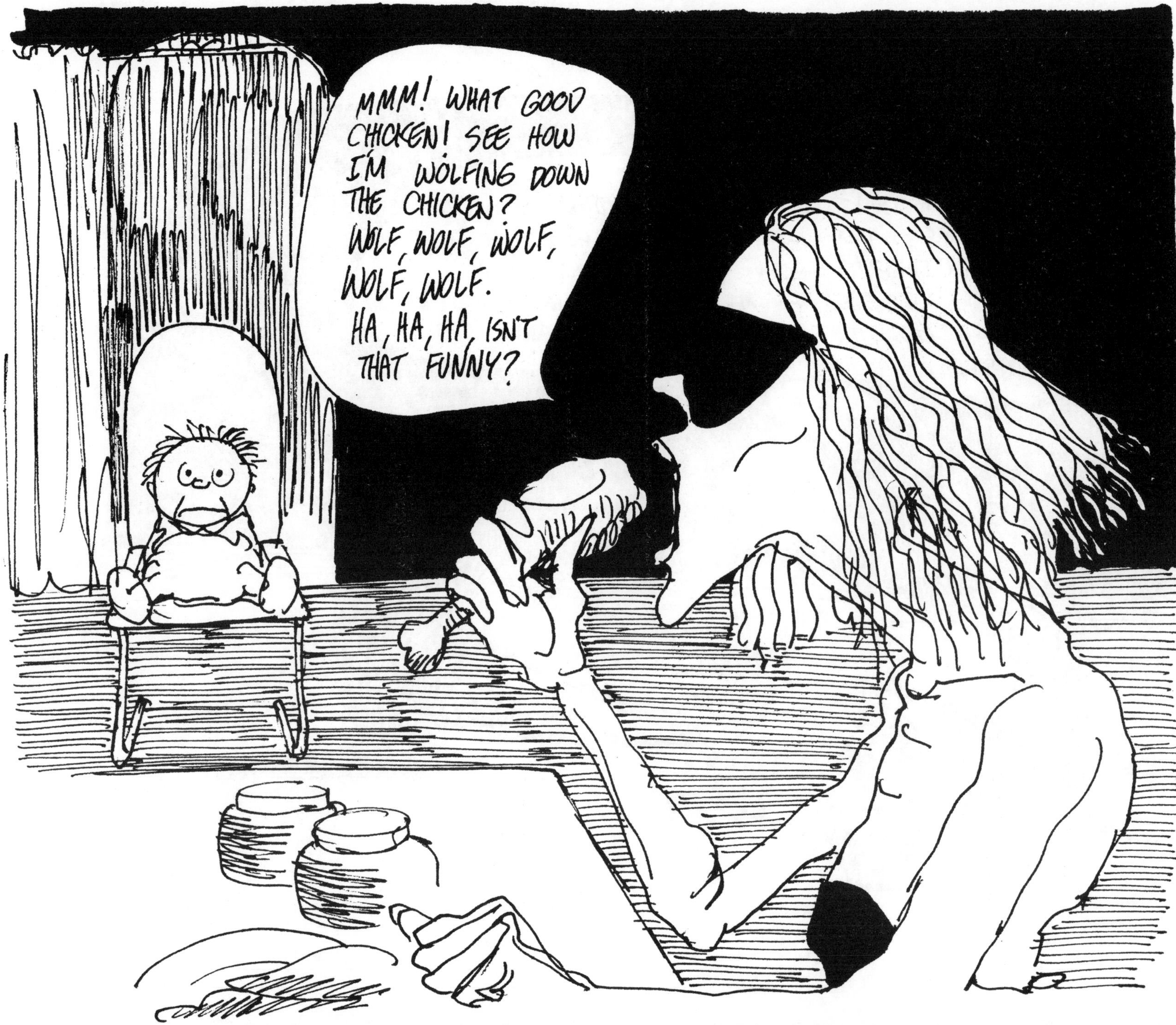
MMM! WHAT GOOD CHICKEN! SEE HOW I'M WOLFING DOWN THE CHICKEN? WOLF, WOLF, WOLF, WOLF, WOLF. HA, HA, HA, ISN'T THAT FUNNY?

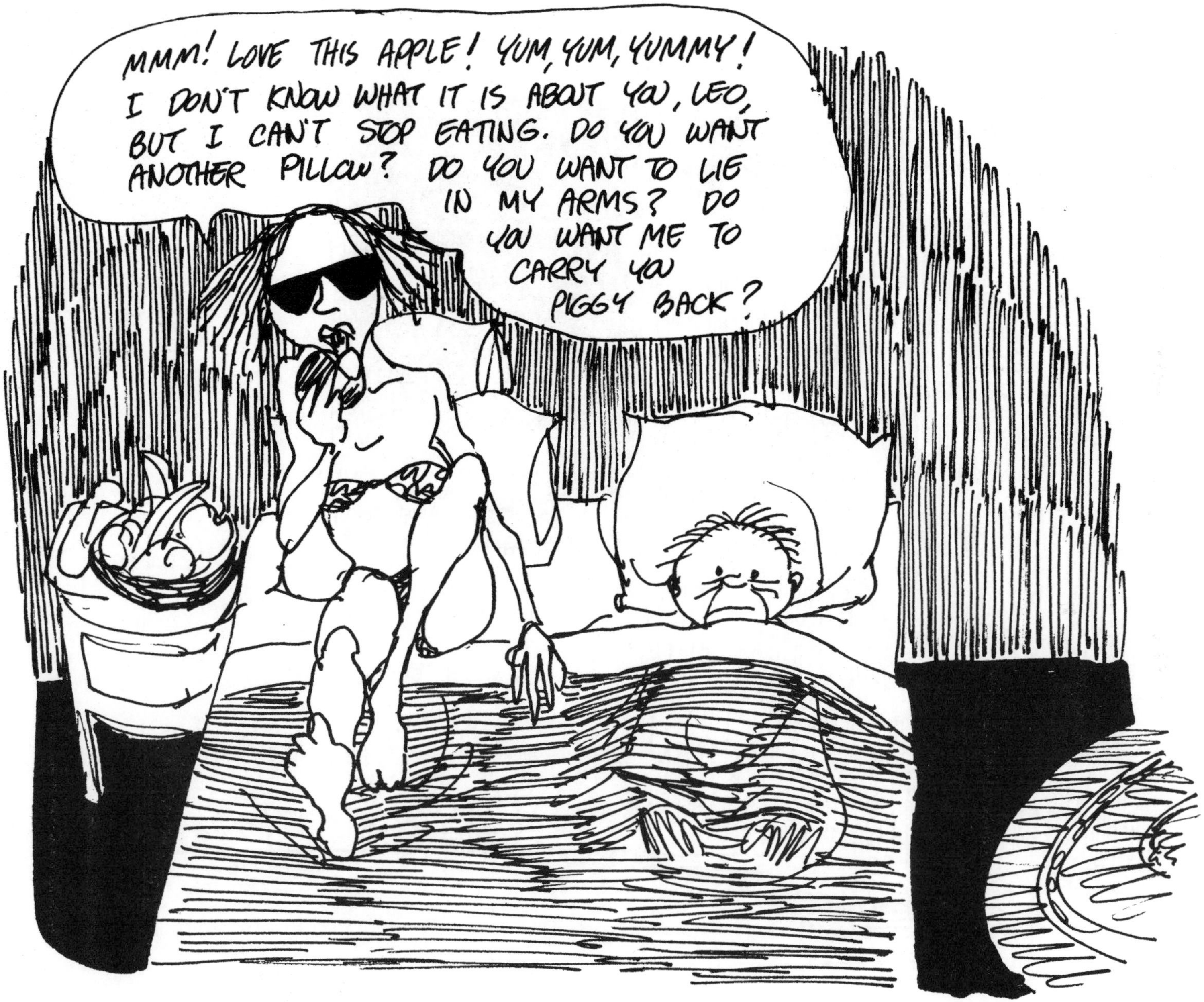
MMM! LOVE THIS APPLE! YUM, YUM, YUMMY! I DON'T KNOW WHAT IT IS ABOUT YOU, LEO, BUT I CAN'T STOP EATING. DO YOU WANT ANOTHER PILLOW? DO YOU WANT TO LIE IN MY ARMS? DO YOU WANT ME TO CARRY YOU PIGGY BACK?

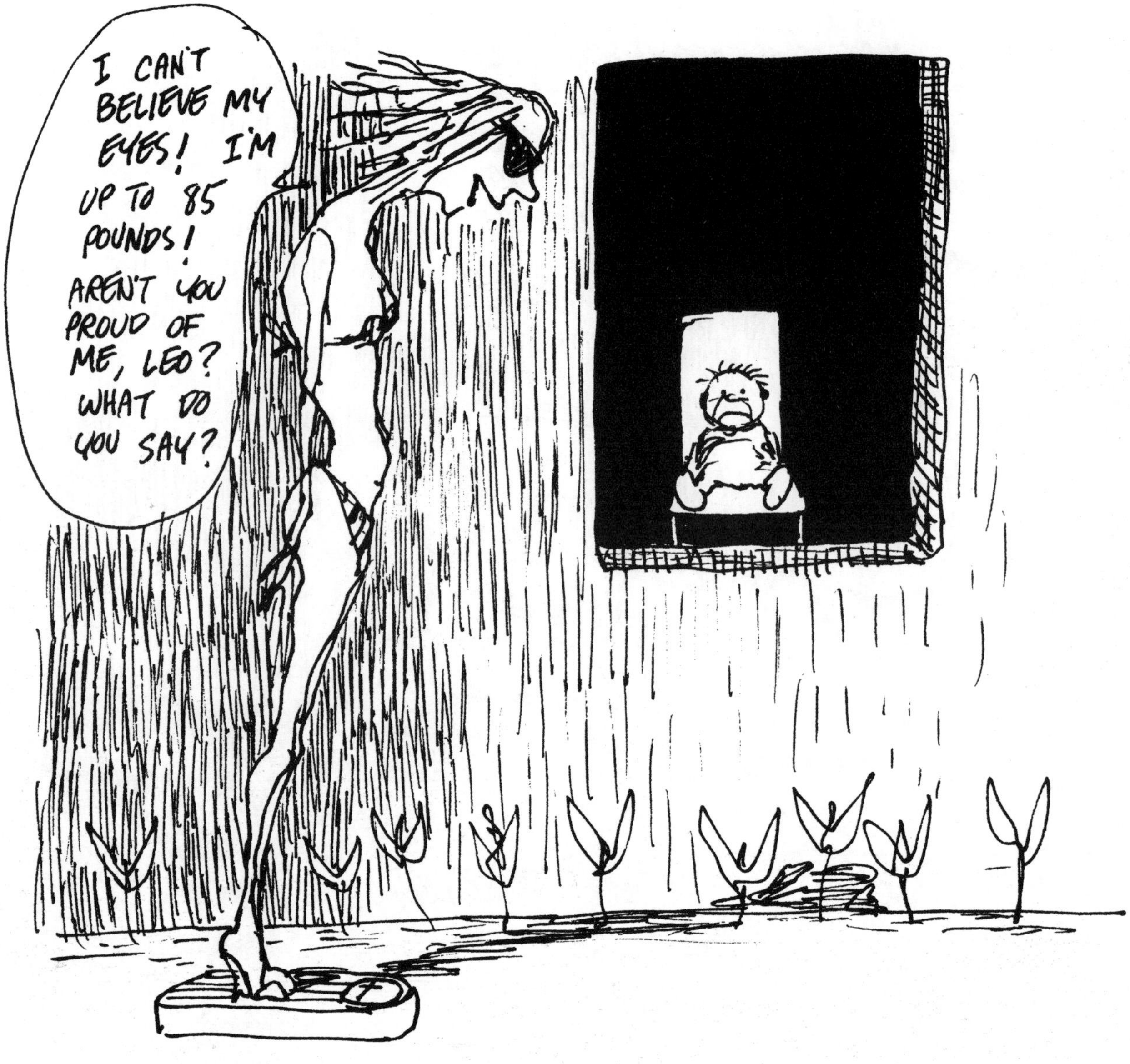
I CAN'T BELIEVE MY EYES! I'M UP TO 85 POUNDS! AREN'T YOU PROUD OF ME, LEO? WHAT DO YOU SAY?

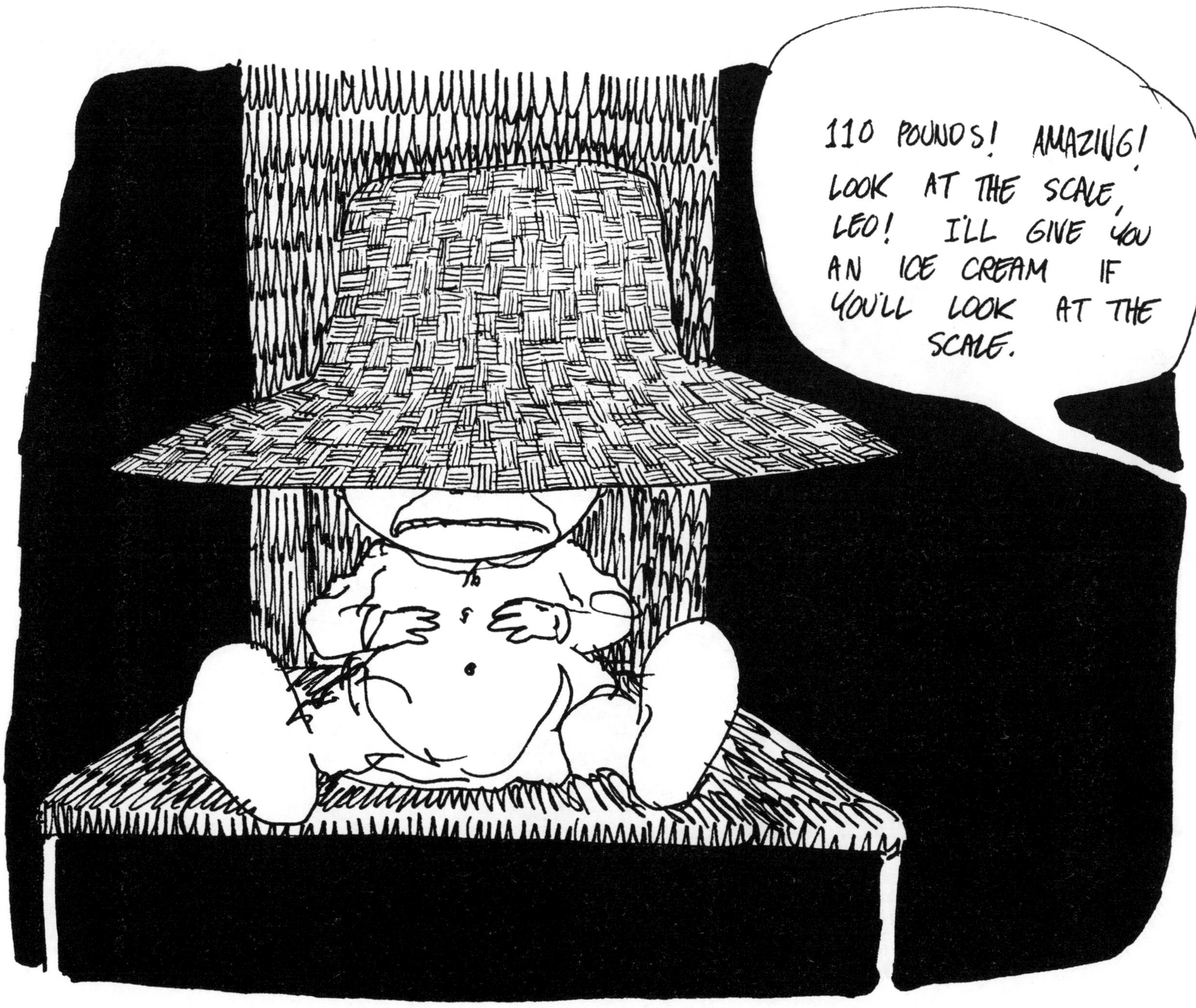
110 POUNDS! AMAZING! LOOK AT THE SCALE, LEO! I'LL GIVE YOU AN ICE CREAM IF YOU'LL LOOK AT THE SCALE.

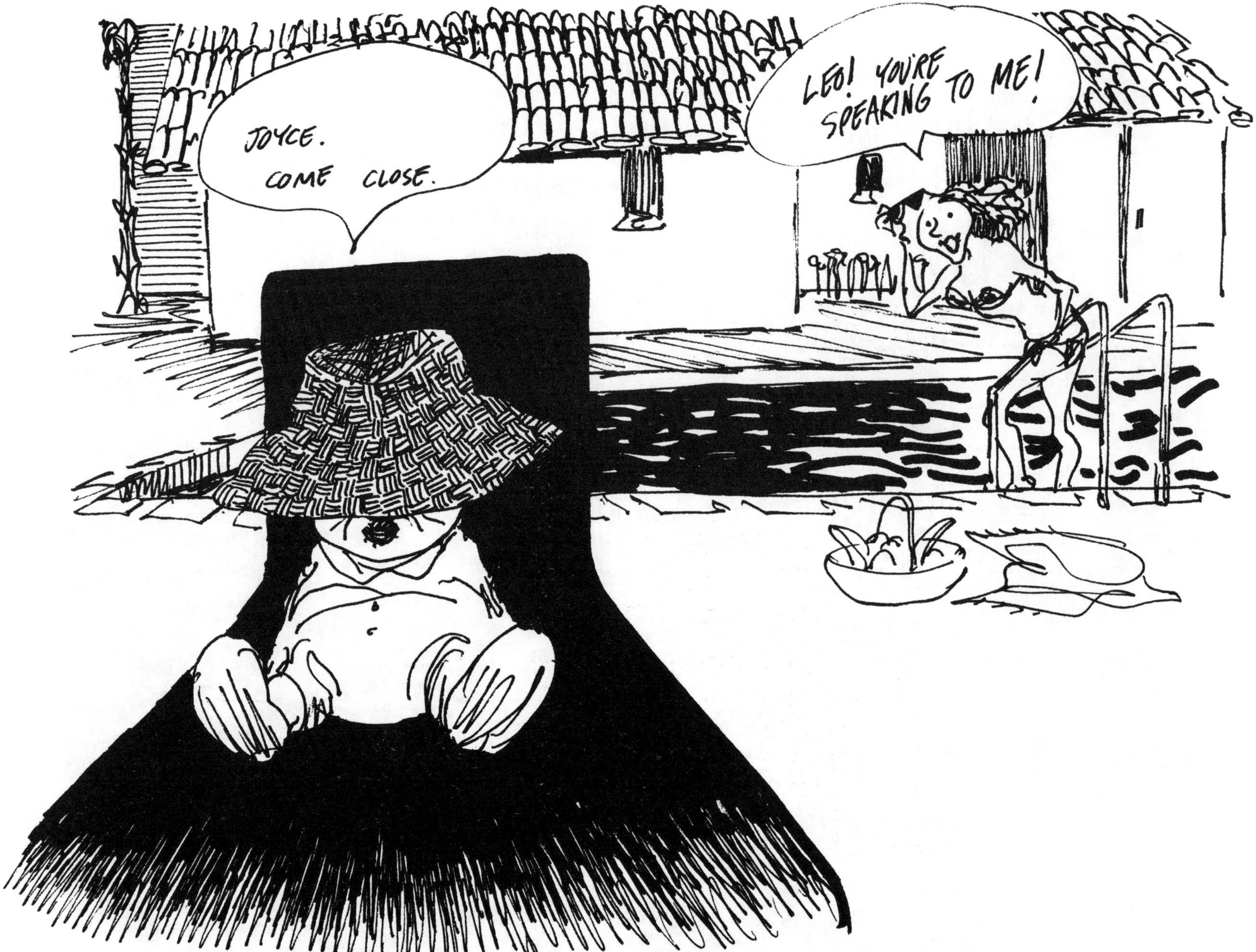
JOYCE. COME CLOSE.
LEO! YOU'RE SPEAKING TO ME!

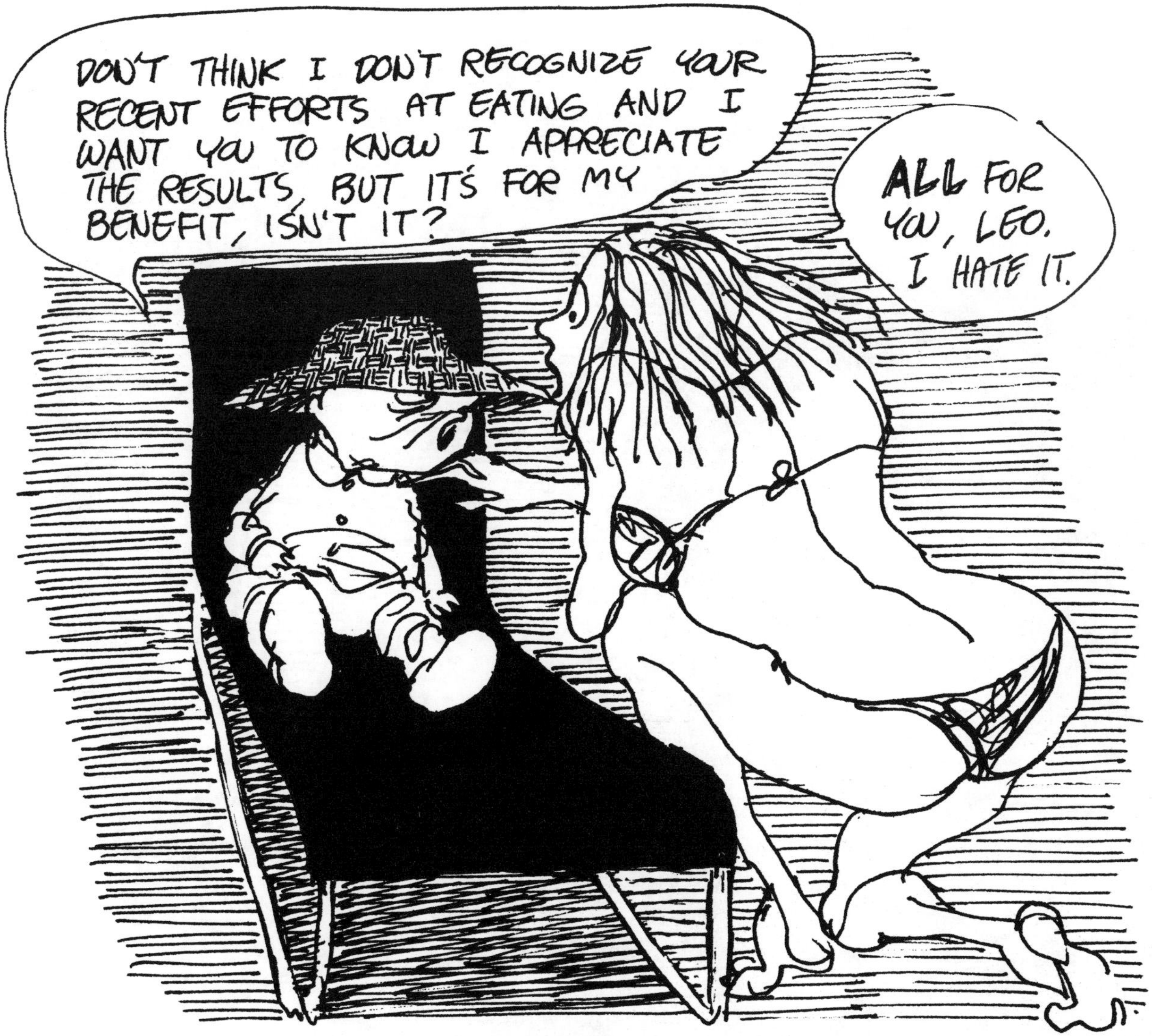
DON'T THINK I DON'T RECOGNIZE YOUR RECENT EFFORTS AT EATING AND I WANT YOU TO KNOW I APPRECIATE THE RESULTS, BUT IT'S FOR MY BENEFIT, ISN'T IT?
ALL FOR YOU, LEO. I HATE IT.

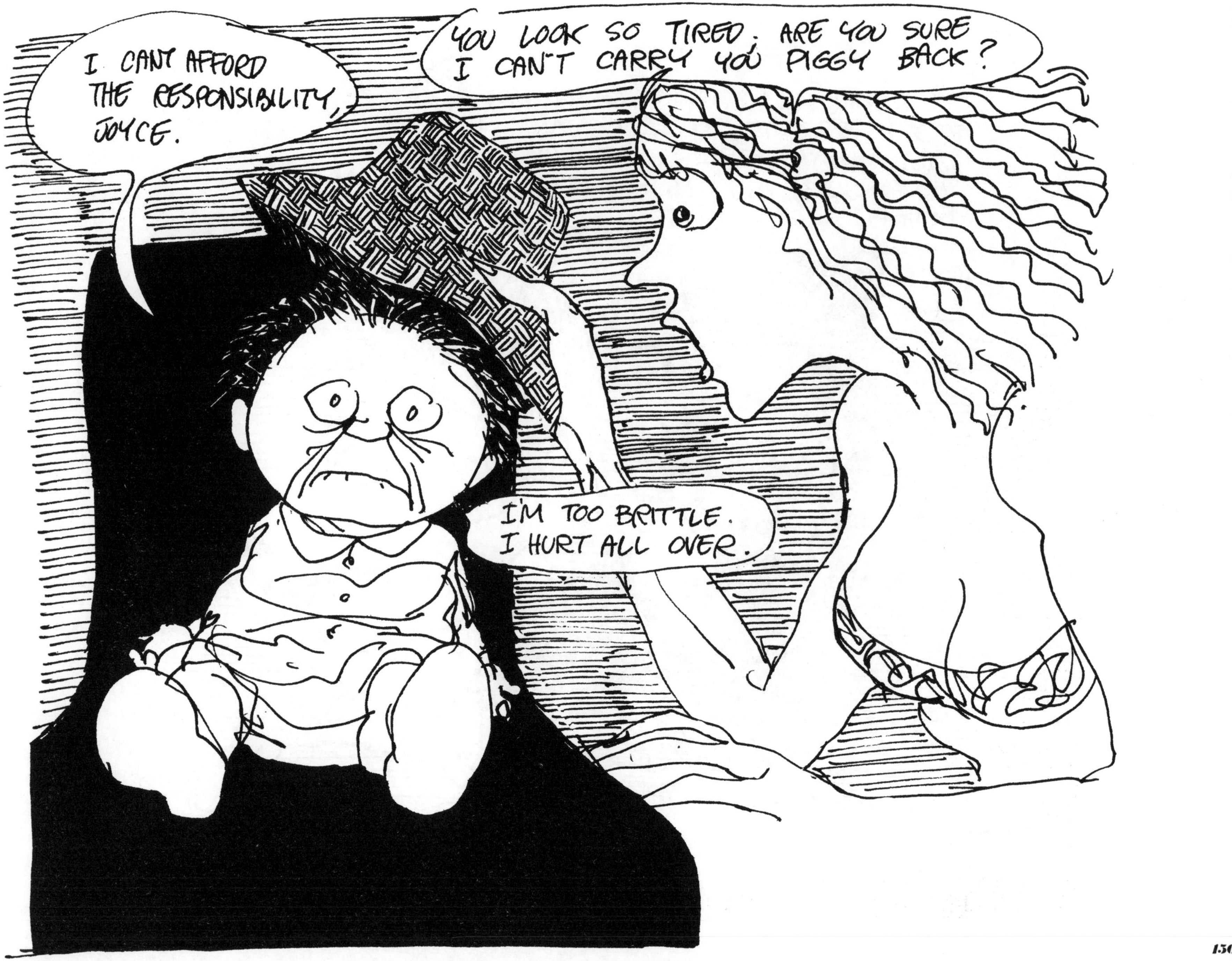
I CANT AFFORD THE RESPONSIBILITY, JOYCE.
YOU LOOK SO TIRED. ARE YOU SURE I CAN'T CARRY YOU PIGGY BACK?
I'M TOO BRITTLE. I HURT ALL OVER.

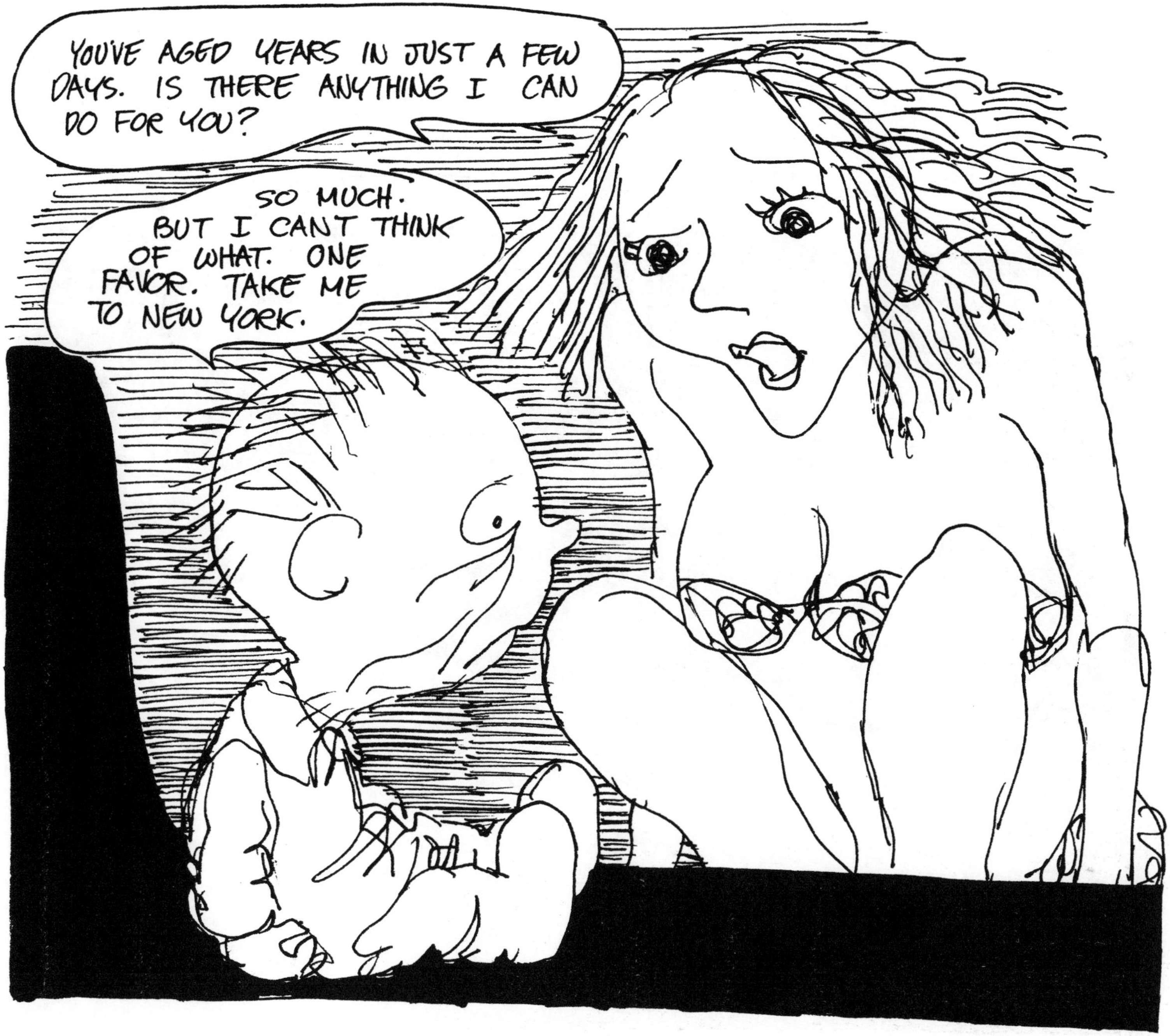
YOU'VE AGED YEARS IN JUST A FEW DAYS. IS THERE ANYTHING I CAN DO FOR YOU?
SO MUCH. BUT I CAN'T THINK OF WHAT. ONE FAVOR. TAKE ME TO NEW YORK.

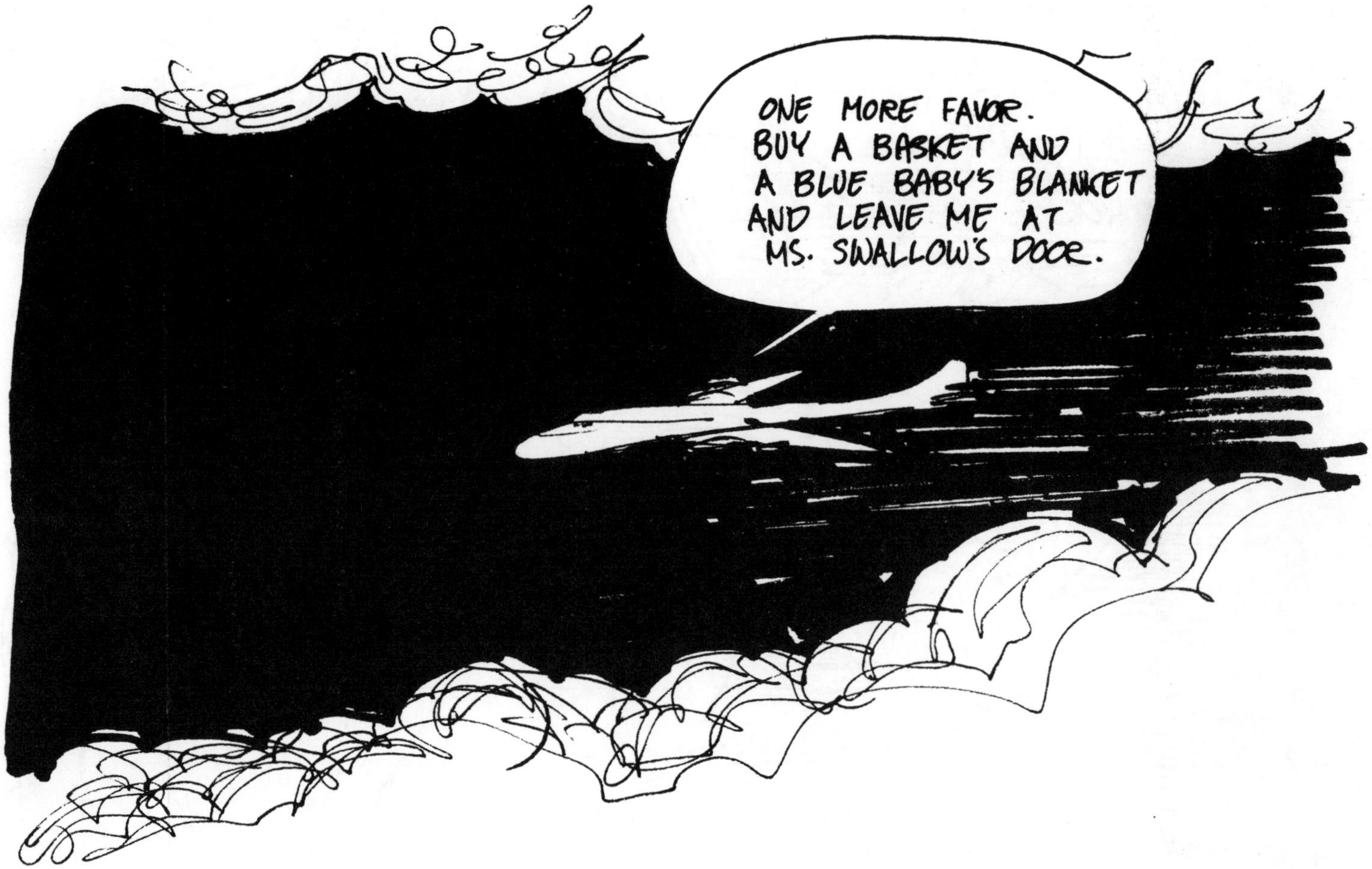
ONE MORE FAVOR. BUY A BASKET AND A BLUE BABY'S BLANKET AND LEAVE ME AT MS. SWALLOW'S DOOR.

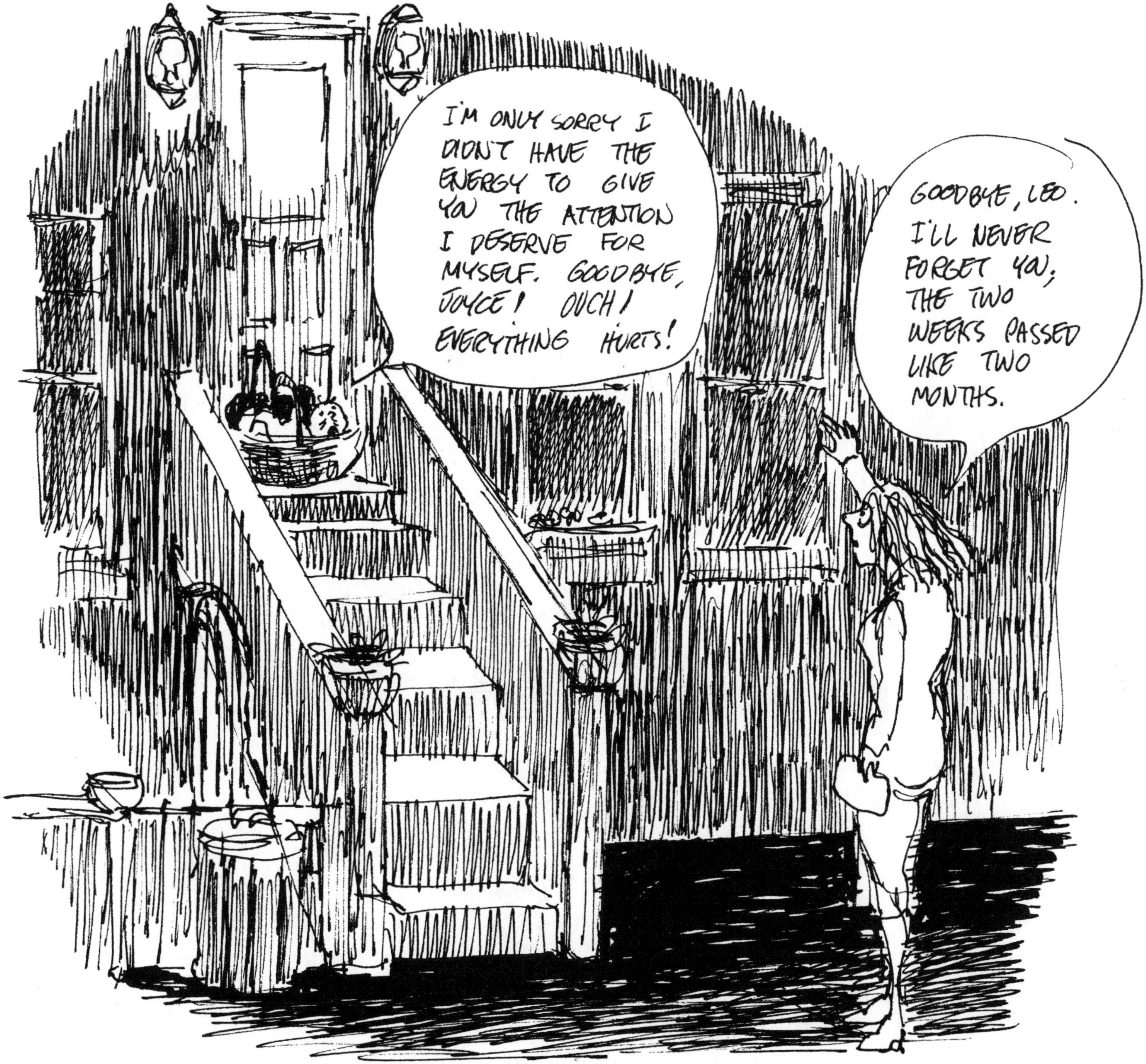
I'M ONLY SORRY I DIDN'T HAVE THE ENERGY TO GIVE YOU THE ATTENTION I DESERVE FOR MYSELF. GOODBYE, JOYCE! OUCH! EVERYTHING HURTS!
GOODBYE, LEO. I'LL NEVER FORGET YOU; THE TWO WEEKS PASSED LIKE TWO MONTHS.

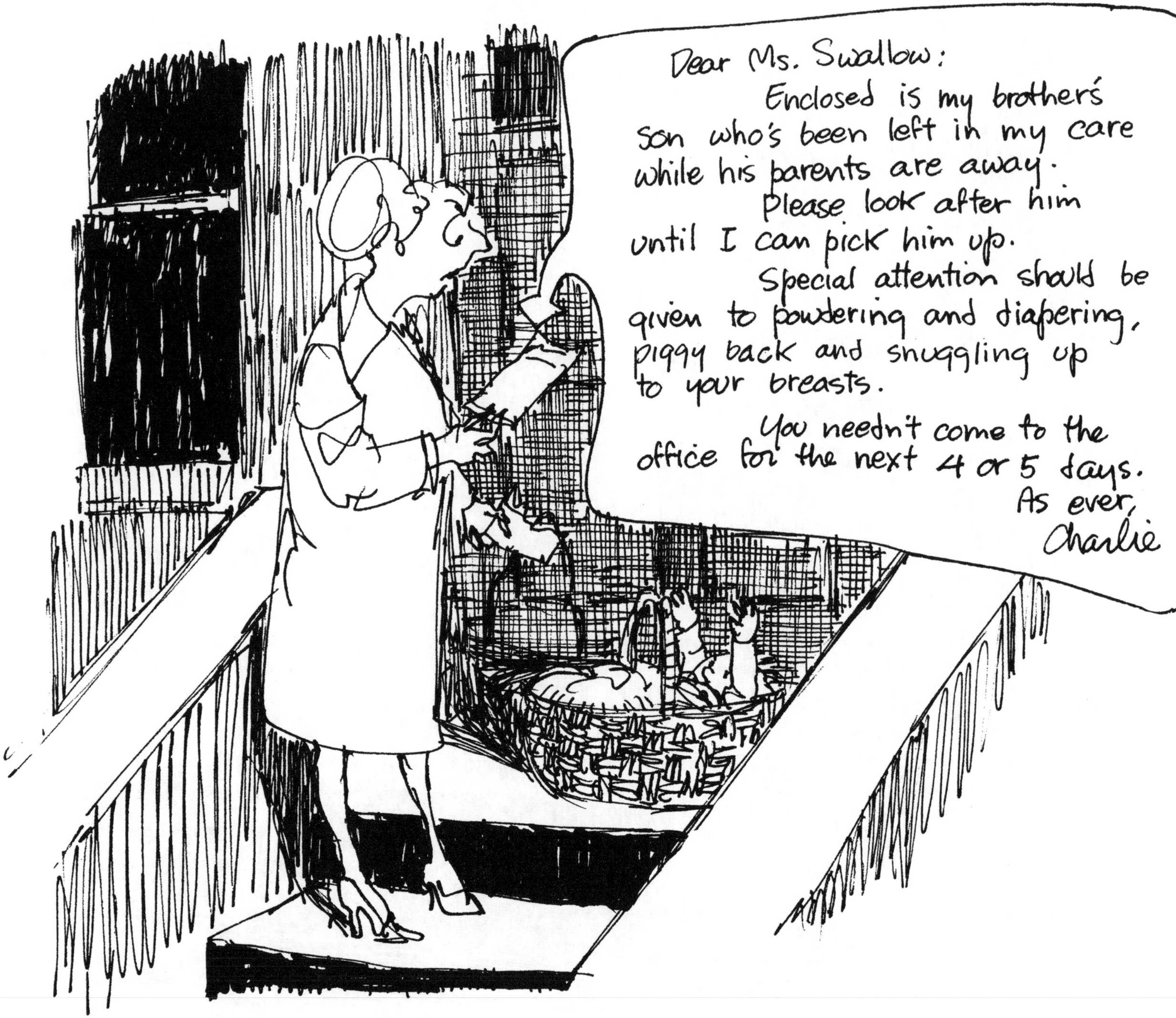
Dear Ms. Swallow:
Enclosed is my brother's son who's been left in my care while his parents are away.
Please look after him until I can pick him up.
Special attention should be given to powdering and diapering, piggy back and snuggling up to your breasts.
You needn't come to the office for the next 4 or 5 days.
As ever,
Charlie

10 EPIPHANY II

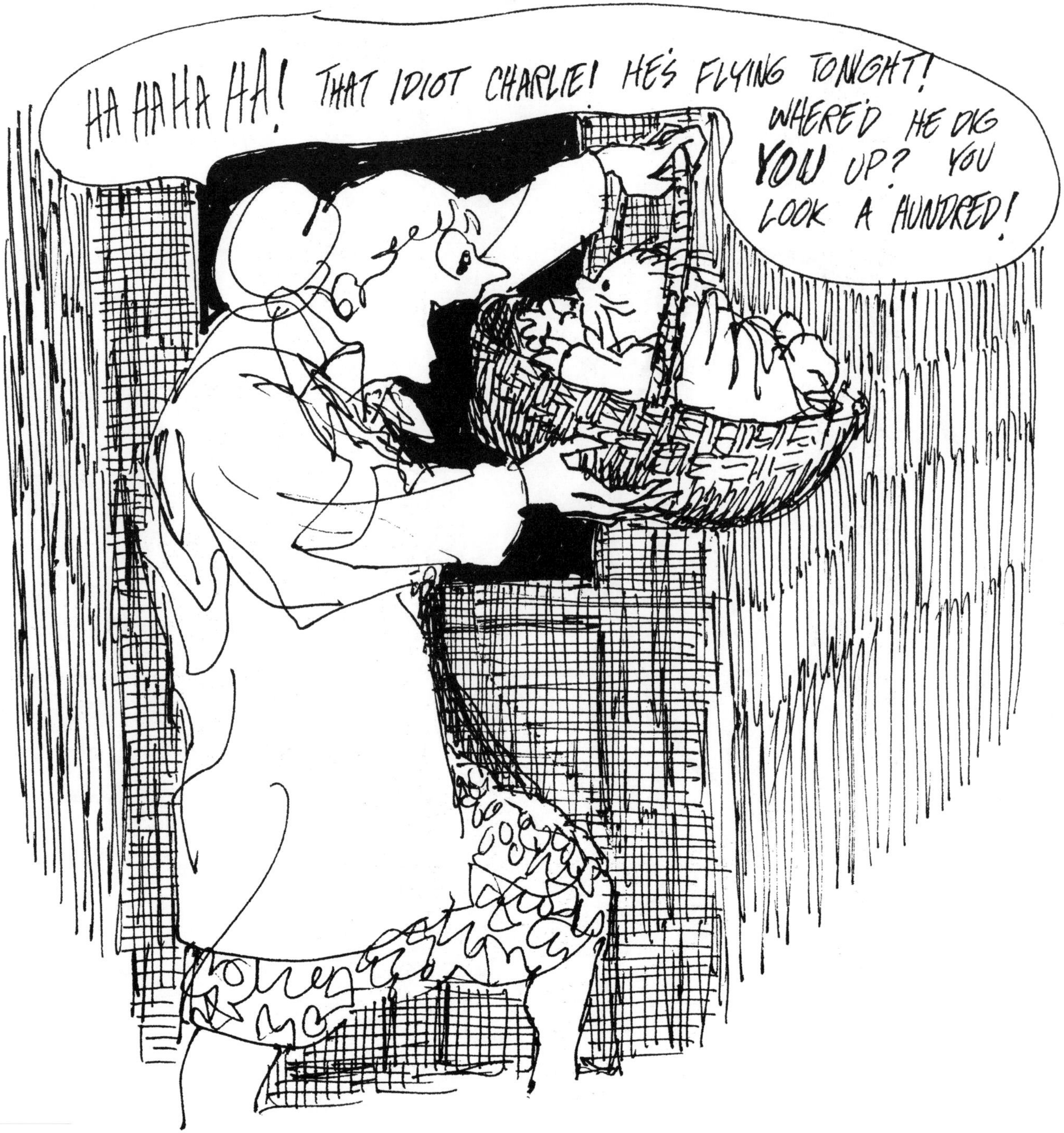
HA HAHA HA! THAT IDIOT CHARLIE! HE'S FLYING TONIGHT! WHERE'D HE DIG YOU UP? YOU LOOK A HUNDRED!

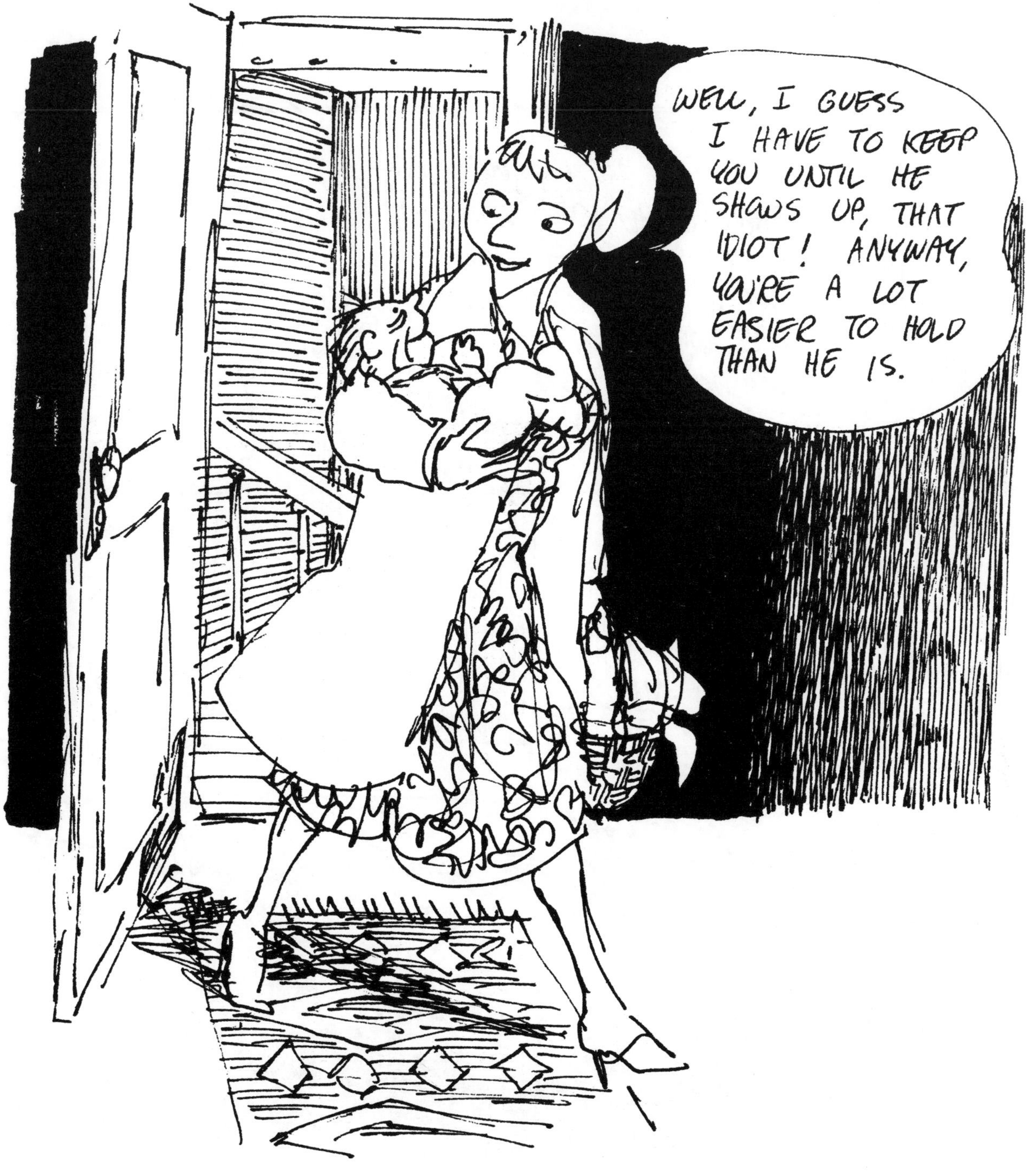
WELL, I GUESS I HAVE TO KEEP YOU UNTIL HE SHOWS UP, THAT IDIOT! ANYWAY, YOU'RE A LOT EASIER TO HOLD THAN HE IS.

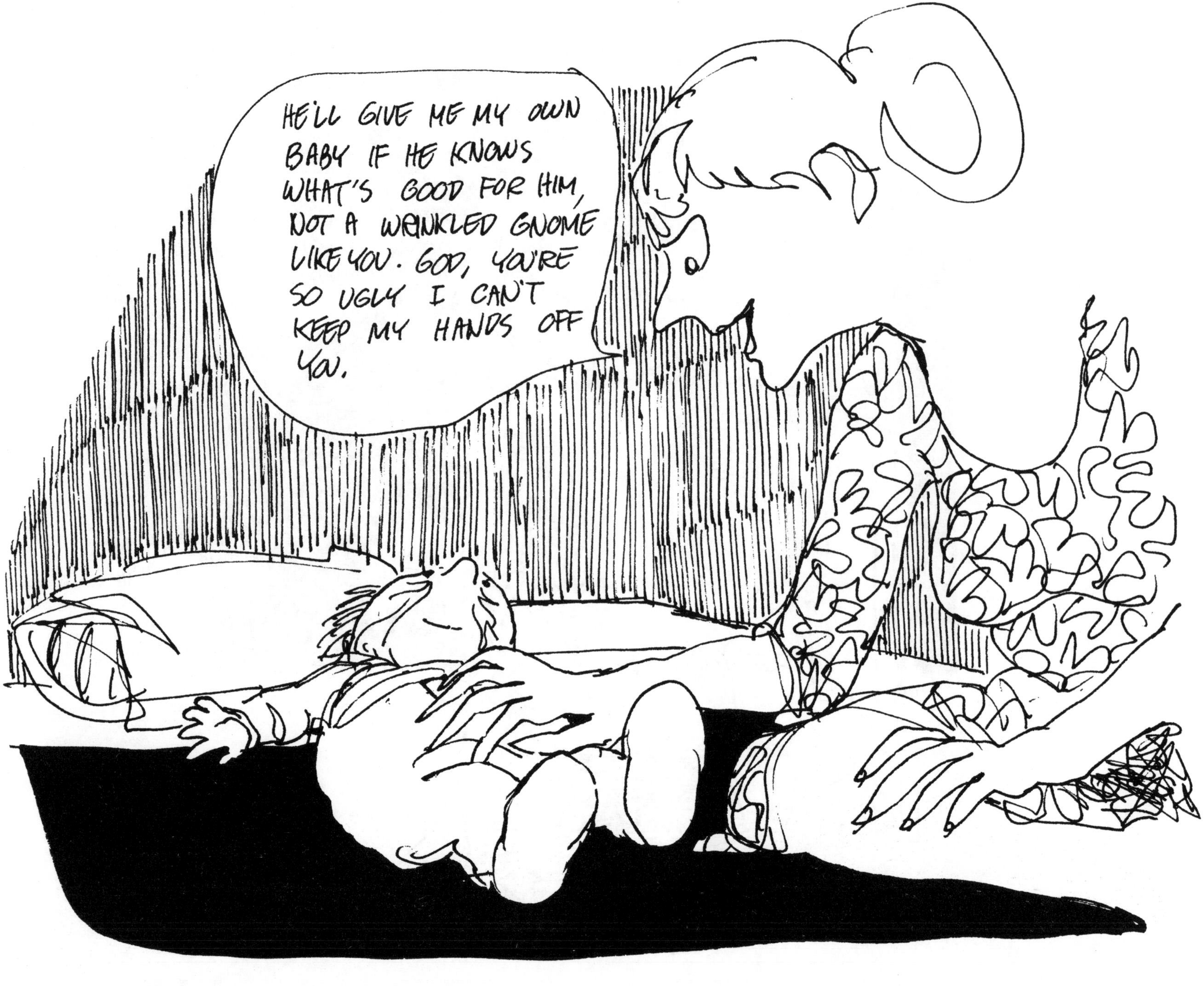
HE'LL GIVE ME MY OWN BABY IF HE KNOWS WHAT'S GOOD FOR HIM, NOT A WRINKLED GNOME LIKE YOU. GOD, YOU'RE SO UGLY I CAN'T KEEP MY HANDS OFF YOU.

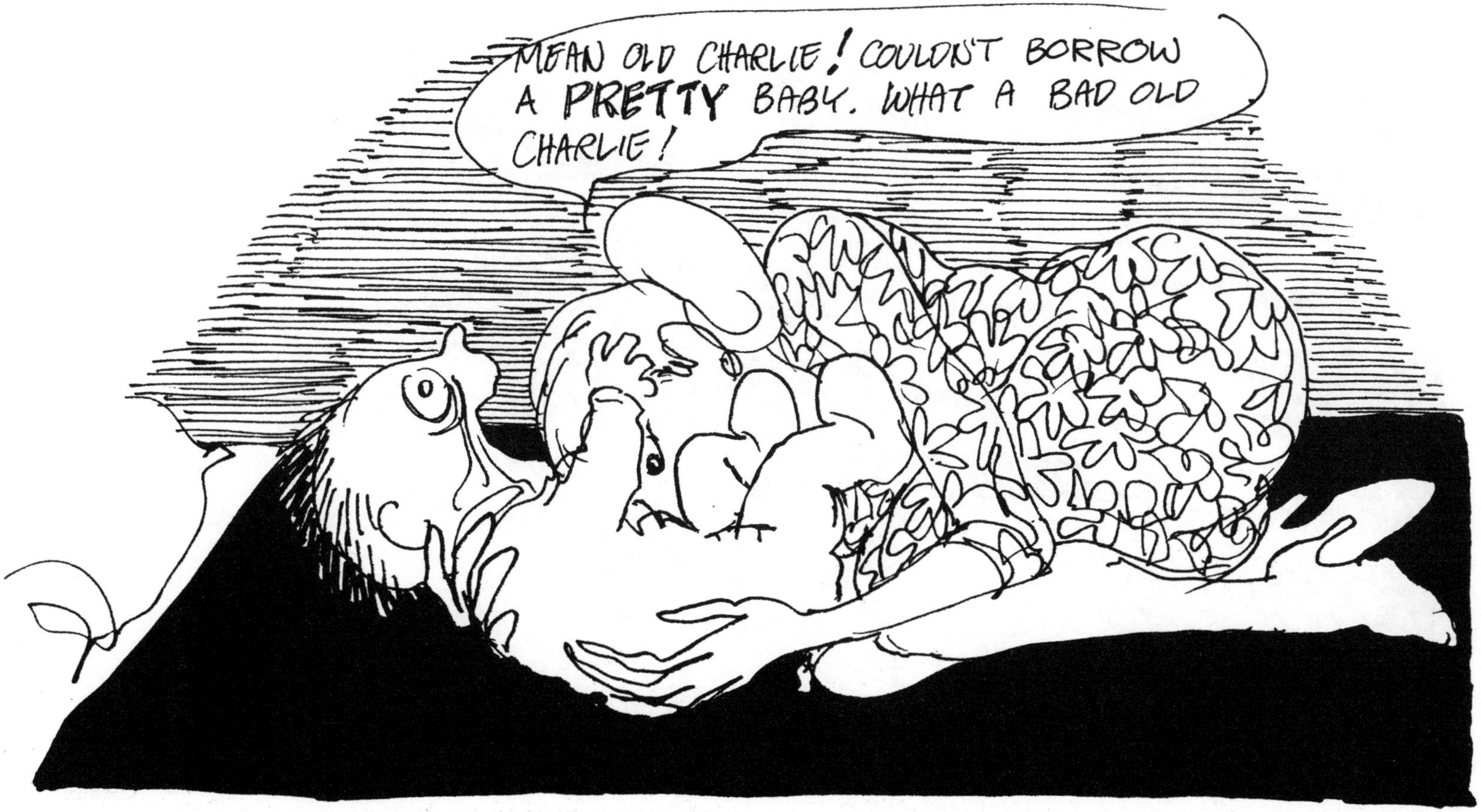
MEAN OLD CHARLIE! COULDN'T BORROW A PRETTY BABY. WHAT A BAD OLD CHARLIE!

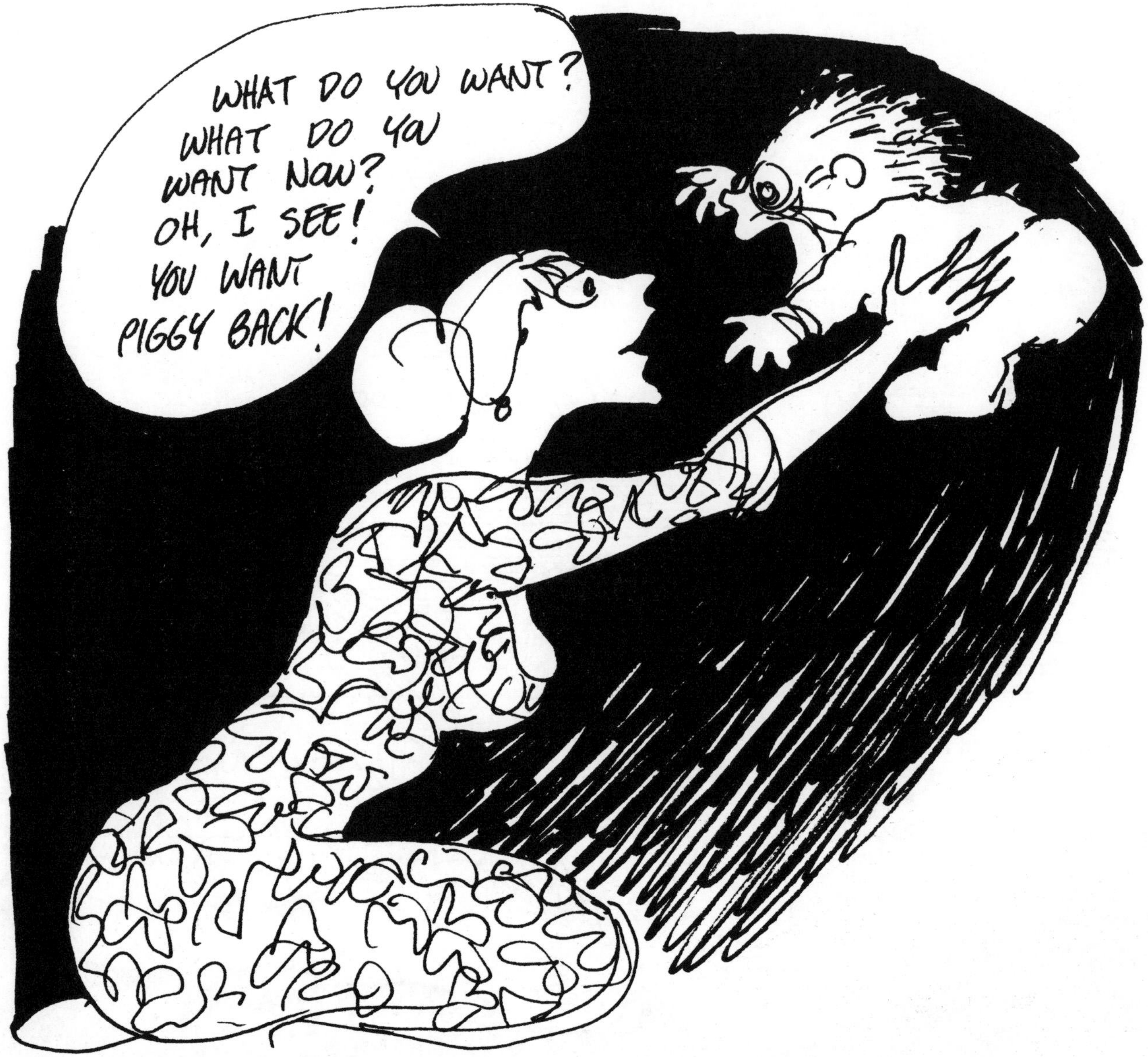
WHAT DO YOU WANT? WHAT DO YOU WANT NOW? OH, I SEE! YOU WANT PIGGY BACK!

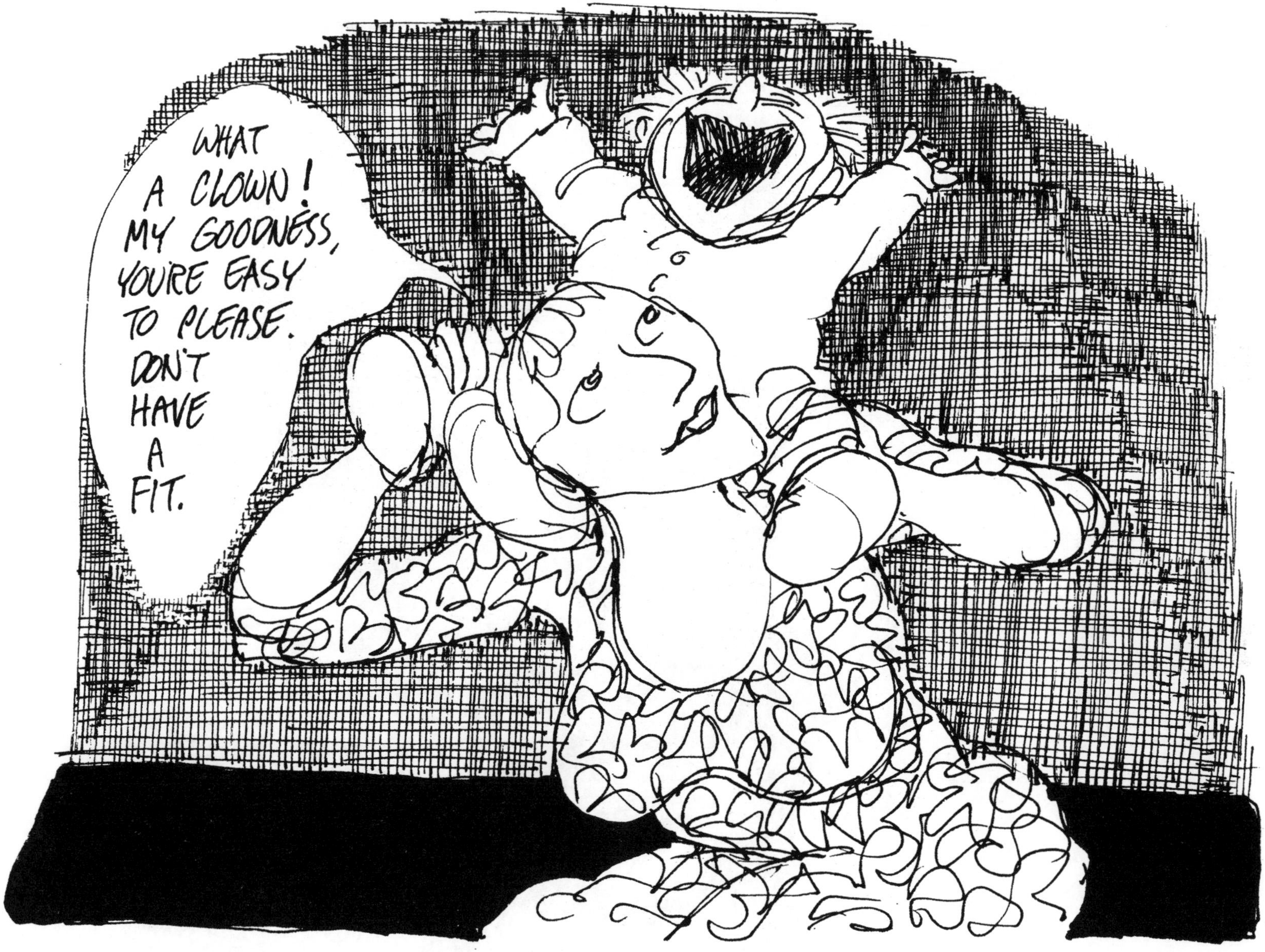
WHAT A CLOWN! MY GOODNESS, YOU'RE EASY TO PLEASE. DON'T HAVE A FIT.

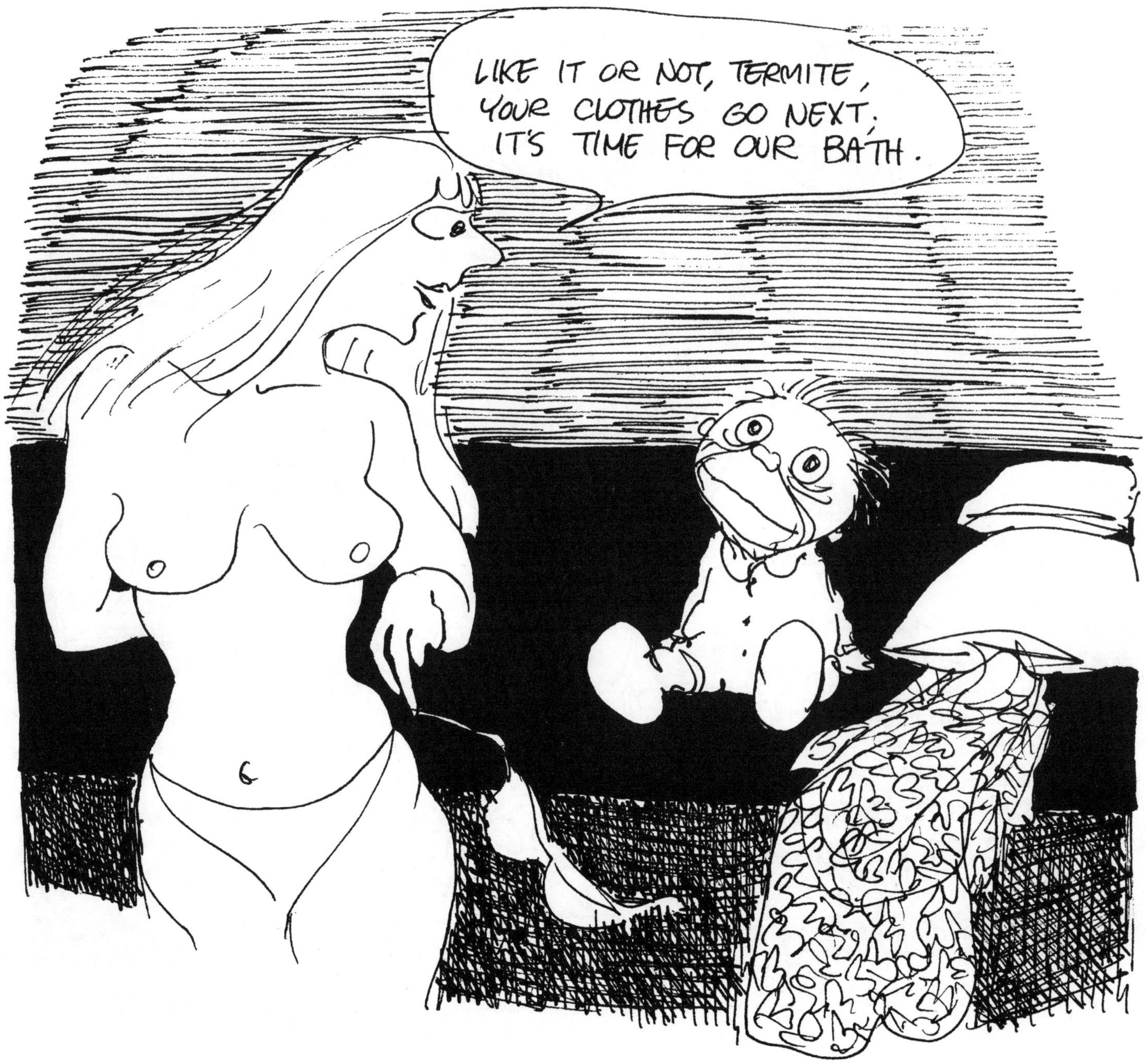
LIKE IT OR NOT, TERMITE, YOUR CLOTHES GO NEXT. IT'S TIME FOR OUR BATH.

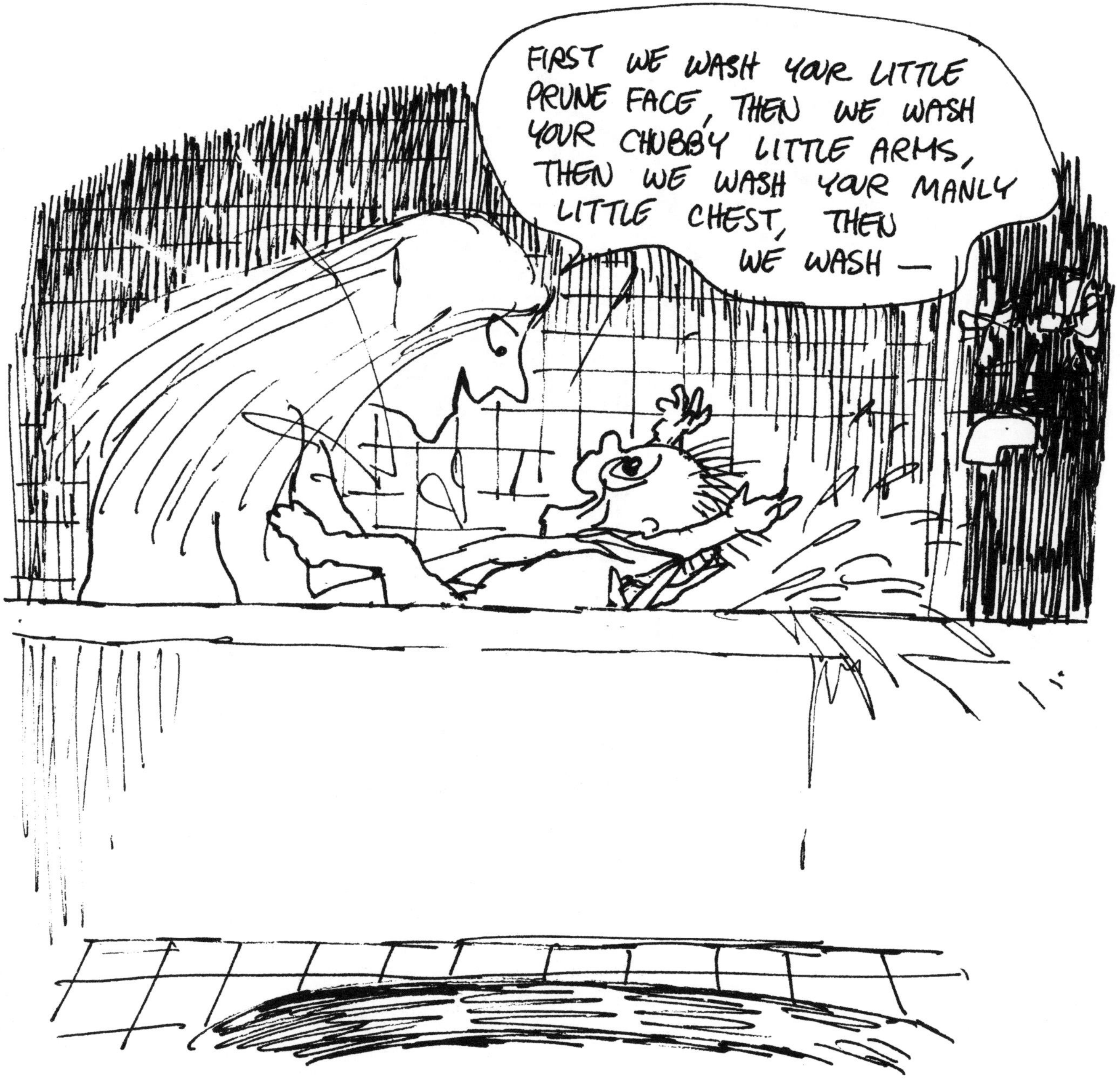
FIRST WE WASH YOUR LITTLE PRUNE FACE, THEN WE WASH YOUR CHUBBY LITTLE ARMS, THEN WE WASH YOUR MANLY LITTLE CHEST, THEN WE WASH —

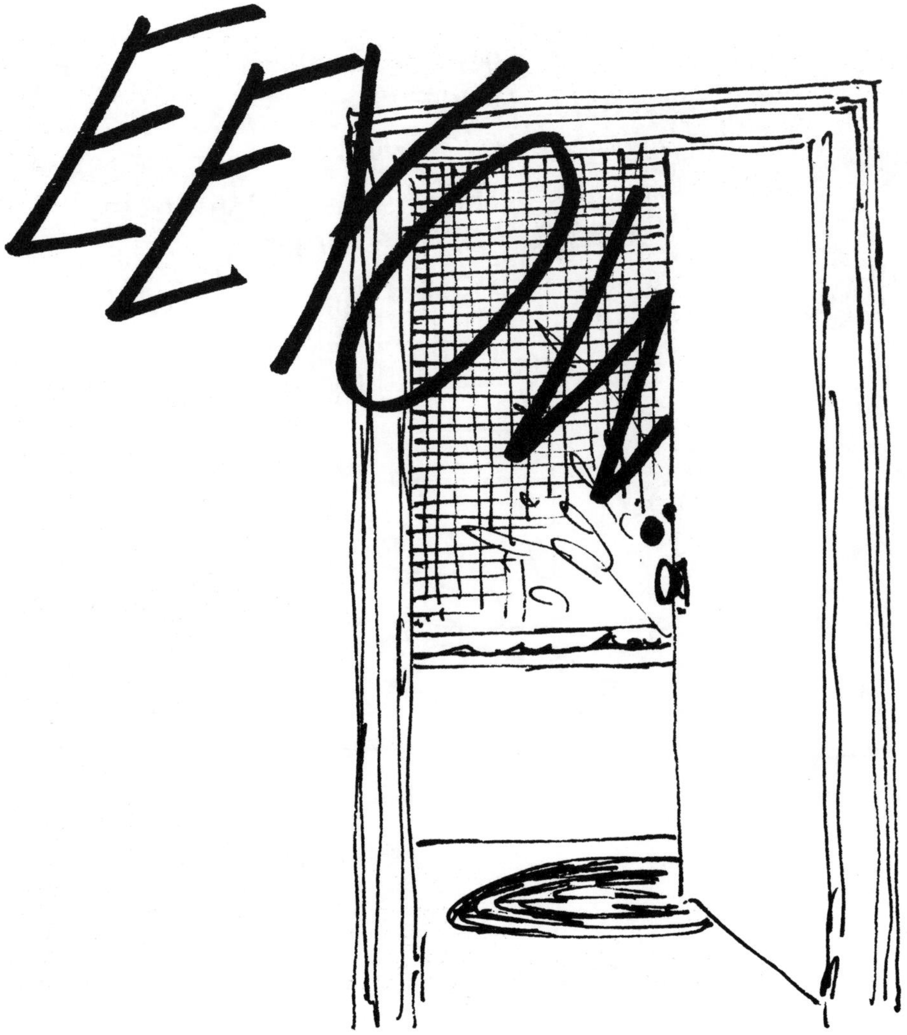
EEYOW

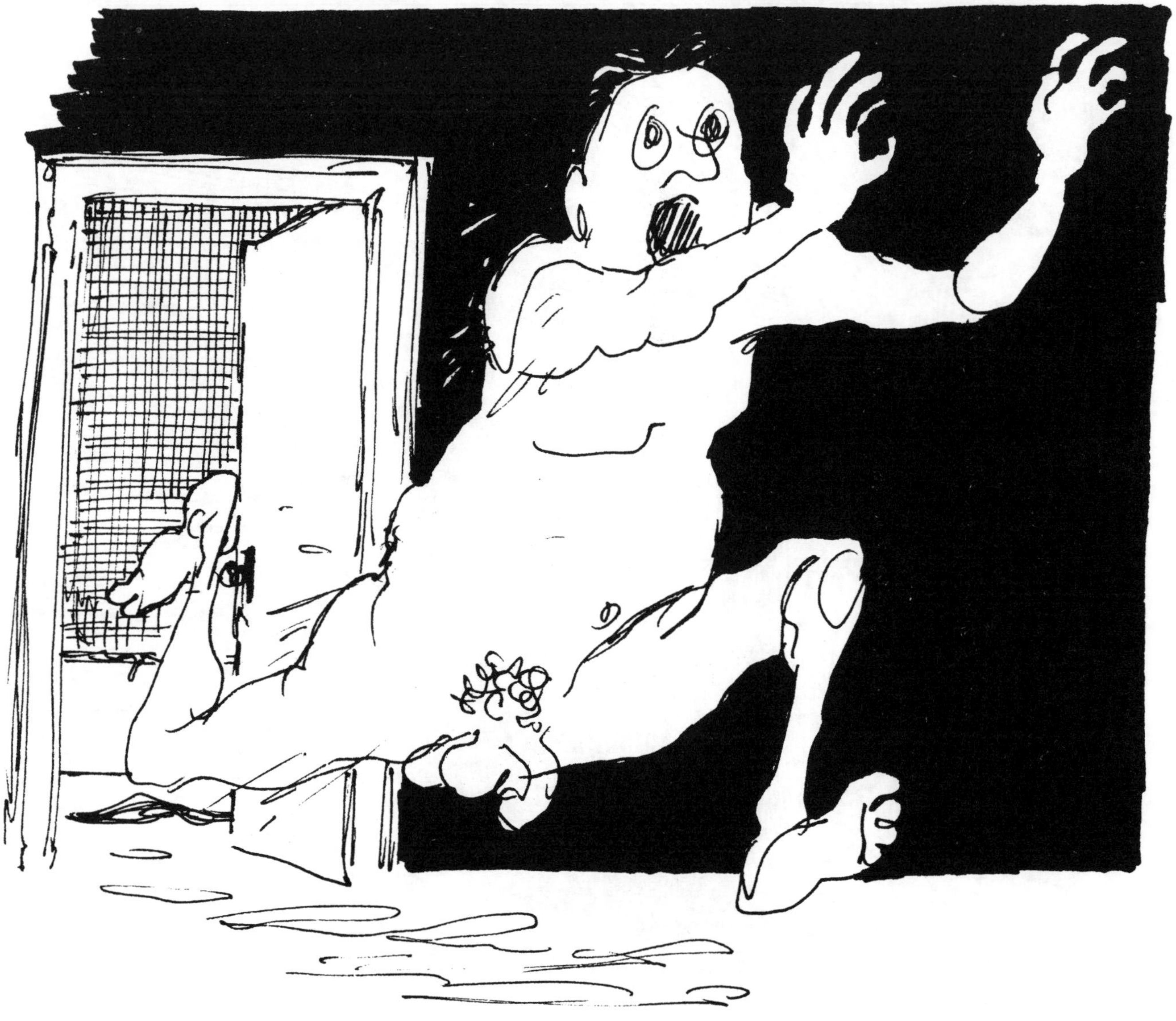

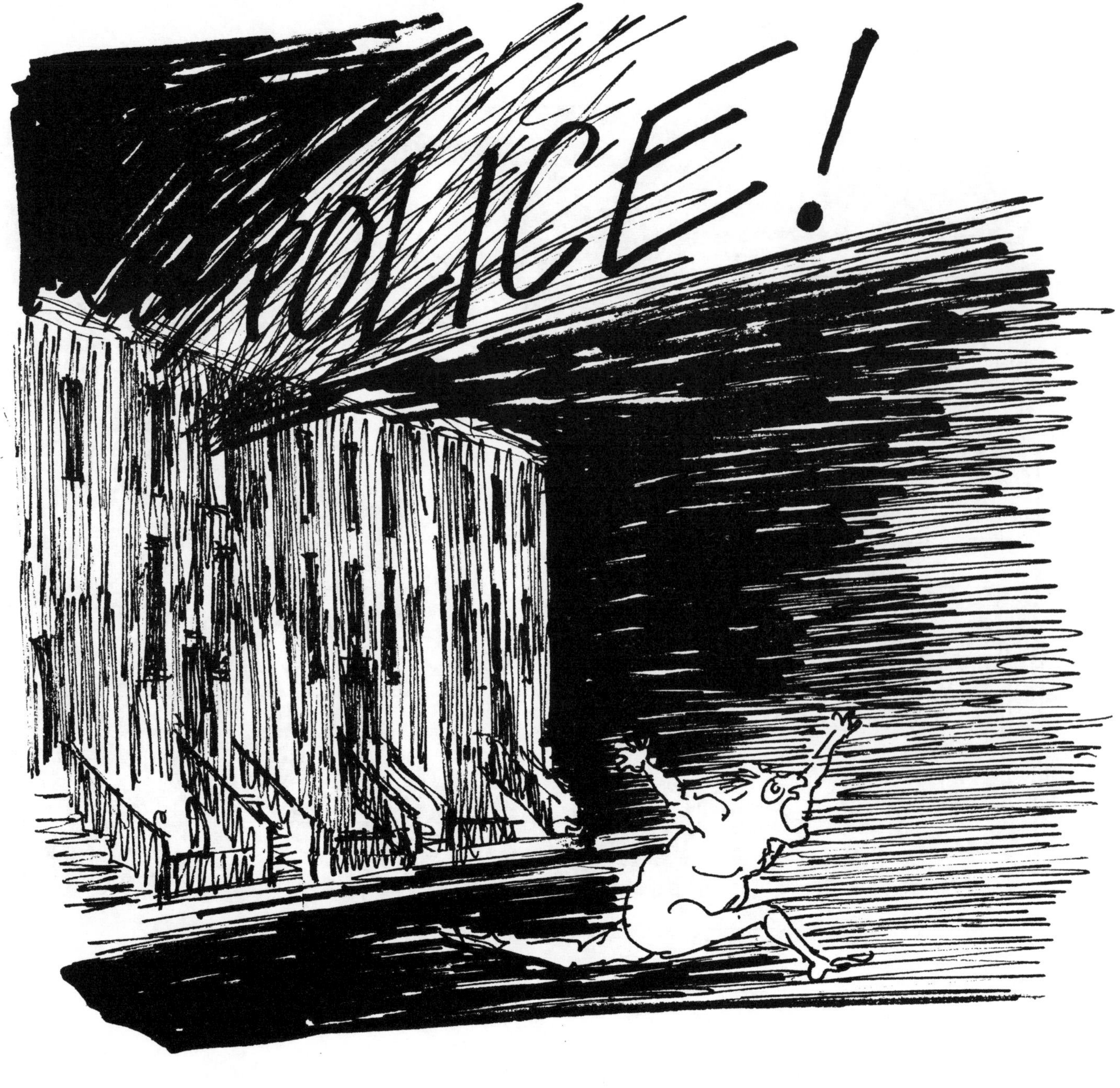
POLICE!

11

COMEUPPANCE

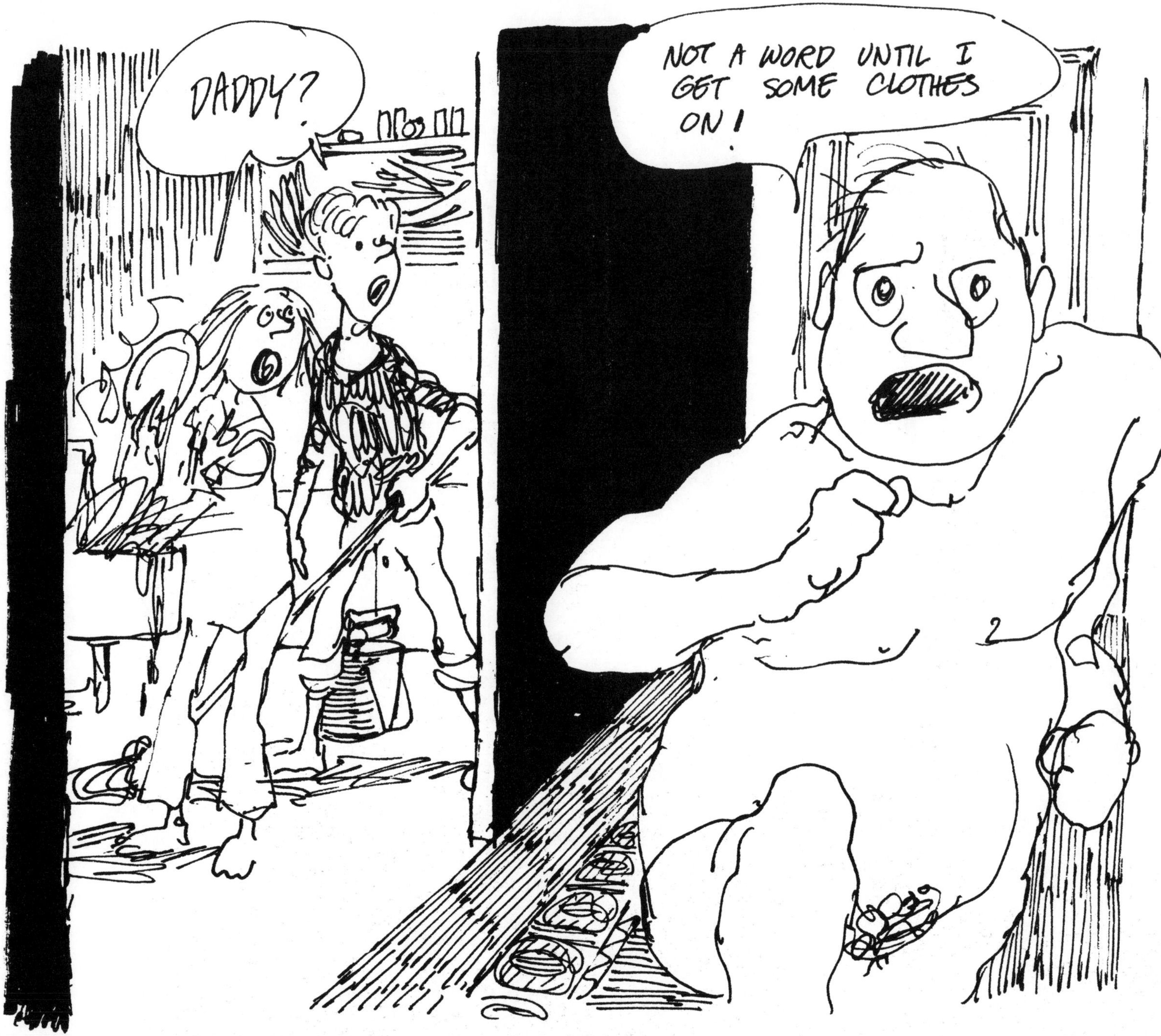
DADDY?
NOT A WORD UNTIL I GET SOME CLOTHES ON!

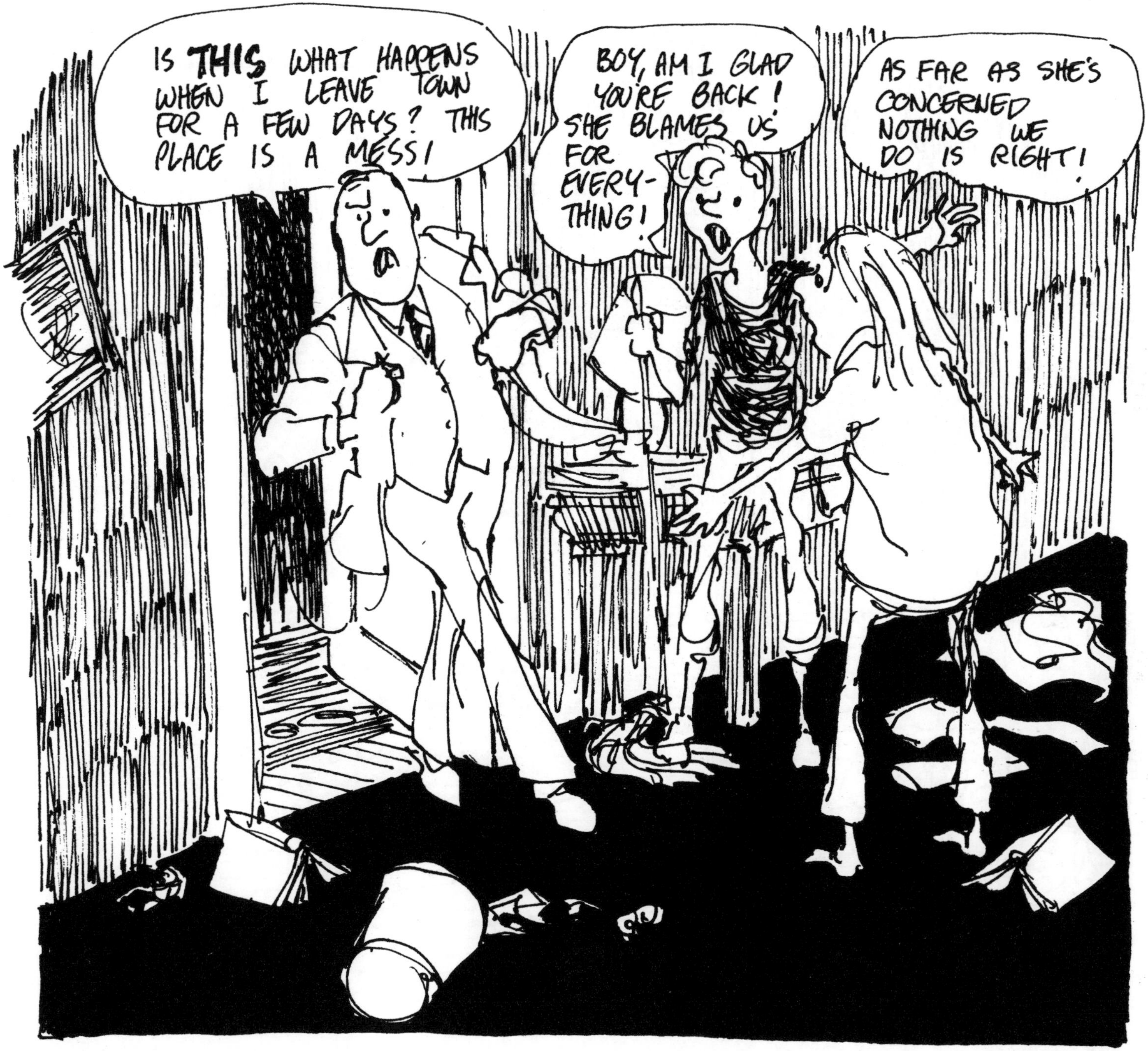
IS THIS WHAT HAPPENS WHEN I LEAVE TOWN FOR A FEW DAYS? THIS PLACE IS A MESS!
BOY, AM I GLAD YOU'RE BACK! SHE BLAMES US FOR EVERY-THING!
AS FAR AS SHE'S CONCERNED NOTHING WE DO IS RIGHT!

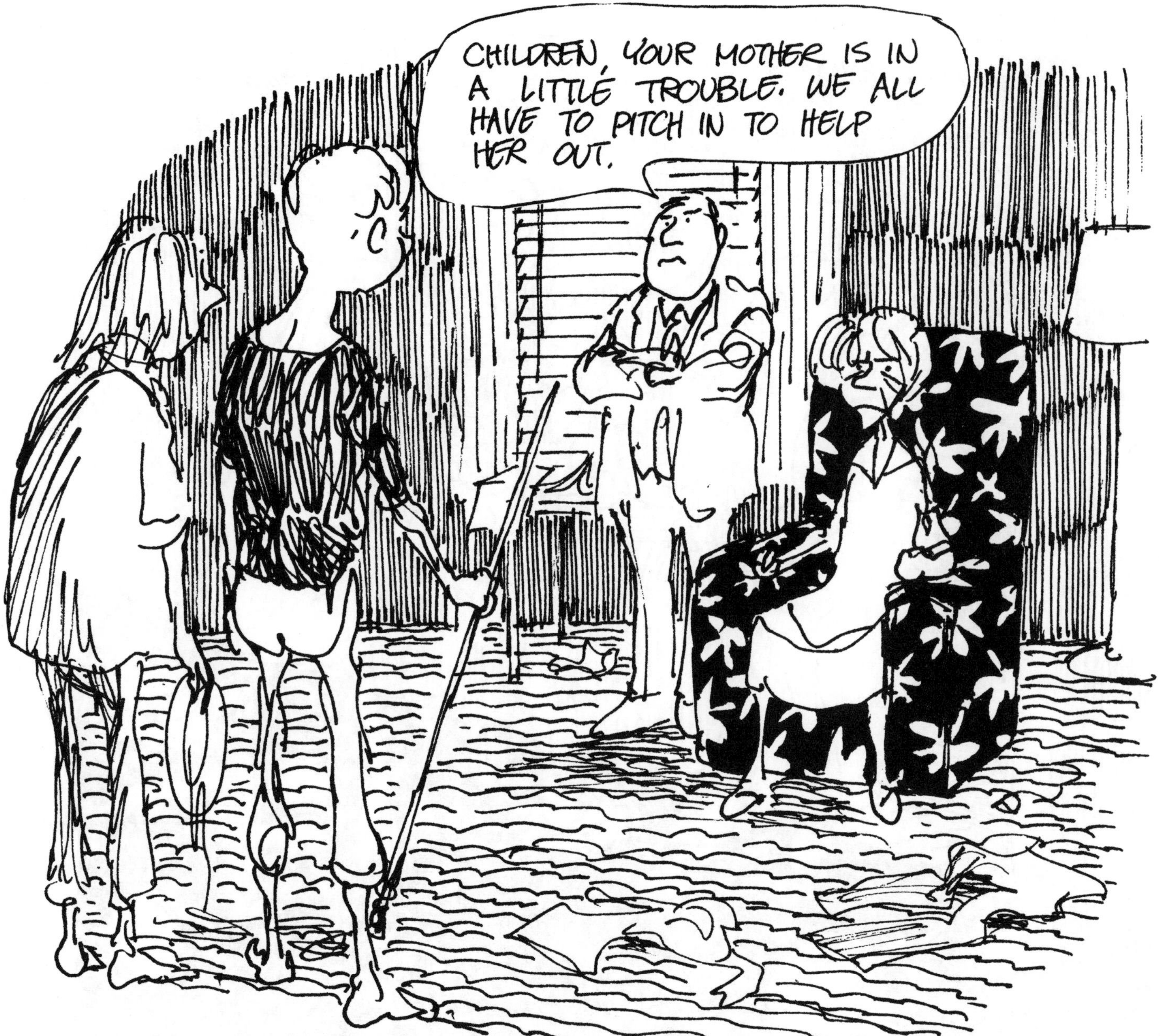
CHILDREN, YOUR MOTHER IS IN A LITTLE TROUBLE. WE ALL HAVE TO PITCH IN TO HELP HER OUT.

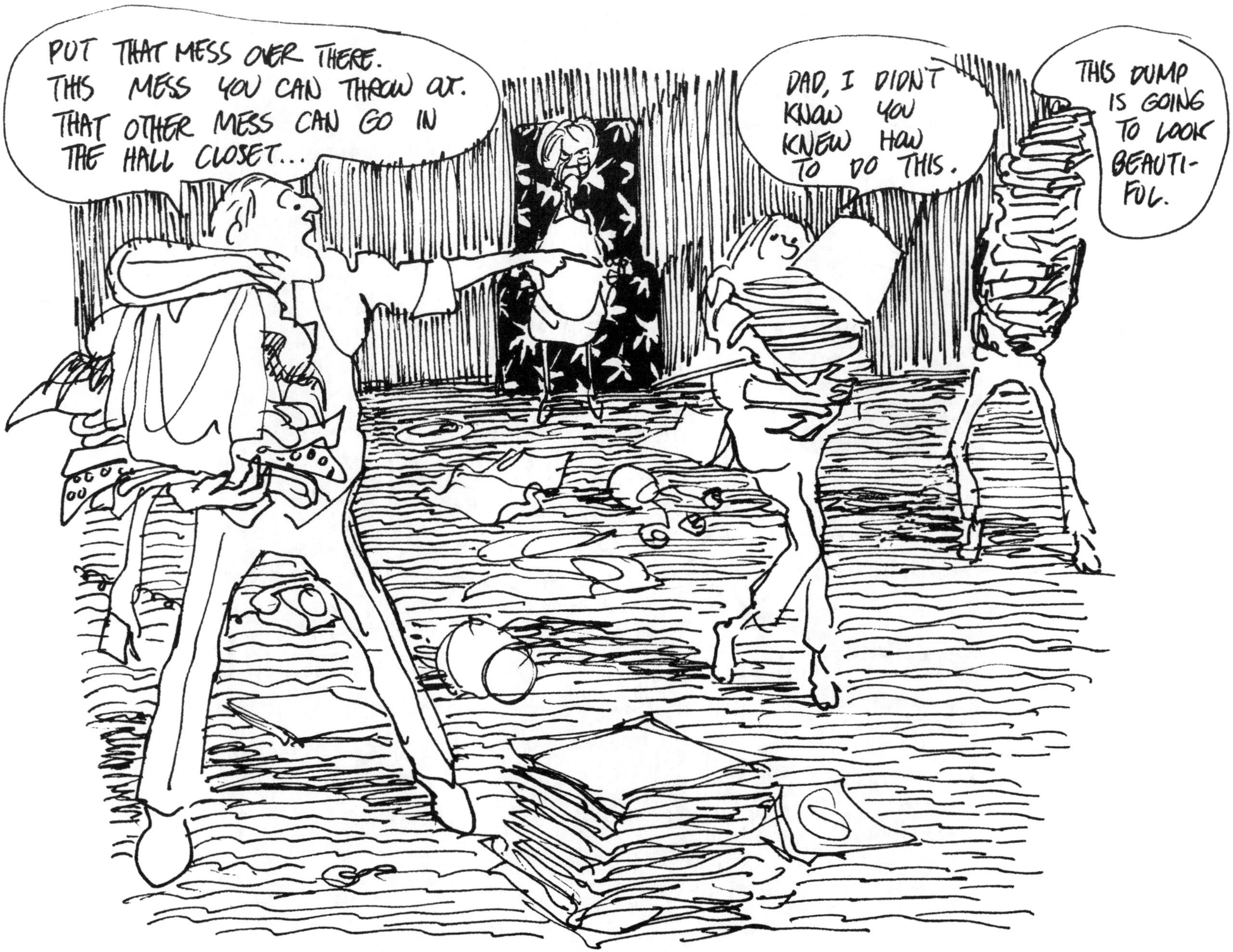
PUT THAT MESS OVER THERE. THIS MESS YOU CAN THROW OUT. THAT OTHER MESS CAN GO IN THE HALL CLOSET...
DAD, I DIDN'T KNOW YOU KNEW HOW TO DO THIS.
THIS DUMP IS GOING TO LOOK BEAUTI-FUL.

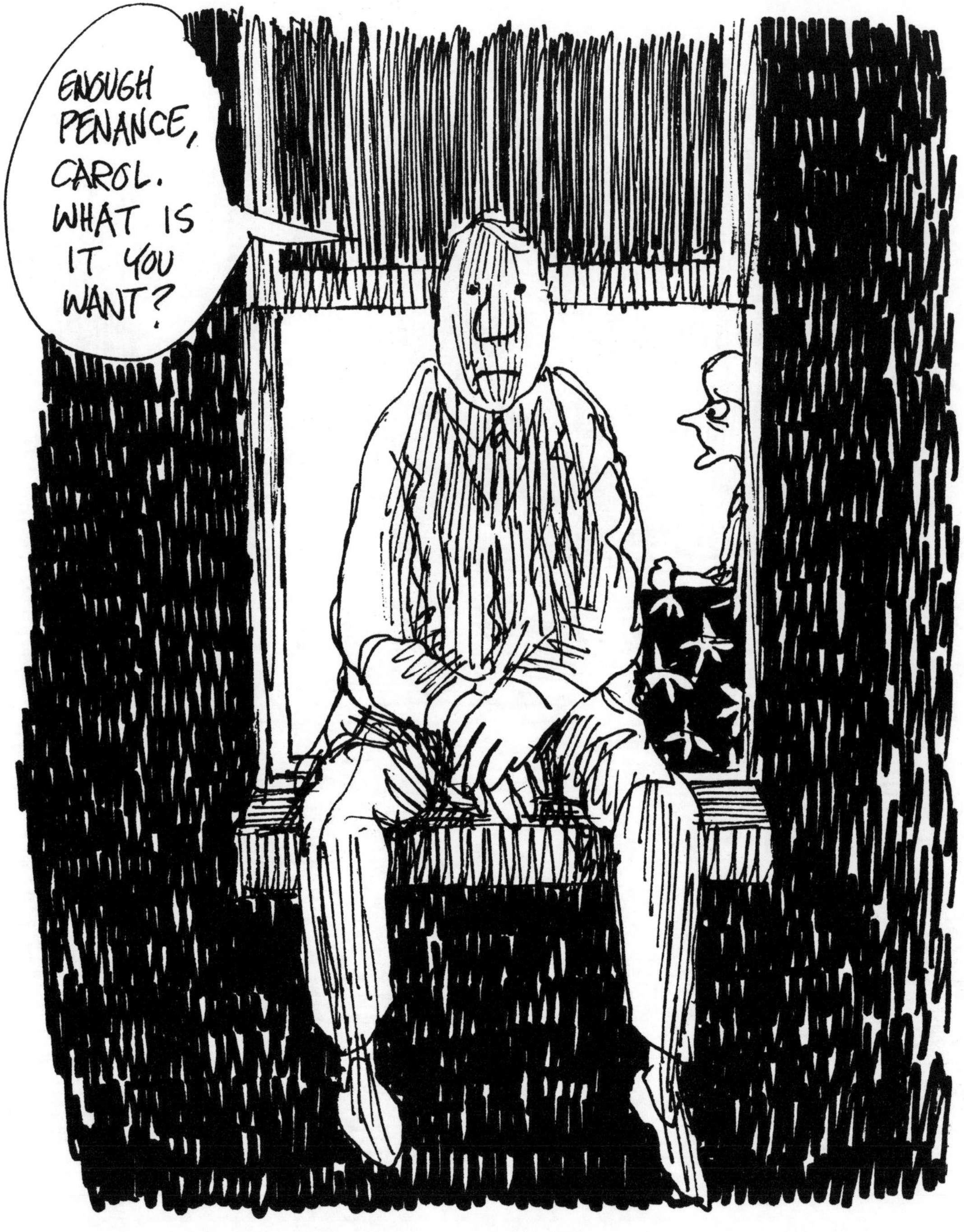
ENOUGH PENANCE, CAROL. WHAT IS IT YOU WANT?

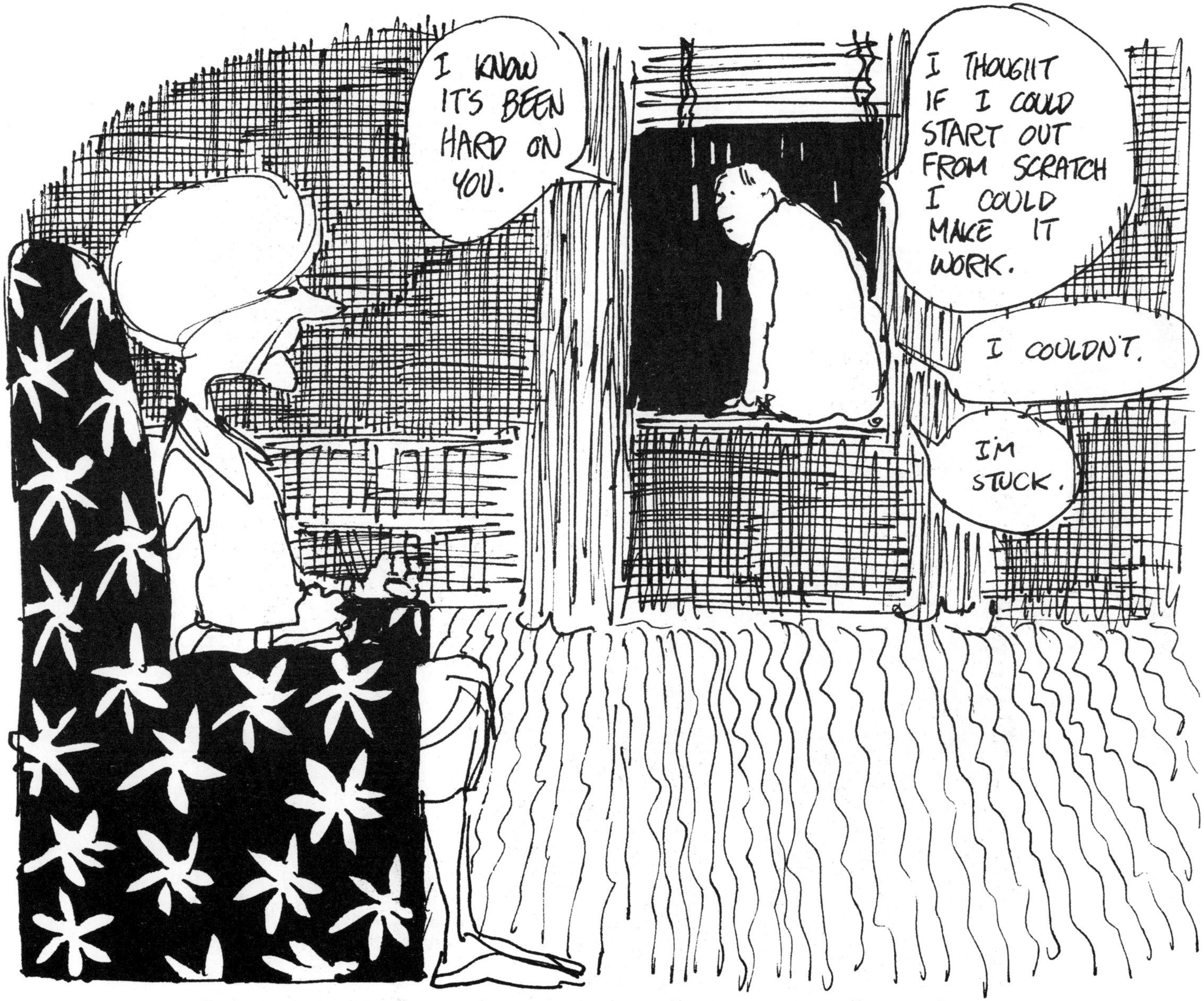
I KNOW IT'S BEEN HARD ON YOU.
I THOUGHT IF I COULD START OUT FROM SCRATCH I COULD MAKE IT WORK.
I COULDN'T.
I'M STUCK.

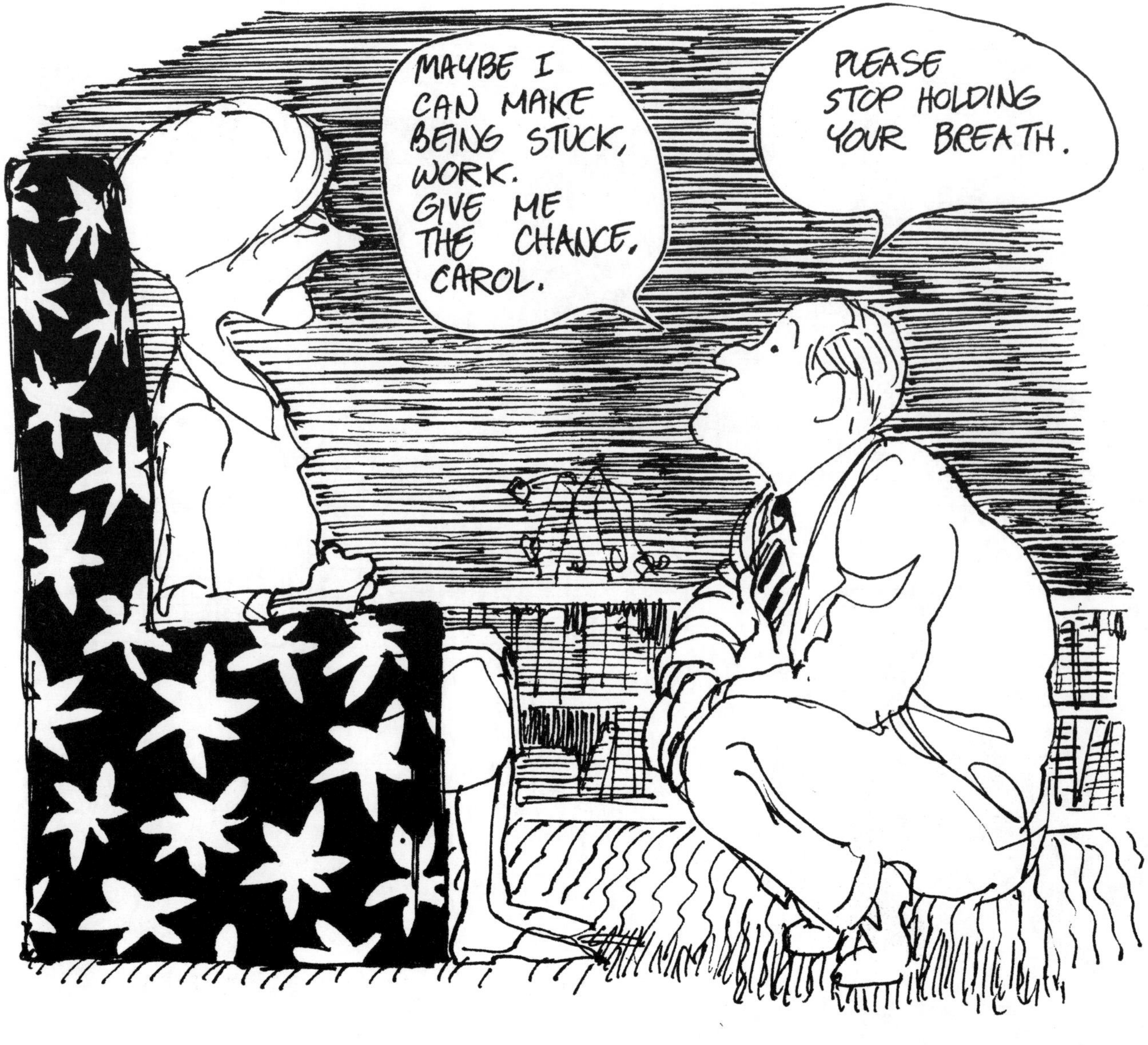
MAYBE I CAN MAKE BEING STUCK, WORK. GIVE ME THE CHANCE, CAROL.
PLEASE STOP HOLDING YOUR BREATH.

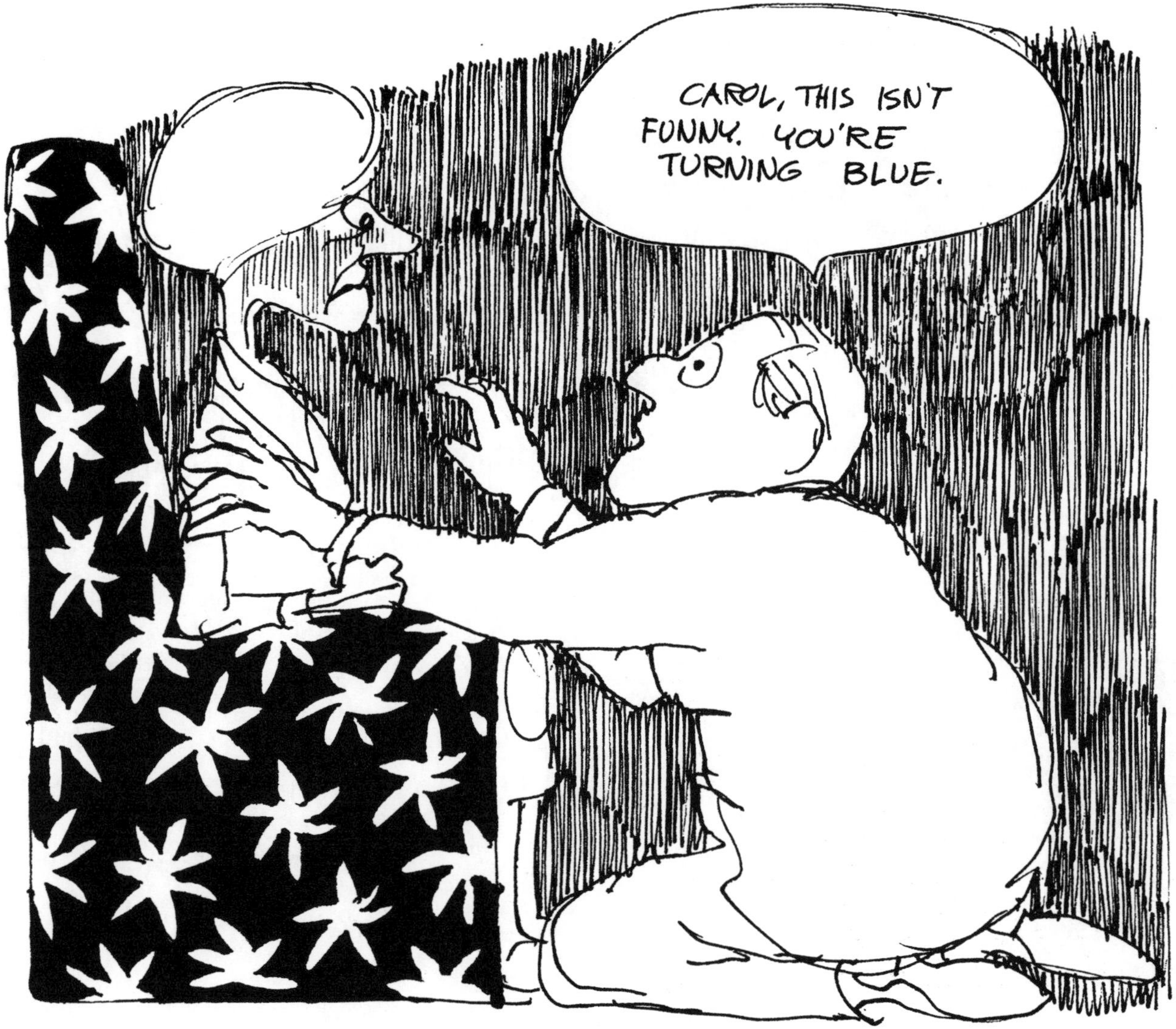
CAROL, THIS ISN'T FUNNY. YOU'RE TURNING BLUE.

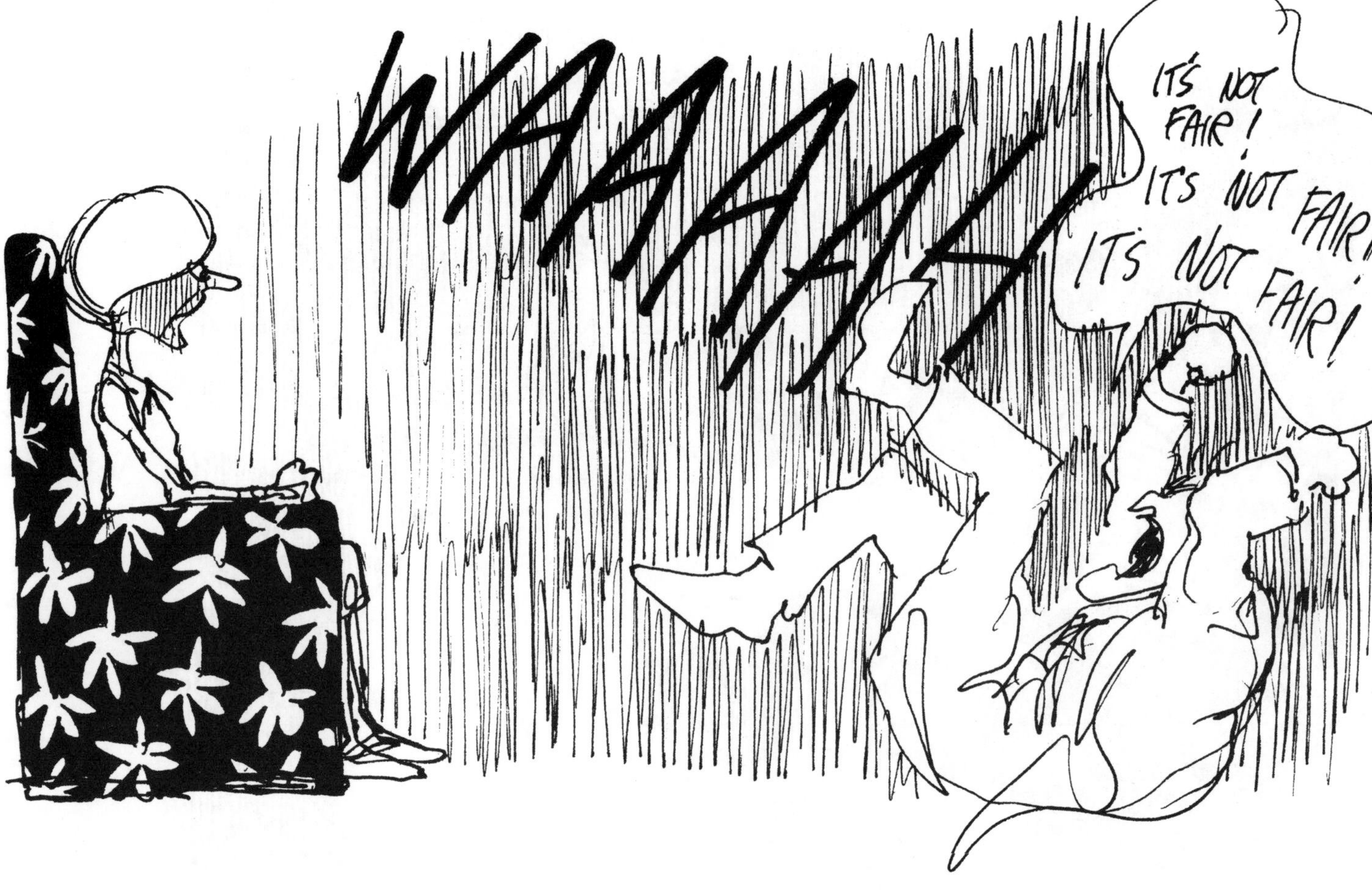
WAAAAAH
IT'S NOT FAIR! IT'S NOT FAIR! IT'S NOT FAIR!

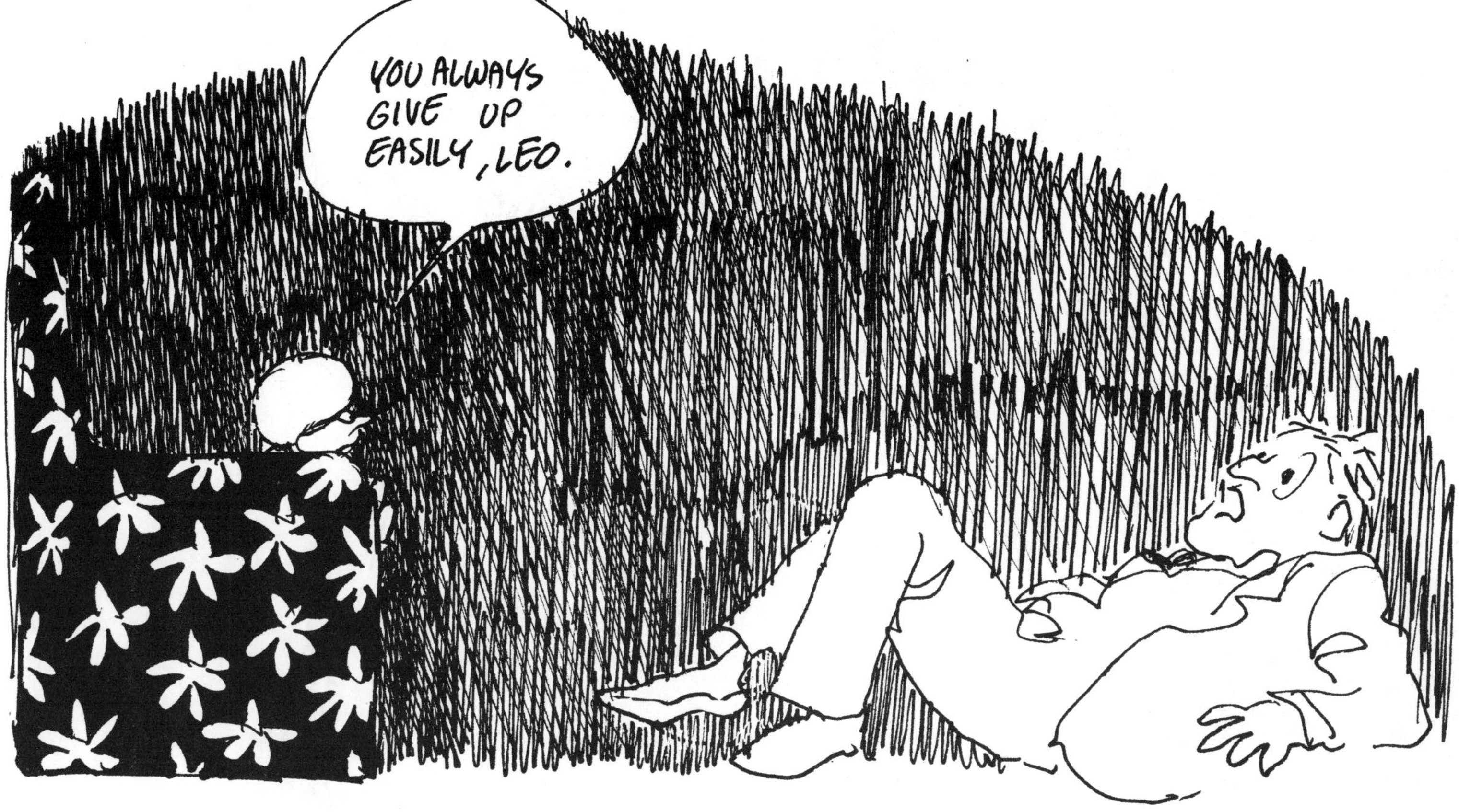
YOU ALWAYS GIVE UP EASILY, LEO.

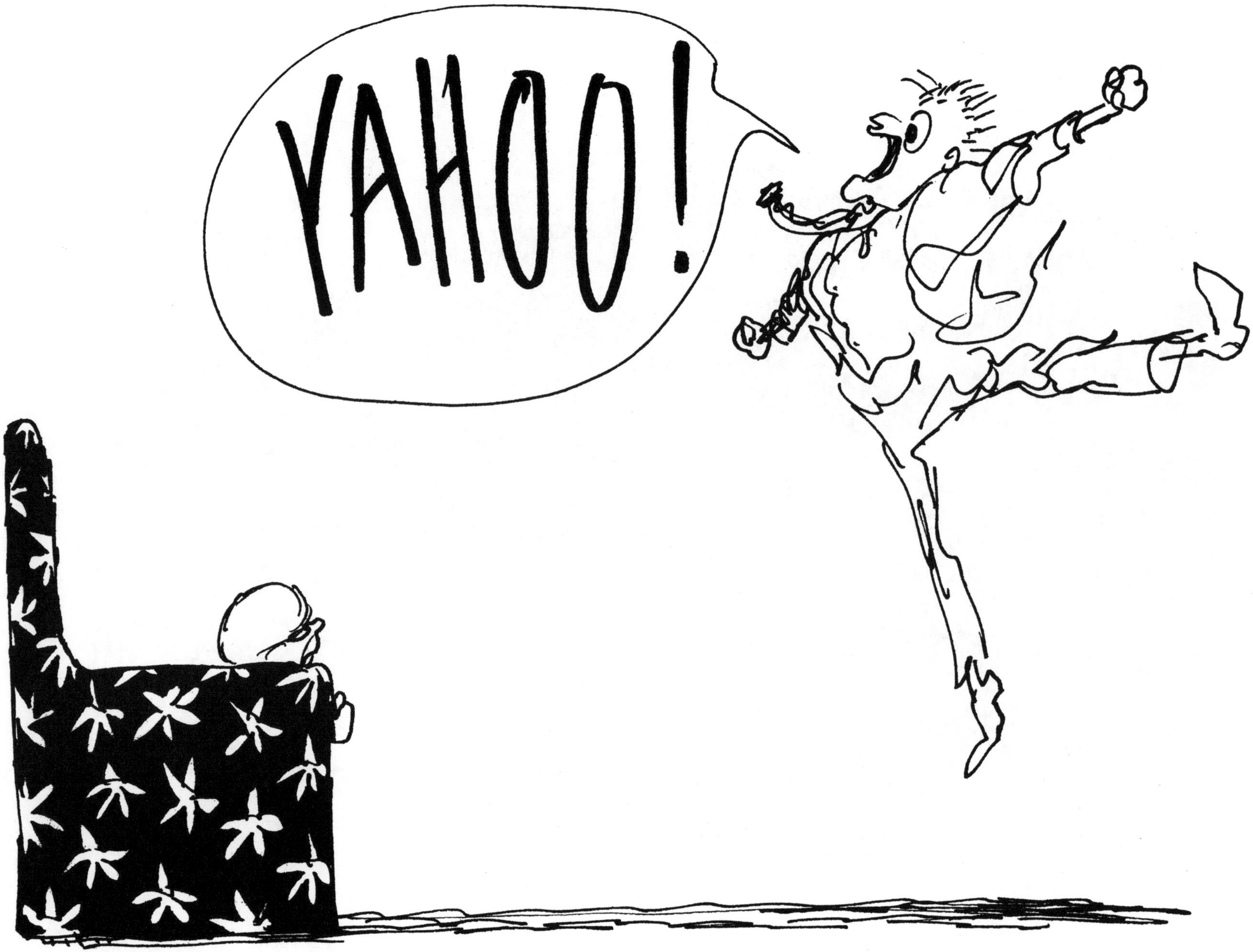
YAHOO!

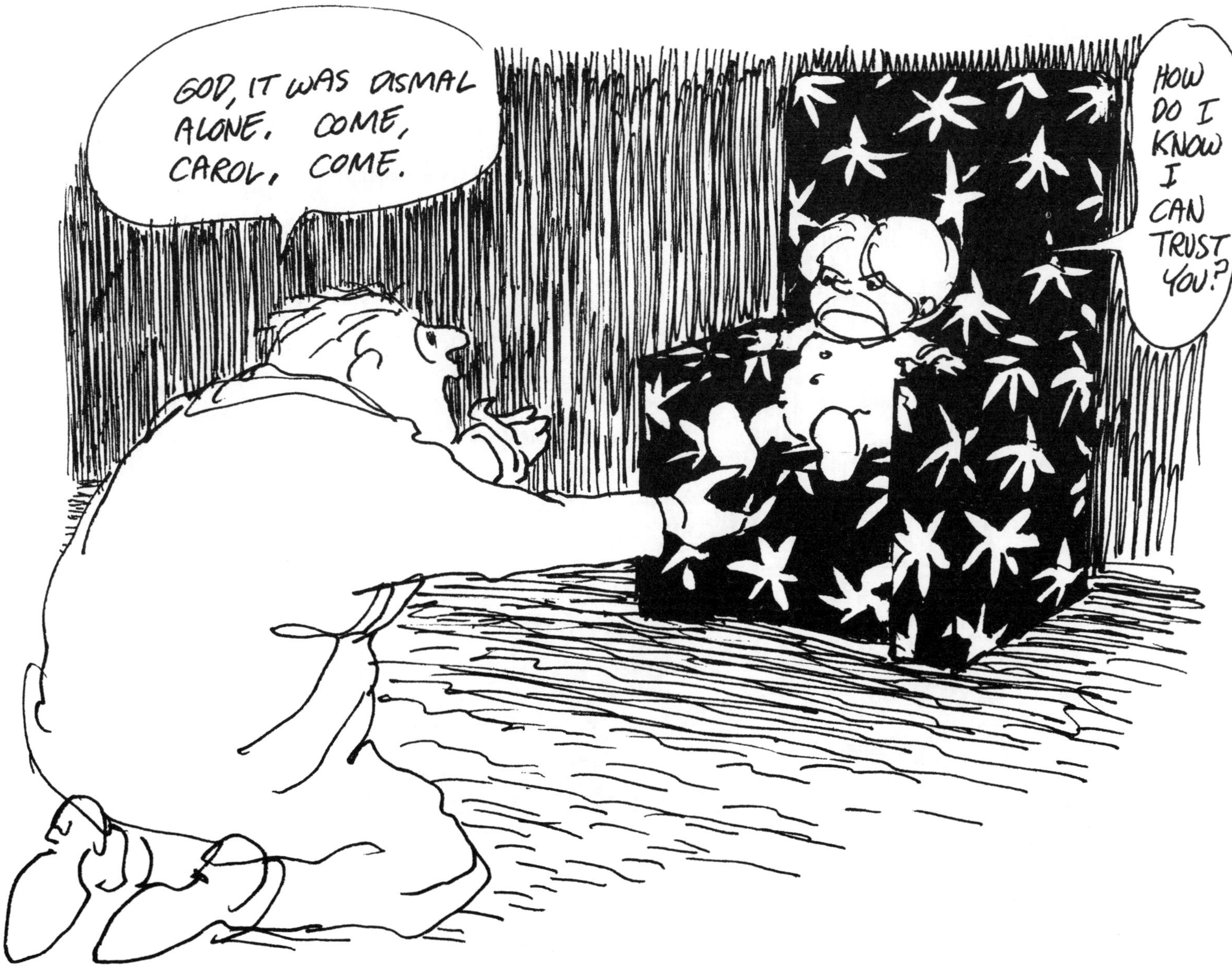
GOD, IT WAS DISMAL ALONE. COME, CAROL, COME.
HOW DO I KNOW I CAN TRUST YOU?

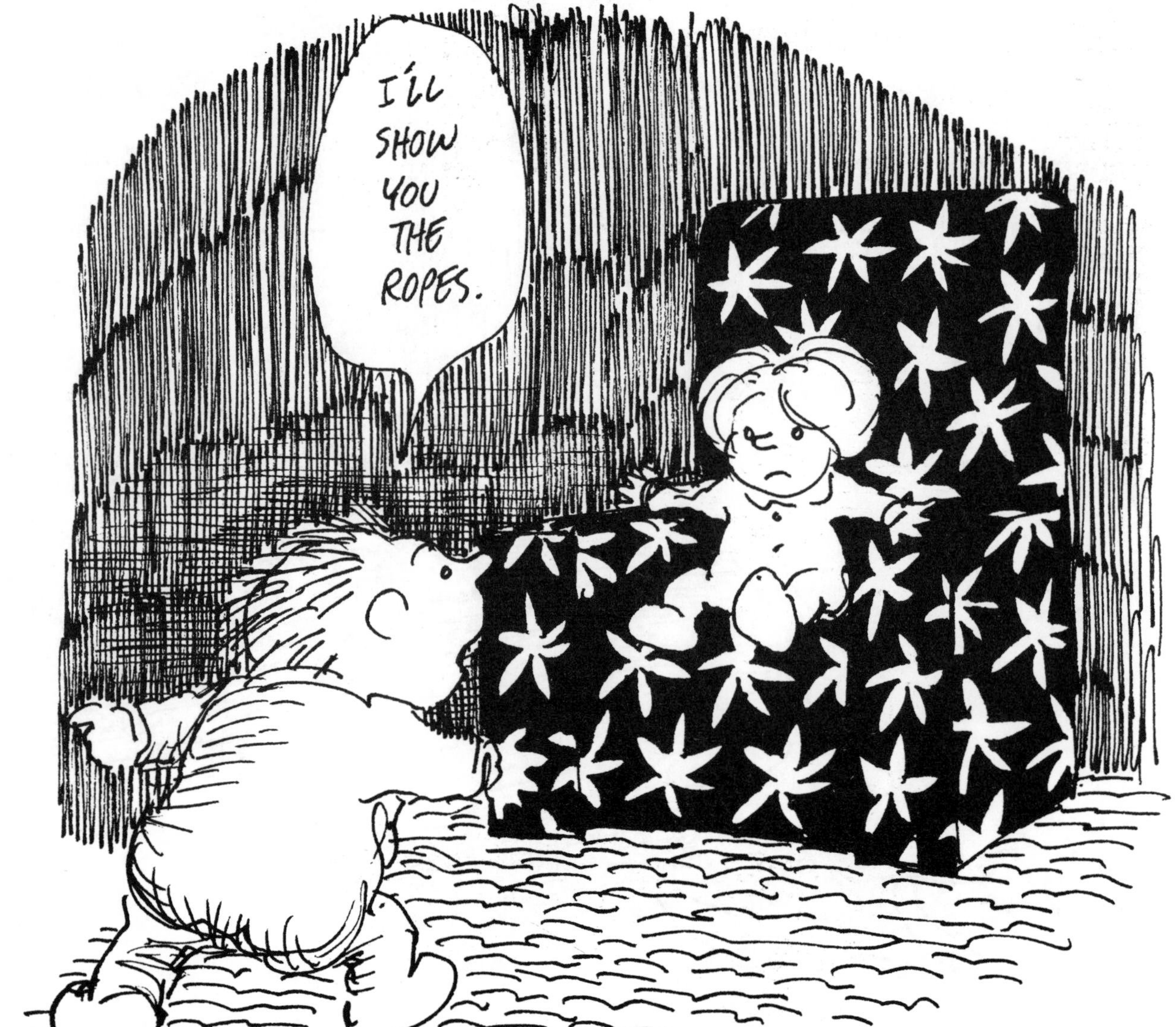
I'LL SHOW YOU THE ROPES.

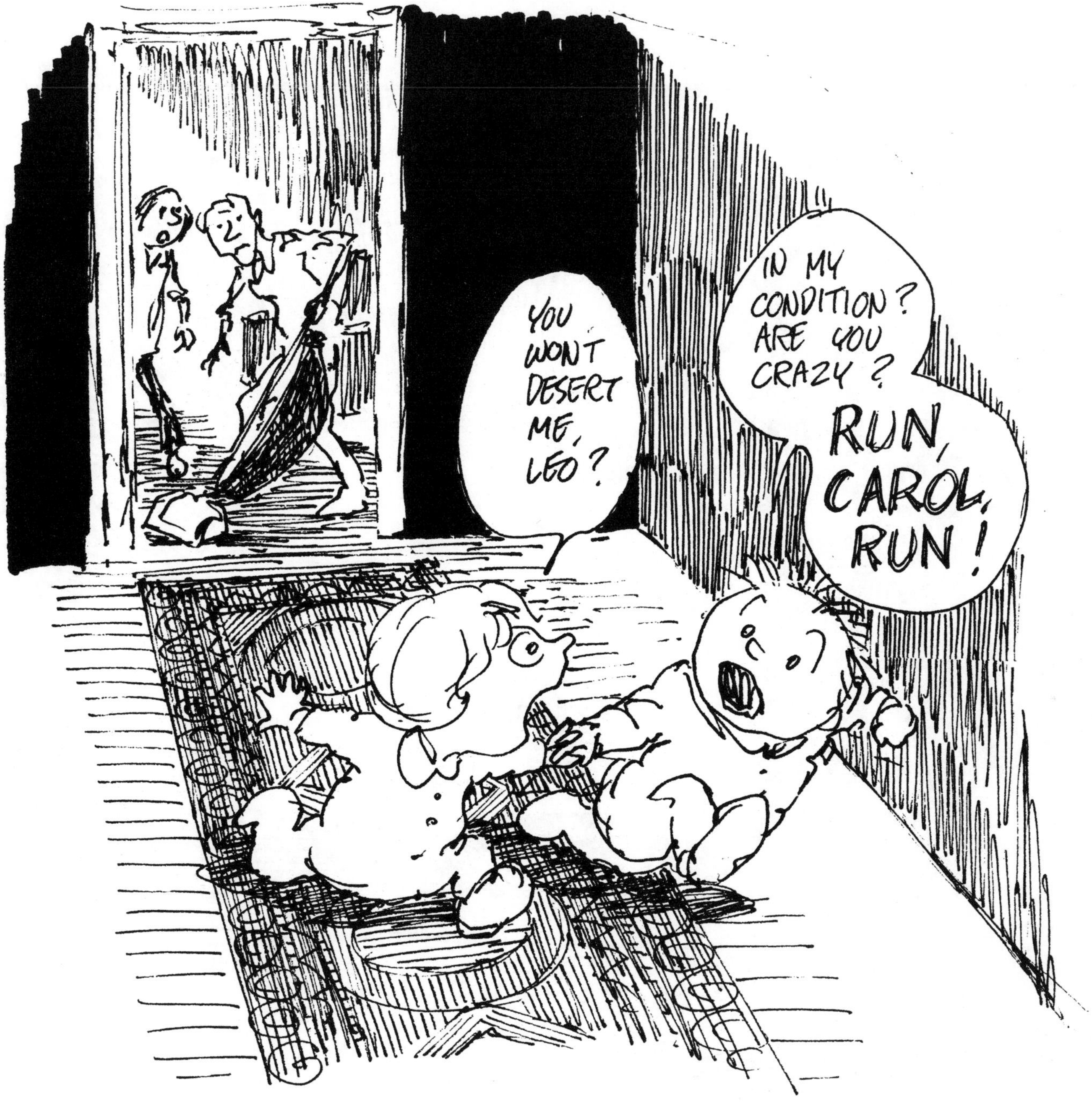
YOU WON'T DESERT ME, LEO?
IN MY CONDITION? ARE YOU CRAZY?
RUN, CAROL, RUN!

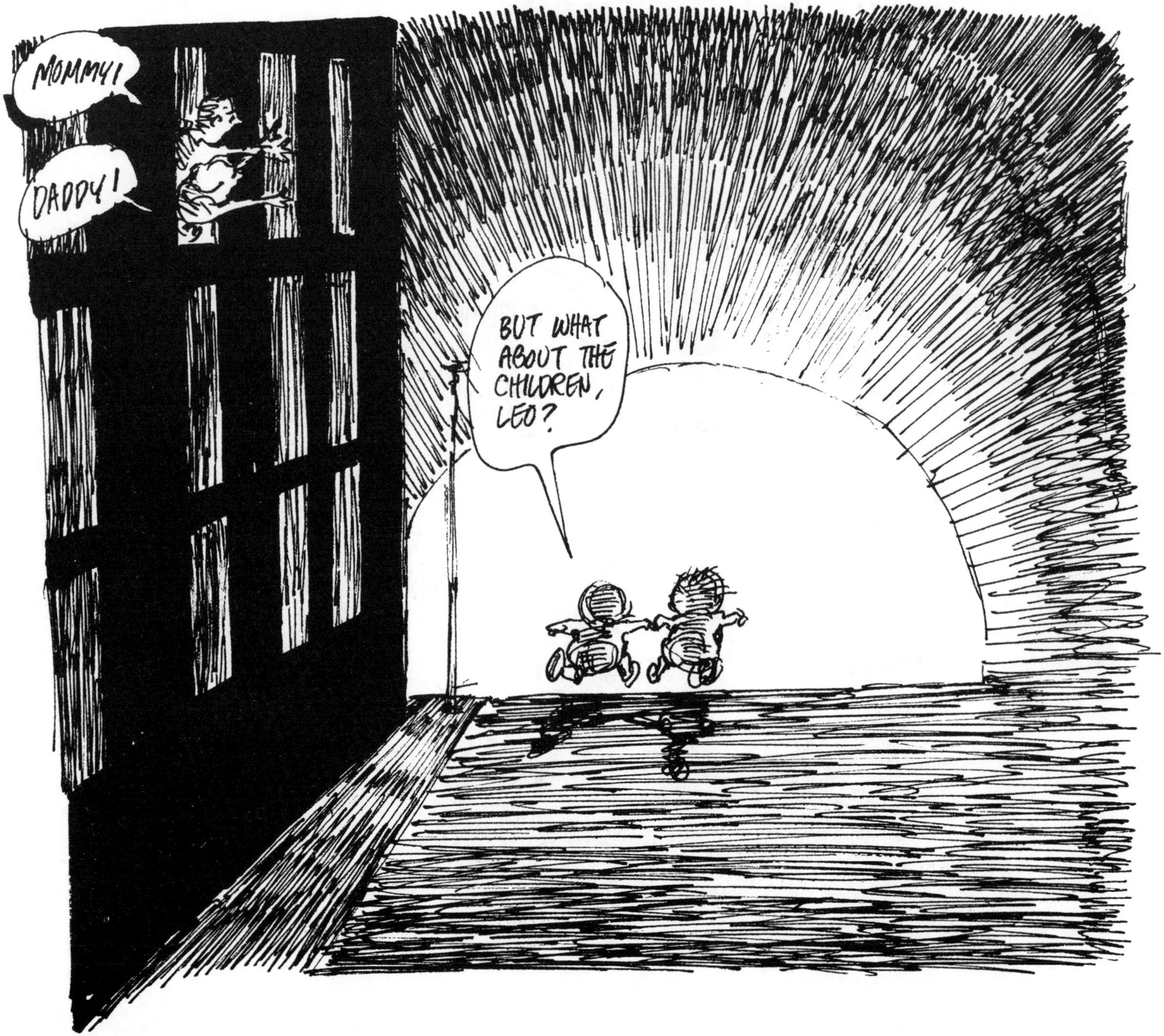
MOMMY!
DADDY!
BUT WHAT ABOUT THE CHILDREN, LEO?

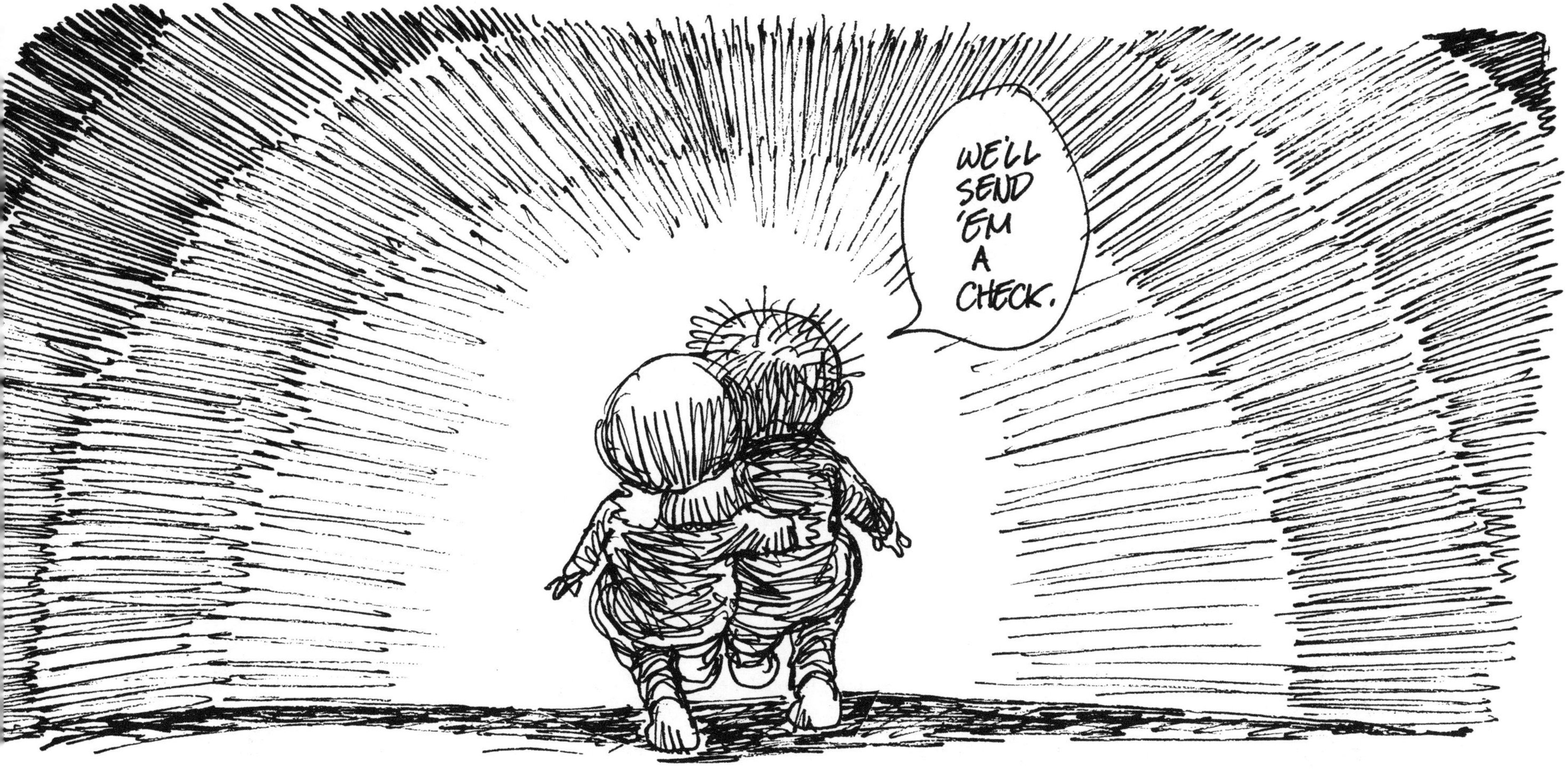
WE'LL SEND 'EM A CHECK.

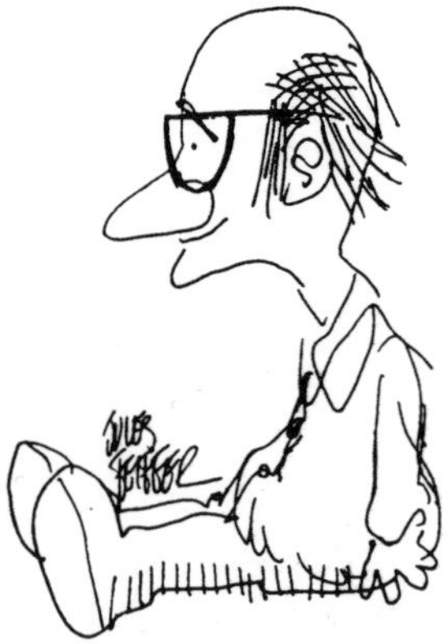
JULES FEIFFER

JULES FEIFFER, inspired by such comic strip grandmasters as Milton Caniff, Roy Crane, and Will Eisner, laid the groundwork for his own cartooning career by attending the Art Students League and Pratt Institute. In 1947, he began a four-year stint assisting Eisner on his syndicated *Spirit* comic book supplement. Eisner soon allotted the teenager a page for his own strip, *Clifford*, instantly exposing his work to an audience of millions; Feiffer also ghost-wrote a number of the later *Spirit* episodes.

After Feiffer was drafted into the army in 1951, his perspective changed radically; once discharged, he resolved to incorporate his convictions into his cartoons. In 1956 he began a 40-year relationship with the *Village Voice*, contributing a weekly strip of social and political satire called *Sick, Sick, Sick*. In 1958 he became a regular contributor to *Playboy*; in 1959 the weekly *Village Voice* strip, redubbed *Feiffer*, was nationally syndicated by the Hall Syndicate, eventually earning Feiffer a Pulitzer.

Over the years, Feiffer has proven himself as formidable a playwright, novelist, screen writer and children's writer as he is a political cartoonist. His plays include *Little Murders*; *Knock, Knock*; *Elliot Loves*; *The White House Murder Case*; and *Grown Ups*, as well as several revues based on his comic strips. In 1961 he won an Academy Award for an animated cartoon based on his story, *Munro*. *Carnal Knowledge*, directed by Mike Nichols from Feiffer's screenplay, became one of the landmark films of the '70s. He also wrote the screenplay for Robert Altman's *Popeye* and the Alain Resnais film *I Want to Go Home*. Feiffer has written two novels, *Harry the Rat with Women* and *Ackroyd*; several children's books, including *A Barrel of Laughs, a Vale of Tears*, *Man in the Ceiling*, and *Meanwhile*; and *The Great Comic Book Heroes*, a tribute to many of the cartoonists who preceded and inspired him.